Violence

MAIN TRENDS OF THE MODERN WORLD

General Editors: Robert Jackall and Arthur J. Vidich

New Tribalisms: The Resurgence of Race and Ethnicity
Edited by Michael W. Hughey

Propaganda
Edited by Robert Jackall

Metropolis: Center and Symbol of Our Times
Edited by Philip Kasinitz

Social Movements: Critiques, Concepts, Case-Studies
Edited by Stanford M. Lyman

Science and the Quest for Reality
Edited by Alfred I. Tauber

**The New Middle Classes: Life-Styles, Status Claims,
and Political Orientations**
Edited by Arthur J.Vidich

**Transformations of Capitalism: Economy, Society,
and the State in Modern Times**
Edited by Harry F. Dahms

Violence: A Reader
Edited by Catherine Besteman

Violence

A Reader

Edited by

Catherine Besteman
Chair and Associate Professor of Anthropology
Colby College
Maine
USA

First published 2002 by
PALGRAVE MACMILLAN
Houndmills, Basingstoke, Hampshire RG21 6XS and
175 Fifth Avenue, New York, N.Y. 10010
Companies and representatives throughout the world.

PALGRAVE MACMILLAN is the global academic imprint of the Palgrave
Macmillan division of St Martin's Press, LLC and of Palgrave Macmillan Ltd.
Macmillan® is a registered trademark in the United States, United Kingdom
and other countries. Palgrave is a registered trademark in the European
Union and other countries.

ISBN 0–333–94775–4 hardback
ISBN 0–333–94776–2 paperback

This book is printed on paper suitable for recycling and
made from fully managed and sustained forest sources.

A catalogue record for this book is available
from the British Library.

Library of Congress Cataloging-in-Publication Data

A catalog record for this book is available from the Library of Congress

Transferred to digital printing 2003

Printed and bound in Great Britain by
Antony Rowe Ltd, Chippenham and Eastbourne

Contents

Acknowledgements   vii

Personal Acknowledgements   ix

Notes on the Contributors   x

1. Introduction   1

I.   Violence and the State

2. Politics as a Vocation
    Max Weber   13

3. Reflections on Violence
    Hannah Arendt   19

4. War Making and State Making as Organized Crime
    Charles Tilly   35

5. The Impact and Function of Terror
    Barrington Moore, Jr.   61

6. The Uniqueness and Normality of the Holocaust
    Zygmunt Bauman   67

II.   Political Violence

7. The Causes of Terrorism
    Martha Crenshaw   99

8. Playing the Game of Love: Passion and
    Martyrdom Among Khalistani Sikhs
    Cynthia Keppley-Mahmood   118

9. A Head for an Eye: Revenge in the Cambodian
    Genocide
    Alexander Laban Hinton   136

10. Dirty Protest: Symbolic Overdetermination and
    Gender in Northern Ireland Ethnic Violence
    Begoña Aretxaga   169

11.   Surfacing Gender: Reconceptualizing Crimes
      Against Women in Time of War
      Rhonda Copelon   193

III.   The Normalization of Violence

12.   Culture of Terror – Space of Death. Roger Casement's
      Putumayo Report and the Explanation of Torture
      Michael Taussig   211

13.   Male Gender and Rituals of Resistance in the
      Palestinian *Intifada*: A Cultural Politics of Violence
      Julie Peteet   244

14.   Terror Warfare and the Medicine of Peace
      Carolyn Nordstrom   273

 IV. Conclusion

15.   Conclusion: Political Violence and the
      Contemporary World   299
Index   313

Acknowledgements

"Politics as a Vocation," pp. 118–26 from *From Max Weber: Essays in Sociology* by Max Weber, edited by H. H. Gerth & C. Wright Mills, translated by H. H. Berth & C. Wright Mills, copyright 1946, 1958 by H. H. Gerth and C. Wright Mills. Used by permission of Oxford University Press, Inc.

Hannah Arendt, "Reflections on Violence." *Journal of International Affairs* 23(1) (1969):1–35. Published by permission of the *Journal of International Affairs* and the Trustees of Columbia University in the City of New York. Minor edits, including deletion of footnotes, were made to accommodate length requirements.

Charles Tilly, "War-Making and State-Making as Organized Crime" from *Bringing the State Back In*, edited by P. Evans, D. Rueschemeyer and T. Skocpol (Cambridge: Cambridge University Press, 1985). Copyright Cambridge University Press 1985. Reprinted with the permission of Cambridge University Press.

Barrington Moore, Jr., "The Impact and Function of Terror" from *Terror and Progress USSR: Some Sources of Change and Stability in the Soviet Dictatorship"* (Cambridge: Harvard University Press, 1954). Reprinted with the permission of Harvard University Press.

Zygmunt Bauman, "The Uniqueness and Normality of the Holocaust," reprinted from Zygmunt Bauman, *Modernity and the Holocaust*, copyright 1989 by Zygmunt Bauman. Used by permission of the publisher, Cornell University Press and Polity Press.

Martha Crenshaw, "The Causes of Terrorism." *Comparative Politics* 12 (1981):379–99. Reprinted with permission.

Cynthia Mahmood, "Playing the Game of Love: Passion and Martyrdom Among Khalistani Sikhs." *Martyrdom and National Resistance Movements: Essays on Asia and Europe*, edited by Joyce Pettigrew. (Amsterdam: VU University Press, 1997:19–34). Reprinted with permission.

Begoña Aretxaga, "Dirty Protest: Symbolic Overdetermination and Gender in Northern Ireland Ethnic Violence." Reproduced by permission of the American Anthropological Association from *Ethos* 23(2). Not for sale or further reproduction.

Alexander Laban Hinton, abridgement of "A Head for an Eye: Revenge in the Cambodian Genocide." Reprinted by permission of the

American Anthropological Association from *American Ethnologist* 25(3). Not for sale or further reproduction.

Rhonda Copelon. "Surfacing Gender: Reconceptualizing Crimes Against Women in Time of War." Reprinted from *Mass Rape: The War Against Women in Bosnia-Herzegovina* edited by Alexandra Stiglmayer by permission of the University of Nebraska Press. Copyright 1993 Verlag GmbH. Copyright 1994 by the University of Nebraska Press.

Michael Taussig, "Culture of Terror – Space of Death. Roger Casement's Putumayo Report and the Explanation of Torture." *Contemporary Studies in Society and History* 26 (1984):467–97. Copyright 1984 Society for Comparative Study of Society and History. Reprinted with the permission of Cambridge University Press.

Julie Peteet, "Male Gender and Rituals of Resistance in the Palestinian Intifada: A Cultural Politics of Violence." Reprinted by permission of the American Anthropological Association from *American Ethnologist* 21(1). Not for sale or further reproduction.

Carolyn Nordstrom, "Terror Warfare and the Medicine of Peace." Reproduced by permission of the American Anthropological Association from *Medical Anthropology Quarterly* 12(1). Not for sale or further reproduction.

Personal acknowledgements

A number of people have contributed to this project over the past several years. The series editors, Robert Jackall and Arthur Vidich, proposed the topic and maintained a close involvement with the project throughout its gestation. Several stellar student research assistants helped compile essays: Jill Kooyoomjian, Andrew Rice, Pia Rice, and Jenny McElhinney. I am grateful to David Nugent and Mary Beth Mills for their careful, critical readings of the Introduction and Conclusion.

Notes on the Contributors

Hannah Arendt (1906–75), one of the twentieth century's leading political theorists, was on the graduate faculty in Philosophy at the New School for Social Research. Among her over twenty books are *Eichmann in Jerusalem, The Origins of Totalitarianism*, and *On Violence*.

Begoña Aretxaga, Associate Professor of Anthropology at the University of Texas, researches political violence, gender, and nationalism in Northern Ireland. She authored *Shattering Silence: Women, Nationalism, and Political Subjectivity in Northern Ireland*.

Zygmunt Bauman is Emeritus Professor of Sociology at the University of Leeds. He is the author of over twenty-five books, including *Postmodern Ethics, Postmodernity and its Discontents*, and *Globalization: The Human Consequences*.

Catherine Besteman, Associate Professor of Anthropology at Colby College, researches political violence in Africa and Latin America. Her books include *Unraveling Somalia: Race, Violence and the Legacy of Slavery* and a forthcoming edited volume on the role of public intellectuals in promoting neo-liberal economics and neo-conservative social agendas.

Rhonda Copelon, a graduate of Yale Law School, worked for twelve years at the Center for Constitutional Rights in New York City, where she is currently a Vice President and volunteer attorney. She is a co-editor of the second edition of the leading legal text, *Sex Discrimination and the Law*.

Martha Crenshaw, the John E. Andrus Professor of Government at Wesleyan University, researches political terrorism. Her books include the *International Encyclopedia of Terrorism in Context*, and *Terrorism, Legitimacy, and Power*.

Alexander Laban Hinton, Assistant Professor in the Department of Anthropology and Sociology at Rutgers University, researches genocide. He is currently completing three book projects: *Cambodia's Shadow: Cultural Dimensions of Genocide, Annihilating Difference: The Anthropology of Genocide*, and *Genocide: An Anthropological Reader*.

Cynthia Mahmood, a Fellow at the Joan B. Kroc Institute for International Peace Studies at the University of Notre Dame, is an expert on Sikh separatism. Her books include *Fighting for Faith and Nation: Dialogues with Sikh Militants* and *The Guru's Gift: An Ethnography Exploring Gender Equality with North American Sikh Women*.

Barrington Moore, Jr. served on the Harvard University faculty for over fifty years as a lecturer in Sociology and a Senior Research Fellow at the Russian Research Center. Among his many publications in the classic study is *Social Origins of Dictatorship and Democracy: Lord and Peasant in the Making of the Modern World*. Other books include *Authority and Inequality Under Capitalism and Socialism* and *Moral Purity and Persecution in History*.

Carolyn Nordstrom is Associate Professor of Anthropology and Fellow at the Kroc Institute of International Peace Studies, University of Notre Dame. Her books, *A Different Kind of War Story, Fieldwork Under Fire: Contemporary Stories of Violence and Survival*, and *The Paths to Domination, Resistance, and Terror* and over three dozen articles focus on political violence and peacebuilding, war economies and transnational criminal systems, cultures of globalization, gender and children in warzones, and creativity.

Julie Peteet is Chair and Associate Professor of Anthropology at the University of Louisville. She is the author of *Gender in Crisis: Women and the Palestinian Resistance Movement*. She has published a number of articles on gender, violence and resistance, and space and identity and is currently completing a book manuscript on the relationship between place and identity in Palestinian refugee camps.

Michael Taussig, Professor of Anthropology at Columbia University, researches colonialism, terror, shamanism, and state in Latin America. His recent books include *The Magic of the State, Mimesis and Alterity*, and *The Nervous System*.

Charles Tilly, the Joseph L. Buttenwieser Professor of Social Science at Columbia University, is a leading historian of the relationship between political conflict and large-scale social change, especially in Western Europe since the 1500s. He has authored more than a dozen books, including *Durable Inequality, Work Under Capitalism* (with Chris Tilly) and *Coercion, Capital, and European States: AD 990–1992*.

Max Weber (1864–1920) was one of the leading founders of modern sociology. His written work addressed the roles of religion, politics, economics, capitalism, and bureaucracy in modern life. Among his many books are *The Protestant Ethic and the Spirit of Capitalism* and *Essays in Economics and Sociology*.

1
Introduction

The chapters in this book address the relationship among power, politics, and violence, examining why the political process of managing power within states sometimes becomes physically violent. Political violence is not new to the contemporary era, but the essays collected here, which primarily focus on political violence in the mid-late twentieth century, illuminate how certain aspects of modernity have contributed to shaping political violence. Many scholars suggest that the changing political and economic parameters of the post-Cold War "new world order" are producing novel forms of political violence in local arenas. Charting the contours of political violence through the 1980s provides a basis for assessing what is new and what is enduring about local violences after the fall of the Berlin Wall. To this end, this volume brings together some of the classic writings on the relationship between states and violence with some of the best new work on political violence in local settings. Many new studies of recent political violence begin at the local level, using close ethnography to link local expressions of political violence to state practices and global processes. As these studies make clear, the state remains the foremost global political institution governing people's lives with universally recognized political legitimacy. This volume takes the state as a reference point, and uses ethnographic cases to examine local interpretations of and motivations for violence. It addresses state-backed violence against citizens and subjects, and violence by citizens against the state and against each other for control of the state.[1]

The volume is organized into three sections. The first section explores the relationship between states and violence and introduces several important themes that reappear in later chapters. One important theme is the origin of political violence. Because states have been responsible for most political violence in the past century, investigating why states utilize violence and how governments justify violence is an important first step in the study of political violence. Other questions about what kinds of states use violence, and what kinds of political ideologies and economic forces sustain or underwrite violence contribute further to this project.

The frame of reference in the second section shifts to those who perpetrate violence against the state or lay claim to a reconstruction of the state, such as terrorists, revolutionaries, and civil war combatants. Recognizing that states are not the only institutions responsible for political violence, a burgeoning area of inquiry focuses on the motivations individuals or groups have for using violence rather than peaceful processes to achieve their goals within their states. Some of this literature demonstrates the rational choices made by perpetrators of violence, arguing that violence is a political instrument to achieve political ends, particularly when perpetrators believe other options have been exhausted. Other studies demonstrate the cultural context of violence, focusing on how local symbolic worlds and belief systems inform perpetrators' understandings of violence. While addressing how political violence may be initiated with rational and instrumental goals, the second section emphasizes the emotional and passionate dimensions of political violence.

The third section shifts the viewpoint again, to the cultural interpretation of violence in contexts that have become thoroughly pervaded by violence. Such violent places are sometimes described as having a "culture of violence" because violence has become normalized as part of the fabric of everyday life, even among the nonviolent members of the society. The chapters in the third section explore this process of normalization.

What motivates political violence? Setting aside the debates within evolutionary psychology about the extent to which humans are innately violent, our authors approach political violence in a variety of ways: as a calculated, rational choice made to achieve particular political goals; as a response to waning power; as motivated by a desire for economic gain; as an act of passion and ideology; and as a cultural performance with intense symbolic and historical references. The contributions overwhelmingly demonstrate that while political violence may be initiated with clearly defined, reasoned goals, these goals may be lost as violence becomes bureaucratically driven, culturally embedded, and/or symbolically elaborated as a normal part of life.

States and violence

In "Politics as a Vocation" (chapter 2 of this volume) Max Weber writes "the relation between the state and violence is an especially intimate one" (p. 13) – so intimate, in fact, that Weber defines a state as "a human community that (successfully) claims the *monopoly of the legitimate use of physical force* within a given territory" (p. 13, italics in original). While Weber was certainly not the first to note the state's involvement with violence, his observations highlight the fact that states are the only social institution that can claim legitimacy in domestic and international law when engaging in violence. Weber argues that violence is inherent to politics, which he defines as groups striving to share or influence the distribution of power, and that obedience to leaders derives in part from the state's monopoly on physical force. Whereas Weber emphasizes the productive aspect of the relationship between power and violence (the legitimate state), Arendt argues that violence is the opposite of power and is never legitimate. The end of violence is not power, she states, but the destruction of power, or terror. Stalin's reign provides a prime example. While Arendt is making a philosophical point about the relationship between power, politics, and violence, other writers have pursued the question of legitimacy identified by Weber by asking how states justify using violence in their pursuit of control and legitimacy.

Some authors address this question by demonstrating how violence may be embedded in the process of state formation. In one of the volume's two contributions about pre-twentieth-century violence, Charles Tilly analyzes the role of violence during the era of European state formation in the seventeenth and eighteenth centuries, a process that set the course for the eventual emergence of an international order of states. Tilly argues that the process of war making among European power-holders produced a distinctive state structure consisting of an administrative apparatus, a military apparatus, a legal apparatus, techniques of extraction, and strong ties with an emerging capitalist class. In short, Tilly concludes that "war makes states," a process historically intertwined in Western Europe with mercantile capitalism. Whereas Tilly emphasizes the links among war making, state making, and capitalism, Barrington Moore Jr.'s focus is the link between terror and socialism, particularly in the Soviet Union.

Addressing concerns prevalent when the essay was written, Moore concludes that socialism does not depend on organized terror, but that certain circumstances incline a socialist regime toward terror. The desire to rapidly alter the structure of society is one, although Moore stresses that the psychological insecurity produced by terror can be destructive to the project of transforming society. Terror had its uses in limiting alternative bases of power within the Soviet system under Stalin, Moore argues, but the regime must offer some semblance of legality to claim legitimacy.

Turning to fascism, Zygmunt Bauman's chapter pursues another dimension of the link between states and violence by addressing the case of a state determined to murder a significant portion of its citizenry as part of the process of state consolidation and modernization. Bauman demonstrates how the conditions of modernity (bureaucracy, science, the organization of knowledge, social engineering) facilitated the Holocaust in Nazi Germany. The chapters by Moore and Bauman suggest that while violence may not be inherent to socialism or fascism, leaders pursuing the task of restructuring a society – such as in Stalinist Russia and Nazi Germany – can utilize the bureaucratic, administrative, and security features of the modern state to complete their projects with efficient, well-organized violence.

Taken together, the five chapters in section I introduce issues that inform the volume. The question of legitimacy raised by Weber and Arendt recurs in several contributions that investigate the language of rationalization and the means–end balance employed by perpetrators of violence. The linked effects of capitalism and modernization explored respectively by Tilly and Bauman affect the spread of and technologies used for political violence. Whereas Tilly's analysis reflects Weber's view that violence is a "means" of politics, however, Bauman's emphasis on modernity shows the endpoint of Arendt's vision of the "rule by nobody" in the context of bureaucratic, technological, modernized state-backed terror. Still, Bauman does not agree with Arendt that the end of violence is not power; he retains a recognition that violence may be a means to a particular political end, and that modernity provides the tools to achieve that end with great efficiency. With Bauman, Moore also emphasizes the ways in which terror may enhance a regime's power, although he notes that the regime must "walk a thin and not always easily discernible line between using too much terror or too little."

In exploring the ways in which violence may be inherent to state building and state consolidation, the authors in section I affirm that states of all political ideologies have engaged in violence against their populations. State-building efforts offer opportunities for violence against internal opponents or undesirables, either to consolidate a particular kind of state citizenry or to control populations for state-backed economic development. State-building projects may support inequalities which benefit a political, economic, or cultural elite, and may establish structural conditions that nurture violence – either by the elite against the marginalized, or by the marginalized in protest against a social order that does not work to their benefit. The task is to determine where such opportunities for violence become available, and how decisions are made to exploit these opportunities violently. Communist and fascist governments clearly have more opportunities, and have been more overt in their use of violence to structure their states. But many scholars – particularly anthropologists – remind us of the violences perpetrated by capitalist states in order to ensure labor supplies and raw materials for capitalist production. Because capitalism is now the singular global economic system, the conclusion to the volume addresses the links between political violence and capitalism in further detail.

Political violence

States are not the only organizations that perpetrate violence, and violence against citizens has many origins besides the state's need for order and control. Certainly, few scholars would defend a definition of the state as purely oppressive, dominating, or monopolizing violence. The contributions in section II take the viewpoint of citizens who utilize violence for their own political purposes.

Martha Crenshaw's chapter, which opens the second section of the volume, provides a general analysis of the causes of terrorism. She suggests that terrorism is facilitated by modernization (particularly urbanization, increased social complexity, and a "permissive" moral environment) and argues that terrorists tend to be distinguished by their normalcy, their elite and minority status, their belief that they speak for a group, and their belief that their concerns are being ignored by their state governments. The "utilitarian" or "instrumental" view of political violence demonstrated in Crenshaw's piece is apparent in many studies of terrorism and revolutionary movements. The Prussian military strategist Clausewitz observed that war is politics continued through other means. Clausewitz's famous aphorism supports the instrumental approach to understanding political violence as a means to an end. The other chapters in section II reveal how much is left out in this approach.

Political violence is never simply instrumental; it is deeply cultural as well. The essays by Cynthia Mahmood, Begoña Aretxaga, Alexander Hinton, and Rhonda Copelon provide case studies of situations where people use terror to challenge state power (militant Sikh nationalists in India, the IRA/INLA in Northern Ireland) or to reconstruct state power (genocidal Khmer Rouge revolutionaries in Cambodia, perpetrators of mass rape in the fragmentation of Yugoslavia). These studies follow the reasoning that people who become terrorists and revolutionary leaders initiate violence to achieve political goals. But they push further than the utilitarian explanation to analyze how violence becomes culturally embedded, absorbing and transforming symbolic constructions of reality, morality, and truth. Weber notes the role of passion in politics; these contributions reveal how passion plays a critical role in political violence, sometimes leading perpetrators of violence to lose sight of their political goals. In these cases, violence can become an end in and of itself.

Mahmood explains how militant Sikh nationalists receive inspiration for their violent acts through their religiously mediated interpretation of history and their culturally elaborated understandings of honor and value. Hinton analyzes how "the Cambodian cultural model of disproportionate revenge" – apparent in socialization practices, ideologies of emotion, popular epics, sayings, and notions of morality – informed genocidal Khmer Rouge policies. Aretxaga explores the psychocultural dimensions of IRA prisoners' use of their own feces and menstrual blood as a form of political protest against prison violence, incarceration, and British political policy. The Northern Irish public read the prisoners' use of human filth as a symbolically rich commentary on British brutality and British colonialism, but also revealing of the gendered dimension of political violence. The violence enacted in all three of these cases has a utilitarian motivation: Sikhs and Northern Irish Catholics desire political and economic autonomy, and the Khmer Rouge utilized class antagonisms in their effort to create a new social order. But what violence means to those who perpetrate or support it is a crucial part of the project of making sense of political violence. These chapters address both arenas: what the perpetrators hope to accomplish in political terms, and how they understand the role of violence in cultural, symbolic terms.

Rhonda Copelon's chapter addresses another dimension of local violence in the modern world – the role of the international community in mediating and adjudicating local processes of state building that utilize terror, genocide, or massive violence. Her contribution suggests how international adjudicators who seek to punish perpetrators of violence must remain attentive to local meanings (what perpetrators thought they were doing, how victims understand their experiences of violence) as well as universal standards of justice. The case of mass rape in Yugoslavia raises questions about how international tribunals set up to punish war crimes can challenge the legitimacy of local political leaders who have used violence in their attempts to build or consolidate their states.

It is imperative to note that analyzing the cultural dimensions of political violence is a very different thing from suggesting that culture motivates violence, that particular cultures are more prone to violence, or that cultural differences produce violence. Rather, these studies (and hundreds of others) suggest that instrumental motivations for political violence can become culturally elaborated; in some cases to the extent that a culture of violence among perpetrators gradually evolves. The chapters in section III turn to the force of symbolism in constructing culturally specific modes of understanding the value, legitimacy, and morality of violence. As a symbolic view justifying and even demanding violence emerges, the utilitarian goals of violence may be lost. The military historian Martin Van Creveld (1991) challenges Clausewitz by arguing that in many contexts violence is not a means to a political end but becomes an end in itself. The endpoint of violence initially pursued for the political goals of power and control can very well become endless violence and the rule by nobody. The agonies of stateless violence apparent in places like Somalia and Sierra Leone provide examples that support Arendt's bleak vision of the political endpoint of violence.

The normalization of violence

The studies in section III analyze contexts where a culture of violence has emerged. The leading contribution by Michael Taussig (one of the first to explore the making of a "culture of terror") demonstrates how acts of terror can be a response to imagined (not actual) terror. The economics of rubber production in colonial Colombia depended on the use of forced labor, a system of control elaborated with great cruelty and torture. Taussig argues that since there was no real economic rationale for such extremely violent labor control policies, "an understanding of the way business can transform the use of terror from the means into an end in itself" (p. 220) must be sought elsewhere. Taussig focuses on the force of narrative in inculcating fear and terror among the rubber station managers, "a trade in terrifying mythologies and fictional realities" (p. 234) that inspired savage cruelty against Indian laborers. Taussig's piece suggests how rumor, innuendo, and gossip can produce a culture of fear through nurturing violent imaginings and inspiring violent action. In an interesting parallel, Barrington Moore, Jr. also noted that the Soviet state utilized terror in response to rumor.

Even in thoroughly violent places, however, ethnographic evidence is clear that most people are not violent, but rather work to avoid or mediate violence. The other chapters in section III turn to the experiences of these people, exploring how people living in the midst of violence manage, how they construct an understanding of the world, of humanity, and of morality.

Like Taussig, Julie Peteet's chapter addresses the poetics of political violence, demonstrating how violence shapes cultural constructions of personhood and personal worth among Palestinian men in the occupied territories. Palestinians have redefined Israeli violence (beatings and detention) as critical rites of passage toward manhood. In this context, the experience of political violence becomes a central component of cultural participation and membership, reconfiguring social relationships and cultural understandings of masculinity. Peteet's analysis illustrates how violence can be normalized through ritualization.

The concluding chapter in the volume offers the most positive analysis. In a world dominated by horrific violence for control of the Mozambican state, Carolyn Nordstrom shows how ordinary people – noncombatants – work symbolically to cleanse combatants and villages of violence. The Mozambique of Nordstrom's description certainly resembles the Hobbesian image of anarchic war – the warring sides are ideologically bereft, soldiers are often children who commit acts of terrible destruction, low-intensity warfare targets civilians and civic leaders – but she shows how civilians show remarkable cultural resilience and are able to maintain order and work toward peace. According to Nordstrom, a culture of peace has emerged from a culture of terror, suggesting that Arendt's endpoint of violence (terror) may be met by locally generated alternatives.

Conclusion

Collectively, the contributions suggest that contemporary political violence may result from the frustrations of a politically or economically disenfranchised group, a regime's fears of losing power, a bureaucratically elaborated nationalist rhetoric of exclusion, or an effort to impose a radically new social order. The social dislocations caused by an economy of extraction or expanding capitalism may contribute to political violence. The most virulent instances of political violence seem to be associated with revolutionary fervor to create a new kind of society (Nazi Germany, Khmer Rouge in Cambodia, the partitioning of Yugoslavia). The violent process of social reconstruction can be made more efficient with modern tools, such as bureaucratized administrative hierarchies, surveillance systems, state control of information, and killing technologies. But the smaller-scale, ongoing conflicts between militant Sikhs and the Indian state, Palestinians and the Israeli state, Northern Irish Catholics and the British government, or Renamo guerrillas and the Mozambican state require a different kind of explanation. Originating in protest against political and/or economic marginalization, these long-term conflicts have absorbed a nonpolitical variety of meanings and motivations. The contributions in sections II and III revealed how political violence is not only instrumental, but is highly emotional, symbolically apprehended, filled with poetics and passions for perpetrators and victims alike. Political goals may recede in the face of the sensuousness of violence. Political goals may initiate violent conflict, but they may not be the only or even the most important force sustaining them.

This is a frightening conclusion. If political violence is not simply instrumental, a means to an end, but is rather an end in itself, then "reason" will not bring about peace (cf. Simons 1999). But the studies collected here also show that the vast majority of people in violent places are not perpetrators; they are victims, accidental bystanders, or complicitous in their silence. In a global world characterized by the rapid movement of information, ideas, and people, this latter group may play an increasingly important role in mobilizing to end political violence. The conclusion to the volume takes up the question of the changing nature of political violence in the globalized contemporary world.

Note

1. International war is obviously political violence, but this volume focuses on political violence within the boundaries of the state. Simons (1999) provides a useful survey of the recent literature on war.

Bibliography

Simons, Anna. "WAR: Back to the Future." *Annual Review of Anthropology* 28 (1999):73–108.
van Creveld, Martin. *The Transformation of War*. (New York: The Free Press, 1991.)

Part I
Violence and the State

2

Politics as a Vocation

Max Weber

We wish to understand by politics only the leadership, or the influencing of the leadership, of a *political* association, hence today, of a *state*.

But what is a "political" association from the sociological point of view? What is a "state"? Sociologically, the state cannot be defined in terms of its ends. There is scarcely any task that some political association has not taken in hand, and there is no task that one could say has always been exclusive and peculiar to those associations which are designated as political ones: today the state, or historically, those associations which have been the predecessors of the modern state. Ultimately, one can define the modern state sociologically only in terms of the specific *means* peculiar to it, as to every political association, namely, the use of physical force.

"Every state is founded on force," said Trotsky at Brest-Litovsk. That is indeed right. If no social institutions existed which knew the use of violence, then the concept of "state" would be eliminated, and a condition would emerge that could be designated as "anarchy," in the specific sense of this word. Of course, force is certainly not the normal or the only means of the state – nobody says that – but force is a means specific to the state. Today the relation between the state and violence is an especially intimate one. In the past, the most varied institutions have known the use of physical force as quite normal. Today, however, we have to say that a state is a human community that (successfully) claims the *monopoly of the legitimate use of physical force* within a given territory. Note that "territory" is one of the characteristics of the state. Specifically, at the present time, the right to use physical force is ascribed to other institutions or to individuals only to the extent to which the state permits it. The state is considered the sole source of the "right" to use violence. Hence, "politics" for us means striving to share

13

power or striving to influence the distribution of power, either among states or among groups within a state.

This corresponds essentially to ordinary usage. When a question is said to be a "political" question, when a cabinet minister or an official is said to be a "political" official, or when a decision is said to be "politically" determined, what is always meant is that interests in the distribution, maintenance, or transfer of power are decisive for answering the questions and determining the decision or the official's sphere of activity. He who is active in politics strives for power either as a means in serving other aims, ideal or egoistic, or as "power for power's sake," that is, in order to enjoy the prestige-feeling that power gives.

Like the political institutions historically preceding it, the state is a relation of men dominating men, a relation supported by means of legitimate (i.e. considered to be legitimate) violence. If the state is to exist, the dominated must obey the authority claimed by the powers that be. When and why do men obey? Upon what inner justifications and upon what external means does this domination rest?

To begin with, in principle, there are three inner justifications, hence basic *legitimations* of domination.

First, the authority of the "eternal yesterday," i.e. of the mores sanctified through the unimaginably ancient recognition and habitual orientation to conform. This is "traditional" domination exercised by the patriarch and the patrimonial prince of yore.

There is the authority of the extraordinary and personal *gift of grace* (charisma), the absolutely personal devotion and personal confidence in revelation, heroism, or other qualities of individual leadership. This is "charismatic" domination, as exercised by the prophet or – in the field of politics – by the elected war lord, the plebiscitarian ruler, the great demagogue, or the political party leader.

Finally, there is domination by virtue of "legality," by virtue of the belief in the validity of legal statute and functional "competence" based on rationally created *rules*. In this case, obedience is expected in discharging statutory obligations. This is domination as exercised by the modern "servant of the state" and by all those bearers of power who in this respect resemble him.

It is understood that, in reality, obedience is determined by highly robust motives of fear and hope – fear of the vengeance of magical powers or of the power-holder, hope for reward in this world or in the beyond – and besides all this, by interests of the most varied sort. Of this we shall speak presently. However, in asking for the "legitimations" of this obedience, one meets with these three "pure" types: "traditional," "charismatic," and "legal."

These conceptions of legitimacy and their inner justifications are of very great significance for the structure of domination. To be sure, the pure types are rarely found in reality. But today we cannot deal with the highly complex variants, transitions, and combinations of these pure types, which problems belong to "political science." Here we are interested above all in the second of these types: domination by virtue of the devotion of those who obey the purely personal "charisma" of the "leader." For this is the root of the idea of a *calling* in its highest expression.

Devotion to the charisma of the prophet, or the leader in war, or to the great demagogue in the *ecclesia* or in parliament, means that the leader is personally recognized as the innerly "called" leader of men. Men do not obey him by virtue of tradition or statute, but because they believe in him. If he is more than a narrow and vain upstart of the moment, the leader lives for his cause and "strives for his work." The devotion of his disciples, his followers, his personal party friends is oriented to his person and to its qualities.

Charismatic leadership has emerged in all places and in all historical epochs. Most importantly in the past, it has emerged in the two figures of the magician and the prophet on the one hand, and in the elected war lord, the gang leader and *condotierre* on the other hand. *Political* leadership in the form of the free "demagogue" who grew from the soil of the city-state is of greater concern to us; like the city-state, the demagogue is peculiar to the Occident and especially to Mediterranean culture. Furthermore, political leadership in the form of the parliamentary "party leader" has grown on the soil of the constitutional state, which is also indigenous only to the Occident.

These politicians by virtue of a "calling," in the most genuine sense of the word, are of course nowhere the only decisive figures in the cross-currents of the political struggle for power. The sort of auxiliary means that are at their disposal is also highly decisive. How do the politically dominant powers manage to maintain their domination? The question pertains to any kind of domination, hence also to political domination in all its forms, traditional as well as legal and charismatic.

Organized domination, which calls for continuous administration, requires that human conduct be conditioned to obedience towards those masters who claim to be the bearers of legitimate power. On the other hand, by virtue of this obedience, organized domination requires the control of those material goods which in a given case are necessary for the use of physical violence. Thus, organized domination requires control of the personal executive staff and the material implements of administration.

The administrative staff, which externally represents the organiza-tion of political domination, is, of course, like any other organization, bound by obedience to the power-holder and not alone by the concept of legitimacy, of which we have just spoken. There are two other means, both of which appeal to personal interests: material reward and social honor. The fiefs of vassals, the prebends of patrimonial officials, the salaries of modern civil servants, the honor of knights, the privil-eges of estates, and the honor of the civil servant comprise their respec-tive wages. The fear of losing them is the final and decisive basis for solidarity between the executive staff and the power-holder. There is honor and booty for the followers in war; for the demagogue's follow-ing, there are "spoils" – that is, exploitation of the dominated through the monopolization of office – and there are politically determined profits and premiums of vanity. All of these rewards are also derived from the domination exercised by a charismatic leader.

To maintain a dominion by force, certain material goods are required, just as with an economic organization. All states may be classified according to whether they rest on the principle that the staff of men themselves *own* the administrative means, or whether the staff is "separated" from these means of administration. This distinction holds in the same sense in which today we say that the salaried employee and the proletarian in the capitalistic enterprise are "sepa-rated" from the material means of production. The power-holder must be able to count on the obedience of the staff members, officials, or whoever else they may be. The administrative means may consist of money, building, war material, vehicles, horses, or whatnot. The ques-tion is whether or not the power-holder himself directs and organizes the administration while delegating executive power to personal ser-vants, hired officials, or personal favorites and confidants, who are non-owners, i.e. who do not use the material means of administration in their own right but are directed by the lord. The distinction runs through all administrative organizations of the past.

These political associations in which the material means of adminis-tration are autonomously controlled, wholly or partly, by the depen-dent administrative staff may be called associations organized in "*estates*." The vassal in the feudal association, for instance, paid out of his own pocket for the administration and judicature of the district enfeoffed to him. He supplied his own equipment and provisions for war, and his subvassals did likewise. Of course, this had consequences for the lord's position of power, which only rested upon a relation of personal faith and upon the fact that the legitimacy of his possession of the fief and the social honor of the vassal were derived from the overlord.

However, everywhere, reaching back to the earliest political formations, we also find the lord himself directing the administration. He seeks to take the administration into his own hands by having men personally dependent upon him: slaves, household officials, attendants, personal "favorites," and prebendaries enfeoffed in kind or in money from his magazines. He seeks to defray the expenses from his own pocket, from the revenues of his patrimonium; and he seeks to create an army which is dependent upon him personally because it is equipped and provisioned out of his granaries, magazines, and armories. In the association of "estates," the lord rules with the aid of an autonomous "aristocracy" and hence shares his domination with it; the lord who personally administers is supported either by members of his household or by plebeians. These are propertyless strata having no social honor of their own; materially, they are completely chained to him and are not backed up by any competing power of their own. All forms of patriarchal and patrimonial domination, Sultanist despotism, and bureaucratic states belong to this latter type. The bureaucratic state order is especially important; in its most rational development, it is precisely characteristic of the modern state.

Everywhere the development of the modern state is initiated through the action of the prince. He paves the way for the expropriation of the autonomous and "private" bearers of executive power who stand beside him, of those who in their own right possess the means of administration, warfare, and financial organization, as well as politically usable goods of all sorts. The whole process is a complete parallel to the development of the capitalist enterprise through gradual expropriation of the independent producers. In the end, the modern state controls the total means of political organization, which actually come together under a single head. No single official personally owns the money he pays out, or the buildings, stores, tools, and war machines he controls. In the contemporary "state" – and this is essential for the concept of state – the "separation" of the administrative staff, of the administrative officials, and of the workers from the material means of administrative organization is completed. Here the most modern development begins, and we see with our own eyes the attempt to inaugurate the expropriation of this expropriator of the political means, and therewith of political power.

The modern state is a compulsory association which organizes domination. It has been successful in seeking to monopolize the legitimate use of physical force as a means of domination within a territory. To this end the state has combined the material means of organization in the hands of its leaders, and it has expropriated all autonomous functionaries of estates who formerly controlled these means in their own right. The state has taken their positions and now stands in the top place.

3

Reflections on Violence

Hannah Arendt

These reflections were provoked by the events and debates of the last few years as seen against the background of the twentieth century, which has become indeed, as Lenin predicted, a century of wars and revolutions, hence a century of that violence which is currently believed to be their common denominator. There is, however, another factor in the present situation which, though predicted by nobody, is of at least equal importance. The technical development of the implements of violence has now reached the point where no political goal could conceivably correspond to their destructive potential or justify their actual use in armed conflict. Hence, warfare – since times immemorial the final merciless arbiter in international disputes – has lost much of its effectiveness and nearly all of its glamor. "The apocalytic" chess game between the superpowers, that is, between those that move on the highest plane of our civilization, is being played according to the rule: "if either 'wins' it is the end of both"; it is a game that bears no resemblance to whatever war games preceded it. Its "rational" goal is deterrence, not victory.

Since violence – in distinction from power, force, or strength – always needs *implements* (as Engels pointed out long ago), the revolution in technology, a revolution in tool-making, was especially marked in warfare. The very substance of violent action is ruled by the means–end category, whose chief characteristic, if applied to human affairs, has always been that the end is in danger of being overwhelmed by the means which it justifies and which are needed to reach it. Since the end of human action, in distinction from the end products of fabrication, can never be reliably predicted, the means used to achieve political goals are more often than

Published by permission of the *Journal of International Affairs* and the Trustees of Columbia University in the City of New York. Footnotes were deleted to accommodate length requirements.

not of greater relevance to the future world than the intended goals. Moreover, all violence harbors within itself an element of arbitrariness; nowhere does Fortuna, good or ill luck, play a more important role in human affairs than on the battlefield, and this intrusion of the "Random Event" can be eliminated by no game theories but only by the certainty of mutual destruction. It is symbolic of this all-pervading unpredictability, which we encounter the moment we approach the realm of violence, that those engaged in the perfection of the means of destruction have finally brought about a level of technical development where their aim, namely warfare, is on the point of disappearing altogether by virtue of the means at its disposal.

No one engaged in thought about history and politics can remain unaware of the enormous role violence has always played in human affairs, and it is at first glance rather surprising that violence has so seldom been singled out for special consideration. (In the last edition of the *Encyclopedia of the Social Sciences* "violence" does not even rate an entry.) This shows to what an extent violence and its arbitrariness were taken for granted and therefore neglected; no one questions or examines what is obvious to all. Those who saw nothing but violence in human affairs, convinced that they were "always haphazard, not serious, not precise" (Renan) or that God was forever with the stronger bayonets, had nothing more to say about either violence or history. Whoever looked for some kind of sense in the records of the past was almost bound to look upon violence as a marginal phenomenon. Whether Clausewitz calls war "the continuation of politics with other means," or Engels defines violence as the accelerator of economic development, the emphasis is on political or economic continuity, on the continuity of a process which remains determined by what preceded violent action. Hence, students of international relations have held until very recently that "it was a maxim that a military resolution in discord with the deeper cultural sources of national power could not be stable," or that, in Engels' words, "wherever the power structure of a country contradicts its economic development" it is political power with its means of violence that will suffer defeat.

Today all these old verities about the relation of war and politics or about violence and power have become inapplicable. We know that "a few weapons could wipe out all other sources of national power in a few moments," that biological weapons are devised which would enable "small groups of individuals ... to upset the strategic balance" and be cheap enough to be produced by "nations unable to develop nuclear striking forces," that "within a very few years" robot soldiers will have made "human soldiers completely obsolete," and that, finally, in conventional warfare the poor countries are much less vulnerable than the great powers precisely because they are "underdeveloped," and because technical superiority can "be much more of a liability than an asset" in guerrilla wars. What all these very uncomfortable novelties add up to is a complete reversal in the relationship between power and violence, foreshadowing another reversal in the future relationship between small and great powers. The amount of violence at the disposal of any given country may soon not be a reliable indication of the country's strength or a reliable guarantee against destruction by a substantially smaller and weaker power. And this again bears an ominous similarity to one of the oldest insights of political science, namely, that power cannot be measured in terms of wealth, that an abundance of wealth may erode power, that riches are particularly dangerous for the power and well-being of republics – an insight that does not lose in validity because it is conveniently forgotten, especially at a time when its truth has acquired a new dimension of validity by becoming applicable to the arsenal of violence as well.

The more doubtful and uncertain of result the use of violence has become in international relations, the more it has gained in reputation and appeal in domestic affairs, specifically in the matter of revolution. The strong Marxist flavor in the rhetoric of the New Left coincides with the steady growth of the entirely non-Marxian conviction, proclaimed by Mao Tse-tung, "Power grows out of the barrel of a gun." To be sure, Marx was aware of the role of violence in history, but this role was to him secondary; not violence but the contradictions inherent in the old society brought about its end. The emergence of a new society was preceded, but not caused, by violent outbreaks, which he likened to the labor pangs that precede, but of course do not cause, the event of organic birth. In the same vein he regarded the state as an instrument of violence at the command of the ruling class; but the actual power of the ruling class did not consist of or rely on violence. It was defined by the role the ruling class played in society, or more exactly, by its role in the process of production. It has often been noticed, and sometimes deplored, that the revolutionary Left under the influence of Marx's teachings ruled out the use of violent means; the "dictatorship of the proletariat" – openly repressive in Marx's writings – came after the revolution and was meant, like the Roman dictatorship, for a strictly limited period. Political assassination, with the exception of a few acts of individual terror perpetuated by small groups of anarchists, was mostly the prerogative of the Right, while organized armed uprisings remained the specialty of the military.

On the level of theory there were a few exceptions. Georges Sorel, who at the beginning of the century tried a combination of Marxism with Bergson's philosophy of life – which on a much lower level of sophistication shows an odd similarity with Sartre's current amalgamation of existentialism and Marxism – thought of class struggle in military terms; but he ended by proposing nothing more violent than the famous myth of the general strike, a form of action which we today would rather think of as belonging to the arsenal of nonviolent politics. Fifty years ago even this modest proposal earned him the reputation of being a fascist, his enthusiastic approval of Lenin and the Russian Revolution notwithstanding. Sartre, who in his Preface to Fanon's *The Wretched of the Earth* goes much farther in his glorification of violence than Sorel in his famous *Reflections on Violence* – farther than Fanon himself, whose argument he wishes to bring to its conclusion – still mentions "Sorel's fascist utterances." This shows to what extent Sartre is unaware of his basic disagreement with Marx on the question of violence, especially when he states that "irrepressible violence … is man recreating himself," that it is "mad fury" through which "the wretched of the earth" can "become men." These notions are all the more remarkable as the idea of man creating himself is strictly in the tradition of Hegelian and Marxian thinking; it is the very basis of all leftist humanism. But according to Hegel man "produces" himself through thought, whereas for Marx, who put Hegel's "idealism" upside down, it was labor, the human form of metabolism with nature, that fulfilled this function. And though one may argue that all notions of man-creating-himself have in common a rebellion against the very factuality of the human condition – nothing is more obvious than that man, be it as member of the species or as an individual, does *not* owe his existence to himself – and that therefore what Sartre, Marx, and Hegel have in common is more relevant than the specific activities through which this non-fact should have come about, it is hardly deniable that a gulf separates the essentially peaceful activities of thinking or laboring from all deeds of violence. "To shoot down a European is to kill two birds with one stone … there remains a dead man and a free man," writes Sartre in his Preface. This is a sentence Marx could never have written.

I quoted Sartre in order to show that this new shift toward violence in the thinking of revolutionaries can remain unnoticed even by one of their most representative and articulate spokesmen. I think this makes it all the more noteworthy insofar as it shows that we do not deal here with some abstract notion in the history of ideas. (If one turns the "idealistic" *concept* of thought upside down one might arrive at the "materialistic" *concept* of labor; one will never arrive at the notion of violence). No doubt this development has a logic of its own, but this logic springs from experience and not from a development of ideas; and this experience was utterly unknown to any generation before.

The pathos and the *élan* of the New Left, their credibility as it were, are closely connected with the weird suicidal development of modern weapons; this is the first generation that grew up under the shadow of the atom bomb. It inherited from the generation of its fathers the experience of a massive intrusion of criminal violence into politics – they learned in high school and in college about concentration and extermination camps, about genocide and torture, about the wholesale slaughter of civilians in war, without which modern military operations are no longer possible even if they remain restricted to "conventional" weapons. Their first reaction was a revulsion against violence in all its forms, an almost matter-of-course espousal of a politics of nonviolence. The successes of this movement, especially with respect to civil rights, were very great, and they were followed by the resistance movement against the war in Vietnam, which again determined to a considerable degree the climate of opinion in this country. But it is a secret to nobody that things have changed since then, and it would be futile to say that only the "extremists" are yielding to a glorification of violence and believe with Fanon that "only violence pays."

The new militants have been denounced as anarchists, red fascists, and, with considerably more justification, "Luddite machine smashers." Their behavior has been blamed on all kinds of social and psychological causes, some of which we shall have to discuss later. Still, it seems absurd, especially in view of the global character of the phenomenon, to ignore the most obvious and perhaps the most potent factor in this development, for which moreover no precedent and no analogy exist – the fact that technological progress seems in so many instances to lead straight into disaster; that the proliferation of techniques and machines, far from threatening only certain classes with unemployment, menaces the very existence of whole nations and conceivably of all mankind. It is only natural that the new generation should live with greater awareness of the possibility of doomsday than those "over thirty," not because they are younger but because this was their first decisive experience in the world. If you ask a member of this generation two simple questions: "How do you wish the world to be in fifty years?" and "What do you want your life to be like five years from now?" the answers are quite often preceded by a "Provided that there is still a world," and "Provided I am still alive."

To be sure, this violence is still mostly a matter of theory and rhetoric, but it is precisely this rhetoric shot through with all kinds of Marxist leftovers that is so baffling. Who could possibly call an ideology Marxist that has put its faith in "the classless idlers," believes that "in the lumpen-proletariat the rebellion will find its urban spearhead," and trusts that the "gangsters light the way for the people?" Sartre in his great felicity with words has given expression to the new faith. "Violence," he now believes on the strength of Fanon's book, "like Achilles' lance, can heal the wounds that it has inflicted." If this were true, revenge would be the cure-all for most of our ills. This myth is more abstract, farther removed from reality than Sorel's myth of a general strike ever was. It is on a par with Fanon's worst rhetorical excesses such as, "Hunger with dignity is preferable to bread eaten in slavery." No history and no theory is needed to refute this statement; the most superficial observer of the processes in the human body knows its untruth. But had he said that bread eaten with dignity is preferable to cake eaten in slavery the rhetorical point would have been lost.

If one reads these irresponsible grandiose statements of the intellectuals – and those I quoted are fairly representative, except that Fanon still manages to stay closer to reality than most – and if one looks at them in the perspective of what we know about the history of rebellions and revolutions, it is tempting to deny their significance, to ascribe them to a passing mood, or to the ignorance and nobility of sentiment of those who are exposed to unprecedented events and developments without any means to handle them mentally, and who therefore bring about a curious revival of thoughts and emotions which Marx had hoped to have buried once and for all. For it is certainly nothing new that those who are being violated dream of violence, that those who are oppressed "dream at least once a day of setting" themselves up in the oppressor's place, that those who are poor dream of the possessions of the rich, the persecuted of exchanging "the role of the quarry for that of the hunter," and the last of the kingdom where "the last shall be first, and the first last." The great rarity of slave-rebellions and of uprisings among the disinherited and downtrodden is notorious; on the rare occasions when they occurred it was precisely "mad fury" that turned dreams into nightmares for everybody. In no case, as far as I know, was the force of these "volcanic" outbursts, in

Sartre's words, "equal to that of the pressure put on them." To believe that we deal with such outbursts in the National Liberation Movements is to prophesy their doom – quite apart from the fact that the unlikely victory would not result in the change of the world (or the system), but only of its personnel. To think, finally, that there is such a thing as the "Unity of the Third World," to which one could address the new slogan in the era of decolonization, "Natives of all underdeveloped countries unite!" (Sartre) is to repeat Marx's worst illusions on a greatly enlarged scale and with considerably less justification.

It is against the background of these experiences that I propose to raise the question of violence in the political realm. This is not easy; for what Sorel remarked sixty years ago, "The problems of violence still remain very obscure," is as true today as it was then. I mentioned the general reluctance to deal with violence as a separate phenomenon in its own right, and I must now qualify this statement. If we turn to the literature on the phenomenon of power, we soon find out that there exists a consensus of opinion among political theorists from Left to Right, to the effect that violence is nothing more than the most flagrant manifestation of power. "All politics is a struggle for power; the ultimate kind of power is violence," said C. Wright Mills, echoing, as it were, Max Weber's definition of the state as "the rule of men over men based on the means of legitimate, that is allegedly legitimate, violence." The consensus is very strange; for to equate political power with "the organization of violence" makes sense only if one follows Marx's estimate of the state as an instrument of suppression in the hands of the ruling class. Let us therefore turn to authors who do not believe that the body politic, its laws and institutions, are merely coercive superstructures, secondary manifestations of some underlying forces. Let us turn, for instance, to Bertrand de Jouvenel, whose book on *Power* is perhaps the most prestigious and, anyway, the most interesting recent treatise on the subject. "To him," he writes, "who contemplates the unfolding of the ages war presents itself as an activity of States, *which pertains to their essence*." Would then, we are likely to ask, the end of warfare mean the end of states? Would the disappearance of violence in the relationships between states spell the end of power?

The answer, it seems, would depend on what we understand by power. And power turns out to be defined as an instrument of rule, while rule, we are told, owes its existence to "the instinct of domination." We are immediately reminded of what Sartre said about violence when we read in Jouvenel that "a man feels himself more of a man when he is imposing himself and making others the instruments of his will," which causes him "incomparable pleasure." "Power," said Voltaire, "consists in making others act as I choose"; it is present wherever I have the chance "to assert my own will against the resistance" of others, said Max Weber, reminding us of Clausewitz' definition of war as "an act of violence to compel the opponent to do as we wish." The word, we are told by Strausz-Hupé, signifies "the power of man over man." To go back to Jouvenel: "To command and to be obeyed: without that, there is no Power – with it no other attribute is needed for it to be ... The thing without which it cannot be: that essence is command." If the essence of power is the effectiveness of command, then there is no greater power than that which grows out of the barrel of a gun. Should Bertrand de Jouvenel and Mao Tse-tung agree on so basic a point in political philosophy as the nature of power?

In terms of our tradition of political thought, these definitions have much to recommend themselves. They coincide with the terms which have been used since Greek antiquity to define the forms of government as the rule of man over man – of one or the few in monarchy and oligarchy, of the best or the many in aristocracy and democracy. Today we ought to add to these terms the latest and perhaps most formidable form of such dominion, bureaucracy or the rule by an intricate system of bureaux in which no men, neither one nor the best, neither the few nor the many, can be held responsible and which could be properly called the rule by Nobody. (If, in accord with traditional political thought, we identify tyranny as the government that is not held to give account of itself, rule by Nobody is clearly the most tyrannical of all, since there is no one left who could even be asked to answer for what is being done. It is this state of affairs which is among the most potent causes for the current world-wide rebellious unrest.)

Moreover, the force of this ancient vocabulary has been considerably strengthened by more modern scientific and philosophical convictions concerning the nature of man. The many recent discoveries of an inborn instinct of domination and an innate aggressiveness in the human animal were preceded by very similar philosophic statements. According to John Stuart Mill "the first lesson of civilization [is] that of obedience," and he speaks of "the two states of the inclinations ... one the desire to exercise power over others; the other ... disinclination to have power exercised over themselves." If we would trust our own experiences in these matters, we should know that the instinct of submission, an ardent desire to obey and be ruled by some strong man, is at least as prominent in human psychology as the will-to-power, and politically, perhaps more relevant. A German saying, to the effect that who wants to command must first learn how to obey, points to the psychological truth in these matters; namely, that the will-to-power and the will-to-submission are interconnected. "Ready submission to tyranny," to use J. S. Mill once more, is by no means always caused by "extreme passiveness." Conversely, a strong disinclination to obey is often accompanied by an equally strong repugnance to dominate and command. Historically speaking, the ancient institution of slave economy would be inexplicable on these grounds. For its express purpose was to liberate the citizens from the burden of household affairs and to permit them to enter the public life of the community where all were equals; if it were true that nothing is sweeter than to give commands and to rule others, the master would never have left his household.

However, there exists another tradition and another vocabulary no less old and time-honored than the one mentioned above. When the Athenian city-state called its constitution an isonomy, or the Romans spoke of the *civitas* as their form of government, they had in mind another concept of power whose essence did not rely upon the command–obedience relationship. It is to these examples that the men of the eighteenth-century revolutions turned when they ransacked the archives of antiquity and constituted a form of government, a republic, where the rule of law, resting on the power of the people, would put an end to the rule of man over man, which they thought was "a government fit for slaves." They too, unhappily, still talked about obedience – obedience to laws instead of men; but what they actually meant was the support of the laws to which the citizenry had given its consent. Such support is never unquestioning, and as far as reliability is concerned it cannot match the indeed "unquestioning obedience" that an act of violence can exact – the obedience every criminal can count on when he snatches my pocketbook with the help of a knife or robs a bank with the help of a gun. It is the support of the people that lends power to the institutions of a country, and this support is but the continuation of the consent which brought the laws into existence to begin with. Under conditions of representative government the people are supposed to rule those who govern them. All political institutions are manifestations and materializations of power; they petrify and decay as soon as the living power of the people ceases to uphold them. This is what Madison meant when he said "all governments rest on opinion," a word that is no less true for the various forms of monarchies than it is for democracies. ("To suppose that majority rule functions only in democracy is a fantastic illusion," as Jouvenel points out: "The king, who is but one solitary individual, stands far more in need of the general support of Society than any other form of government.") Even the tyrant, the One who rules against all, needs helpers in the business of violence, though their number may be more restricted. However, the strength of opinion, that is, the power of the government, depends on numbers; it is "in proportion to the number with which it is associated," and tyranny, as Montesquieu discovered, is therefore the most violent and the least powerful among the forms of government. It is indeed one of the most obvious distinctions between power and violence that power always stands in need of numbers, whereas relying on implements, violence up to a point can manage without them. A legally unrestricted majority rule, that is, a democracy without a constitution, can be very formidable indeed in the suppression of the rights of minorities and very effective in the suffocation of dissent without any use of violence. Undivided and unchecked power can bring about a "consensus" of opinion which is hardly less coercive than suppression by means of violence. But that does not mean than violence and power are the same.

It is, I think, a rather sad reflection on the present state of political science that our terminological language does not distinguish between such key terms as power, strength, force, authority, and, finally, violence – all of which refer to distinct, different phenomena and would hardly exist unless they did. To use them as synonyms indicates not only a certain deafness to linguistic meanings, which would be serious enough; it has also resulted in a kind of blindness with respect to the realities they correspond to. In such a situation it is always tempting to introduce new definitions, but I am afraid this would not help; the definitions would lack in plausibility. There is behind the apparent confusion a firm conviction in whose light all distinctions would actually be of, at best, minor importance; namely, the conviction that the most crucial political issue is, and always has been, the question of Who rules Whom? It is only after one eliminates this disastrous reduction of public affairs to the business of dominion, that the original data in the realm of human affairs will appear or rather reappear in their authentic diversity.

With this we cannot concern ourselves here. And it must be admitted that it is particularly tempting to think of power in terms of command and obedience, and hence to equate power with violence, in a discussion of what actually is only one of power's special cases –

namely, the power of government. Since in foreign relations as well as in domestic affairs violence appears as a kind of last resort to keep the power structure intact against individual challengers – the foreign enemy, the native criminal – it looks indeed as though power were nothing but a façade, the velvet glove which either conceals the iron hand or will turn out to belong to a paper tiger. However, upon closer inspection this presentation loses much of its plausibility. For our purpose, the gap between theory and reality is perhaps best illustrated by the phenomenon of revolution.

Since the beginning of the century theoreticians of revolution have told us that the chances of revolution have significantly decreased in proportion to the increased destructive capacities of weapons at the unique disposition of governments. The history of the last seventy years, with its extraordinary record of successful and unsuccessful revolutions, tells a different story. Were people mad who even tried against such overwhelming odds? And, quite apart from instances of full success, how can even a temporary success be explained? The fact is that the gap between state-owned means of violence and what people can muster by themselves – from beer bottles to Molotov cocktails and guns – has always been so enormous that technical improvements make hardly any difference. Textbook recommendations of "how to make a revolution" in a step-by-step progression from dissent to conspiracy, from resistance to armed uprising, are all based on the mistaken notion that revolutions are being "made." In a contest of violence against violence the superiority of the government has always been absolute; but this superiority lasts only so long as the power structure of the government is intact – that is, so long as commands are obeyed and the army or police forces are prepared to use their weapons. When this is no longer the case, the situation changes abruptly. Not only is the rebellion not put down, the arms themselves change hands – sometimes as in the Hungarian Revolution within a few hours. (We should know about such things after all these years of futile fighting in Vietnam where for a long time, prior to massive aid from Russia, the National Liberation Front fought us with weapons that were made in the United States.) Only after this has happened, when the disintegration of the government in power has permitted the rebels to arm themselves, can one speak of an "armed uprising," which often does not take place at all or occurs when it is no longer necessary. Where commands are no longer obeyed, the means of violence are of no use; and the question of this obedience is not decided by the command–obedience relation but by opinion, and, of course, by the

number of those who share it. Everything depends upon the power
behind the violence. The sudden dramatic breakdown of power, which
ushers in revolutions, reveals in a flash how civil obedience – to the
laws, to the rulers, to the institutions – is but the outward manifestation of support and consent.

Where power has disintegrated, revolutions are possible but not necessary. We know of many instances when utterly impotent regimes
were permitted to continue in existence for long periods of time –
either because there was no one to test their strength and to reveal
their weakness, or because they were lucky enough not to be engaged
in war and suffer defeat. For disintegration often becomes manifest
only in direct confrontation; and even then, when power is already in
the street, some group of men, prepared for such an eventuality, is
needed to pick it up and assume responsibility. We have just witnessed
how the relatively harmless, essentially non-violent French students'
rebellion was sufficient to reveal the vulnerability of the whole political system which rapidly disintegrated before the astonished eyes of
the young rebels. Without knowing it they had tested the system. They
intended no more than to challenge the ossified university system, and
down came the system of governmental power together with that of
the huge party bureaucracies – "une sorte de désintégration de toutes
les hiérarchies." It was a textbook case of a revolutionary situation
which did not develop into a revolution because there was nobody,
least of all the students, who was prepared to seize power and the
responsibility that goes with it. Nobody except, of course, de Gaulle.
Nothing was more characteristic of the seriousness of the situation
than his appeal to the army, his ride to see Massu and the generals in
the dark of the night, a walk to Canossa if there ever was one in view
of what had happened only a few years before. But what he sought and
received was support, not obedience, and the means to obtain it were
not commands but concessions. If commands had been enough he
would never have had to leave Paris.

No government exclusively based upon the means of violence has
ever existed. Even the totalitarian ruler, whose chief instrument of rule
is torture, needs a power basis, the secret police and its net of inform-
ers. Only the above-mentioned development of robot soldiers, which
would eliminate the human factor completely and, conceivably,
permit one man with a pushbutton at his disposal to destroy
whomever he pleases, could change this fundamental ascendancy of
power over violence. Even the most despotic domination we know of,
the rule of master over slaves, who always outnumbered him, did not

rest upon superior means of coercion as such but upon a superior organization of power – that is, upon the organized solidarity of the masters. Single men without others to support them never have enough power to use violence. Hence, in domestic affairs, violence functions as the last resort of power against criminals or rebels – that is, against single individuals who, as it were, refuse to be overpowered by the consensus of the majority. And even in actual warfare, we have seen in Vietnam how an enormous superiority in the means of violence can become helpless if confronted with an ill-equipped but well organized opponent who is much more powerful. This lesson, to be sure, could have been learned since the beginnings of guerrilla warfare, which is at least as old as the defeat of Napoleon's still unvanquished army in Spain.

To switch for a moment to conceptual language: Power is indeed of the essence of all government, but violence is not. Violence is by nature instrumental; like all means, it always stands in need of guidance and justification through the end it pursues. And what needs justification through something else cannot be the essence of anything. The end of war – end taken in its twofold meaning – is peace or victory; but to the question, And what is the end of peace? there is no answer. Peace is an absolute, even though in recorded history the periods of warfare have nearly always outlasted the periods of peace. Power is in the same category; it is, as the saying goes, "an end in itself." (This, of course, is not to deny that governments pursue policies and employ their power to achieve prescribed goals. But the power structure itself precedes and outlasts all aims, so that power, far from being the means to an end, is actually the very condition that enables a group of people to think and act in terms of the means–end category.) And since government is essentially organized and institutionalized power, the current question, What is the end of government? does not make much sense either. The answer will be either question-begging – to enable men to live together – or dangerously utopian: to promote happiness or to realize a classless society or some other non-political ideal, which if tried out in earnest cannot but end in the worst kind of government, that is, tyranny.

Power needs no justification, as it is inherent in the very existence of political communities; what, however, it does need is legitimacy. The common usage of these two words as synonyms is no less misleading and confusing than the current equation of obedience and support. Power springs up whenever people get together and act in concert, but it derives its legitimacy from the initial getting together rather than from any action that then may follow. Legitimacy, when challenged, is claimed by an appeal to the past, while justification relates to an end which lies in the future. Violence can be justifiable, but it never will be legitimate. Its justification loses in plausibility the farther away its intended end recedes into the future. No one will question the use of violence in self-defence because the danger is not only clear but present, and the end to justify the means is immediate.

Power and violence, though they are distinct phenomena, usually appear together. Up to now, we have discussed such combinations and found that wherever they are so combined, power is the primary and predominant factor. The situation, however, is entirely different when we deal with them in their pure states – as for instance in cases of foreign invasion and occupation. We saw that the current equation of violence and power rests on the understanding of government as domination of man over man by means of violence. Such domination is easy to achieve if the conqueror is confronted by an impotent government and by a nation unused to the exercise of political power. In all other cases the difficulties are very great indeed, and the occupying invader will try immediately to establish Quisling governments, that is, to find a native power base with which to support his dominion. The head-on clash between Russian tanks and the entirely non-violent resistance of the people in Czechoslovakia is a textbook case of a confrontation of violence and power in their pure states. But while this kind of domination is difficult, it is not impossible. Violence, we must remember, does not depend on numbers or opinions but on implements, and the implements of violence share with all other tools that they increase and multiply human strength. Those who oppose violence with mere power will soon find out that they are confronted not with men but with men's artifacts, whose inhumanity and destructive effectiveness increase in proportion to the distance that separates the opponents. Violence can always destroy power; out of the barrel of a gun grows the most effective command, resulting in the most instant and perfect obedience. What never can grow out of it is power.

In a head-on clash between violence and power, the outcome is hardly in doubt. If Gandhi's enormously powerful and successful strategy of nonviolent resistance had met with a different enemy – Stalin's Russia, Hitler's Germany, even pre-war Japan, instead of England – the outcome would not have been decolonization but massacre and submission. However, England in India or France in Algeria had good reasons for their restraint. Rule by sheer violence comes into play where power is being lost; it is precisely the shrinking power of the Russian government, internally and externally, that became manifest in its "solution" of the Czechoslovak problem – just as it was the shrinking power of European imperialism that became manifest in the alternative between decolonization and massacre. To substitute violence for power can bring victory, but its price is very high; for it is not only paid by the vanquished, it is paid by the victor in terms of his own power. The much-feared boomerang effect of the "government of subject races" (Lord Cromer) upon the home government during the imperialist era meant that rule by violence in far-away lands would end by affecting the government of England, that the last "subject race" would be the English themselves. It has often been said that impotence breeds violence, and psychologically this is quite true. Politically speaking, the point is that loss of power tempts into substituting violence for power – we could watch this process on television during the Democratic Convention in Chicago – and that violence itself results in impotence. Where violence is no longer backed and restrained by power, the well-known reversal in the reckoning with means and ends has taken place. It is the means, the means of destruction, that now determine the end – with the result that the end will be the destruction of all power.

Nowhere is the self-defeating factor in the victory of violence over power more evident than in the use of terror for purposes of domination, about whose weird successes and eventual failures we know perhaps more than any generation before us. Terror is not the same as violence; it is rather the form of government that comes into being when violence, having destroyed all power, does not abdicate but, on the contrary, remains in full control. It has often been noticed that the effectiveness of terror depends almost entirely on the degree of social atomization, the disappearance of every kind of organized opposition, which must be achieved before the full force of terror can be let loose. This atomization – an outrageously pale, academic word for the horror it implies – is maintained and intensified through the ubiquity of the informer, who can be literally omnipresent because he no longer is merely a professional agent in the pay of the police but potentially every person one comes into contact with. How such a fully developed police state is established and how it works can now be learned by everybody in Aleksandr I. Solzhenitsyn's *The First Circle*, which will probably remain one of the masterpieces of twentieth-century literature and certainly contains the best documentation on Stalin's regime in existence. The decisive difference between totalitarian domination, based on terror, and tyrannies and dictatorships, established by violence, is that only the former turns not only against its enemies but against its friends and supporters as well, being afraid of all power, even the power of its friends. The climax of terror is reached when the police state begins to devour its own children , when yesterday's executioner becomes today's victim. And this is also the moment when power disappears entirely. There exist now a great many plausible reasons to explain the de-Stalinization of Russia – none, I believe, so compelling as the realization by the Stalinist functionaries themselves that a continuation of the regime would lead, not to an insurrection, against which terror is indeed the best safeguard, but to a paralyzation of the whole country.

To sum up: politically speaking, it is not enough to say that power and violence are not the same. Power and violence are opposites; where the one rules absolutely, the other is absent. Violence appears where power is in jeopardy, but left to its own course its end is the disappearance of power. This implies that it is not correct to say, the opposite of violence is non-violence: to speak of nonviolent power is actually redundant. Violence can destroy power; it is utterly incapable of creating it. Hegel's and Marx's great trust in the dialectical "power of negation," by virtue of which opposites do not destroy but smoothly develop into each other because contradictions promote and do not paralyze development, rests on a much older philosophical prejudice, on the prejudice that evil is no more than a privative modus of the good, that good can come out of evil; that, in short, evil is but the temporary manifestation of a still hidden good. Such time-honored opinions have become dangerous. They are shared by many, who have never heard of the names of Hegel or Marx, for the simple reason that they inspire hope and dispel fear – a treacherous hope used to dispel legitimate fears. By this, I don't mean to equate violence with evil; I only want to stress that violence can't be derived from its opposite, which is power, and that in order to understand it for what it is, we shall have to examine its roots and nature.

4

War Making and State Making as Organized Crime

Charles Tilly

Warning

If protection rackets represent organized crime at its smoothest, then war making and state making – quintessential protection rackets with the advantage of legitimacy – qualify as our largest examples of organized crime. Without branding all generals and statesmen as murderers or thieves, I want to urge the value of that analogy. At least for the European experience of the past few centuries, a portrait of war makers and state makers as coercive and self-seeking entrepreneurs bears a far greater resemblance to the facts than do its chief alternatives: the idea of a social contract, the idea of an open market in which operators of armies and states offer services to willing consumers, the idea of a society whose shared norms and expectations call forth a certain kind of government.

The reflections that follow merely illustrate the analogy of war making and state making with organized crime from a few hundred years of European experience and offer tentative arguments concerning principles of changes and variation underlying the experience. My reflections grow from contemporary concerns: worries about the increasing destructiveness of war, the expanding role of great powers as suppliers of arms and military organization to poor countries, and the growing importance of military rule in those same countries. They spring from the hope that the European experience, properly understood, will help us to grasp what is happening today, perhaps even to do something about it.

The Third World of the twentieth century does not greatly resemble Europe of the sixteenth or seventeenth century. In no simple sense can we read the future of Third World countries from the pasts of European countries. Yet a thoughtful exploration of European experience will serve us well. It will show us that coercive exploitation played a large part in the creation of the European states. It will show us that popular resistance to coercive exploitation forced would-be power-holders to concede protection and constraints on their own action. It will therefore help us to eliminate faulty implicit comparisons between today's Third World and yesterday's Europe. That clarification will make it easier to understand exactly how today's world is different and what we therefore have to explain. It may even help us to explain the current looming presence of military organization and action throughout the world. Although that result would delight me, I do not promise anything so grand.

This chapter, then, concerns the place of organized means of violence in the growth and change of those peculiar forms of government we call national states: relatively centralized, differentiated organizations the officials of which more or less successfully claim control over the chief concentrated means of violence within a population inhabiting a large, contiguous territory. The argument grows from historical work on the formation of national states in Western Europe, especially on the growth of the French state from 1600 onward. But it takes several deliberate steps away from that work, wheels, and stares hard at it from theoretical ground. The argument brings with it few illustrations and no evidence worthy of the name.

Just as one repacks a hastily filled rucksack after a few days on the trail – throwing out the waste, putting things in order of importance, and balancing the load – I have repacked my theoretical baggage for the climb to come; the real test of the new packing arrives only with the next stretch of the trail. The trimmed-down argument stresses the interdependence of war making and state making and the analogy between both of those processes and what, when less successful and smaller in scale, we call organized crime. War makes states, I shall claim. Banditry, piracy, gangland rivalry, policing, and war making all belong on the same continuum – that I shall claim as well. For the historically limited period in which national states were becoming the dominant organizations in Western countries, I shall also claim that mercantile capitalism and state making reinforced each other.

Double-edged protection

In contemporary American parlance, the word "protection" sounds two contrasting tones. One is comforting, the other ominous. With one tone, "protection" calls up images of the shelter against danger provided by a powerful friend, a large insurance policy, or a sturdy roof. With the other, it evokes the racket in which a local strong man forces merchants to pay tribute in order to avoid damage – damage the strong man himself threatens to deliver. The difference, to be sure, is a matter of degree: A hell-and-damnation priest is likely to collect contributions from his parishioners only to the extent that they believe his predictions of brimstone for infidels; our neighborhood mobster may actually be, as he claims to be, a brothel's best guarantee of operation free of police interference.

Which image the word "protection" brings to mind depends mainly on our assessment of the reality and externality of the threat. Someone who produces both the danger and, at a price, the shield against it is a racketeer. Someone who provides a needed shield but has little control over the danger's appearance qualifies as a legitimate protector, especially if his price is no higher than his competitors'. Someone who supplies reliable, low-priced shielding both from local racketeers and from outside marauders makes the best offer of all.

Apologists for particular governments and for government in general commonly argue, precisely, that they offer protection from local and external violence. They claim that the prices they charge barely cover the costs of protection. They call people who complain about the price of protection "anarchists," "subversives," or both at once. But consider the definition of a racketeer as someone who creates a threat and then charges for its reduction. Governments' provision of protection, by this standard, often qualifies as racketeering. To the extent that the threats against which a given government protects its citizens are imaginary or are consequences of its own activities, the government has organized a protection racket. Since governments themselves commonly simulate, stimulate, or even fabricate threats of external war and since the repressive and extractive activities of governments often constitute the largest current threats to the livelihoods of their own citizens, many governments operate in essentially the same ways as racketeers. There is, of course, a difference: Racketeers, by the conventional definition, operate without the sanctity of governments.

How do racketeer governments themselves acquire authority? As a question of fact and of ethics, that is one of the oldest conundrums of political analysis. Back to Machiavelli and Hobbes, nevertheless, political observers have recognized that, whatever else they do, governments organize and, wherever possible, monopolize violence. It matters little whether we take violence in a narrow sense, such as damage to persons and objects, or in a broad sense, such as violation of people's desires and interests; by either criterion, governments stand out from other organizations by their tendency to monopolize the concentrated means of violence. The distinction between "legitimate" and "illegitimate" force, furthermore, makes no difference to the fact. If we take legitimacy to depend on conformity to an abstract principle or on the assent of the governed (or both at once), these conditions may serve to justify, perhaps even to explain, the tendency to monopolize force; they do not contradict the fact.

In any case, Arthur Stinchcombe's agreeably cynical treatment of legitimacy serves the purposes of political analysis much more efficiently. Legitimacy, according to Stinchcombe, depends rather little on abstract principle or assent of the governed: "The person *over whom power is exercised is* not usually as important as *other power-holders.*"[1] Legitimacy is the probability that other authorities will act to confirm the decisions of a given authority. Other authorities, I would add, are much more likely to confirm the decisions of a challenged authority that controls substantial force; not only fear of retaliation, but also desire to maintain a stable environment recommend that general rule. The rule underscores the importance of the authority's monopoly of force. A tendency to monopolize the means of violence makes a government's claim to provide protection, in either the comforting or the ominous sense of the word, more credible and more difficult to resist.

Frank recognition of the central place of force in governmental activity does not require us to believe that governmental authority rests "only" or "ultimately" on the threat of violence. Nor does it entail the assumption that a government's only service is protection. Even when a government's use of force imposes a large cost, some people may well decide that the government's other services outbalance the costs of acceding to its monopoly of violence. Recognition of the centrality of force opens the way to an understanding of the growth and change of governmental forms.

Here is a preview of the most general argument: Power-holders' pursuit of war involved them willy-nilly in the extraction of resources for war making from the populations over which they had control and in the promotion of capital accumulation by those who could help them borrow and buy. War making, extraction, and capital accumulation interacted to shape European state making. Power-holders did not undertake those three momentous activities with the intention of creating national states – centralized, differentiated, autonomous, extensive political organizations. Nor did they ordinarily foresee that national states would emerge from war making, extraction, and capital accumulation.

Instead, the people who controlled European states and states in the making warred in order to check or overcome their competitors and thus to enjoy the advantages of power within a secure or expanding territory. To make more effective war, they attempted to locate more capital. In the short run, they might acquire that capital by conquest, by selling off their assets, or by coercing or dispossessing accumulators of capital. In the long run, the quest inevitably involved them in establishing regular access to capitalists who could supply and arrange credit and in imposing one form of regular taxation or another on the people and activities within their spheres of control.

As the process continued, state makers developed a durable interest in promoting the accumulation of capital, sometimes in the guise of direct return to their own enterprises. Variations in the difficulty of collecting taxes, in the expense of the particular kind of armed force adopted, in the amount of war making required to hold off competitors, and so on resulted in the principal variations in the forms of European states. It all began with the effort to monopolize the means of violence within a delimited territory adjacent to a power-holder's base.

Violence and government

What distinguished the violence produced by states from the violence delivered by anyone else? In the long run, enough to make the division between "legitimate" and "illegitimate" force credible. Eventually, the personnel of states purveyed violence on a larger scale, more effectively, more efficiently, with wider assent from their subject populations, and with readier collaboration from neighboring authorities than did the personnel of other organizations. But it took a long time for that series of distinctions to become established. Early in the state-making process, many parties shared the right to use violence, the practice of using it routinely to accomplish their ends, or both at once. The continuum ran from bandits and pirates to kings via tax collectors, regional power-holders, and professional soldiers.

The uncertain, elastic line between "legitimate" and "illegitimate" violence appeared in the upper reaches of power. Early in the state-making process, many parties shared the right to use violence, its actual employment, or both at once. The long love–hate affair between aspiring state makers and pirates or bandits illustrates the division. "Behind piracy on the seas acted cities and city-states," writes

Fernand Braudel of the sixteenth century. "Behind banditry, that terrestrial piracy, appeared the continual aid of lords."[2] In times of war, indeed, the managers of full-fledged states often commissioned privateers, hired sometime bandits to raid their enemies, and encouraged their regular troops to take booty. In royal service, soldiers and sailors were often expected to provide for themselves by preying on the civilian population: commandeering, raping, looting, taking prizes. When demobilized, they commonly continued the same practices, but without the same royal protection; demobilized ships became pirate vessels, demobilized troops bandits.

It also worked the other way: A king's best source of armed supporters was sometimes the world of outlaws. Robin Hood's conversion to royal archer may be a myth, but the myth records a practice. The distinctions between "legitimate" and "illegitimate" users of violence came clear only very slowly, in the process during which the state's armed forces became relatively unified and permanent.

Up to that point, as Braudel says, maritime cities and terrestrial lords commonly offered protection, or even sponsorship, to freebooters. Many lords who did not pretend to be kings, furthermore, successfully claimed the right to levy troops and maintain their own armed retainers. Without calling on some of those lords to bring their armies with them, no king could fight a war; yet the same armed lords constituted the king's rivals and opponents, his enemies' potential allies. For that reason, before the seventeenth century, regencies for child sovereigns reliably produced civil wars. For the same reason, disarming the great stood high on the agenda of every would-be state maker.

The Tudors, for example, accomplished that agenda through most of England. "The greatest triumph of the Tudors," writes Lawrence Stone,

> was the ultimately successful assertion of a royal monopoly of violence both public and private, an achievement which profoundly altered not only the nature of politics but also the quality of daily life. There occurred a change in English habits that can only be compared with the further step taken in the nineteenth century, when the growth of a police force finally consolidated the monopoly and made it effective in the greatest cities and the smallest villages.[3]

Tudor demilitarization of the great lords entailed four complementary campaigns: eliminating their great personal bands of armed retainers, razing their fortresses, taming their habitual resort to violence for the settlement of disputes, and discouraging the cooperation of their dependents and tenants. In the Marches of England and Scotland, the task was more delicate, for the Percys and Dacres, who kept armies and castles along the border, threatened the Crown but also provided a buffer against Scottish invaders. Yet they, too, eventually fell into line.

In France, Richelieu began the great disarmament in the 1620s. With Richelieu's advice, Louis XIII systematically destroyed the castles of the great rebel lords, Protestant and Catholic, against whom his forces battled incessantly. He began to condemn dueling, the carrying of lethal weapons, and the maintenance of private armies. By the later 1620s, Richelieu was declaring the royal monopoly of force as doctrine. The doctrine took another half-century to become effective:

> Once more the conflicts of the Fronde had witnessed armies assembled by the "grands." Only the last of the regencies, the one after the death of Louis XIV, did not lead to armed uprisings. By that time Richelieu's principle had become a reality. Likewise in the Empire after the Thirty Years' War only the territorial princes had the right of levying troops and of maintaining fortresses ... . Everywhere the razing of castles, the high cost of artillery, the attraction of court life, and the ensuing domestication of the nobility had its share in this development.[4]

By the later eighteenth century, through most of Europe, monarchs controlled permanent, professional military forces that rivaled those of their neighbors and far exceeded any other organized armed force within their own territories. The state's monopoly of large-scale violence was turning from theory to reality.

The elimination of local rivals, however, posed a serious problem. Beyond the scale of a small city-state, no monarch could govern a population with his armed force alone, nor could any monarch afford to create a professional staff large and strong enough to reach from him to the ordinary citizen. Before quite recently, no European government approached the completeness of articulation from top to bottom achieved by imperial China. Even the Roman Empire did not come close. In one way or another, every European government before the French Revolution relied on indirect rule via local magnates. The magnates collaborated with the government without becoming officials in any strong sense of the term, had some access to government-backed force, and exercised wide discretion within their own territories: junkers, justices of the peace, lords. Yet the same magnates were potential rivals, possible allies of a rebellious people.

Eventually, European governments reduced their reliance on indirect rule by means of two expensive but effective strategies: (*a*) extending their officialdom to the local community and (*b*) encouraging the creation of police forces that were subordinate to the government rather than to the individual patrons, distinct from war-making forces, and therefore less useful as the tools of dissident magnates. In between, however, the builders of national power all played a mixed strategy: eliminating, subjugating, dividing, conquering, cajoling, buying as the occasions presented themselves. The buying manifested itself in exemptions from taxation, creations of honorific offices, the establishment of claims on the national treasury, and a variety of other devices that made a magnate's welfare dependent on the maintenance of the existing structure of power. In the long run, it all came down to massive pacification and monopolization of the means of coercion.

Protection as business

In retrospect, the pacification, cooptation, or elimination of fractious rivals to the sovereign seems an awesome, noble, prescient enterprise, destined to bring peace to a people; yet it followed almost ineluctably from the logic of expanding power. If a power-holder was to gain from the provision of protection, his competitors had to yield. As economic historian Frederic Lane put it twenty-five years ago, governments are in the business of selling protection ... whether people want it or not. Lane argued that the very activity of producing and controlling violence favored monopoly, because competition within that realm generally raised costs, instead of lowering them. The production of violence, he suggested, enjoyed large economies of scale.

Working from there, Lane distinguished between (*a*) the monopoly profit, or *tribute*, coming to owners of the means of producing violence as a result of the difference between production costs and the price exacted from "customers" and (*b*) the *protection rent* accruing to those customers – for example, merchants – who drew effective protection against outside competitors. Lane, a superbly attentive historian of Venice, allowed specifically for the case of a government that generates protection rents for its merchants by deliberately attacking their competitors. In their adaptation of Lane's scheme, furthermore, Edward Ames and Richard Rapp substitute the apt word "extortion" for Lane's "tribute." In this model, predation, coercion, piracy, banditry, and racketeering share a home with their upright cousins in responsible government.

This is how Lane's model worked: If a prince could create a sufficient armed force to hold off his and his subjects' external enemies and to keep the subjects in line for 50 megapounds but was able to extract 75 megapounds in taxes from those subjects for that purpose, he gained a tribute of (75 – 50 =) 25 megapounds. If the 10-pound share of those taxes paid by one of the prince's merchant-subjects gave him assured access to world markets at less than the 15-pound shares paid by the merchant's foreign competitors to *their* princes, the merchant also gained a protection rent of (15–10 =) 5 pounds by virtue of his prince's greater efficiency. That reasoning differs only in degree and in scale from the reasoning of violence-wielding criminals and their clients. Labor racketeering (in which, for example, a ship owner holds off trouble from longshoremen by means of a timely payment to the local union boss) works on exactly the same principle: The union boss receives tribute for his no-strike pressure on the longshoremen, while the ship owner avoids the strikes and slowdowns longshoreman impose on his competitors.

Lane pointed out the different behavior we might expect of the managers of a protection-providing government owned by

1. Citizens in general
2. A single self-interested monarch
3. The managers themselves

If citizens in general exercised effective ownership of the government – O distant ideal! – we might expect the managers to minimize protection costs and tribute, thus maximizing protection rent. A single self-interested monarch, in contrast, would maximize tribute, set costs so as to accomplish that maximization of tribute, and be indifferent to the level of protection rent. If the managers owned the government, they would tend to keep costs high by maximizing their own wages, to maximize tribute over and above those costs by exacting a high price from their subjects, and likewise to be indifferent to the level of protection rent. The first model approximates a Jeffersonian democracy, the second a petty despotism, and the third a military junta.

Lane did not discuss the obvious fourth category of owner: a dominant class. If he had, his scheme would have yielded interesting empirical criteria for evaluating claims that a given government was "relatively autonomous" or strictly subordinate to the interests of a dominant class. Presumably, a subordinate government would tend to maximize monopoly profits – returns to the dominant class resulting from the difference between the costs of protection and the price received for it – as well as tuning protection rents nicely to the economic interests of the dominant class. An autonomous government, in contrast, would tend to maximize managers' wages and its own size as well and would be indifferent to protection rents. Lane's analysis immediately suggests fresh propositions and ways of testing them.

Lane also speculated that the logic of the situation produced four successive stages in the general history of capitalism:

1. A period of anarchy and plunder
2. A stage in which tribute takers attracted customers and established their monopolies by struggling to create exclusive, substantial states
3. A stage in which merchants and landlords began to gain more from protection rents than governors did from tribute
4. A period (fairly recent) in which technological changes surpassed protection rents as sources of profit for entrepreneurs

In their new economic history of the Western world, Douglass North and Robert Paul Thomas make stages 2 and 3 – those in which state makers created their monopolies of force and established property rights that permitted individuals to capture much of the return from their own growth-generating innovations – the pivotal moment for sustained economic growth. Protection, at this point, overwhelms tribute. If we recognize that the protected property rights were mainly those of capital and that the development of capitalism also facilitated the accumulation of the wherewithal to operate massive states, that extension of Lane's analysis provides a good deal of insight into the coincidence of war making, state making, and capital accumulation.

Unfortunately, Lane did not take full advantage of his own insight. Wanting to contain his analysis neatly within the neoclassical theory of industrial organization, Lane cramped his treatment of protection: treating all taxpayers as "customers" for the "service" provided by protection-manufacturing governments, brushing aside the objections to the idea of a forced sale by insisting that the "customer" always had the choice of not paying and taking the consequences of nonpayment, minimizing the problems of divisibility created by the public-goods character of protection, and deliberately neglecting the distinction between the costs of producing the means of violence in general and the costs of giving "customers" protection by means of that violence. Lane's ideas suffocate inside the neoclassical box and breathe easily outside it. Nevertheless, inside or outside, they properly draw the economic analysis of government back to the chief activities that real governments have carried on historically: war, repression, protection, adjudication.

More recently, Richard Bean has applied a similar logic to the rise of European national states between 1400 and 1600. He appeals to economies of scale in the production of effective force, counteracted by diseconomies of scale in command and control. He then claims that the improvement of artillery in the fifteenth century (cannon made small medieval forts much more vulnerable to an organized force) shifted the curve of economies and diseconomies to make larger armies, standing armies, and centralized governments advantageous to their masters. Hence, according to Bean, military innovation promoted the creation of large, expensive, well-armed national states.

History talks

Bean's summary does not stand up to historical scrutiny. As a matter of practice, the shift of infantry-backed artillery sieges of fortified cities occurred only during the sixteenth and seventeenth centuries. Artillery did improve during the fifteenth century, but the invention of new fortifications, especially the *trace italienne*, rapidly countered the advantage of artillery. The arrival of effective artillery came too late to have *caused* the increase in the viable size of states. (However, the increased cost of fortifications to defend against artillery did give an advantage to states enjoying larger fiscal bases.)

Nor is it obvious that changes in land war had the sweeping influence Bean attributes to them. The increasing decisiveness of naval warfare, which occurred simultaneously, could well have shifted the military advantage to small maritime powers such as the Dutch Republic. Furthermore, although many city-states and other microscopic entities disappeared into larger political units before 1600, such events as the fractionation of the Habsburg Empire and such facts as the persistence of large but loosely knit Poland and Russia render ambiguous the claim of a significant increase in geographic scale. In short, both Bean's proposed explanation and his statement of what must be explained raise historical doubts.

Stripped of its technological determinism, nevertheless, Bean's logic provides a useful complement to Lane's, for different military formats do cost substantially different amounts to produce and do provide substantially different ranges of control over opponents, domestic and foreign. After 1400 the European pursuit of larger, more permanent, and more costly varieties of military organization did, in fact, drive spectacular increases in princely budgets, taxes, and staffs. After 1500 or so, princes who managed to create the costly varieties of military organization were, indeed, able to conquer new chunks of territory.

The word "territory" should not mislead us. Until the eighteenth century, the greatest powers were maritime states, and naval warfare remained crucial to international position. Consider Fernand Braudel's roll call of successive hegemonic powers within the capitalist world: Venice and its empire, Genoa and its empire, Antwerp–Spain, Amsterdam–Holland, London–England, New York–the United States. Although Brandenburg–Prussia offers a partial exception, only in our own time have such essentially landbound states as Russia and China achieved preponderant positions in the world's system of states. Naval warfare was by no means the only reason for that bias toward the sea. Before the later nineteenth century, land transportation was so expensive everywhere in Europe that no country could afford to supply a large army or a big city with grain and other heavy goods without having efficient water transport. Rulers fed major inland centers such as Berlin and Madrid only at great effort and at considerable cost to their hinterlands. The exceptional efficiency of waterways in the Netherlands undoubtedly gave the Dutch great advantages at peace and at war.

Access to water mattered in another important way. Those metropolises on Braudel's list were all major ports, great centers of commerce, and outstanding mobilizers of capital. Both the trade and the capital served the purposes of ambitious rulers. By a circuitous route, that observation brings us back to the arguments of Lane and Bean. Considering that both of them wrote as economic historians, the greatest weakness in their analyses comes as a surprise: Both of them understate the importance of capital accumulation to military expansion. As Jan de Vries says of the period after 1600:

> Looking back, one cannot help but be struck by the seemingly symbiotic relationship existing between the state, military power, and the private economy's efficiency in the age of absolutism. Behind every successful dynasty stood an array of opulent banking families. Access to such bourgeois resources proved crucial to the princes' state-building and centralizing policies. Princes also needed direct access to agricultural resources, which could be mobilized only when agricultural productivity grew and an effective administrative and military power existed to enforce the princes' claims. But the

lines of causation also ran in the opposite direction. Successful state-building and empire-building activities plus the associated tendency toward concentration of urban population and government expenditure, offered the private economy unique and invaluable opportunities to capture economies of scale. These economies of scale occasionally affected industrial production but were most significant in the development of trade and finance. In addition, the sheer pressure of central government taxation did as much as any other economic force to channel peasant production into the market and thereby augment the opportunities for trade creation and economic specialization.[5]

Nor does the "symbiotic relationship" hold only for the period after 1600. For the precocious case of France, we need only consider the increase in royal expenditures and revenues from 1515 to 1785. Although the rates of growth in both regards accelerated appropriately after 1600, they also rose substantially during the sixteenth century. After 1550, the internal Wars of Religion checked the work of international expansion that Francis I had begun earlier in the century, but from the 1620s onward Louis XIII and Louis XIV (aided and abetted, to be sure, by Richelieu, Mazarin, Colbert, and other state-making wizards) resumed the task with a vengeance. "As always," comments V. G. Kiernan, "war had every political recommendation and every financial drawback."[6]

Borrowing and then paying interest on the debt accounts for much of the discrepancy between the two curves. Great capitalists played crucial parts on both sides of the transaction: as the principal sources of royal credit, especially in the short term, and as the most important contractors in the risky but lucrative business of collecting royal taxes. For this reason, it is worth noticing that

> for practical purposes the national debt began in the reign of Francis I. Following the loss of Milan, the key to northern Italy, on September 15, 1522, Francis I borrowed 200,000 frances ... at 12.5 percent from the merchants of Paris, to intensify the war against Charles V. Administered by the city government, this loan inaugurated the famous series of bonds based on revenues from the capital and known as *rentes sur l'Hôtel de Ville.*[7]

(The government's failure to pay those *rentes*, incidentally, helped align the Parisian bourgeoisie against the Crown during the Fronde, some twelve decades later.) By 1595, the national debt had risen to 300 million francs; despite governmental bankruptcies, currency manipulations, and the monumental rise in taxes, by Louis XIV's death in 1715 war-induced borrowing had inflated the total to about 3 billion francs, the equivalent of about eighteen years in royal revenues.[8] War, state apparatus, taxation, and borrowing advanced in tight cadence.

Although France was precocious, it was by no means alone. "Even more than in the case of France," reports the ever-useful Earl J. Hamilton,

> the national debt of England originated and has grown during major wars. Except for an insignificant carry-over from the Stuarts, the debt began in 1689 with the reign of William and Mary. In the words of Adam Smith, "it was in the war which began in 1688, and was concluded by the treaty of Ryswick in 1697, that the foundation of the present enormous debt of Great Britain was first laid."[9]

Hamilton, it is true, goes on to quote the mercantilist Charles Davenant, who complained in 1698 that the high interest rates promoted by government borrowing were cramping English trade. Davenant's complaint suggests, however, that England was already entering Frederic Lane's third stage of state–capital relations, when merchants and landowners receive more of the surplus than do the suppliers of protection.

Until the sixteenth century, the English expected their kings to live on revenues from their own property and to levy taxes only for war. G. R. Elton marks the great innovation at Thomas Cromwell's drafting of Henry VIII's subsidy bills for 1534 and 1540: "1540 was very careful to continue the real innovation of 1534, namely that extraordinary contributions could be levied for reasons other than war."[10] After that point as before, however, war making provided the main stimulus to increases in the level of taxation as well as of debt. Rarely did debt and taxes recede. What A. T. Peacock and J. Wiseman call a "displacement effect" (and others sometimes call a "ratchet effect") occurred: When public revenues and expenditures rose abruptly during war, they set a new, higher floor beneath which peacetime revenues and expenditures did not sink. During the Napoleonic Wars, British taxes rose from 15 to 24 percent of national income and to almost three times the French level of taxation.[11]

True, Britain had the double advantage of relying less on expensive land forces than its Continental rivals and of drawing more of its tax revenues from customs and excise – taxes that were, despite evasion, significantly cheaper to collect than land taxes, property taxes, and poll taxes. Nevertheless, in England as well as elsewhere, both debt and taxes rose enormously from the seventeenth century onward. They rose mainly as a function of the increasing cost of war making.

What do states do?

As should now be clear, Lane's analysis of protection fails to distinguish among several different uses of state-controlled violence. Under the general heading of organized violence, the agents of states characteristically carry on four different activities:

1. War making: Eliminating or neutralizing their own rivals outside the territories in which they have clear and continuous priority as wielders of force
2. State making: Eliminating or neutralizing their rivals inside those territories
3. Protection: Eliminating or neutralizing the enemies of their clients
4. Extraction: Acquiring the means of carrying out the first three activities – war making, state making, and protection

The third item corresponds to protection as analyzed by Lane, but the other three also involve the application of force. They overlap incompletely and to various degrees; for example, war making against the commercial rivals of the local bourgeoisie delivers protection to that bourgeoisie. To the extent that a population is divided into enemy classes and the state extends its favors partially to one class or another, state making actually reduces the protection given some classes.

War making, state making, protection, and extraction each take a number of forms. Extraction, for instance, ranges from outright plunder to regular tribute to bureaucratized taxation. Yet all four depend on the state's tendency to monopolize the concentrated means of coercion. From the perspectives of those who dominate the state, each of them – if carried on effectively – generally reinforces the others. Thus, a state that successfully eradicates its internal rivals strengthens its ability to extract resources, to wage war, and to protect its chief supporters. In the earlier European experience, broadly speaking, those supporters were typically landlords, armed retainers of the monarch, and churchmen.

Each of the major uses of violence produced characteristic forms of organization. War making yielded armies, navies, and supporting services. State making produced durable instruments of surveillance and control within the territory. Protection relied on the organization of war making and state making but added to it an apparatus by which the protected called forth the protection that was their due, notably through courts and representative assemblies. Extraction brought fiscal and accounting structures into being. The organization and deployment of violence themselves account for much of the characteristic structure of European states.

The general rule seems to have operated like this: The more costly the activity, all other things being equal, the greater was the organizational residue. To the extent, for example, that a given government invested in large standing armies – a very costly, if effective, means of war making – the bureaucracy created to service the army was likely to become bulky. Furthermore, a government building a standing army while controlling a small population was likely to incur greater costs, and therefore to build a bulkier structure, than a government within a populous country. Brandenburg–Prussia was the classic case of high cost for available resources. The Prussian effort to build an army matching those of its larger Continental neighbors created an immense structure; it militarized and bureaucratized much of German social life.

In the case of extraction, the smaller the pool of resources and the less commercialized the economy, other things being equal, the more difficult was the work of extracting resources to sustain war and other governmental activities; hence, the more extensive was the fiscal apparatus. England illustrated the corollary of that proposition, with a relatively large and commercialized pool of resources drawn on by a relatively small fiscal apparatus. As Gabriel Ardant has argued, the choice of fiscal strategy probably made an additional difference. On the whole, taxes on land were expensive to collect as compared with taxes on trade, especially large flows of trade past easily controlled checkpoints. Its position astride the entrance to the Baltic gave Denmark an extraordinary opportunity to profit from customs revenues.

With respect to state making (in the narrow sense of eliminating or neutralizing the local rivals of the people who controlled the state), a territory populated by great landlords or by distinct religious groups generally imposed larger costs on a conqueror than one of fragmented power or homogeneous culture. This time, fragmented and homogeneous Sweden, with its relatively small but effective apparatus of control, illustrates the corollary.

Finally, the cost of protection (in the sense of eliminating or neutralizing the enemies of the state makers' clients) mounted with the range over which that protection extended. Portugal's effort to bar the Mediterranean to its merchants' competitors in the spice trade provides a textbook case of an unsuccessful protection effort that nonetheless built up a massive structure.

Thus, the sheer size of the government varied directly with the effort devoted to extraction, state making, protection, and, especially, war making but inversely with the commercialization of the economy and the extent of the resource base. What is more, the relative bulk of different features of the government varied with the cost/resource ratios of extraction, state making, protection, and war making. In Spain we see hypertrophy of Court and courts as the outcome of centuries of effort at subduing internal enemies, whereas in Holland we are amazed to see how small a fiscal apparatus grows up with high taxes within a rich, commercialized economy.

Clearly, war making, extraction, state making, and protection were interdependent. Speaking very, very generally, the classic European state-making experience followed this causal pattern:

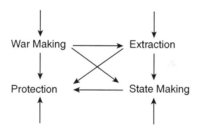

In an idealized sequence, a great lord made war so effectively as to become dominant in a substantial territory, but that war making led to increased extraction of the means of war – men, arms, food, lodging, transportation, supplies, and/or the money to buy them – from the population within that territory. The building up of war-making capacity likewise increased the capacity to extract. The very activity of extraction, if successful, entailed the elimination, neutralization, or cooptation of the great lord's local rivals; thus, it led to state making. As a by-product, it created organization in the form of tax-collection agencies, police forces, courts, exchequers, account keepers; thus it again led to state making. To a lesser extent, war making likewise led to state making through the expansion of military organization itself, as a standing army, war industries, supporting bureaucracies, and (rather later) schools grew up within the state apparatus. All of these structures checked potential rivals and opponents. In the course of making war, extracting resources, and building up the state apparatus, the managers of states formed alliances with specific social classes. The members of those classes loaned resources, provided technical services, or helped ensure the compliance of the rest of the population, all in return for a measure of protection against their own rivals and enemies. As a result of these multiple strategic choices, a distinctive state apparatus grew up within each major section of Europe.

How states formed

This analysis, if correct, has two strong implications for the development of national states. First, popular resistance to war making and state making made a difference. When ordinary people resisted vigorously, authorities made concessions: guarantees of rights, representative institutions, courts of appeal. Those concessions, in their turn, constrained the later paths of war making and state making. To be sure, alliances with fragments of the ruling class greatly increased the effects of popular action; the broad mobilization of gentry against Charles I helped to give the English Revolution of 1640 a far greater impact on political institutions than did any of the multiple rebellions during the Tudor era.

Second, the relative balance among war making, protection, extraction, and state making significantly affected the organization of the states that emerged from the four activities. To the extent that war making went on with relatively little extraction, protection, and state making, for example, military forces ended up playing a larger and more autonomous part in national politics. Spain is perhaps the best European example. To the extent that protection, as in Venice or Holland, prevailed over war making, extraction, and state making, oligarchies of the protected classes tended to dominate subsequent national politics. From the relative predominance of state making sprang the disproportionate elaboration of policing and surveillance; the Papal States illustrate that extreme. Before the twentieth century, the range of viable imbalances was fairly small. Any state that failed to put considerable effort into war making was likely to disappear. As the twentieth century wore on, however, it became increasingly common for one state to lend, give, or sell war-making means to another; in those cases, the recipient state could put a disproportionate effort into extraction, protection, and/or state making and yet survive. In our own time, clients of the United States and the Soviet Union provide numerous examples.

This simplified model, however, neglects the external relations that shaped every national state. Early in the process, the distinction between "internal" and "external" remained as unclear as the distinction between state power and the power accruing to lords allied with the state. Later, three interlocking influences connected any given national state to the European network of states. First, there were the flows of resources in the form of loans and supplies, especially loans and supplies devoted to war making. Second, there was the competition among states for hegemony in disputed territories, which stimulated war making and temporarily erased the distinctions among war making, state making, and extraction. Third, there was the intermittent creation of coalitions of states that temporarily combined their efforts to force a given state into a certain form and position within the international network. The war-making coalition is one example, but the peace-making coalition played an even more crucial part: From 1648, if not before, at the ends of wars all effective European states coalesced temporarily to bargain over the boundaries and rulers of the recent belligerents. From that point on, periods of major reorganization of the European state system came in spurts, at the settlement of widespread wars. From each large war, in general, emerged fewer national states than had entered it.

War as international relations

In these circumstances, war became the normal condition of the international system of states and the normal means of defending or enhancing a position within the system. Why war? No simple answer will do; war as a potent means served more than one end. But surely part of the answer goes back to the central mechanisms of state making: The very logic by which a local lord extended or defended the perimeter within which he monopolized the means of violence, and thereby increased his return from tribute, continued on a larger scale into the logic of war. Early in the process, external and internal rivals overlapped to a large degree. Only the establishment of large perimeters of control within which great lords had checked their rivals sharpened the line between internal and external. George Modelski sums up the competitive logic cogently:

Global power ... strengthened those states that attained it relatively to all other political and other organizations. What is more, other states competing in the global power game developed similar organizational forms and similar hardiness: they too became nation-states – in a defensive reaction, because forced to take issue with or to confront a global power, as France confronted Spain and later Britain, or in imitation of its obvious success and effectiveness, as Germany followed the example of Britain in Weltmacht, or as earlier Peter the Great had rebuilt Russia on Dutch precepts and examples. Thus not only Portugal, the Netherlands, Britain and the United States became nation-states, but also Spain, France, Germany, Russia and Japan. The short, and the most parsimonious, answer to the question of why these succeeded where "most of the European efforts to build states failed" is that they were either global powers or successfully fought with or against them.[12]

This logic of international state making acts out on a large scale the logic of local aggrandizement. The external complements the internal.

If we allow that fragile distinction between "internal" and "external" state-making processes, then we might schematize the history of European state making as three stages: (*a*) The differential success of some power-holders in "external" struggles establishes the difference between an "internal" and an "external" arena for the deployment of force; (*b*) "external" competition generates "internal" state making; (*c*) "external" compacts among states influence the form and locus of particular states ever more powerfully. In this perspective, state-certifying organizations such as the League of Nations and the United Nations simply extended the European-based process to the world as a whole. Whether forced or voluntary, bloody or peaceful, decolonization simply completed that process by which existing states leagued to create new ones.

The extension of the Europe-based state-making process to the rest of the world, however, did not result in the creation of states in the strict European image. Broadly speaking, internal struggles such as the checking of great regional lords and the imposition of taxation on peasant villages produced imported organizational features of European states: the relative subordination of military power to civilian control, the extensive bureaucracy of fiscal surveillance, the representation of wronged interests via petition and parliament. On the whole, states elsewhere developed differently. The most telling feature of that difference appears in military organization. European states built up their military apparatuses through sustained struggles with their subject populations and by means of selective extension of protection to different classes within those populations. The agreements on protection constrained the rulers themselves, making them vulnerable to courts, to assemblies, to withdrawals of credit, services, and expertise.

To a larger degree, states that have come into being recently through decolonization or through reallocations of territory by dominant states have acquired their military organization from outside, without the same internal forging of mutual constraints between rulers and ruled. To the extent that outside states continue to supply military goods and expertise in return for commodities, military alliance or both, the new states harbor powerful, unconstrained organizations that easily overshadow all other organizations within their territories. To the extent that outside states guarantee their boundaries, the managers of those military organizations exercise extraordinary power within them. The advantages of military power become enormous, the incentives to seize power over the state as a whole by means of that advantage very strong. Despite the great place that war making occupied in the making of European states, the old national states of Europe almost never experienced the great disproportion between military organization and all other forms of organization that seems the fate of client states throughout the contemporary world. A century ago, Europeans might have congratulated themselves on the spread of civil government throughout the world. In our own time, the analogy between war making and state making, on the one hand, and organized crime, on the other, is becoming tragically apt.

Notes

1. Arthur L. Stinchocombe, *Constructing Social Theories* (New York: Harcourt, Brace & World, 1968), p. 150; italics in the original.
2. Fernand Braudel, *La Méditerranée et le monde méditerranéen à l'époque de Philippe II* (Paris: Armand Colin, 1966), vol. 2, pp. 88–9.
3. Lawrence Stone, *The Crisis of the Aristocracy* (Oxford: Clarendon Press, 1965), p. 200.
4. Dietrich Gerhard, *Old Europe: A Study of Continuity, 1000–1800* (New York: Academic Press, 1981), pp. 124–5.
5. Jan de Vries, *The Economy of Europe in an Age of Crisis, 1600–1750* (Cambridge: Cambridge University Press, 1976).
6. V. G. Kiernan, *State and Society in Europe, 1550–1650* (Oxford: Blackwell, 1980), p. 104. For French finances, see Alain Guery, "Les Finances de la Monarchie Française sous l'Ancien Regime," *Annales Economies, Societés, Civilisations* 33 (1978), p. 227.

7. Earl J. Hamilton, "Origin and Growth of the National Debt in France and England," in *Studi in onore di Gino Luzzato* (Milan: Giuffre, 1950), vol. 2, p. 254.
8. Ibid., pp. 247, 249.
9. Ibid., p. 254.
10. G. R. Elton, "Taxation for War and Peace in Early-Tudor England," in *War and Economic Development: Essays in Memory of David Joslin*, ed. J. M. Winter (Cambridge: Cambridge University Press, 1975), p. 42.
11. Peter Mathias, *The Transformation of England: Essays in the Economic and Social History of England in the Eighteenth Century* (New York: Oxford University Press, 1979), p. 122.
12. George Modelski, "The Long Cycle of Global Politics and the Nation State," *Comparative Studies in Society and History* 20 (1978): 231.

Bibliography

Ames, Edward, and Richard T. Rapp. "The Birth and Death of Taxes: A Hypothesis." *Journal of Economic History* 37 (1977):161–78.

Ardent, Gabriel. "Financial Policy and Economic Infrastructure of Modern States and Nations." In *The Formation of National States in Western Europe*, edited by Charles Tilly. Princeton, N.J.: Princeton University Press, 1975.

Badie, Bertrand, and Pierre Birnbaum. *Sociologie de l'Etat*. Paris: Bernard Grasset, 1979.

Badie, Bertrand. *Le développment politique*. 2nd ed. Paris: Economica, 1980.

Bayard, Francoise. "Fermes et traités en France dans la première moitié du XVIIe siècle (première esquisse 1631–1653)." *Bulletin du Centre d'Histoire, Economique et Sociale de la Region Lyonnaise*, no. 1 (1976):45–80.

Bean, Richard. "War and the Birth of the Nation State." *Journal of Economic History* 33 (1973):203–21.

Blockmans, W. P. "A Typology of Representative Institutions in Late Medieval Europe." *Journal of Medieval History* 4 (1978):189–215.

Blok, Anton. *The Mafia of a Sicilian Village, 1860–1960: A Study of Violent Peasant Entrepreneurs*. Oxford: Blackwell, 1974.

Booney, Richard. *Political Change under Richelieu and Mazarin, 1624–1661*. Oxford: Oxford University Press, 1978.

Braudel, Fernand. *La Méditerranée et le monde méditerranéen à l'époque de Philippe II*. 2d ed. 2 vols. Paris: Armand Colin, 1966.

— *Civilisation materielle, économie, et capitalisme, XVe–XVIIIe siècle*. 3 vols. Paris: Armand Colin, 1979.

Braun, Rudolf. "Taxation, Sociopolitical Structure, and State-Building: Great Britain and Brandenburg-Prussia." In *The Formation of National States in Western Europe*, edited by Charles Tilly. Princeton, N.J.: Princeton University Press, 1975.

— "Steuern und Staatsfinanzierung als Modernisierungsfaktoren: Ein deutsch-englischer Vergleich." In *Studien zum Beginn der modernen Welt*, edited by Reinhard Koselleck. Stuttgart: Klett-Cotta, 1977.

Carneiro, Robert. "Political Expansion as an Expression of the Principle of Competitive Exclusion." In *Origins of the State*, edited by Ronald Cohen and Elman R. Service. Philadelphia: Institute for the Study of Human Issues, 1978.

Carsten, F. L. *The Origins of Prussia*. Oxford: Clarendon Press, 1954.

Chapman, Brian. *Police State.* London: Pall Mall, 1970.

Cipolla, Carlo M. *Guns, Sails, and Empires: Technological Innovation and the Early Phases of European Expansion 1400–1700.* New York: Pantheon Press, 1965.

Clark, Sir George. "The Social Foundations of States." In *The New Cambridge Modern History*, vol. 5, *The Ascendancy of France, 1648–88,* edited by F. L. Carsten. Cambridge: Cambridge University Press, 1969.

Cooper, J. P. "Differences between English and Continental Governments in the Early Seventeenth Century." In *Britain and the Netherlands,* edited by J. S. Bromley and E. H. Kossmann. London: Chatto & Windus, 1960.

— "General Introduction." In *The New Cambridge Modern History*, vol. 4, *The Decline of Spain and Thirty Years War, 1609–58/59,* edited by J. P. Cooper, Cambridge: Cambridge University Press, 1970.

Davis, Lance E. "It's a Long, Long Road to Tipperary, or Reflections on Organized Violence, Protection Rates, and Related Topics: The New Political History." *Journal of Economic History* 40 (1980):1–16.

Dent, Julian. *Crisis in Finance: Crown, Financiers, and Society and Seventeenth-Century France.* Newton Abbot, United Kingdom: David & Charles, 1973.

Dickson, P. G. M. *The Financial Revolution in England: A Study in the Development of Public Credit, 1688–1756.* London: St. Martin's Press, 1967.

Elton, G. R. "Taxation for War and Peace in Early-Tudor England." In *War and Economic Development: Essays in Memory of David Joslin,* edited by J. M. Winter. Cambridge: Cambridge University Press, 1975.

Finer, Samuel E. "State-building, State Boundaries, and Border Control." *Social Science Information* 13 (1974):79–126.

— "State- and Nation-Building in Europe: The Role of the Military." In *The Formation of National States in Western Europe,* edited by Charles Tilly, Princeton, N.J.: Princeton University Press, 1975.

Fueter, Edward. *Geschichte des europäischen Staatensystems von 1492–1559.* Munich: Oldenbourg, 1919.

Gerhard, Dietrich. *Old Europe: A Study of Continuity, 1000–1800.* New York: Academic Press, 1981.

Gooch, John, *Armies in Europe.* London: Routledge & Kegan Paul. 1980.

Guenee, Bernard. "Y a-t-il un Etat des XIVe et XVe siècles?" *Annales Economies, Sociétés, Civilisations* 36 (1981):399–406.

Guery, Alain. "Les finances de la monarchie francaise sous l'Ancien Regime, *Annales Economies, Sociétés, Civilisations* 33 (1978):216–39.

Hale, J. R. "Armies, Navies, and the Art of War." In *The New Cambridge Modern History, vol. 2, The Reformation 1520–1559,* edited by G. R. Elton. Cambridge: Cambridge University Press, 1968.

— "Armies, Navies, and the Art of War." In *The New Cambridge Modern History, vol. 3, The Counter-Reformation and Price Revolution, 1559–1610,* edited by R. B. Wernham. Cambridge: Cambridge University Press, 1968.

Hamilton, Earl J. "Origin and Growth of the National Debt in France and England." In *Studi in onore di Gino Luzzato,* vol. 2. Milan: Giuffre, 1950.

Harding, Robert R. *Anatomy of a Power Elite: The Provincial Governors of Early Modern France.* New Haven, Conn.: Yale University Press, 1978.

Hechter, Michael, and William Brustein. "Regional Modes of Production and Patterns of State Formation in Western Europe." *American Journal of Sociology* 85 (1980):1061–94.

Hintze, Otto. *Staat und Verfassung: Gesammelte Abhandlungen zur allgemeinen Verfas-sungsgeschichte.* Edited by Gerhard Oestreich. Gottingen: Vandenhoeck & Ruprecht, 1962; originally 1910.

Howard, Michael. *War in European History.* Oxford: Oxford University Press, 1976.

James, M. E. *Change and Continuity in the Tudor North: The Rise of Thomas First Lord Wharton.* Borthwick Papers no. 27. York: St. Anthony's Press, 1965.

— "The First Earl of Cumberland (1493–1542) and the Decline of Northern Feudalism." *Northern History* 1 (1966):43–69.

— "The Concept of Order and the Northern Rising, 1569." *Past and Present* 60 (1973):49–83.

John, A. H. "Wars and the British Economy, 1700–1763." *Economic History Review,* 2d ser., 7 (1955):329–44.

Kiernan, V. G. "Conscription and Society in Europe before the War of 1914–18." In *War and Society: Historical Essays in Honour and Memory of J. R. Western, 1928–1971,* edited by M. R. D. Foot. London: Elek Books, 1973.

— *State and Society in Europe, 1550–1650.* Oxford: Blackwell, 1980.

van Klaveren, Jacob. "Die historische Erscheinung der Korruption." *Vierteljahrschrift für Sozial- und Wirtschaftsgeschichte* 44 (1957):289–324.

— "Fiskalismus – Merkantilismus – Korruption: Drei Aspekte der Finanz- und Wirtschafts-politik während des Ancien Regime." *Vierteljahrschrift für Sozial- und Wirtschaftsgeschichte* 47 (1960):333–53.

Ladero Quesado, Miguel Angel. "Les finances royales de Castille à la veille des temps modernes." *Annales Economies, Sociétés, Civilisations* 25 (1970):775–88.

Lane, Frederic C. "Force and Enterprise in the Creation of Oceanic Commerce." In *The Tasks of Economic History* (Supplemental issue of the *Journal of Economic History* 10 [1950]), pp. 19–31.

— "Economic Consequences of Organized Violence." *Journal of Economic History* 18 (1958):401–17.

— "The Economic Meaning of War and Protection." In *Venice and History: The Collected Papers of Frederic C. Lane.* Baltimore, Md.: Johns Hopkins University Press, 1966; originally 1942.

— "The Role of Government in Economic Growth in Early Modern Times." *Journal of Economic History* 35 (1975):8–17; with comment by Douglass C. North and Robert Paul Thomas, pp. 18–19.

Levi, Margaret. "The Predatory Theory of Rule." In *The Microfoundations of Macrosociology,* edited by Michael Hechter. Philadelphia: Temple University Press, 1983.

Ludtke, Alf. "Genesis und Durchsetzung des modernen Staates: Zur Analyse von Herrschaft und Verwaltung." *Archiv für Sozialgeschichte* 20 (1980):470–91.

Lyons, G. M. "Exigences militaires et budgets militaires aux U.S.A." *Revue Française de Sociologie* 2 (1961):66–74.

Mathias, Peter. "Taxation and Industrialization in Britain, 1700–1870." In *The Transformation of England: Essays in the Economic and Social History of England in the Eighteenth Century,* edited by Peter Mathias, New York: Oxford University Press, 1979.

Michaud, Claude. "Finances et guerres de religion en France." *Revue d'Histoire Moderne et Contemporaine* 28 (1981):572–96.

Modelski, George. "The Long Cycle of Global Politics and the Nation-State." *Comparative Studies in Society and History* 20 (1978):214–35.

Nef, John U. *War and Human Progress: An Essay on the Rise of Industrial Civilization.* Cambridge: Harvard University Press, 1952.
— *Industry and Government in France and England, 1540–1640.* Ithaca, N.Y.: Cornell University Press, 1965; originally 1940.
North, Douglass C. and Robert Paul Thomas, *The Rise of the Western World: A New Economic History.* Cambridge: Cambridge University Press, 1973.
O'Donnell, Guillermo. "Comparative Historical Formations of the State Apparatus and Socio-economic Change in the Third World." *International Social Science Journal* 32 (1980):717–29.
Parker, Geoffrey. *The Army of Flanders and the Spanish Road 1567–1659.* Cambridge: Cambridge University Press, 1972.
Peacock, Alan T., and Jack Wiseman. *The Growth of Public Expenditure in the United Kingdom.* Princeton, N.J.:Princeton University Press, 1961.
Poggi, Gianfranco. *The Development of the Modern State: A Sociological Introduction.* Stanford, Calif.: Stanford University press, 1978.
Polisensky, Josef V. *War and Society in Europe, 1618–1648.* Cambridge: Cambridge University Press, 1978.
Pounds, Norman J. G., and Sue Simons Ball. "Core-Areas and the Development of the European States System." *Annals of the Association of American Geographers* 54 (1964):24–40.
Ramsey, G. D. *The City of London in International Politics at the Accession of Elizabeth Tudor.* Manchester: Manchester University Press, 1975.
Redlich, Fritz. *The German Military Enterpriser and His Work Force.* 2 vols. Wiesbaden: Steiner, 1964–65. *Vierteljahrschrift für Sozial- und Wirtschaftsgeschichte,* Beiheften 47, 48.
Riemersma, Jelle C. "Government Influence on Company Organization in Holland and England (1550–1650)." *The Tasks of Economic History* (Supplemental issue of the *Journal of Economic History* 10 [1950]), pp. 31–9.
Romano, Salvatore Francesco. *Storia della mafia.* Milan: Sugar, 1963.
Rosenberg, Hans. *Bureaucracy, Aristocracy and Autocracy: The Prussian Experience, 1660–1815.* Cambridge: Harvard University Press, 1958.
Russett, Bruce M. *What Price Vigilance? The Burdens of National Defense.* New Haven, Conn.: Yale University Press, 1970.
Schelling, Thomas C. "Economics and Criminal Enterprise." *The Public Interest* 7 (1967):61–78.
Steensgaard, Niels. *The Asian Trade Revolution of the Seventeenth Century: The East India Companies and the Decline of the Caravan Trades.* Chicago: University of Chicago Press, 1974.
Stein, Arthur A., and Bruce M. Russett. "Evaluating War: Outcomes and Consequences." In *Handbook of Political Conflict: Theory and Research,* edited by Ted Robert Gurr. New York: Free Press, 1980.
Stinchcombe, Arthur L. *Constructing Social Theories.* New York: Harcourt, Brace & World, 1968.
Stone, Lawrence. "State Control in Sixteenth-Century England." *Economic History Review* 17 (1947):103–20.
— *The Crisis of the Aristocracy, 1558–1641.* Oxford: Clarendon Press, 1965.
Tenenti, Alberto. *Piracy and the Decline of Venice, 1580–1615.* Berkeley: University of California Press, 1967.

Torsvik, Per, ed. *Mobilization, Center-Periphery Structures and Nation-Building: A Volume in Commemoration of Stein Rokkan.* Bergen: Universitetsforlaget, 1981.

de Vries, Jan. "On the Modernity of the Dutch Republic." *Journal of Economic History* 33 (1973):191–202.

— *The Economy of Europe in an Age of Crisis, 1600–1750.* Cambridge: Cambridge University Press, 1976.

— "Barges and Capitalism: Passenger Transportation in the Dutch Economy, 1632–1839," *A. A. G. Bijdragen* 21 (1978):33–398.

Wijn, J. W. "Military Forces and Warfare 1610–48." In *The New Cambridge Modern History,* vol. 4, *The Decline of Spain and the Thirty Years War 1609–58/59,* edited by J. P. Cooper. Cambridge: Cambridge University Press, 1970.

Williams, Penry, "Rebellion and Revolution in Early Modern England." In *War and Society: Historical Essays in Honour and Memory of J. R. Western, 1928–1971,* edited by M. R. D. Foot. London: Elek Books, 1973.

Wolfe, Martin. *The Fiscal System of Renaissance France.* New Haven, Conn.: Yale University Press, 1972.

Zolberg, Aristide R. "Strategic Interactions and the Formation of Modern States: France and England." *International Social Science Journal* 32 (1980):687–716.

5

The Impact and Function of Terror

Barrington Moore, Jr.

Anyone who has studied the Soviet Union for more than a few years is likely to be aware of considerable change in the kinds of statements about the USSR that require or do not require extensive proof. The shifts in what is taken for granted, even among professional students of Soviet affairs, derive only partly from the increase and diffusion of firm factual knowledge. They reflect also the changing tides of public hopes and fears about this huge power. Both factors are extremely influential in any attempt to assess the part played by organized terror in the Soviet system. It also happens that in recent years both factors have tended to push judgments on this question in the same, and possibly an extreme, direction. The tense rivalry for world leadership, together with the stream of new information from Soviet refugees, tend to produce a Western image of the Soviet system in which organized terror is seen as the chief driving force and the main source of motivation in the daily behavior of every Soviet citizen. Because of the still fragmentary nature of the evidence any appraisal of this major factor must face very great difficulties. Here we shall try to examine the terror primarily with two problems in mind. The first is to discover, so far as possible, the significance of terror in the daily life and ordinary actions of Soviet citizens. The second is to ascertain to what extent, if any, mass terror represents an inherent and inevitable feature of the socialist organization of society generally, as well as of the rather special forms that socialism has taken in the Soviet Union.

The following features of the impact of mass terror upon the population stand out, at least provisionally, in connection with the broader problem of stability or change within the Soviet system. One of them is that the terror appears to the population as capricious. As the Soviet leadership alters its policies in the effort to adapt to changing circumstances at home and abroad, its definition of the sources of internal danger necessarily varies over time. Perhaps the greatest variations, the "elimination of the kulaks as a class" and the blood-bath of the Great Purge, both of which may be regarded as part of the violent establishment and consolidation of the Stalinist system, are already past. But even if no such upheaval is in store for the future, smaller and less dramatic policy changes carry with them their redefinitions of the sources of internal danger and the categories of potential victims. Most of the population, busy with their own affairs, cannot possibly foresee these changes. Therefore an element of apparent capriciousness and arbitrariness is bound to remain as long as terror is a prominent instrument. It is of course impossible to draw a sharp line by asserting that when a certain number of people, or certain strategic groups in the population, no longer believe that this society operates according to their subjective definitions of fairness and justice, this society is doomed. Furthermore, the Soviet government, as we have seen, apparently has considerable capital on which it can draw, in the willingness of many people to overlook the harshness of their own treatment, or to regard it as an accidental matter. With all these qualifications the propositions may be offered that organized terror necessarily seems capricious to the subjects of a totalitarian society and that this capriciousness in turn undermines the essential bases of social organization.

Finally, we may take brief note of some of the dynamic consequences of the restriction and control of the flow of information in the Soviet Union, the typical totalitarian counterpart of terror. The rationalist utopian hope that the masses would follow the "correct" course of action if they were in possession of full information has always been treated ambivalently by Marxists and particularly by Russian Marxists. The practice of the latter has indeed swung to the opposite extreme of maximum restriction of the flow of certain kinds of information. To some extent, and in varying proportions among different groups, rumor and gossip serve as a substitute for the information that is restricted. In turn, and as part of a vicious circle, terror must be used to stamp out the substitute.

Now it may be useful to examine the other side of the coin, by considering the pressures upon the rulers of a socialist state to employ terror as an instrument of policy. This is a problem that transcends the Soviet experience, but upon which the Soviet case sheds some valuable light. It is frequently argued that socialism inevitably brings about the widespread use of terror and the disappearance of legal and other safeguards on the freedom of the individual. Socialism may be defined as a form of economic organization in which the decisions concerning the kinds of commodities to be produced and their manner of distribution to the population are made by a central authority instead of by private individuals with property rights in the means of production. Such a definition excludes states such as Britain under the Labor government, where a substantial portion of the economy remained in private hands. The discussion will also be confined to the problems specific to an industrial society.

In its most persuasive form the argument that terror is the blood relative of socialism runs somewhat as follows. The freedom of the individual in society and his defense against arbitrary attacks upon his person ultimately depend upon the competition of independent interest groups within the society. The struggle among workers, managers, farmers, as well as among noneconomic groups such as organized religion, the military forces, and others, provides the necessary basis for a constitutional order. This play of interests takes place within the framework of general acceptance of the rules of the game, expressed in law, and particularly constitutional law. The latter provides certain permissible methods, such as free elections and the organization of political parties, for carrying on the struggle in the political arena, and prohibits others, such as the use of organized violence. Whatever destroys the play of interest groups within the society and permits a single group to dominate inevitably destroys the only realistic guarantee that organized violence will not be used against dissenting persons or groups in the society. Power is the only effective check on power. Socialism destroys this check. The concentration of economic authority in the hands of a single body inevitably carries with it the concentration of political authority. The economic institutions of socialism, by definition, imply the destruction of independent foci of power and authority within the state and their subordination to a single will.

The reply of the democratic socialist holds that socialism provides both a procedure for making economic decisions in a way that will distribute more goods and services to a greater proportion of the population, and a method through which the population may share in the making of these decisions. Socialists have tended to concentrate on the economic technicalities of the way in which these results might be achieved and to ignore the political side of the question.[1] Nevertheless, the essential point of their argument may be expressed as a claim that socialism provides the individual with a more realistic opportunity for making his wishes felt than does a system of private property.

I do not think that the socialist argument comes to grips with the liberal point that power is the only effective check on power. But it does draw attention to a major aspect of the problem: the necessity to distinguish between centralized economic control that is forcibly imposed in order to carry out a policy opposed by most of the population and one that is the consequence of an attempt to find a more satisfactory way of meeting the wishes of the population. Organized terror in the Soviet Union belongs quite clearly in the first of these two categories. The Soviet case cannot therefore be made to support the argument that *any* form of socialism will require organized terror to maintain it.

Under what circumstances, then, may socialism, or any similar form of centralized economy, be expected to develop the features of organized and more or less permanent terror? The answer may be hazarded that organized terror, in its beginning stages at any rate, does not stem from any particular type of economic structure, but from the attempt to alter the structure of society at a rapid rate and from above through forceful administrative devices. The essence of the situation appears to lie in the crusading spirit, the fanatical conviction in the justice and universal applicability of some ideal about the way life should be organized, along with a lack of serious concern about the consequences of the methods used to pursue this ideal. The liberal suspicion of fanatical and self-righteous utopianism is well founded in this respect, though there is very great difficulty in specifying in concrete terms what is utopian and what is practicable. The attempt to change institutions rapidly nearly always results in opposition by established interests. The more rapid and more thorough the change, the more extensive and bitter is the opposition likely to be. Hence organized terror becomes necessary. It may be employed either by the opponents or the advocates of change, or by both if the society becomes polarized around two camps strongly upholding and opposing the *status quo*.

Insofar as socialism requires terror, it does so primarily in order to change the situation that it inherits from its predecessors. Economic and social change that is not the spontaneous product of attitudes and social relationships widely prevalent throughout the society require terror and enthusiasm as their motive force. Whether spontaneous or forced, a rapid pace of change is likely to produce widespread human suffering. Hence the situation in which a socialist regime comes to power is crucial in determining the probabilities of terror, as is widely recognized in socialist writings. If the socialists are content to take over the situation left by their predecessors without making fundamental changes, relatively little terror may be needed. This was the situation originally anticipated in Marxist theory, where terror would merely brush away the remnants of the old order. If, on the other hand, socialism is to be dynamic after it has come to power, it is likely to require the constant application of terror, both against the population at large and dissidents within its own ranks. Its commitment to terror is as great as its commitment to change that goes against the habits and desires of various sectors of the population.

Revolutionary leaders on this account are frequently faced with a dilemma. If they display too little "revolutionary courage" in the use of force, their opponents may rally and overthrow them. The weakness of the German socialists in this respect is often cited as one of the major elements in the Nazi counterrevolution. If, on the other hand, the revolutionists display too much "revolutionary courage" in destroying the bases of the old order and creating a new one, they may find that their original objectives of greater human freedom have been sacrificed to the necessities of keeping power.

If terror is the product of enthusiasm and one of the necessary instruments of a dynamic regime, it is likewise one of the elements that can destroy this dynamism.

There are, on the other hand, a number of services that organized terror performs for the regime. In the first place, it helps to generate in some people a sort of generalized fear, a sensation of guilt, that in many cases results in feats of prodigious effort.[2] These exceptional efforts must be balanced against the loss of initiative and the escape from responsibility that the background of terror produces in others. Yet they are immediate evidence that the consequences are by no means altogether negative from the regime's standpoint. In the second place, since the terror hits heavily at the instruments of the dictatorship, it helps to prevent them from obtaining too much independent power and thereby frustrating the will of the dictator. The Great Purge of the late thirties struck heavily at the Party, for which there is fairly detailed evidence, and also at the secret police itself, for which the evidence is much scantier.[3] Terror is a necessary ingredient in the dictator's ability to "shake up the apparatus" and reach down to interfere with its operations at any level. It therefore contitutes an essential element in the dictator's control. It also constitutes a device, albeit an extreme one, through which the Soviet system can handle the problem of initiating shifts in policy and personnel and making the new policy stick. Likewise, the purges help to clear the road for talent, keeping open channels of upward mobility, a necessary feature in any dynamic industrial society. Without more precise statistical information, it is difficult to estimate the significance of the purge in this connection, but it is probably considerable. Finally, one should not overlook its effect in destroying and preventing the formation of organized opposition. Former Soviet citizens, who as a group have the greatest stake in the possibilities of such opposition, are nearly unanimous in their denial that any such opposition exists. In this respect, terror is a necessary counterpart to the cult of an infallible leadership in preventing alternative appraisals of the situation at home and abroad from splitting the Party. This infallibility, for which the seeds were planted by Lenin, was fully cultivated by Stalin, and upon his death transferred to a collective leadership, which so far has presented itself as a rather anonymous and impersonal body to the Soviet public.

Summing up the advantages and disadvantages of organized terror to the Soviet system, one can offer the conclusion that the new regime still requires terror as an essential aspect of its power and that it is unlikely to give it up of its own accord. The regime has to walk a thin and not always easily discernible line between using too much terror or too little. Too much can destroy the minimal framework of regularity and legality necessary to maintain the total system upon which the regime's power depends. Too little terror diminishes control at the center by permitting the growth of independent centers of authority within the bureaucracy. Whether the new leaders will be able to solve this problem remains to be seen.

Notes

1. Cf. Benjamin E. Lippincott, ed., *On the Economic Theory of Socialism* (Minneapolis, 1938). For a critical survey of the literature see Joseph A. Schumpeter, *Capitalism, Socialism and Democracy* (3rd ed.; New York, 1947), Part III.
2. Cf. Dicks, "Observations on Contemporary Russian Behaviour," *Human Relations*, V, no. 2, esp. pp. 127, 155–6.
3. See Z. Brzezinski, "The Permanent Purge and Soviet Totalitarianism" (Ph.D. thesis, Harvard University, 1953), particularly for evidence concerning the impact of the purge on the Party.

6
The Uniqueness and Normality of the Holocaust

Zygmunt Bauman

"Wouldn't you be happier if I had been able to show you that all the perpetrators were crazy?" asks the great historian of the Holocaust, Raul Hilberg. Yet this is precisely what he is *unable* to show. The truth he does show brings no comfort. It is unlikely to make anybody happy. They were educated men of their time. That is the crux of the question whenever we ponder the meaning of Western Civilization after Auschwitz. Our evolution has outpaced our understanding; we can no longer assume that we have a full grasp of the workings of our social institutions, bureaucratic structures, or technology.[1]

This is certainly bad news for philosophers, sociologists, theologians and all the other learned men and women who are professionally concerned with understanding and explaining. Hilberg's conclusions mean that they have not done their job well; they cannot explain what has happened and why, and they cannot help us to understand it. This charge is bad enough as far as the scientists go (it is bound to make the scholars restless, and may even send them, as they say, back to the drawing board), but in itself it is not a cause for public alarm. There have been, after all, many other important events in the past that we feel we do not fully understand. Sometimes this makes us angry; most of the time, however, we do not feel particularly perturbed. After all – so we console ourselves – these past events are matters of *academic interest*.

But are they? It is not the Holocaust which we find difficult to grasp in all its monstrosity. *It is our Western Civilization which the occurrence of the Holocaust has made all but incomprehensible* – and this at a time when we thought we had come to terms with it and seen through its innermost drives and even through its prospects, and at a time of its worldwide, unprecedented cultural expansion. If Hilberg is right, and our most crucial social institutions elude our mental and practical grasp, then it is not just the professional academics who ought to be worried.

True, the Holocaust occurred almost half a century ago. True, its immediate results are fast receding into the past. The generation that experienced it at first hand has almost died out. But – and this is an awesome, sinister "but" – these once-familiar features of our civilization, which the Holocaust had made mysterious again, are still very much part of our life. They have not gone away. Neither has, therefore, the *possibility* of the Holocaust.

We shrug off such a possibility. We pooh-pooh the few obsessed people riled by our balance of mind. We have a special, derisive name for them – "prophets of doom." It comes easy to dismiss their anguished warnings. Are we not vigilant already? Do we not condemn violence, immorality, cruelty? Do we not muster all our ingenuity and considerable, constantly growing resources to fight them? And besides, is there anything at all in our life that points to the sheer possibility of a catastrophe? Life is getting better and more comfortable. On the whole, our institutions seem to cope. Against the enemy, we are well protected, and our friends surely won't do anything nasty. Granted, we hear from time to time of atrocities that some not particularly civilized, and for this reason spiritually far-away people, visit upon their equally barbaric neighbors. Ewe massacre a million Ibos, having first called them vermin, criminals, money-grabbers and subhumans without culture;[2] Iraqis poison-gas their Kurdish citizens without even bothering to call them names; Tamils massacre Singhalese; Ethiopians exterminate Eritreans; Ugandans exterminate themselves (or was it the other way round?). It is all sad, of course, but what can it possibly have to do with us? If it proves anything at all, it certainly proves how bad it is to be unlike us, and how good it is to be safe and sound behind the shield of our superior civilization.

Just how untoward our complacency may prove in the end becomes apparent once we recall that still in 1941 the Holocaust was not expected; that, given the extant knowledge of the "facts of the case," it was not expectable; and that, when it finally came to pass one year later, it met with universal incredulity. People refused to believe the facts they stared at. Not that they were obtuse or ill-willed. It was just that nothing they had known before had prepared them to believe. For all they had known and believed, the mass murder for which they did not even have a name yet was, purely and simply, unimaginable. In

1988, it is unimaginable again. In 1988, however, we know what we did not know in 1941; that also *the unimaginable ought to be imagined.*

The problem

There are two reasons for which the Holocaust, unlike many other topics of academic study, cannot be seen as a matter of solely academic interest; and for which the problem of the Holocaust cannot be reduced to the subject-matter of historical research and philosophical contemplation.

The first reason is that the Holocaust, even if it is plausible that, "as a central historical event – not unlike the French Revolution, the discovery of America, or the discovery of the wheel – it has changed the course of subsequent history,"[3] has most certainly changed little, if anything, in the course of the subsequent history of our collective consciousness and self-understanding.

The second reason is that whatever happened to the "course of history," nothing much happened to those products of history which in all probability contained the potentiality of the Holocaust – or at least we cannot be sure that it did. For all we know (or, rather, for all we do not know) they may still be with us, waiting for their chance. We can only suspect that the conditions that once before gave birth to the Holocaust have not been radically transformed. If there was something in our social order which made the Holocaust possible in 1941, we cannot be sure that it has been eliminated since then.

The real cause for concern, one that cannot be easily argued away, nor dismissed as a natural yet misleading outcome of post-Holocaust trauma, lies elsewhere. It can be gleaned from two related facts.

First, ideational processes that by their own inner logic may lead to genocidal projects, and the technical resources that permit implementation of such projects, not only have been proved fully compatible with modern civilization, but have been conditioned, created and supplied by it. The Holocaust did not just, mysteriously, avoid clash with the social norms and institutions of modernity. It was these norms and institutions that made the Holocaust feasible. Without modern civilization and its most central essential achievements, there would be no Holocaust.

Second, all those intricate networks of checks and balances, barriers and hurdles which the civilizing process has erected and which, as we hope and trust, would defend us from violence and constrain all over ambitious and unscrupulous powers, have been proven ineffective.

When it came to mass murder, the victims found themselves alone. Not only had they been fooled by an apparently peaceful and humane, legalistic and orderly society – their sense of security became a most powerful factor of their downfall.

To put it bluntly, there are reasons to be worried because we know now that *we live in a type of society that made the Holocaust possible, and that contained nothing which could stop the Holocaust from happening.* For these reasons alone it is necessary to study the lessons of the Holocaust. Much more is involved in such a study than the tribute to the memory of murdered millions, settling the account with the murderers and healing the still-festering moral wounds of the passive and silent witnesses.

Obviously, the study itself, even a most diligent study, is not a sufficient guarantee against the return of mass murderers and numb bystanders. Yet without such a study, we would not even know how likely or improbable such a return may be.

Genocide extraordinary

Mass murder is not a modern invention. History is fraught with communal and sectarian enmities, always mutually damaging and potentially destructive, often erupting into overt violence, sometimes leading to massacre, and in some cases resulting in extermination of whole populations and cultures. On the face of it, this fact denies the uniqueness of the Holocaust. In particular, it seems to deny the intimate link between the Holocaust and modernity, the "elective affinity" between the Holocaust and modern civilization. It suggests instead that murderous communal hatred has always been with us and will probably never go away; and that the only significance of modernity in this respect is that, contrary to its promise and to the widespread expectations, it did not file smooth the admittedly rough edges of human coexistence and thus has not put a definite end to man's inhumanity to man. Modernity has not delivered on its promise. Modernity has failed. But modernity bears no responsibility for the episode of the Holocaust – as genocide accompanied human history from the start.

This is not, however, the lesson contained in the experience of the Holocaust. No doubt the Holocaust was another episode in the long series of attempted mass murders and the not much shorter series of accomplished ones. It also bore features that it did not share with any of the past cases of genocide. It is these features which deserve special attention. They had a distinct modern flavor. Their presence suggests that modernity contributed to the Holocaust more directly than through its own weakness and ineptitude. It suggests that the role of modern civilization in the incidence and the perpetration of the Holocaust was active, not passive. It suggests that the Holocaust was as much a product, as it was a failure, of modern civilization. Like everything else done in the modern – rational, planned, scientifically informed, expert, efficiently managed, co-ordinated – way, the Holocaust left behind and put to shame all its alleged pre-modern equivalents, exposing them as primitive, wasteful and ineffective by comparison. Like everything else in our modern society, the Holocaust was an accomplishment in every respect superior, if measured by the standards that this society has preached and institutionalized. It towers high above the past genocidal episodes in the same way as the modern industrial plant towers above the craftsman's cottage workshop, or the modern industrial farm, with its tractors, combines and pesticides, towers above the peasant farmstead with its horse, hoe and hand-weeding.

On 9 November 1938 an event took place in Germany which went down in history under the name of *Kristallnacht*. Jewish businesses, seats of worship, and homes were attacked by an unruly, though officially encouraged and surreptitiously controlled, mob; they were broken down, set on fire, vandalized. About one hundred persons lost their lives. *Kristallnacht* was the only large-scale pogrom that occurred on the streets of German towns throughout the duration of the Holocaust. It was also the one episode of the Holocaust that followed the established, centuries-old tradition of anti-Jewish mob violence. It did not differ much from past pogroms; it hardly stood out from the long line of crowd violence stretching from ancient time, through the Middle Ages and up to the almost contemporary, but still largely pre-modern, Russia, Poland or Rumania. Were the Nazis treatment of the Jews composed only of *kristallnacht* and suchlike events, it would hardly add anything but an extra paragraph, a chapter at best, to the multi-volume chronicle of emotions running amok, of lynching mobs, of soldiers looting and raping their way through the conquered towns. This was not, however, to be.

This was not to be for a simple reason: one could neither conceive of, nor make, mass murder on the Holocaust scale of no matter how many *Kristallnachte*.

Consider the numbers. The German state annihilated approximately six million Jews. At the rate of 100 per day this would have required nearly 200 years. Mob violence rests on the wrong psychological basis, on violent emotion. People can be manipulated into fury, but fury cannot be maintained for 200 years. Emotions, and their biological basis, have a natural time course, lust, even blood lust, is eventually sated. Further, emotions are notoriously fickle, can be turned. A lynch mob is unreliable, it can sometimes be moved by sympathy – say by a child's suffering. To eradicate a 'race' it is essential to kill the children.

Thorough, comprehensive, exhaustive murder required the replacement of the mob with a bureaucracy, the replacement of shared rage with obedience to authority. The requisite bureaucracy would be effective whether manned by extreme or tepid anti-Semites, considerably broadening the pool of potential recruits; it would govern the actions of its members not by arousing passions but by organizing routines; it would only make distinctions it was designed to make, not those its members might be moved to make, say, between children and adults, scholar and thief, innocent and guilty; it would be responsive to the will of the ultimate authority through a hierarchy of responsibility – whatever that will might be.[4]

Rage and fury are pitiably primitive and inefficient as tools of mass annihilation. They normally peter out before the job is done. One cannot build grand designs on them. Certainly not such designs as reach beyond momentary effects like a wave of terror, the breakdown of an old order, clearing the ground for a new rule. Ghengis Khan and Peter the Hermit did not need modern technology and modern, scientific methods of management and co-ordination. Stalin or Hitler did. It is the adventurers and dilletantes like Ghengis Khan and Peter the Hermit that our modern, rational society has discredited and, arguably, put paid to. It is the practitioners of cool, thorough and systematic genocide like Stalin and Hitler for whom the modern, rational society paved the way.

Most conspicuously, the modern cases of genocide stand out for their sheer scale. On no other occasion but during Hitler's and Stalin's rule were so many people murdered in such a short time. This is not, however, the only novelty, perhaps not even a primary one – merely a by-product of other, more seminal features. Contemporary mass murder is distinguished by a virtual absence of all spontaneity on the one hand, and the prominence of rational, carefully calculated design on the other. It is marked by an almost complete elimination of contingency and chance, and independence from group emotions and personal motives. It is set apart by its merely sham or marginal – disguising or decorative – role of ideological mobilization. But first and foremost, it stands out by its purpose.

Murderous motives in general, and motives for mass murder in particular, have been many and varied. They range from pure, cold-blooded calculation of competitive gain, to equally pure, disinterested hatred or heterophobia. Most communal strifes and genocidal campaigns against aborigines lie comfortably within this range. If accompanied by an ideology, the latter does not go much further than a simple "us or them" vision of the world, and a precept "There is no room for both of us," or "The only good injun is a dead injun." The adversary is expected to follow mirror-image principles only if allowed to. Most genocidal ideologies rest on a devious symmetry of assumed intentions and actions.

Truly modern genocide is different. *Modern genocide is genocide with a purpose.* Getting rid of the adversary is not an end in itself. It is a means to an end: a necessity that stems from the ultimate objective, a step that one has to take if one wants ever to reach the end of the road. *The end itself is a grand vision of a better, and radically different, society.* Modern genocide is an element of social engineering, meant to bring about a social order conforming to the design of the perfect society.

To the initiators and the managers of modern genocide, society is a subject of planning and conscious design. One can and should do more about the society than change one or several of its many details, improve it here and there, cure some of its troublesome ailments. One can and should set oneself goals more ambitious and radical: one can and should remake the society, force it to conform to an overall, scientifically conceived plan. One can create a society that is objectively better than the one "merely existing" – that is, existing without conscious intervention. Invariably, there is an aesthetic dimension to the design: the ideal world about to be built conforms to the standards of superior beauty. Once built, it will be richly satisfying, like a perfect work of art; it will be a world which, in Alberti's immortal words, no adding, diminishing or altering could improve.

This is a gardener's vision, projected upon a world-size screen. The thoughts, feelings, dreams and drives of the designers of the perfect world are familiar to every gardener worth his name, though perhaps on a somewhat smaller scale. Some gardeners hate the weeds that spoil their design – that ugliness in the midst of beauty, litter in the midst of serene order. Some others are quite unemotional about them: just a problem to be solved, an extra job to be done. Not that it makes a difference to the weeds; both gardeners exterminate them. If asked or given a chance to pause and ponder, both would agree; weeds must die not so much because of what they are, as because of what the beautiful, orderly garden ought to be.

Modern culture is a garden culture. It defines itself as the design for an ideal life and a perfect arrangement of human conditions. If constructs its own identity out of distrust of nature. In fact, it defines itself and nature, and the distinction between them, through its endemic distrust of spontaneity and its longing for a better, and necessarily artificial, order. Apart from the overall plan, the artificial *order* of the garden needs tools and raw materials. It also needs defense – against the unrelenting danger of what is, obviously, a disorder. The order, first conceived of as a design, determines what is a tool, what is a raw material, what is useless, what is irrelevant, what is harmful, what is a weed or a pest. It classifies all elements of the universe by their relation to itself. This relation is the only meaning it grants them and tolerates – and the only justification of the gardener's actions, as differentiated as the relations themselves. From the point of view of the design all actions are instrumental, while all the objects of action are either facilities or hindrances.

Modern genocide, like modern culture in general, is a gardener's job. It is just one of the many chores that people who treat society as a garden need to undertake. If garden design defines its weeds, there are weeds wherever there is a garden. And weeds are to be exterminated. Weeding out is a creative, not a destructive activity. It does not differ in kind from other activities which combine in the construction and sustenance of the perfect garden. All visions of society-as-garden define parts of the social habitat as human weeds. Like all other weeds, they must be segregated, contained, prevented from spreading, removed and kept outside the society boundaries; if all these means prove insufficient, they must be killed.

Stalin's and Hitler's victims were not killed in order to capture and colonize the territory they occupied. Often they were killed in a dull, mechanical fashion with no human emotions – hatred included – to enliven it. They were killed because they did not fit, for one reason or another, the scheme of a perfect society. Their killing was not the work of destruction, but creation. They were eliminated, so that an objectively better human world – more efficient, more moral, more beautiful – could be established. A Communist world. Or a racially pure, Aryan world. In both cases, a harmonious world, conflict-free, docile in the hands of their rulers, orderly, controlled. People tainted with ineradicable blight of their past or origin could not be fitted into such an unblemished, healthy and shining world. Like weeds, their nature could not be changed. They could not be improved or re-educated. They had to be eliminated for reasons of genetic or ideational heredity – of a natural mechanism, resilient and immune to cultural processing.

The two most notorious and extreme cases of modern genocide did not betray the spirit of modernity. They did not deviously depart from the main track of the civilizing process. They were the most consistent, uninhibited expressions of that spirit. They attempted to reach the most ambitious aims of the civilizing process most other processes stop short of, not necessarily for the lack of good will. They showed what the rationalizing, designing, controlling dreams and efforts of modern civilization are able to accomplish if not mitigated, curbed or counteracted.

These dreams and efforts have been with us for a long time. They spawned the vast and powerful arsenal of technology and managerial skills. They gave birth to institutions which serve the sole purpose of instrumentalizing human behavior to such an extent that any aim may be pursued with efficiency and vigor, with or without ideological dedication or moral approval on the part of the pursuers. They legitimize the rulers' monopoly on ends and the confinement of the ruled to the role of means. They define most actions as means, and means as subordination – to the ultimate end, to those who set it, to supreme will, to supra-individual knowledge.

Emphatically, this does not mean that we all live daily according to Auschwitz principles. From the fact that the Holocaust is modern, it does not follow that modernity is a Holocaust. The Holocaust is a by-product of the modern drive to a fully designed, fully controlled world, once the drive is getting out of control and running wild. Most of the time, modernity is prevented from doing so. Its ambitions clash with the pluralism of the human world; they stop short of their fulfillment for the lack of an absolute power absolute enough and a monopolistic agency monopolistic enough to be able to disregard, shrug off, or overwhelm all autonomous, and thus countervailing and mitigating, forces.

Peculiarity of modern genocide

When the modernist dream is embraced by an absolute power able to monopolize modern vehicles of rational action, and when that power attains freedom from effective social control, genocide follows. A modern genocide – like the Holocaust. The short circuit (one almost wishes to say: a chance encounter) between an ideologically obsessed power elite and the tremendous facilities of rational, systemic action developed by modern society, may happen relatively seldom. Once it does happen, however, certain aspects of modernity are revealed which under different circumstances are less visible and hence may be easily "theorized away."

Modern Holocaust is unique in a double sense. *It is unique among other historic cases of genocide because it is modern. And it stands unique against the quotidianity of modern society because it brings together some ordinary factors of modernity which normally are kept apart.* Is this second sense of its uniqueness, only the combination of factors is unusual and rare, not the factors that are combined. Separately, each factor is common and normal. As the knowledge of saltpetre, sulphur or charcoal is not complete unless one knows and remembers that, if mixed, they turn into gunpowder.

The simultaneous uniqueness and normality of the Holocaust has found excellent expression in the summary of Sarah Gordon's findings:

> systematic extermination, as opposed to sporadic pogroms, could be carried out only by extremely powerful government, and probably could have succeeded only under the cover of wartime conditions. It was only the advent of Hitler and his radical anti-Semitic followers and their subsequent centralization of power that made the extermination of European Jewry possible ...
>
> The process of organized exclusion and murder required cooperation by huge sections of the military and bureaucracy, as well as acquiescence among the German people, whether or not they approved of Nazi persecution and extermination.[5]

Gordon names several factors which had to come together to produce the Holocaust; radical (and modern: racist and exterminatory) antisemitism of the Nazi type; transformation of that antisemitism into the practical policy of a powerful, centralized state; that state being in command of a huge, efficient bureaucratic apparatus; "state of emergency" – an extraordinary, wartime condition, which allowed that government and the bureaucracy it controlled to get away with things which could, possibly, face more serious obstacles in time of peace; and the non-interference, the passive acceptance of those things by the population at large. Two among those factors (one can argue that the two can be reduced to one: with Nazis in power, war was virtually inevitable) could be seen as coincidental – not necessary attributes of a modern society, though always its possibility. The remaining factors, however, are fully "normal." They are constantly present in every modern society, and their presence has been made both possible and inescapable by those processes which are properly associated with the rise and entrenchment of modern civilization.

Here I intend to focus on one only, yet arguably the most crucial among the constituent factors of the Holocaust: the typically modern, technological-bureaucratic patterns of action and the mentality they institutionalize, generate, sustain and reproduce.

There are two antithetical ways in which one can approach the explanation of the Holocaust. One can consider the horrors of mass murder as evidence of the fragility of civilization, or one can see them as evidence of its awesome potential. One can argue that, with criminals in control, civilized rules of behavior may be suspended, and thus the eternal beast always hiding just beneath the skin of the socially drilled being may break free. Alternatively, one can argue that, once armed with the sophisticated technical and conceptual products of modern civilization, men can do things their nature would otherwise prevent them from doing. To put it differently; one can, following the Hobbesian tradition, conclude that the inhuman pre-social state has not yet been fully eradicated, all civilizing efforts notwithstanding. Or one can, on the contrary, insist that the civilizing process has succeeded in substituting artificial and flexible patterns of human conduct for natural drives, and hence made possible a scale of inhumanity and destruction which had remained inconceivable as long as natural predispositions guided human action. I propose to opt for the second approach, and substantiate it in the following discussion.

The fact that most people (including many a social theorist) instinctively choose the first, rather than the second, approach, is a testimony to the remarkable success of the etiological myth which, in one variant or another, Western civilization has deployed over the years to legitimize its spatial hegemony by projecting it as temporal superiority. Western civilization has articulated its struggle for domination in terms of the holy battle of humanity against barbarism, reason against ignorance, objectivity against prejudice, progress against degeneration, truth against superstition, science against magic, rationality against passion. It has interpreted the history of its ascendance as the gradual yet relentless substitution of human mastery over nature for the mastery of nature over man. It has presented its own accomplishment as, first and foremost, a decisive advance in human freedom of action, creative potential ad security. It has identified freedom and security with its own type of social order: Western, modern society is defined as *civilized* society, and a civilized society in turn is understood as a state from which most of the natural ugliness and morbidity, as well as most of the immanent human propensity to cruelty and violence, have been eliminated or at least suppressed. The popular image of civilized society is, more than anything else, that of the absence of violence; of a gentle, polite, soft society.

All in all, the overall nonviolent character of modern civilization is an illusion. More exactly, it is an integral part of its self-apology and self-apotheosis; in short, of its legitimizing myth. It is not true that our civilization exterminates violence due to the inhuman, degrading or immoral character of the latter. If modernity

> is indeed antithetical to the wild passions of barbarism, it is not at all antithetical to efficient, dispassionate destruction, slaughter, and torture ... As the quality of thinking grows more rational, the quantity of destruction increases. In our time, for example, terrorism and torture are no longer instruments of passions; they have become instruments of political rationality.[6]

What in fact has happened in the course of the civilizing process, is the redeployment of violence, and the redistribution of access to violence. Like so many other things which we have been trained to abhor and detest, violence has been taken out of sight, rather than forced out of existence. It has become invisible, that is, from the vantage point of narrowly circumscribed and privatized personal experience. It has been enclosed instead in segregated and isolated territories, on the whole inaccessible to ordinary members of society; or evicted to the "twilight areas", off-limits for a large majority (and the majority which counts) of society's members; or exported to distant places which on the whole are irrelevant for the life-business of civilized humans (one can always cancel holiday bookings).

The ultimate consequence of all this is the concentration of violence. Once centralized and free from competition, means of coercion would be capable of reaching unheard of results even if not technically perfected. Their concentration, however, triggers and boosts the escalation of technical improvements, and thus the effects of concentration are further magnified. As Anthony Giddens repeatedly emphasized (see, above all, his *Contemporary Critique of Historical Materialism* (1981), and *The Constitution of Society* (1984)), the removal of violence from the daily life of civilized societies has always been intimately associated with a thoroughgoing militarization of inter-societal exchange and inner-societal production of order; standing armies and police forces brought together technically superior weapons and superior technology of bureaucratic management. For the last two centuries, the number of people who have suffered violent death as the result of such militarization has been steadily growing to reach a volume unheard of before.

The Holocaust absorbed an enormous volume of means of coercion. Having harnessed them in the service of a single purpose, it also added stimulus to their further specialization and technical perfection. More, however, than the sheer quantity of tools of destruction, and even their technical quality, what mattered was the way in which they were deployed. Their formidable effectiveness relied mostly on the subjection of their use to purely bureaucractic, technical considerations (which made their use all but totally immune to the countervailing pressures, such as they might have been submitted to if the means of violence were controlled by dispersed and unco-ordinated agents and deployed in a diffuse way). Violence has been turned into a technique. Like all techniques, it is free from emotions and purely rational. "It is, in fact, entirely reasonable, if 'reason' means instrumental reason, to apply American military force, B-52's napalm, and all the rest to 'communist-dominated' Viet-Nam (clearly an 'undesirable object'), as the 'operator' to transform it into a 'desirable object'."[7]

Effects of the hierarchical and functional divisions of labor

Use of violence is most efficient and cost effective when the means are subjected to solely instrumental-rational criteria, and thus dissociated from moral evaluation of the ends. Such dissociation is an operation all bureaucracies are good at. One may even say that it provides the essence of bureaucratic structure and process, and with it the secret of that tremendous growth of mobilizing and co-ordinating potential, and of the rationality and efficiency of action, which modern civilization has achieved thanks to the development of bureaucratic administration. The dissociation is by and large an outcome of two parallel processes, which are both central to the bureaucratic model of action. The first is the *meticulous functional division of labor* (as additional to, and distinct in its consequences from, linear graduation of power and subordination); the second is the *substitution of technical for a moral responsibility*.

All division of labor (also such division as results from the mere hierarchy of command) creates a distance between most of the contributors to the final outcome of collective activity, and the outcome itself. Before the last links in the bureaucratic chain of power (the direct executors) confront their task, most of the preparatory operations which brought about that confrontation have been already performed by persons who had no personal experience, and sometimes not the knowledge either, of the task in question. Unlike in a pre-modern unit of work, in which all steps of the hierarchy share in the same occupational skills, and the practical knowledge of working operations actually grows towards the top of the ladder (the master knows the same as his journeyman or apprentice, only more and better), persons occupying successive rungs of modern bureaucracy differ sharply in the kind of expertise and professional training their jobs require. They may be able to put themselves imaginatively into their subordinates' position; this may even help in maintaining "good human relations" inside the office – but it is not the condition of proper performance of the task, nor of the effectiveness of the bureaucracy as a whole. In fact, most bureaucracies do not treat seriously the romantic recipe that requires every bureaucrat, and particularly those who occupy the top, to "start from the bottom" so that on the way to the summit they should acquire, and memorize, the experience of the entire slope. Mindful of the multiplicity of skills which the managerial jobs of various magnitudes demand, most bureaucracies practice instead separate avenues of recruitment for different levels of the hierarchy. Perhaps it is true that each soldier carries a marshal's baton in his knapsack, but few marshals, and few colonels or captains for that matter, keep soldiers' bayonets in their briefcases.

What such practical and mental distance from the final product means is that most functionaries of the bureaucratic hierarchy may give commands without full knowledge of their effects. In many cases they would find it difficult to visualize those effects. Usually, they only have an abstract, detached awareness of them; the kind of knowledge which is best expressed in statistics, which measure the results without passing any judgment, and certainly not moral ones. In their files and their minds the results are at best diagramatically represented as curves or sectors of a circle; ideally, they would appear as a column of numbers. Graphically or numerically represented, the final outcomes of their commands are devoid of substance. The graphs measure the *progress* of work, they say nothing about the nature of the operation or its objects. The graphs make tasks of widely different character mutually exchangeable; only the quantifiable success or failure matter, and seen from that point of view, the tasks do not differ.

All these effects of distance created by the hierarchical division of labor are radically magnified once the division becomes functional.

Now it is not just the lack of direct, personal experience of the actual execution of the task to which successive command contribute their share, but also the lack of similarity between the task at hand and the task of the office as a whole (one is not a miniature version, or an icon, of the other), which distances the contributor from the job performed by the bureaucracy of which he is a part. The psychological impact of such distantiation is profound and far-reaching. It is one thing to give a command to load bombs on the plane, but quite different to take care of regular steel supply in a bomb factory. In the first case, the command-giver may have no vivid, visual impression of the devastation the bomb is about to cause. In the second case, however, the supply manager does not, if he chooses to, have to think about the use to which bombs are put at all. Even an abstract, purely notional knowledge of the final outcome is redundant, and certainly irrelevant as far as the success of his own part of the operation goes. In a functional division of labor, everything one does is in principle *multifinal*; that is, it can be combined and integrated into more than one meaning-determining totality. By itself, the function is devoid of meaning, and the meaning which will be eventually bestowed on it is in no way pre-empted by the actions of its perpetrators. It will be "the others" (in most cases anonymous and out of reach) who will some time, some-where, decide that meaning. "Would workers in the chemical plants that produced napalm accept responsibility for burned babies?" ask Kren and Rappoport. "Would such workers even be aware that others might reasonably think they were responsible?"[8] Of course they wouldn't. And there is no bureaucratic reason why they should. The splitting of the baby-burning process in minute functional tasks and then separating the tasks from each other have made such awareness irrelevant – and exceedingly difficulty to achieve. Remember as well that it is chemical plants that produce napalm, not any of their individual workers ...

The second process responsible for distantiation is closely related to the first. The substitution of technical for moral responsibility would not be conceivable without the meticulous functional dissection and separation of tasks. At least it would not be conceivable to the same extent. The substitution takes place, to a degree, already within the purely linear graduation of control. Each person within the hierarchy of command is accountable to his immediate superior, and thus is naturally interested in his opinion and his approval of the work. However much this approval matters to him, he is still, though only theoretically, aware of what the ultimate outcome of his work is bound to be.

And so there is at least an abstract chance of one awareness being measured against the other; benevolence of superiors being confronted with repulsiveness of the effects. And whenever comparison is feasible, so is the choice. Within a purely linear division of command, technical responsibility remains, at least in theory, vulnerable; it may still be called to justify itself in moral terms and to compete with moral conscience. A functionary may, for instance, decide that by giving a particular command his superior overstepped his terms of reference, as he moved from the domain of purely technical interest to that charged with ethical significance (shooting soldiers is OK; shooting babies is a different matter); and that the duty to obey an authoritative command does not extend so far as to justify what the functionary considers as morally unacceptable deeds. All these theoretical possibilities disappear, however, or are considerably weakened, once the linear hierarchy of command is supplemented, or replaced, by functional division and separation of tasks. The triumph of technical responsibility is then complete, unconditional, and for all practical purposes, unassailable.

Technical responsibility differs from moral responsibility in that it forgets that the action is a means to something other than itself. As outer connections of action are effectively removed from the field of vision, the bureaucrat's own act becomes an end in itself. It can be judged only by its intrinsic criteria of propriety and success. Hand-in-hand with the vaunted relative autonomy of the official conditioned by his functional specialization, comes his remoteness from the overall effects of the divided yet co-ordinated labor of the organization as a whole. Once isolated from their distant consequences, most functionally specialized acts either pass the moral test easily, or are morally indifferent. When unencumbered by moral worries, the act can be judged on unambiguously rational grounds. What matters then is whether the act has been performed according to the best available technological know-how, and whether its output has been cost-effective. Criteria are clear-cut and easy to operate.

For our topic, two effects of such a context of bureaucratic action are most important. First is the fact that the skills, expert knowledge, inventiveness and dedication of actors, complete with their personal motives that prompted them to deploy these qualities in full, can be fully mobilized and put to the service of the overall bureaucratic purpose even if (or perhaps because) the actors retain relative functional autonomy towards this purpose and even if this purpose does not agree with the actors' own moral philosophy. To put it bluntly, *the result is the irrelevance of moral standards for the technical success of the bureaucratic operation.* The instinct of workmanship, which according to Thorstein Veblen is present in every actor, focuses fully on proper performance of the job in hand. The practical devotion to the task may be further enhanced by the actor's craven character and the severity of his superiors, or by the actor's interest in promotion, the actor's ambition or disinterested curiosity, or by many other personal circumstances, motives, or character features – but, on the whole, workmanship will suffice even in their absence. By and large, the actors want to excel; whatever they do, they want to do well. Once, thanks to the complex functional differentiation within bureaucracy, they have been distantiated from the ultimate outcomes of the operation to which they contribute, their moral concerns can concentrate fully on the good performance of the job at hand. Morality boils down to the commandment to be a good, efficient and diligent expert and worker.

Dehumanization of bureaucratic objects

Another, equally important effect of bureaucratic context of action is *dehumanization of the objects of bureaucratic operation*; the possibility to express these objects in purely technical, ethically neutral terms.

Dehumanization starts at the point when, thanks to the distantiation, the objects at which the bureaucratic operation is aimed can, and are, reduced to a set of quantitative measures. For railway managers, the only meaningful articulation of their object is in terms of tonnes per kilometre. They do not deal with humans, sheep, or barbed wire; they only deal with the cargo, and this means an entity consisting entirely of measurements and devoid of quality. For most bureaucrats, even such a category as cargo would mean too strict a quality-bound restriction. They deal only with the financial effects of their actions. Their object is money. Money is the sole object that appears on both input and output ends, and *pecunia*, as the ancients shrewdly observed, definitely *non olet*. As they grow, bureaucratic companies seldom allow themselves to be confined to one qualitatively distinct area of activity. They spread sideways, guided in their movements by a sort of *lucrotropism* – a sort of gravitational pulling force of the highest returns on their capital. As we remember, the whole operation of the Holocaust was managed by the Economic Administration Section of the *Reichsicherheithauptamt*. We know that this one assignment, exceptionally, was not intended as a strategem or a camouflage.

Reduced, like all other objects of bureaucratic management, to pure, quality-free measurements, human objects lose their distinctiveness. They are already dehumanized – in the sense that the language in which things that happen to them (or are done to them) are narrated, safeguards its referents from ethical evaluation. In fact, this language is unfit for normative-moral statements. It is only humans that may be objects of ethical propositions. (True, moral statements do extend sometimes to other, nonhuman living beings; but they may do so only by expanding from their original anthropomorphic foothold.) Humans lose this capacity once they are reduced to ciphers.

Dehumanization is inextricably related to the most essential, rationalizing tendency of modern bureaucracy. As all bureaucracies affect in some measure some human objects, the adverse impact of dehumanization is much more common than the habit to identify it almost totally with its genocidal effects would suggest. Soldiers are told to shoot *targets*, which *fall* when they are *hit*. Employees of big companies are encouraged to destroy *competition*. Officers of welfare agencies operate *discretionary awards* at one time, *personal credits* at another. Their objects are *supplementary benefit recipients*. It is difficult to perceive and remember the humans behind all such technical terms. The point is that as far as the bureaucratic goals go, they are better not perceived and not remembered.

Once effectively dehumanized, and hence cancelled as potential subjects of moral demands, human objects of bureaucratic task-performance are viewed with ethical indifference, which soon turns into disapprobation and censure when their resistance, or lack of cooperation, slows down the smooth flow of bureaucratic routine. Dehumanized objects cannot possibly possess a "cause," much less a "just" one; they have no "interests" to be considered, indeed no claim to subjectivity. Human objects become therefore a "nuisance factor." Their obstreperousness further strengthens the self-esteem and the bonds of comradeship that unite the functionaries. The latter see themselves now as companions in a difficult struggle, calling for courage, self-sacrifice and selfless dedication to the cause. It is not the objects of bureaucratic action, but its subjects who suffer and deserve compassion and moral praise. They may justly derive pride and assurance of their own dignity from crushing the recalcitrance of their victims – much as they are proud of overriding any other obstacle. Dehumanization of the objects and positive moral self-evaluation reinforce each other. The functionaries may faithfully serve any goal while their moral conscience remains unimpaired.

The overall conclusion is that the bureaucratic mode of action, as it has been developed in the course of the modernizing process, contains all the technical elements which proved necessary in the execution of genocidal tasks. This mode can be put to the service of a genocidal objective without major revision of its structure, mechanisms and behavioral norms.

Moreover, contrary to widespread opinion, bureaucracy is not merely a tool, which can be used with equal facility at one time for cruel and morally contemptible, at another for deeply humane purposes. Even if it does move in any direction which it is pushed, bureaucracy is more like a loaded dice. It has a logic and a momentum of its own. It renders some solutions more, and other solutions less, probable. Given an initial push (being confronted with a purpose), it will – like the brooms of the sorcerer's apprentice – easily move beyond all thresholds at which many of those who gave it the push would have stopped, were they still in control of the process they triggered. Bureaucracy is programmed to seek the optimal solution. It is programmed to measure the optimum in such terms as would not distinguish between one human object and another or between human and inhuman objects. What matters is the efficiency and lowering of costs of their processing.

The role of bureaucracy in the Holocaust

It so happened in Germany half a century ago that bureaucracy was given the task of making Germany *judenrein* – clean of Jews. Bureaucracy started from what bureaucracies start with: the formulation of a precise definition of the object, then registering those who fitted the definition and opening a file for each. It proceeded to segregate those in the files from the rest of the population, to which the received brief did not apply. Finally, it moved to evicting the segregated category from the land of the Aryans which was to be cleansed – by nudging it to emigrate first, and deporting it to non-German territories once such territories found themselves under German control. By that time bureaucracy developed wonderful cleansing skills, not to be wasted and left to rust. *Bureaucracy which acquitted itself so well of the task of cleansing Germany made more ambitious tasks feasible, and their choice well-high natural.* With such a superb cleaning facility, why stop at the *Heimat* of the Aryans? Why refrain from cleaning the whole of their empire? True, as the empire was now ecumenical, it had no "outside" left where the dumping ground for the Jewish litter could be disposed of. Only one direction of deportation remained; upward, in smoke.

For many years now historians of the Holocaust have been split into the "intentionalist" and the "functionalist" camps. The first insist that killing the Jews was from the start Hitler's firm decision, waiting only for opportune conditions to emerge. The second credit Hitler with only a general idea of "finding a solution" to the "Jewish problem": clear only as far as the vision of "clean Germany" goes, but vague and muddled as to the practical steps to be taken to bring that vision closer. Historical scholarship ever more convincingly supports the functionalist view. Whatever the ultimate outcome of the debate, however, there is hardly any doubt that the space extending between the idea and its execution was filled wall-to-wall with bureaucratic action. Neither is there any doubt that however vivid was Hitler's imagination, it would have accomplished little if it had not been taken over, and translated into a routine process of problem-solving, by a huge and rational bureaucratic apparatus. Finally, and perhaps most importantly, the bureaucratic mode of action left its indelible impression of the Holocaust process. Its fingerprints are all over the Holocaust history, for everyone to see. True, bureaucracy did not hatch the fear of racial contamination and the obsession with racial hygiene. For that it needed visionaries, as bureaucracy picks up where visionaries stop. But bureaucracy made the Holocaust. And it made it in its own image.

Hilberg has suggested that the moment the first German official had written the first rule of Jewish exclusion, the fate of the European Jews was sealed. There is a most profound and terrifying truth in this comment. What bureaucracy needed was the definition of its task. Rational and efficient as it was, it could be trusted to see the task to its end.

Bureaucracy contributed to the perpetuation of the Holocaust not only through its inherent capacities and skills, but also through its immanent ailments. The tendency of all bureaucracies to lose sight of the original goal and to concentrate on the means instead – the means which turn into the ends – has been widely noted, analyzed and described. The Nazi bureaucracy did not escape its impact. Once set in motion, the machinery of murder developed its own impetus: the more it excelled in cleansing the territories it controlled of the Jews, the more actively it sought new lands where it could exercise its newly acquired skills. With the approaching military defeat of Germany, the original purpose of the *Endlösung* was becoming increasingly unreal. What kept the murdering machine going then was solely its own routine and impetus. The skills of mass murder had to be used simply because they were there. The experts created the objects for their own expertise. We remember the experts of Jewish Desks in Berlin introducing every new petty restriction on German Jews who had long before all but disappeared from German soil; we remember the SS commanders who forbade the *Wehrmacht* generals from keeping alive the

Jewish craftsmen they badly needed for military operations. But nowhere was the morbid tendency of substituting the means for the ends more visible than in the uncanny and macabre episode of the murder of Romanian and Hungarian Jews, perpetrated with the Eastern Front just a few miles away, and at an enormous cost to the war effort: priceless rail carriages and engines, troops and administrative resources were diverted from military tasks in order to cleanse distant parts of Europe for the German habitat which was never to be.

Bureaucracy is intrinsically *capable* of genocidal action. To *engage* in such an action, it needs an encounter with another invention of modernity: a bold design of a better, more reasonable and rational social order – say a racially uniform, or a classless society – and above all the capacity of drawing such designs and determination to make them efficacious. Genocide follows when two common and abundant inventions of modern times meet. It is only their meeting which has been, thus far, uncommon and rare.

Bankruptcy of modern safeguards

Physical violence and its threat

> is no longer a perpetual insecurity that it brings into the life of the individual, but a peculiar form of security ... a continuous, uniform pressure is exerted on individual life by the physical violence stored behind the scenes of everyday life, a pressure totally familiar and hardly perceived, conduct and drive economy having been adjusted from earliest youth to this social structure.[9]

In these words, Norbert Elias restated the familiar self-definition of civilized society. Elimination of violence from daily life is the main assertion around which that definition revolves. As we have seen, the apparent elimination is in fact merely an eviction, leading to the reassembly of resources and disposition of centers of violence in new locations within the social system. According to Elias, the two developments are closely interdependent. The area of daily life is comparatively free from violence precisely because somewhere in the wings physical violence is stored – in quantities that put it effectively out of the control of ordinary members of society and endow it with irresistible power to suppress unauthorized outbursts of violence. Daily manners mellowed mainly because people are now threatened with violence in case they are violent – with violence they cannot match or reasonably hope to repel. The disappearance of violence from the horizon of daily life is thus one more manifestation of the centralizing and monopolizing tendencies of modern power; violence is absent from individual intercourse because it is now controlled by forces definitely outside the individual reach. But the forces are not outside *everybody's* reach. Thus the much vaunted mellowing of manners (which Elias, following the etiological myth of the West, celebrates with such a relish), and the cosy security of daily life that follows have their price. A price which we, dwellers in the house of modernity, may be called to pay at any time. Or made to pay, without being called first.

Pacification of daily life means at the same time its defenselessness. By agreeing, or being forced to renounce the use of physical force in their reciprocal relations, members of modern society disarm themselves in front of the unknown and normally invisible, yet potentially sinister and always formidable managers of coercion. Their weakness is worrying not so much because of the high probability that the managers of coercion will indeed take advantage of it and hurry to turn the means of violence they control against the disarmed society, as for the simple fact that whether such advantage will or will not be taken, does not in principle depend on what ordinary men and women do. By themselves, the members of modern society cannot prevent the use of massive coercion from happening. Mellowing of manners goes hand-in-hand with a radical shift in control over violence.

Awareness of the constant threat which the characteristically modern imbalance of power contains would make life unbearable, were it not for our trust in safeguards which we believe have been built into the fabric of modern, civilized society. Most of the time we have no reason to think that the trust is misguided. Only on a few dramatic occasions a doubt is cast on the reliability of the safeguards. Perhaps the main significance of the Holocaust lies in its having been one of the most redoubtable of such occasions to date. *In the years leading to the Final Solution the most trusted of the safeguards had been put to a test. They all failed – one by one, and all together.*

Perhaps the most spectacular was the failure of science – as a body of ideas, and as a network of institutions of enlightenment and training. The deadly potential of the most revered principles and accomplishments of modern science has been exposed. The emancipation of reason from emotions, of rationality from normative pressures, of effectiveness from ethics have been the battle-cries of science since its inception. Once implemented, however, they made science, and the formidable technological applications it spawned, into docile instruments in the hands of unscrupulous power. The dark and ignoble role which science played in the perpetuation of the Holocaust was both direct and indirect.

Indirectly (though centrally to its general social function), science cleared the way to genocide through sapping the authority, and questioning the binding force, of all normative thinking, particularly that of religion and ethics. Science looks back at its history as the long and victorious struggle of reason over superstition and irrationality. In as far as religion and ethics could not rationally legitimize the demands they made on human behavior, they stood condemned and found their authority denied. As values and norms had been proclaimed immanently and irreparably subjective, instrumentality was left as the only field where the search for excellence was feasible. Science wanted to be value-free and took pride in being such. By institutional pressure and by ridicule, it silenced the preachers of morality. In the process, it made itself morally blind and speechless. It dismantled all the barriers that could stop it from cooperating, with enthusiasm and abandon, in designing the most effective and rapid methods of mass sterilization or mass killing; or from conceiving of the concentration camps' slavery as a unique and wonderful opportunity to conduct medical research for the advancement of scholarship and – of course – of mankind.

Science (or this time, rather the scientists) helped the Holocaust perpetrators directly as well. Modern science is a gigantic and complex institution. Research costs dear, as it requires huge buildings, expensive equipment and large teams of highly paid experts. Thus science depends on a constant flow of money and non-monetary resources, which only equally large institutions are able to offer and to guarantee. Science is not, however, mercantile, nor are the scientists avaricious. Science is about truth, and scientists are about pursuing it. Scientists are overwhelmed with curiosity and excited by the unknown. If measured by all other earthly concerns, including monetary, curiosity is disinterested. It is only the value of knowledge and truth which scientists preach and search. It is just a coincidence, and preferably a minor irritant, that curiosity cannot be sated, and the truth found, without ever-growing funds, ever-more costly laboratories, ever-larger salary bills. What scientists want is merely to be allowed to go where their thirst for knowledge prompts them.

A government which stretches its helpful hand and offers just that can count on the scientists' gratitude and cooperation. Most scientists would be prepared in exchange to surrender quite a long list of lesser precepts. They would be prepared, for instance, to make do with the sudden disappearance of some of their colleagues with the wrong shape of nose or biographical entry. If they object at all, it will be that taking all these colleagues away in one swoop may put the research schedule in jeopardy. (This is not a slur nor a squib; this is what the protests of German academics, medics and engineers, if recorded at all, boiled down to. Less still was heard from their Soviet equivalents during the purges.) With relish, German scientists boarded the train drawn by the Nazi locomotive towards the brave, new, racially purified and German-dominated world. Research projects grew more ambitious by the day, and research institutes grew more populous and resourceful by the hour. Little else mattered.

In his fascinating new study of the contribution of biology and medical science to the designing and implementing of Nazi racial policy, Robert Proctor puts paid to the popular myth of science under Nazism as, first and foremost, the victim of persecution and an object of intense indoctrination from above (a myth dating at least from Joseph Needham's influential *The Nazi Attack on International Science*, published in 1941). In the light of Proctor's meticulous research, the widespread opinion sorely underestimates the degree to which political initiatives (indeed, some of the most gruesome among them) were generated by the scientific community itself, rather than imposed from outside on reluctant yet craven boffins, and the extent to which racial policy itself was initiated and managed by the recognized scientists with academically impeccable credentials. If there was coercion, "it often took the form of one part of the scientific community coercing another." On the whole, "many of the social and intellectual foundations [for racial programs] were laid down long before the rise of Hitler to power," and biomedical scientists "played an active, even leading role in the initiation, administration, and execution of the Nazi racial programmes."[10] That the biomedical scientists in question were by no standards a lunatic or fanatical fringe of the profession is shown by Proctor's painstaking study of the composition of the editorial boards of 147 medical journals published in Nazi Germany. After Hitler's rise to power, the boards remained either unchanged or they replaced only a small minority of their members (in all probability, the change is accounted for by the removal of Jewish scholars).[11]

At best, the cult of rationality, institutionalized as modern science, proved impotent to prevent the state from turning into organized crime; at worst, it proved instrumental in bringing the transformation about. Its rivals, however, did not earn a higher score either. In their silence German academics had plenty of companions. Most conspicuously, they were joined by the Churches – all of them. Silence in the face of the organized inhumanity was the only item on which the Churches, so often at loggerheads, found themselves in agreement. None of them attempted to reclaim its flouted authority. None of the Churches (as distinct from single, and mostly isolated churchmen) acknowledged its responsibility for deeds perpetrated in a country it claimed as its domain, and by people in its pastoral charge. (Hitler never left the Catholic Church; neither was he excommunicated.) None upheld its right to pass moral judgments on its flock and impose penitence on the wayward.

Most pertinently, the culturally trained revulsion against violence proved a poor safeguard against organized coercion, while civilized manners showed an astounding ability to cohabit, peacefully and harmoniously, with mass murder. The protracted, and often painful, civilizing process failed to erect a single foolproof barrier against the genocide. Those mechanisms needed the civilized code of behavior to coordinate criminal actions in such a way that they seldom clashed with the self-righteousness of the perpetrators. Among the bystanders, the civilized disgust of inhumanity did not prove strong enough to encourage an active resistance to it. Most bystanders reacted as civilized norms advise and prompt us to react to things unsightly and barbaric; they turned their eyes the other way. The few who stood up against cruelty did not have norms or social sanctions to support them and reassure. They were loners, who in justification of their fight against evil could only quote one of their distinguished ancestors: "Ich kann nicht anders."

In the face of an unscupulous team saddling the powerful machine of the modern state with its monopoly of physical violence and coercion, the most vaunted accomplishments of modern civilization failed as safeguards against barbarism. *Civilization proved incapable of guaranteeing moral use of the awesome powers it brought into being.*

Conclusions

If we ask now what the original sin was which allowed this to happen, the collapse (or non-emergence) of democracy seems to be the most convincing answer. In the absence of traditional authority, the only checks and balances capable of keeping the body politic away from extremities can be supplied by political democracy. The latter is not, however, quick to arrive, and it is slower still to take root once the hold of the old authority and system of control has been broken – particularly if the breaking was done in a hurry. Such situations of interregnum and instability tend to occur during and after deep-reaching revolutions, which succeed in paralyzing old seats of social power without as yet replacing them with new ones – and create for this reason a state of affairs in which *political and military forces are neither counterbalanced nor restrained by resourceful and influential social ones.*

Such situations emerged, arguably, in pre-modern times as well – in the wake of bloody conquests or protracted internecine strifes which led on occasion to well-nigh complete self-annihilation of established elites. The expectable consequences of such situations were, however, different. A general collapse of the larger social order normally followed. War destruction seldom reached as low as the grass-root, communal networks of social control; communally regulated local islands of social order were now exposed to erratic acts of violence and pillage, but they had themselves to fall back upon once the social organization above the local level disintegrated. In most cases, even the most profound blows to traditional authorities in pre-modern societies differed from modern unheavals in two crucial aspects; first, they left the primeval, communal controls of order intact or at least still viable; and second, they weakened, rather than strengthened the possibility of organized action on a supra-communal level, as the social organization of the higher order fell apart and whatever exchange was left between localities was once again subjected to a free play of unco-ordinated forces.

Under modern conditions, on the contrary, upheavals of a similar kind occur, on the whole, after communal mechanisms of social regulation have all but disappeared and local communities ceased to be self-sufficient and self-reliant. Instead of an instinctive reflex of "falling back" upon one's own resources, the void tends to be filled by new, but again supra-communal, forces, which seek to deploy the state monopoly of coercion to impose a new order on the societal scale. Instead of collapsing, political power becomes therefore virtually the only force behind the emerging order. In its drive it is neither stopped nor restrained by economic and social forces, seriously undermined by the destruction or paralysis of old authorities.

This is, of course, a theoretical model, seldom implemented in full in historical practice. Its use consists however in drawing attention to those social dislocations that seem to make the surfacing of genocidal tendencies more likely. Dislocations may differ in form and intensity, but they are united by the general effect of *the pronounced supremacy of political over economic and social power, of the state over the society.* They went perhaps deepest and farthest in the case of the Russian Revolution and the subsequent prolonged monopoly of the state as the only factor of social integration and order-reproduction. Yet also in

Germany they went farther and deeper than it is popularly believed. Arriving after the brief Weimar interlude, the Nazi rule undertook and completed the revolution that the Weimar Republic – that uneasy interplay of old and new (but immature) elites which only at the surface resembled political democracy – was, for various reasons, incapable of administering. Old elites were considerably weakened or pushed aside. One by one, the forms of articulation of economic and social forces were dissembled and replaced with new, centrally supervised forms emanating from, and legitimized by, the state. All classes were profoundly affected, but the most radical blow was delivered to the classes that can carry non-political power only collectively, i.e. to the non-proprietary classes, and to the working class above all. Etatization or disbanding of all autonomous labor institutions coupled with the subjection of local government to almost total central control, left the popular masses virtually powerless and, for all practical purposes, excluded from the political process. Resistance of social forces was prevented additionally by the surrounding of state activity with an impenetrable wall of secrecy – indeed, the state conspiracy of silence against the very population it ruled. The overall and ultimate effect was the replacement of traditional authorities not by the new vibrant forces of self-governing citizenship, but by an almost total monopoly of the political state, with social powers prevented from self-articulation, and thus from forming a structural foundation of political democracy.

Modern conditions made possible the emergence of a resourceful state, capable of replacing the whole network of social and economic controls by political command and administration. More importantly still, modern conditions provide substance for that command and administration. Modernity, as we remember, is an age of artificial order and of grand societal designs, the era of planners, visionaries, and – more generally – "gardeners" who treat society as a virgin plot of land to be expertly designed and then cultivated and doctored to keep to the designed form.

Periods of deep social dislocations are times when this most remarkable feature of modernity comes into its own. Indeed, at no other time does society seem to be so formless – "unfinished," indefinite and pliable – literally waiting for a vision and a skillful and resourceful designer to give it a form. At no other time does society seem so devoid of forces and tendencies of its own, and hence incapable of resisting the hand of the gardener, and ready to be squeezed into any form he chooses. *The combination of malleability and helplessness constitutes an attraction which few self-confident, adventurous visionaries could resist. It also constitutes a situation in which they cannot be resisted.*

The carriers of the grand design at the helm of modern state bureaucracy, emancipated from the constraints of nonpolitical (economic, social, cultural) powers; this is the recipe for genocide. Genocide arrives as an integral part of the process through which the grand design is implemented. *The design gives it the legitimation; state bureaucracy gives it the vehicle; and the paralysis of society gives it the "road clear" sign.*

The conditions propitious to the perpetration of genocide are thus special, yet not at all exceptional. Rare, but not unique. Not being an immanent attribute of modern society, they are not an alien phenomenon either. As far as modernity goes, genocide is neither abnormal nor a case of malfunction. It demonstrates what the rationalizing, engineering tendency of modernity is capable of if not checked and mitigated, if the pluralism of social powers is indeed eroded – as the modern ideal of purposefully designed, fully controlled, conflict-free, orderly and harmonious society would have it. Any impoverishment of grass-root ability to articulate interests and self-govern, every assault on social and cultural pluralism and the opportunities of its political expression, every attempt to fence off the untrammelled freedom of the state by a wall of political secrecy, each step towards the weakening of the social foundations of political democracy make a social disaster on a Holocaust scale just a little bit more feasible. Criminal designs need social vehicles to be effective. But so does the vigilance of those who want to prevent their implementation.

Thus far the vehicles for vigilance seem in short supply, while there is no shortage of institutions that seem capable of serving criminal designs or – worse still – incapable of preventing an ordinary task-oriented activity from acquiring a criminal dimension. Joseph Weizenbaum, one of the most acute observers and analysts of the social impact of information technology (admittedly a recent development, not available at the time of the Nazi Holocaust), suggests that the capacity for genocidal action has been, if anything, increased:

> Germany implemented the "final solution" of its "Jewish Problem" as a textbook exercise in instrumental reasoning. Humanity briefly shuddered when it could no longer avert its gaze from what had happened, when the photographs taken by the killers themselves began to circulate, and when the pitiful survivors re-emerged into the light. But in the end, it made no difference. The same logic, the same cold and ruthless application of calculating reason, slaugh-

tered at least as many people during the next twenty years as had fallen victim to the technicians of the thousand-year Reich. We have learned nothing. Civilization is as imperilled today as it was then.[12]

And the reasons why instrumental rationality, and the human networks developed to serve it, remain morally blind now as they were then, are virtually unchanged. In 1966, more than twenty years after the gruesome discovery of the Nazi crime, a group of distinguished scholars designed the scientifically elegant and exemplary rational project of the *electronic battlefield* for the use of the generals of the Vietnam war. "These men were able to give the counsel they gave because they were operating at an enormous psychological distance from the people who would be maimed and killed by the weapons systems that would result from the idea they communicated to their sponsors."[13]

Thanks to rapidly advancing new information technology, which more than any technology that preceded it has succeeded in obliterating the humanity of its human objects ("People, things, events are 'programmed', one speaks of 'inputs' and 'outputs', of feedback loops, variables, percentages, processes, and so on, until eventually all contact with concrete situations is abstracted away. Then only graphs, data sets, printouts are left"[14]) – the psychological distance grows unstoppably and at an unprecedented pace. So does the autonomy of purely technological progress from any deliberately chosen and discursively agreed human purposes. Today more than at any other time, available, technological means undermine their own applications and subordinate the evaluation of the latter to their own criteria of efficiency and effectiveness. By the same token, the authority of political and moral evaluation of action has been reduced to a minor consideration – if not discredited and rendered irrelevant. Action can hardly need any other justification than the recognition that the available technology has made it feasible. Jacques Ellul has warned that, having emancipated itself from the constraint of discursively-set social tasks, technology

never advances toward anything but *because* it is pushed from behind. The technician does not know why he is working, and generally he does not care. He works *because* he has instruments allowing him to perform a certain task, to succeed in a new operation ... there is no call towards a goal; there is constraint by an engine placed in the back and not tolerating any halt to the machine.[15]

There seems to be less hope than before that the civilized guarantees against inhumanity can be relied upon to control the application of human instrumental–rational potential, once the calculation of efficiency has been awarded supreme authority in deciding political purposes.

Notes

1. Raul Hilberg, "Significance of the Holocaust", in *The Holocaust: Ideology, Bureaucracy, and Genocide*, ed. Henry Friedlander and Sybil Milton (Millwood, NY: Kraus International Publications, 1980), pp. 101–2.
2. Cf. Colin Legum in the *Observer*, October 12, 1966.
3. Henry L. Feingold, "How Unique is the Holocaust?" in *Genocide: Critical Issues of the Holocaust*, ed. Alex Grobman and David Landes (Los Angeles: Simon Wiesenthal Centre, 1983), p. 397.
4. John P. Sabini and Mary Silver, "Destroying the Innocent with a Clear Conscience: A Sociopsychology of the Holocaust", in *Survivors, Victims, and Perpetrators: Essays in the Nazi Holocaust*, ed. Joel E. Dinsdale (Washington: Hemisphere Publishing Corporation, 1980), pp. 329–30.
5. Sarah Gordon, *Hitler, Germans, and the "Jewish Question"* (Princeton: Princeton University Press, 1984), pp. 48–9.
6. Kren and Rappoport, *The Holocaust and the Crisis*, p. 140.
7. Joseph Weizenbaum, *Computer Power and Human Reason: From Judgment to Calculation* (San Francisco: W. H. Freeman, 1976), p. 252.
8. George A. Kren and Leon Rappoport, *The Holocaust and the Crisis of Human Behavior* (New York: Holmes and Meier, 1980), p. 140.
9. Norbert Elias, *The Civilizing Process: State Formation and Civilization*, trans. Edmund Jephcott (Oxford: Basil Blackwell, 1982), pp. 238–9.
10. Robert Proctor, *Racial Hygiene: Medicine under the Nazis* (Cambridge Mass.: Harvard University Press, 1988), pp. 4, 6.
11. Proctor, *Racial Hygiene*, pp. 315–24.
12. Weizenbaum, *Computer Power*, p. 256.
13. Weizenbaum, *Computer Power*, p. 275.
14. Weizenbaum, *Computer Power*, p. 253.
15. Jacques Ellul, *Technological System*, trans. Joachim Neugroschel (New York: Continuum, 1980), pp. 272, 273.

Part II
Political Violence

7
The Causes of Terrorism

Martha Crenshaw

Terrorism occurs both in the context of violent resistance to the state as well as in the service of state interests. If we focus on terrorism directed against governments for purposes of political change, we are considering the premeditated use or threat of symbolic, low-level violence by conspiratorial organizations. Terrorist violence communicates a political message; its ends go beyond damaging an enemy's material resources.[1] The victims or objects of terrorist attack have little intrinsic value to the terrorist group but represent a larger human audience whose reaction the terrorists seek. Violence characterized by spontaneity, mass participation, or a primary intent of physical destruction can therefore be excluded from our investigation.

The study of terrorism can be organized around three questions: why terrorism occurs, how the process of terrorism works, and what its social and political effects are. Here the objective is to outline an approach to the analysis of the causes of terrorism, based on comparison of different cases of terrorism, in order to distinguish a common pattern of causation from the historically unique.

The subject of terrorism has inspired a voluminous literature in recent years. However, nowhere among the highly varied treatments does one find a general theoretical analysis of the causes of terrorism. This may be because terrorism has often been approached from historical perspectives, which, if we take Laqueur's work as an example, dismiss explanations that try to take into account more than a single case as "exceedingly vague or altogether wrong."[2] Certainly existing general accounts are often based on assumptions that are neither explicit nor factually demonstrable. We find judgments centering on social factors such as the permissiveness and affluence in which Western youth are raised or the imitation of dramatic models encouraged by television. Alternatively, we encounter political explanations that blame revolutionary ideologies, Marxism–Leninism or nationalism, governmental weakness in giving in to terrorist demands, or conversely government oppression, and the weakness of the regime's opponents. Individual psychopathology is often cited as a culprit.

Even the most persuasive of statements about terrorism are not cast in the form of testable propositions, nor are they broadly comparative in origin or intent. Many are partial analyses, limited in scope to revolutionary terrorism from the Left, not terrorism that is a form of protest or a reaction to political or social change. A narrow historical or geographical focus is also common; the majority of explanations concern modern phenomena. Some focus usefully on terrorism against the Western democracies.[3] In general, propositions about terrorism lack logical comparability, specification of the relationship of variables to each other, and a rank-ordering of variables in terms of explanatory power.

We would not wish to claim that a general explanation of the sources of terrorism is a simple task, but it is possible to make a useful beginning by establishing a theoretical order for different types and levels of causes. We approach terrorism as a form of political behavior resulting from the deliberate choice of a basically rational actor, the terrorist organization. A comprehensive explanation, however, must also take into account the environment in which terrorism occurs and address the question of whether broad political, social, and economic conditions make terrorism more likely in some contexts than in others. What sort of circumstances lead to the formation of a terrorist group? On the other hand, only a few of the people who experience a given situation practice terrorism. Not even all individuals who share the goals of a terrorist organization agree that terrorism is the best means. It is essential to consider the psychological variables that may encourage or inhibit individual participation in terrorist actions. The analysis of these three levels of causation will center first on situational variables, then on the strategy of the terrorist organization, and last on the problem of individual participation.

This chapter represents only a preliminary set of ideas about the problem of causation; historical cases of terrorism are used as illustrations, not as demonstrations of hypotheses. The historical examples referred to here are significant terrorist campaigns since the French Revolution of 1789; terrorism is considered as a facet of secular modern politics, principally associated with the rise of nationalism, anarchism, and revolutionary socialism.[4] The term *terrorism* was coined to describe the systematic inducement of fear and anxiety to control and direct a civilian population, and the phenomenon of terrorism as a challenge to the authority of the state grew from the difficulties revolutionaries experienced in trying to recreate the mass uprisings of the French Revolution. Most references provided here are drawn from the best-known and most-documented examples: Narodnaya Volya and the Combat Organization of the Socialist-Revolutionary party in Russia, from 1878 to 1913; anarchist terrorism of the 1890s in Europe, primarily France; the Irish Republican Army (IRA) and its predecessors and successors from 1919 to the present; the Irgun Zwai Leumi in Mandate Palestine from 1937 to 1947; the Front de Libération Nationale (FLN) in Algeria from 1954 to 1962; the Popular Front for the Liberation of Palestine from 1968 to the present; the Rote Armee Fraktion (RAF) and the June 2 Movement in West Germany since 1968; and the Tupamaros of Uruguay, 1968 to 1974.

The setting for terrorism

An initial obstacle to identification of propitious circumstances for terrorism is the absence of significant empirical studies of relevant cross-national factors. There are a number of quantitative analyses of collective violence, assassination, civil strife, and crime,[5] but none of these phenomena is identical to a campaign of terrorism. Little internal agreement exists among such studies, and the consensus one finds is not particularly useful for the study of terrorism.[6] For example, Ted Robert Gurr found that "modern" states are less violent than developing countries and that legitimacy of the regime inhibits violence. Yet, Western Europe experiences high levels of terrorism. Surprisingly, in the 1961–70 period, out of eighty-seven countries, the United States was ranked as having the highest number of terrorist campaigns.[7] Although it is impractical to borrow entire theoretical structures from the literature on political and criminal violence, some propositions can be adapted to the analysis of terrorism.

To develop a framework for the analysis of likely settings for terrorism, we must establish conceptual distinctions among different types of factors. First, a significant difference exists between *preconditions*, factors that set the stage for terrorism over the long run, and *precipitants*, specific events that immediately precede the occurrence of terrorism. Second, a further classification divides preconditions into enabling or permissive factors, which provide opportunities for terrorism to happen, and situations that directly inspire and motivate terrorist campaigns. Precipitants are similar to the direct causes of terrorism.[8]

Furthermore, no factor is neatly compartmentalized in a single nation-state; each has a transnational dimension that complicates the analysis.

First, modernization produces an interrelated set of factors that is a significant permissive cause of terrorism, as increased complexity on all levels of society and economy creates opportunities and vulnerabilities. Sophisticated networks of transportation and communication offer mobility and the means of publicity for terrorists. The terrorists of Narodnaya Volya would have been unable to operate without Russia's newly established rail system, and the Popular Front for the Liberation of Palestine could not indulge in hijacking without the jet aircraft. In Algeria, the FLN only adopted a strategy of urban bombings when they were able to acquire plastic explosives. In 1907, the Combat Organization of the Socialist-Revolutionary party paid 20,000 rubles to an inventor who was working on an aircraft in the futile hope of bombing the Russian imperial palaces from the air.[9] Today we fear that terrorists will exploit the potential of nuclear power, but it was in 1867 that Nobel's invention of dynamite made bombings a convenient terrorist tactic.

Urbanization is part of the modern trend toward aggregation and complexity, which increases the number and accessibility of targets and methods. The popular concept of terrorism as "urban guerrilla warfare" grew out of the Latin American experience of the late 1960s.[10] Yet, as Hobsbawm has pointed out, cities became the arena for terrorism after the urban renewal projects of the late nineteenth century, such as the boulevards constructed by Baron Haussman in Paris, which made them unsuitable for a strategy based on riots and the defense of barricades.[11] In preventing popular insurrections, governments have exposed themselves to terrorism. P. N. Grabosky has recently argued that cities are a significant cause of terrorism in that they provide an opportunity (a multitude of targets, mobility, communications, anonymity, and audiences) and a recruiting ground among the politicized and volatile inhabitants.[12]

Social "facilitation," which Gurr found to be extremely powerful in bringing about civil strife in general, is also an important permissive factor. This concept refers to social habits and historical traditions that sanction the use of violence against the government, making it morally and politically justifiable, and even dictating an appropriate form, such as demonstrations, coups, or terrorism. Social myths, traditions, and habits permit the development of terrorism as an established political custom. An excellent example of such a tradition is the case of Ireland, where the tradition of physical force dates from the eighteenth century, and the legend of Michael Collins in 1919–21 still inspires and partially excuses the much less discriminate and less effective terrorism of the contemporary Provisional IRA in Northern Ireland.

Moreover, broad attitudes and beliefs that condone terrorism are communicated transnationally. Revolutionary ideologies have always crossed borders with ease. In the nineteenth and early twentieth centuries, such ideas were primarily a European preserve, stemming from the French and Bolshevik Revolutions. Since the Second World War, Third World revolutions – China, Cuba, Algeria – and intellectuals such as Frantz Fanon and Carlos Marighela[13] have significantly influenced terrorist movements in the developed West by promoting the development of terrorism as routine behavior.

The most salient political factor in the category of permissive causes is a government's inability or unwillingness to prevent terrorism. The absence of adequate prevention by police and intelligence services permits the spread of conspiracy. However, since terrorist organizations are small and clandestine, the majority of states can be placed in the permissive category. Inefficiency or leniency can be found in a broad range of all but the most brutally efficient dictatorships, including incompetent authoritarian states such as tsarist Russia on the eve of the emergence of Narodnaya Volya as well as modern liberal democratic states whose desire to protect civil liberties constrains security measures. The absence of effective security measures is a necessary cause, since our limited information on the subject indicates that terrorism does not occur in the communist dictatorships; and certainly repressive military regimes in Uruguay, Brazil, and Argentina have crushed terrorist organizations. For many governments, however, the cost of disallowing terrorism is too high.

Turning now to a consideration of the direct causes of terrorism, we focus on background conditions that positively encourage resistance to the state. These instigating circumstances go beyond merely creating an environment in which terrorism is possible; they provide motivation and direction for the terrorist movement. We are dealing here with reasons rather than opportunities.

The first condition that can be considered a direct cause of terrorism is the existence of concrete grievances among an identifiable subgroup of a larger population, such as an ethnic minority discriminated against by the majority. A social movement develops in order to redress these grievances and to gain either equal rights or a separate state; terrorism is then the resort of an extremist faction of this broader movement. In practice, terrorism has frequently arisen in such situations: in modern states, separatist nationalism among Basques,

Bretons, and Québeçois has motivated terrorism. In the colonial era, nationalist movements commonly turned to terrorism.

This is not to say, however, that the existence of a dissatisfied minority or majority is a necessary or a sufficient cause of terrorism. Not all those who are discriminated against turn to terrorism, nor does terrorism always reflect objective social or economic deprivation. In West Germany, Japan, and Italy, for example, terrorism has been the chosen method of the privileged, not the downtrodden. Some theoretical studies have suggested that the essential ingredient that must be added to real deprivation is the perception on the part of the deprived that this condition is not what they deserve or expect, in short, that discrimination is unjust. An attitude study, for example, found that "the idea of justice or fairness may be more centrally related to attitudes toward violence than are feelings of deprivation. It is the perceived injustice underlying the deprivation that gives rise to anger or frustration."[14] The intervening variables, as we have argued, lie in the terrorists' perceptions. Moreover, it seems likely that for terrorism to occur the government must be singled out to blame for popular suffering.

The second condition that creates motivations for terrorism is the lack of opportunity for political participation. Regimes that deny access to power and persecute dissenters create dissatisfaction. In this case, grievances are primarily political, without social or economic overtones. Discrimination is not directed against any ethnic, religious, or racial subgroup of the population. The terrorist organization is not necessarily part of a broader social movement; indeed, the population may be largely apathetic. In situations where paths to the legal expression of opposition are blocked, but where the regime's repression is inefficient, revolutionary terrorism is doubly likely, as permissive and direct causes coincide. An example of this situation is tsarist Russia in the 1870s.

Context is especially significant as a direct cause of terrorism when it affects an elite, not the mass population. Terrorism is essentially the result of elite disaffection; it represents the strategy of a minority, who may act on behalf of a wider popular constituency who have not been consulted about, and do not necessarily approve of, the terrorists' aims or methods. There is remarkable relevance in E. J. Hobsbawm's comments on the political conspirators of post-Napoleonic Europe: "All revolutionaries regarded themselves, with some justification, as small elites of the emancipated and progressive operating among, and for the eventual benefit of, a vast and inert mass of the ignorant and misled common people, which would no doubt welcome liberation when it came, but could not be expected to take much part in preparing it."[15] Many terrorists today are young, well-educated, and middle class in background. Such students or young professionals, with prior political experience, are disillusioned with the prospects of changing society and see little chance of access to the system despite their privileged status. Much terrorism has grown out of student unrest; this was the case in nineteenth-century Russia as well as post-World War II West Germany, Italy, the United States, Japan and Uruguay.

Perhaps terrorism is most likely to occur precisely where mass passivity and elite dissatisfaction coincide. Discontent is not generalized or severe enough to provoke the majority of the populace to action against the regime, yet a small minority, without access to the bases of power that would permit overthrow of the government through coup d'état or subversion, seeks radical change. Terrorism may thus be a sign of a stable society rather than a symptom of fragility and impending collapse. Terrorism is the resort of an elite when conditions are not revolutionary. Luigi Bonanate has blamed terrorism on a "blocked society" that is strong enough to preserve itself (presumably through popular inertia) yet resistant to innovation. Such self-perpetuating *immobilisme* invites terrorism.[16]

The last category of situational factors involves the concept of a precipitating event that immediately precedes outbreaks of terrorism. Although it is generally thought that precipitants are the most unpredictable of causes, there does seem to be a common pattern of government actions that act as catalysts for terrorism. Government use of unexpected and unusual force in response to protest or reform attempts often compels terrorist retaliation. The development of such an action–reaction syndrome then establishes the structure of the conflict between the regime and its challengers. There are numerous historical examples of a campaign of terrorism precipitated by a government's reliance on excessive force to quell protest or squash dissent. The tsarist regime's severity in dealing with the populist movement was a factor in the development of Narodnaya Volya as a terrorist organization in 1879. The French government's persecution of anarchists was a factor in subsequent anarchist terrorism in the 1890s. The British government's execution of the heros of the Easter Rising set the stage for Michael Collins and the IRA. The Protestant violence that met the Catholic civil rights movement in Northern Ireland in 1969 pushed the Provisional IRA to retaliate. In West Germany, the death of Beno

Ohnesorg at the hands of the police in a demonstration against the Shah of Iran in 1968 contributed to the emergence of the RAF.

This analysis of the background conditions for terrorism indicates that we must look at the terrorist organization's perception and interpretation of the situation. Terrorists view the context as permissive, making terrorism a viable option. In a material sense, the means are placed at their disposal by the environment. Circumstances also provide the terrorists with compelling reasons for seeking political change. Finally, an event occurs that snaps the terrorists' patience with the regime. Government action is now seen as intolerably unjust, and terrorism becomes not only a possible decision but a morally acceptable one. The regime has forfeited its status as the standard of legitimacy. For the terrorist, the end may now excuse the means.

The reasons for terrorism

Significant campaigns of terrorism depend on rational political choice. As purposeful activity, terrorism is the result of an organization's decision that it is a politically useful means to oppose a government. The argument that terrorist behavior should be analyzed as "rational" is based on the assumption that terrorist organizations possess internally consistent sets of values, beliefs, and images of the environment. Terrorism is seen collectively as a logical means to advance desired ends. The terrorist organization engages in decision-making calculations that an analyst can approximate. In short, the terrorist group's reasons for resorting to terrorism constitute an important factor in the process of causation.[17]

Terrorism serves a variety of goals, both revolutionary and subrevolutionary. Terrorists may be revolutionaries (such as the Combat Organization of the Socialist-Revolutionary Party in the nineteenth century or the Tupamaros of the twentieth); nationalists fighting against foreign occupiers (the Algerian FLN, the IRA of 1919–21, or the Irgun); minority separatists combatting indigenous regimes (such as the Corsican, Breton, and Basque movements, and the Provisional IRA); reformists (the bombing of nuclear construction sites, for example, is meant to halt nuclear power, not to overthrow governments); anarchists or millenarians (such as the original anarchist movement of the nineteenth century and modern millenarian groups such as the Red Army faction in West Germany, the Italian Red Brigades, and the Japanese Red Army); or reactionaries acting to prevent change from the top (such as the Secret Army Organization during the Algerian war or the contemporary Ulster Defence Association in Northern Ireland).[18]

Saying that extremist groups resort to terrorism in order to acquire political influence does not mean that all groups have equally precise objectives or that the relationship between means and ends is perfectly clear to an outside observer. Some groups are less realistic about the logic of means and ends than others. The leaders of Narodnaya Volya, for example, lacked a detailed conception of how the assassination of the tsar would force his successor to permit the liberalization they sought. Other terrorist groups are more pragmatic: the IRA of 1919–21 and the Irgun, for instance, shrewdly foresaw the utility of a war of attrition against the British. Menachem Begin, in particular, planned his campaign to take advantage of the "glass house" that Britain operated in.[19] The degree of skill in relating means to ends seems to have little to do with the overall sophistication of the terrorist ideology. The French anarchists of the 1890s, for example, acted in light of a well-developed philosophical doctrine but were much less certain of how violence against the bourgeoisie would bring about freedom. It is possible that anarchist or millenarian terrorists are so preoccupied with the splendor of the future that they lose sight of the present. Less theoretical nationalists who concentrate on the short run have simpler aims but sharper plans.

However diverse the long-run goals of terrorist groups, there is a common pattern of proximate or short-run objectives of a terrorist strategy. Proximate objectives are defined in terms of the reactions that terrorists want to achieve in their different audiences.[20] The most basic reason for terrorism is to gain recognition or attention – what Thornton called advertisement of the cause. Violence and bloodshed always excite human curiosity, and the theatricality, suspense, and threat of danger inherent in terrorism enhance its attention-getting qualities. In fact, publicity may be the highest goal of some groups. For example, terrorists who are fundamentally protesters might be satisfied with airing their grievances before the world. Today, in an interdependent world, the need for international recognition encourages transnational terrorist activities, with escalation to ever more destructive and spectacular violence. As the audience grows larger, more diverse, and more accustomed to terrorism, terrorists must go to extreme lengths to shock.

Terrorism is also often designed to disrupt and discredit the processes of government, by weakening it administratively and impairing normal operations. Terrorism as a direct attack on the regime aims at the insecurity and demoralization of government officials, independent of any impact on public opinion. An excellent example of this strategy is Michael Collins's campaign against the British intelligence system in Ireland in 1919–21. This form of terrorism often accompanies rural guerrilla warfare, as the insurgents try to weaken the government's control over its territory.

Terrorism also affects public attitudes in both a positive and a negative sense, aiming at creating either sympathy in a potential constituency or fear and hostility in an audience identified as the "enemy." These two functions are interrelated, since intimidating the "enemy" impresses both sympathizers and the uncommitted. At the same time, terrorism may be used to enforce obedience in an audience from whom the terrorists demand allegiance. The FLN in Algeria, for example, claimed more Algerian than French victims. Fear and respect were not incompatible with solidarity against the French.[21] When terrorism is part of a struggle between incumbents and challengers, polarization of public opinion undermines the government's legitimacy.

Terrorism may also be intended to provoke a counterreaction from the government, to increase publicity for the terrorists' cause and to demonstrate to the people that their charges against the regime are well founded. The terrorists mean to force the state to show its true repressive face, thereby driving the people into the arms of the challengers. For example, Carlos Marighela argued that the way to win popular support was to provoke the regime to measures of greater repression and persecution.[22] Provocative terrorism is designed to bring about revolutionary conditions rather than to exploit them. The FLN against the French, the Palestinians against Israel, and the RAF against the Federal Republic all appear to have used terrorism as provocation.

In addition, terrorism may serve internal organizational functions of control, discipline, and morale building within the terrorist group and even become an instrument of rivalry among factions in a resistance movement. For example, factional terrorism has frequently characterized the Palestinian resistance movement. Rival groups have competed in a vicious game where the victims are Israeli civilians or anonymous airline passengers, but where the immediate goal is influence within the resistance movement rather than the intimidation of the Israeli public or international recognition of the Palestinian cause.

Terrorism is a logical choice when oppositions have such goals and when the power ratio of government to challenger is high. The observation that terrorism is a weapon of the weak is hackneyed but apt. At least when initially adopted, terrorism is the strategy of a minority that by its own judgment lacks other means. When the group perceives its options as limited, terrorism is attractive because it is a relatively inexpensive and simple alternative, and because its potential reward is high.

Weakness and consequent restriction of choice can stem from different sources. On the one hand, weakness may result from the regime's suppression of opposition. Resistance organizations which lack the means of mounting more extensive violence may then turn to terrorism because legitimate expression of dissent is denied. Lack of popular support at the outset of a conflict does not mean that the terrorists' aims lack general appeal. Even though they cannot immediately mobilize widespread and active support, over the course of the conflict they may acquire the allegiance of the population. For example, the Algerian FLN used terrorism as a significant means of mobilizing mass support.[23]

On the other hand, it is wrong to assume that where there is terrorism there is oppression. Weakness may mean that an extremist organization deliberately rejects nonviolent methods of opposition open to them in a liberal state. Challengers then adopt terrorism because they are impatient with time-consuming legal methods of eliciting support or advertising their cause, because they distrust the regime, or because they are not capable of, or interested in, mobilizing majority support. Most terrorist groups operating in Western Europe and Japan in the past decade illustrate this phenomenon. The new millenarians lack a readily identifiable constituency and espouse causes devoid of mass appeal. Similarly, separatist movements represent at best only a minority of the total population of the state.

Thus, some groups are weak because weakness is imposed on them by the political system they operate in, others because of unpopularity. We are therefore making value judgments about the potential legitimacy of terrorist organizations. In some cases resistance groups are genuinely desperate, in others they have alternatives to violence. Nor do we want to forget that nonviolent resistance has been chosen in other circumstances, for example, by Gandhi and by Martin Luther King. Terrorists may argue that they had no choice, but their perceptions may be flawed.[24]

In addition to weakness, an important rationale in the decision to adopt a strategy of terrorism is impatience. Action becomes imperative. For a variety of reasons, the challenge to the state cannot be left to the future. Given a perception of limited means, the group often sees the choice as between action as survival and inaction as the death of resistance.

One reason for haste is external: the historical moment seems to present a unique chance. For example, the resistance group facing a colonial power recently weakened by a foreign war exploits a temporary vulnerability: the IRA against Britain after World War I, the Irgun against Britain after World War II, and the FLN against France after the Indochina war. We might even suggest that the stalemate between the United States and North Vietnam stimulated the post-1968 wave of anti-imperialist terrorism, especially in Latin America. There may be other pressures or catalysts provided by the regime, such as the violent precipitants discussed earlier or the British decision to introduce conscription in Ireland during World War I.

A sense of urgency may also develop when similar resistance groups have apparently succeeded with terrorism and created a momentum. The contagion effect of terrorism is partially based on an image of success that recommends terrorism to groups who identify with the innovator. The Algerian FLN, for example, was pressured to keep up with nationalists in Tunisia and Morocco, whose violent agitation brought about independence in 1956. Terrorism spread rapidly through Latin America in the post-1968 period as revolutionary groups worked in terms of a continental solidarity.

Dramatic failure of alternative means of obtaining one's ends may also fuel a drive toward terrorism. The Arab defeat in the 1967 war with Israel led Palestinians to realize that they could no longer depend on the Arab states to further their goals. In retrospect, their extreme weakness and the historical tradition of violence in the Middle East made it likely that militant nationalists should turn to terrorism. Since international recognition of the Palestinian cause was a primary aim (given the influence of outside powers in the region) and since attacks on Israeli territory were difficult, terrorism developed into a transnational phenomenon.

These external pressures to act are often intensified by internal politics. Leaders of resistance groups act under constraints imposed by their followers. They are forced to justify the organization's existence, to quell restlessness among the cadres, to satisfy demands for revenge, to prevent splintering of the movement, and to maintain control. Pressures may also come from the terrorists' constituency.

In conclusion, we see that terrorism is an attractive strategy to groups of different ideological persuasions who challenge the state's authority. Groups who want to dramatize a cause, to demoralize the government, to gain popular support, to provoke regime violence, to inspire followers, or to dominate a wider resistance movement, who are weak vis-à-vis the regime, and who are impatient to act, often find terrorism a reasonable choice. This is especially so when conditions are favorable, providing opportunities and making terrorism a simple and rapid option, with immediate and visible payoff.

Individual motivation and participation

In their intense commitment, separation from the outside world, and intolerance of internal dissent, terrorist groups resemble religious sects or cults. Michael Barkun has explained the continued commitment of members of millenarian movements, a conviction frequently expressed in proselytizing in order to validate beliefs, in terms of the reinforcement and reassurance of rightness that the individual receives from other members of the organization. He also notes the frequent practice of initiation rites that involve violations of taboos, or "bridge-burning acts," that create guilt and prevent the convert's return to society. Thus the millenarian, like the terrorist group, constitutes "a community of common guilt."[25] J. Bowyer Bell has commented on the religious qualities of dedication and moral fervor characterizing the IRA: "In the Republican Movement, the two seemingly opposing traditions, one of the revolution and physical force, and the other of pious and puritanical service, *combine into a secular vocation.*"[26]

If there is a single common emotion that drives the individual to become a terrorist, it is vengeance on behalf of comrades or even the constituency the terrorist aspires to represent. (At the same time, the demand for retribution serves as public justification or excuse.) A regime thus encourages terrorism when it creates martyrs to be avenged. Anger at what is perceived as unjust persecution inspires demands for revenge, and as the regime responds to terrorism with greater force, violence escalates out of control.

There are numerous historical demonstrations of the central role vengeance plays as motivation for terrorism. It is seen as one of the principal causes of anarchist terrorism in France in the 1890s. The infamous Ravachol acted to avenge the "martyrs of Clichy," two possibly innocent anarchists who were beaten by the police and sentenced to prison. Subsequent bombings and assassinations, for instance that of President Carnot, were intended to avenge Ravachol's execution.[27] The cruelty of the sentences imposed for minor offenses at the "Trial of the 193," the hanging of eleven southern revolutionaries after Soloviev's unsuccessful attack on the tsar in 1879, and the "Trial of the 16" in 1880 deeply affected the members of Narodnaya Volya. Kravchinski (Stepniak) explained that personal resentment felt after the Trial of the 193 led to killing police spies; it then seemed unreasonable to spare their employers, who were actually responsible for the repression. Thus, intellectually the logic first inspired by resentment compelled them to escalate terrorism by degrees.[28] During the Algerian war, the French execution of FLN prisoners; in Northern Ireland, British troops firing on civil rights demonstrators; in West Germany, the death of a demonstrator at the hands of the police – all served to precipitate terrorism as militants sought to avenge their comrades.

The terrorists' willingness to accept high risks may also be related to the belief that one's death will be avenged. The prospect of retribution gives the act of terrorism and the death of the terrorist meaning and continuity, even fame and immortality. Vengeance may be not only a function of anger but of a desire for transcendence.

Shared guilt is surely a strong force in binding members of the terrorist group together. Almost all terrorists seem compelled to justify their behavior, and this anxiety cannot be explained solely by reference to their desire to create a public image of virtuous sincerity. Terrorists usually show acute concern for morality, especially for sexual purity, and believe that they act in terms of a higher good. Justifications usually focus on past suffering, on the glorious future to be created, and on the regime's illegitimacy and violence, to which terrorism is the only available response. Shared guilt and anxiety increase the group's interdependence and mutual commitment and may also make followers more dependent on leaders and on the common ideology as sources of moral authority.

Guilt may also lead terrorists to seek punishment and danger rather than avoid it. The motive of self-sacrifice notably influenced many Russian terrorists of the nineteenth century. Kaliayev, for example, felt that only his death could atone for the murder he committed. Even to Camus, the risk of death for the terrorist is a form of personal absolution.[29] In other cases of terrorism, individuals much more pragmatic than Kaliayev, admittedly a religious mystic, seemed to welcome capture because it brought release from the strains of underground existence and a sense of content and fulfillment. For example, Meridor, a member of the Irgun High Command, felt "high spirits" and "satisfaction" when arrested by the British because he now shared the suffering that all fighters had to experience. He almost welcomed the opportunity to prove that he was prepared to sacrifice himself for the cause. In fact, until his arrest he had felt "morally uncomfortable" whereas afterwards he felt "exalted."[30] Menachem Begin expressed similar feelings. Once, waiting as the British searched the hotel where he was staying, he admitted anxiety and fear, but when he knew there was "no way out," his "anxious thoughts evaporated." He "felt a peculiar serenity mixed with incomprehensible happiness" and waited "composedly," but the police passed him by.[31]

Vera Figner, a leader of the Narodnaya Volya, insisted on physically assisting in acts of terrorism, even though her comrades accused her of seeking personal satisfaction instead of allowing the organization to make the best use of her talents. She found it intolerable to bear a moral responsibility for acts that endangered her comrades. She could not encourage others to commit acts she would not herself commit; anything less than full acceptance of the consequences of her decisions would be cowardice.[32]

It is possible that the willingness to face risk is related to what Robert J. Lifton has termed "survivor-guilt" as well as to feelings of group solidarity or of guilt at harming victims.[33] Sometimes individuals who survive disaster or escape punishment when others have suffered feel guilty and may seek relief by courting a similar fate. This guilt may also explain why terrorists often take enormous risks to rescue imprisoned comrades, as well as why they accept danger or arrest with equanimity or even satisfaction.

It is clear that once a terrorist group embarks on a strategy of terrorism, whatever its purpose and whatever its successes or failures, psychological factors make it very difficult to halt. Terrorism as a process gathers its own momentum, independent of external events.

Conclusions

Terrorism per se is not usually a reflection of mass discontent or deep cleavages in society. More often it represents the disaffection of a fragment of the elite, who may take it upon themselves to act on the behalf of a majority unaware of its plight, unwilling to take action to remedy grievances, or unable to express dissent. This discontent, however subjective in origin or minor in scope, is blamed on the government and its supporters. Since the sources of terrorism are manifold, any society or polity that permits opportunities for terrorism is vulnerable. Government reactions that are inconsistent, wavering between tolerance and repression, seem most likely to encourage terrorism.

Given some source of disaffection – and in the centralized modern state with its faceless bureaucracies, lack of responsiveness to demands is ubiquitous – terrorism is an attractive strategy for small organizations of diverse ideological persuasions who want to attract attention for their cause, provoke the government, intimidate opponents, appeal for sympathy, impress an audience, or promote the adherence of the faithful.

Terrorists perceive an absence of choice. Whether unable or unwilling to perceive a choice between terrorist and nonterrorist action, whether unpopular or prohibited by the government, the terrorist group reasons that there is no alternative. The ease, simplicity, and rapidity with which terrorism can be implemented and the prominence of models of terrorism strengthen its appeal, especially since terrorist groups are impatient to act. Long-standing social traditions that sanction terrorism against the state, as in Ireland, further enhance its attractiveness.

There are two fundamental questions about the psychological basis of terrorism. The first is why the individual takes the first step and chooses to engage in terrorism: why join? Does the terrorist possess specific psychological predispositions, identifiable in advance, that suit him or her for terrorism? That terrorists are people capable of intense commitment tells us little, and the motivations for terrorism vary immensely. Many individuals are potential terrorists, but few actually make that commitment. To explain why terrorism happens, another question is more appropriate: Why does involvement continue? What are the psychological mechanisms of group interaction? We are not dealing with a situation in which certain types of personalities suddenly turn to terrorism in answer to some inner call. Terrorism is the result of a gradual growth of commitment and opposition, a group development that furthermore depends on government action. The psychological relationships within the terrorist group – the interplay of commitment, risk, solidarity, loyalty, guilt, revenge, and isolation – discourage terrorists from changing the direction they have taken. This may explain why – even if objective circumstances change when, for example, grievances are satisfied, or if the logic of the situation changes when, for example, the terrorists are offered other alternatives for the expression of opposition – terrorism may endure until the terrorist group is physically destroyed.

Notes

1. For discussions of the meaning of the concept of terrorism, see Thomas P. Thornton,"Terror as a Weapon of Political Agitation," in Harry Eckstein, ed. *Internal War* (New York, 1964), pp. 71–99; Martha Crenshaw Hutchinson, "The Concept of Revolutionary Terrorism," *Revolutionary Terrorism: The FLN in Algeria, 1954–1962* (Stanford: The Hoover Institution Press, 1978) chap. 2; and E. Victor Walter, *Terror and Resistance* (New York, 1969).

2. Walter Laqueur, "Interpretations of Terrorism – Fact, Fiction and Political Science," *Journal of Contemporary History*, 12 (January 1977), 1–42. See also his major work *Terrorism* (London: Weidenfeld and Nicolson, 1977).

3. See, for example, Paul Wilkinson, *Terrorism and the Liberal State* (London: Macmillan, now Palgrave, 1977), or J. Bowyer Bell, *A Time of Terror: How Democratic Societies Respond to Revolutionary Violence* (New York, 1978).
4. This is not to deny that some modern terrorist groups, such as those in West Germany, resemble premodern millenarian movements. See specifically Conor Cruise O'Brien, "Liberty and Terrorism," *International Security*, 2 (1977), 56–67. In general, see Norman Cohn, *The Pursuit of the Millennium* (London: Secker and Warburg, 1957), and E. J. Hobsbawm, *Primitive Rebels: Studies in Archaic Forms of Social Movement in the 19th and 20th Centuries* (Manchester: Manchester University Press, 1971).
5. A sampling would include Douglas Hibbs, Jr., *Mass Political Violence: A Cross-National Causal Analysis* (New York, 1973); William J. Crotty, ed. *Assassinations and the Political Order* (New York, 1971); Ted Robert Gurr, *Why Men Rebel* (Princeton, 1971), and Gurr, Peter N. Grabosky, and Richard C. Hula, *The Politics of Crime and Conflict* (Beverly Hills, 1977).
6. For a summary of these findings, see Gurr, "The Calculus of Civil Conflict," *Journal of Social Issues*, 28 (1972), 27–47.
7. Gurr, "Some Characteristics of Political Terrorism in the 1960s," in Michael Stohl, ed. *The Politics of Terrorism* (New York, 1979), pp. 23–50 and 46–7.
8. A distinction between preconditions and precipitants is found in Eckstein, "On the Etiology of Internal Wars," *History and Theory*, 4 (1965), 133–62. Kenneth Waltz also differentiates between the framework for action as a permissive or underlying cause and special reasons as immediate or efficient causes. In some cases we can say of terrorism, as he says of war, that it occurs because there is nothing to prevent it. See *Man, the State and War* (New York, 1959), p. 232.
9. Boris Savinkov, *Memoirs of a Terrorist*, trans. Joseph Shaplen (New York: A. & C. Boni, 1931), pp. 286–7.
10. The major theoreticians of the transition from the rural to the urban guerrilla are Carlos Marighela, *For the Liberation of Brazil* (Harmondsworth: Penguin Books, 1971), and Abraham Guillen, *Philosophy of the Urban Guerrilla: The Revolutionary Writings of Abraham Guillen,* trans. and edited by Donald C. Hodges (New York, 1973).
11. Hobsbawm, *Revolutionaries: Contemporary Essays* (New York, 1973), pp. 226–7.
12. Grabosky, "The Urban Context of Political Terrorism," in Michael Stohl, ed., pp. 51–76.
13. See Amy Sands Redlick, "The Transnational Flow of Information as a Cause of Terrorism," in Yonah Alexander, David Carlton, and Wilkinson, eds. *Terrorism: Theory and Practice* (Boulder, 1979), pp. 73–95. See also Manus I. Midlarsky, Martha Crenshaw, and Fumihiko Yoshida, "Why Violence Spreads: The Contagion of International Terrorism," *International Studies Quarterly*, 24 (June 1980), 262–98.
14. Monica D. Blumenthal, et al., *More About Justifying Violence: Methodological Studies of Attitudes and Behavior* (Ann Arbor: Survey Research Center, Institute for Social Research, University of Michigan, 1975), p. 108. Similarly, Peter Lupsha, "Explanation of Political Violence: Some Psychological Theories Versus Indignation," *Politics and Society*, 2 (1971), 89–104, contrasts the concept of "indignation" with Gurr's theory of relative deprivation, which holds that expectations exceed rewards (see *Why Men Rebel*, esp. pp. 24–30).

15. Hobsbawm, *Revolutionaries*, p. 143.

16. Luigi Bonanate, "Some Unanticipated Consequences of Terrorism," *Journal of Peace Research*, 16 (1979), 197–261. If this theory is valid, we then need to identify such blocked societies.

17. See Barbara Salert's critique of the rational choice model of revolutionary participation in *Revolutions and Revolutionaries* (New York, 1976). In addition, Abraham Kaplan discusses the distinction between reasons and causes in "The Psychodynamics of Terrorism," *Terrorism – An International Journal*, 1, 3 and 4 (1978), 237–54.

18. For a typology of terrorist organizations, see Wilkinson, *Political Terrorism* (New York, 1975). These classes are not mutually exclusive, and they depend on an outside assessment of goals. For example, the Basque ETA would consider itself revolutionary as well as separatist. The RAF considered itself a classic national liberation movement, and the Provisional IRA insists that it is combatting a foreign oppressor, not an indigenous regime.

19. Bell presents a succinct analysis of Irgun strategy in "The Palestinian Archetype: Irgun and the Strategy of Leverage," in *On Revolt: Strategies of National Liberation* (Cambridge [Ma.], 1976), chap. 3.

20. See Thornton's analysis of proximate goals in "Terror as a Weapon of Political Agitation," in Eckstein, ed., pp. 82–8.

21. Walter's discussion of the concept of "forced choice" explains how direct audiences, from whom the victims are drawn, may accept terrorism as legitimate: see *Terror and Resistance*, pp. 285–9.

22. See Marighela, *For the Liberation of Brazil*, pp. 94–5. The West German RAF apparently adopted the idea of provocation as part of a general national liberation strategy borrowed from the Third World.

23. See Hutchinson, *Revolutionary Terrorism*, chap. 3 pp. 40–60.

24. See Michael Walzer's analysis of the morality of terrorism in *Just and Unjust Wars* (New York, 1977), pp. 197–206. See also Bernard Avishai, "In Cold Blood," *The New York Review of Books*, March 8, 1979, pp. 41–4, for a critical appraisal of the failure of recent works on terrorism to discuss moral issues. The question of the availability of alternatives to terrorism is related to the problem of discrimination in the selection of victims. Where victims are clearly responsible for a regime's denial of opportunity, terrorism is more justifiable than where they are not.

25. Michael Barkun, *Disaster and the Millennium* (New Haven, 1974), pp. 14–16. See also Leon Festinger, et al., *When Prophecy Fails* (New York, 1964).

26. Bell, *The Secret Army* (London: Anthony Blond, 1970), p. 379.

27. Jean Maitron, *Histoire du mouvement anarchiste en France (1880–1914)* (Paris: Société universitaire d'éditions et de librairie, 1955), pp. 242–3.

28. S. Stepniak (pseudonym for Kravchinski), *Underground Russia: Revolutionary Profiles and Sketches from Life* (London: Smith, Elder, and Co., 1882), pp. 36–7; see also Venturi, pp. 639 and 707–8.

29. See "Les meurtriers delicats" in *L'Homme Révolté* (Paris: Gallimard, 1965), pp. 571–9.

30. Ya'acov Meridor, *Long is the Road to Freedom* (Tujunga [Ca.]: Barak Publications, 1961), pp. 6 and 9.

31. Begin, p. 111.

32. Vera Figner, *Memoires d'une revolutionnaire*, trans. Victor Serge (Paris: Gallimard, 1930), pp. 131 and 257–62.
33. Such an argument is applied to Japanese Red Army terrorist Kozo Okamoto by Patricia Steinhof in "Portrait of a Terrorist," *Asian Survey*, 16 (1976), 830–45.

8
Playing the Game of Love: Passion and Martyrdom among Khalistani Sikhs

Cynthia Keppley-Mahmood

> Let me say, with the risk of appearing ridiculous, that the true
> revolutionary is guided by strong feelings of love. It is impossible
> to think of an authentic revolutionary without this quality.
>
> Che Guevara (1969:389)

In an essay on the break-up of the Soviet Union called "Why Were We Surprised?" W. R. Connor proposes that the "realist" model of politics long dominant in the West was, in fact, highly unreal in that it neglected what he calls "the passions" of ethnic and religious loyalties, affirmations of cultural identities, and yearnings for a moral state (Connor 1991:175–85). This was not the first time Western social science had failed to predict a major socio-political upheaval (the over-throw of the Shah of Iran comes to mind, for example), and only now is it dawning on theorists across the disciplines that something must be wrong with the way we have traditionally done business. Martyrdom, as often a matter of "passion" as of rational calculation, is part of this radical re-evaluation of what matters in the realm of polit-ics. Always enigmatic, usually frightening, martyrs intrigue and repel us in their refusal to play by the rules that most of us live by. Young men who crash trucks through the gates of Marine Corps barracks are part of the picture of unpredictability, of incommensurability, that haunts us when we try to analyze political conflicts that don't progress according to mainline Clausewitzian strategy.

The government of India currently claims to have contained the Sikh militant movement aimed at the creation of a sovereign state of Khalistan in Punjab. Though the abuses that occurred during this containment were widely condemned by human rights groups (Asia Watch 1991, Amnesty International 1992, Human Rights

Watch/Physicians for Human Rights 1994), it is clear that a situation of quiet now obtains in Punjab, where farmers are back in their fields, shopkeepers in their shops, children at schools, and so on. The militants, imagined as criminals, extremists, and terrorists, are marginalized in current Indian portrayals of Punjab; indeed, the way things now look it seems difficult to remember that just a few years ago they were virtually in control of the state, their separatist aspirations a serious threat to the integrity of India. However, this picture, as Joyce Pettigrew notes (1995), is a highly superficial one. It fails to take into account the issues that prompted the militant uprising in the first place, and fails to consider the passions that continue to animate the militants, now in exile, in hiding, or beneath the mask of that farmer in his field who smiles on the nightly news.

I propose here to talk about matters of passion, always a problem for academics who easily turn questions of faith into questions of psychology, philosophical stances into cultural traditions, and assertions of dignity into political movements. These frames of discourse are more graspable in terms of the rationality we continue to hope runs the world and, in being graspable, appear controllable also. Hannah Arendt (1965), in her calculated use of the concept of evil in exploring the dynamics of genocide, was trying to push the terms of analysis to this other insistent level, and this is why her work continues to intrigue despite myriad empirical and political criticisms of it. We sense that there is something more going on when humans put other humans into gas ovens or light themselves on fire. The Enlightenment dream behind both academia and politics stumbles against it, flails out in frustration, throws up words like "terrorism" that obscure more than they reveal, and eventually resorts to talk of psychopathology. One can't be a *human being* and do things like that.

Agreeing with J. R. Corbin (1977) that human violence is in fact mostly conceptual, not meaningless, customary or blind, I spent the past three years researching the conceptual order of expatriate Khalistani Sikhs, conducting about thirty extensive interviews with militants in eight cities across the U.S. and Canada. Some of the people with whom I talked reside in those cities, while others travelled there for the purpose of the interview. I stayed in Sikh homes, spoke in gurudwaras, and attended meetings of various kinds of Sikh organizations. My interlocutors in this project have been on both the receiving and the initiating ends of acts of violence in Punjab, and I hoped to learn from them what makes the courage of Sikh soldiers the envy of the military world and the determination of Sikh "terrorists" the night-mare of the modern state of India.

The potency of massacres

During the first week of June 1984, the Indian armed forces launched a massive assault on the "Golden Temple" complex in Amritsar, the sacred heart of the Sikh religion and the temporal centre of the Sikh people. Indicative of Sikhism's welding together of spiritual and political matters, the Golden Temple complex contains both the Harimandir Sahib, the holiest shrine, and the Akal Takht, the "throne" from which worldly decisions are made. The gold leaf of the Harimandir Sahib and the vaulted domes of the Akal Takht mirror and amplify each other, nested amongst a concert of smaller buildings including rest houses for visiting pilgrims, offices of various Sikh organizations, and the Sikh Reference Library.

The reason why the government of India ordered the attack on the Golden Temple complex in June 1984 was to flush out a band of armed militants led by Sant ("Saint") Jarnail Singh Bhindranwale, who as head of a key Sikh seminary gave voice to not only a string of economic and political grievances but also to the sense that Sikhism as a religion was threatened by encroaching Hinduism. A generally over-looked aspect of the assault on the complex is the great discrepancy between government rhetoric about Bhindranwale and his group and the actual seriousness with which the attack was carried out. In the months preceding Operation Blue Star, as the army assault was called, the militants were routinely described as a small band of criminals with no popular support, extremists who were as despised by the mass of Sikhs as they were by the rest of India. They were not portrayed as spearheading any kind of a serious movement or representing any serious political threat.

Thus people were all the more shocked when it became clear, after the media blackout during the military operation against Bhindranwale, that it had taken not only crack ground forces but even tanks to subdue him. What kind of "criminal" was it who could inflict so many casualties on highly trained troops of the Indian army? Even Lt. Gen. K. S. Brar, in command of the assault, remarked that the militants had fought far harder, better, and longer than anybody had expected (Brar 1993).

This making light of militants while at the same time launching large-scale offensives against them is not restricted to Punjab, but is characteristic of government responses to insurgency. For example, Egypt's President Hosni Mubarak recently referred to Islamic militants as "belly dancers [and] drummers from the slums," while keeping some twenty thousand of them in prison (Elon 1995:33). Making light of, criminalizing, psychologizing, and otherwise peripheralizing such movements is obviously part of a strategy of domination. It is wholly logical that a government wishing to retain its power would not want to accord legitimacy to those hoping to overthrow it. But the divergence between public rhetoric and actual operations (the mass jailing of "belly dancers") does more than make a government look duplicitous; it pushes those whose credibility as political actors is being undermined to further demonstrations of strength, to further proofs that one is, in fact, more than "a drummer from the slums." In the space created by insult, the most dramatic actions – violent actions – are experienced by perpetrators as simple reclamations of dignity.

What people heard from government sources after Operation Blue Star was that the band of extremists who had illegitimately taken over the Golden Temple complex had been effectively subdued in a successful military operation that was carried out with full respect for Sikh religious sentiments. But what they saw, in photographs that quickly made the rounds in the Sikh community, passed from hand to hand with shocked horror, was the Akal Takht with a gaping hole in its dome, its walls pock-marked with bullets, the pavement in front soaked with blood and littered with bodies. The Sikh Reference Library, containing irreplaceable manuscripts and copies of the Sikh holy book, had burned to the ground. However, with all of this physical destruction, I suggest that it was the Indian government's continuing denial of substantial harm that was in a way the most psychologically damaging aspect of the entire event. Sikhs felt they were not being taken seriously, and their militancy, then nascent, got an enormous boost. Sikh militants would force the government to take them seriously, to pay attention.

India and the world were brought to rapt attention when two Sikhs assassinated Prime Minister Indira Gandhi five months after Operation Blue Star. The post-assassination backlash against the Sikhs brought shock. Hindu mobs, ignored by and in cases it seems led by police, slaughtered some 3,000 to 6,000 Sikhs in cities across India. People started using the world "holocaust" (*ghallughara*) to describe what was happening, a term that hadn't been applied since Ahmed Shah Abdali's invasion of Punjab centuries before.

And again, ridicule. Sikh bodies, shaking as they burned in the streets of Delhi, were said to be "dancing the *bhangra*" (a Punjabi folk dance). As one woman described it, it was not only the sight of humans on fire that was horrific, but the terrible asynchrony of this vision with ongoing radio commentary that was painting a wildly different picture. Was one going crazy? One doubted one's own perceptions.

Against this kind of ambiguity, the strong assertions of the militants must have come as a kind of relief to the housewife mentioned above. Whatever else they might have done with which one disagreed, in a field of outright lies and propaganda they were telling it as many people in fact witnessed it. The Golden Temple complex was heavily damaged, thousands of people *did* burn in the streets, the police *did* look the other way. Human rights organizations in India, with great courage, investigated all of these things, but their reports were not as accessible to the masses of uneducated Sikhs as the house-to-house, village-to-village campaigns of the militants. People had a sense of homecoming when they embraced the militancy, able then to reject government rhetoric as enemy rhetoric and to cease the constant attempt to reconcile what they heard with what they knew.

In an atmosphere of deceit and denial, the massacres surrounding the assault on the Golden Temple complex and following the assassination of Indira Gandhi seem in themselves to be assertions of truth. Massacre art, in particular showing the torn, broken, and seeping bodies lying before the Akal Takht, was distributed and hung in Sikh homes. In their very gruesomeness these paintings, drawings and photos assert themselves in a room; they are impossible to ignore, and intrude in conversation, meditation, and everyday activities. Their potency derives only in part from their blood; it derives also from their unwillingness to be masked, covered, or distorted. The slaughter is there for all to see, whatever statistics are released or policies promulgated. Hanging such a painting in one's home is therefore a continuing assertion of the unsuppressible quality of truth – a truth which, in the vision of the militants, is worth killing and dying for.

Martyrdom and truth

Bhindranwale, embattled with his core group of dedicated militants in the Akal Takht in June 1984, had the chance to escape, but didn't take it. Though in fact the majority of the militants who were defending the Takht did leave by a back route before the final onslaught, some 35 remained until the bitter end, when they were all killed. Bhindranwale is said to have compared himself to a historical hero of the Sikhs, Baba Deep Singh, who lost his head in battle with the Afghans but who is believed by religious Sikhs to have carried it in his hands to lay it down at the Golden Temple complex. "Baba Deep Singh had to struggle for several miles to lay down his head in this place," Bhindranwale is reported to have said, "while I am privileged to be able to give mine right here."

Bhindranwale was a man who knew the value of history. He carried a silver arrow around with him, symbol of the last Sikh Guru, and talked about the current opposition to the Indian government in the same terms as historical Sikh struggles against Afghans and Mughals. But the comparison with Baba Deep Singh resonated even further, back to the first Guru and founder of Sikhism, Guru Nanak, who had advised his sikhs or disciples that selflessness was a prerequisite to spiritual fulfillment. "If you want to play this game of love," he said, "come to my street with your head in your palms." The story of Baba Deep Singh concretizes this notion admirably, and Bhindranwale, calling upon his historical example, added another layer to the martyrdom-as-selflessness theme when he gave his head in 1984. His portrait now hangs in militant Sikh homes beside photographs of the devastated Akal Takht, inspiring fresh martyrdoms in his wake.

After Guru Nanak, the tradition's founder, there were nine other Gurus who led the Sikh *panth* (community) from the fifteenth through eighteenth centuries. The fifth, Guru Arjun, was the first to be martyred for the Sikh faith, succumbing to torture during the reign of Mughal emperor Jehangir. It was not only the fact of his death, however, but the manner it which he greeted it, which have become critical to Sikh consciousness. Guru Arjun, dying of horrific tortures, was described by his companion Mian Mir as "unruffled," "calm and unperturbed like the sea," and "in absolute bliss." He had, that is, already achieved such a state of spiritual detachment from the world, through attachment to God, that he lived life as a lotus in water, unaffected by its waves, crossing the ocean of the world in safety through meditation on God's name (drawing on a metaphor favored by Guru Nanak). The same elevated state was believed to have characterized Bhai Mani Singh, another famous historical martyr, whose Mughal torturer, ordered to slice him limb from limb, sought to spare his victim by starting at the wrist. "You were ordered to cut me joint by joint," Mani Singh is said to have responded, "so start at the little finger and work your way up." Guru Arjun is believed to have shown the same defiance in voluntarily wading into a river subsequent to his tortures, where he "blended with the Divine Light" (died).

These classic examples illustrate the important but elusive connection between dying and witnessing in Sikhism, only superficially construed as masculine bravado. The tradition of wanggar (inform and challenge) in the early phases of the Khalistani insurgency was an element of this, in which a fighter would call out his identity to his enemies and challenge them to respond, rather than simply eliminating them quietly. As Pettigrew points out, this kind of swagger, resulting as it did in numerous unnecessary casualties, was later discouraged as a routine tactic (1992:396). But she notes appropriately that the point of this behavior was to deny the enemy's claim that one did not exist, that one was a Pakistani agent or a criminal, and to affirm loudly, clearly, and at risk to oneself that one was a Sikh, resisting injustice as *a Sikh*. "The martyr is one whom terror does not silence," she concludes (op. cit.:400).

Sikhs who have been initiated into the siblinghood of the *Khalsa* or "pure," established by Guru Gobind Singh in 1699, use their very bodies to refuse the silence of submission or complicity. Guru Gobind Singh began the tradition of the so-called 'five Ks," the five signs which must be kept by every Khalsa Sikh (the "Ks" describe their names in Punjabi). These external symbols of faith, including most conspicuously unshorn hair bound up into a turban and the carrying of swords, make Sikhs a noticeable presence in any crowd, even an Indian crowd in which a multitude of religious adornments and paraphernalia compete raucously for attention. Khalsa Sikhs take these external symbols quite seriously; people have died for the right to wear them, and today Sikhs are involved in legal battles in several nations surrounding the carrying of swords in schools, the wearing of turbans in military service, and so on. How can we account for this deep attachment to the externalities of faith, in a tradition which began when Guru Nanak questioned similar externalities in Islam and Hinduism?

When Sikhs are initiated into the Khalsa, they sip *amrit* or nectar, and in the imbibing of this *amrit* dedicate themselves to lives of service. Of importance here is the special heritage bequeathed to the Sikhs by Guru Gobind Singh, founder of the Khalsa, who was the last Guru in the spiritual lineage. Rather than passing on the Guruship to some other individual, Gobind Singh vested the religious authority of the Guru in the holy book of the Sikhs, the Adi Granth (henceforth Guru Granth Sahib), and he vested the temporal authority of the Guru in the entire Sikh *panth*. In this dualism of Guru Granth and Guru Panth, Gobind Singh was carrying to fruition the earlier conception of the interrelatedness of *miri* and *piri*, temporal and spiritual authority, represented in the double swords symbolic of Sikhism since the days of Guru Hargobind. But in Gobind Singh's formulation it was divinity itself which was embodied in both the word (Guru Granth) and in the nation (Guru Panth) of the Sikhs. For an *amritdhari* Sikh, one who has undergone the initiation of *amrit*, praising the Word and defending the Nation would be complementary modes of worship. "The way they handle their weapons, it's like they are praying," one women whose household sheltered Sikh militants commented. Frightening as this image may be to the secular West, it is entirely in line with Khalsa Sikh tradition.

The *amritdhari* Sikh, having committed him- or herself to both Granth and Panth, is in a sense already a martyr; he or she has offered his or her head to the service of Guru. It is the moment of initiation, the moment of taking *amrit*, that is actually the key moment in the creation of the Sikh martyr; from that point on he or she lives utterly for the faith, in tune with Guru, and hence fearless of bodily or worldly consequences. The literal moment of death is in a way something of an afterthought, since the *amritdhari* Sikh is to have "died" to his or her personal self already. "He who is fearless is a Sikh and he who is fearful is not a Sikh," said Bhindranwale. This sense of being beyond fear accounts for the classic grace under fire of the Sikhs, noted by virtually every observer, friend or foe, through the tumultuous history of this community. It is expressed in the serenity of historical heroes under torture and in the otherwise insanely bold actions of Khalistani militants in combat.

The *amritdhari* Sikh, in simply being there in an inescapably obvious saffron turban, is using his or her own body as a witness to truth. In this perpetual challenge *amritdhari* Sikhs are particularly unnerving to governments trying to control them, as stated explicitly in the Indian army's newsletter just after the 1984 events in which *amritdhari* Sikhs are declared outright to be "dangerous." The five Ks, as symbols of truth in which people have invested their very lives, become then critical aspects of witness; relinquishing them under any circumstances appears to *amritdhari* Sikhs as unforgivable capitulation. And insults to the five Ks, a common experience of Khalistani Sikhs in custody, are unerasable components of militant consciousness. "Truth is pure steel," the Guru Granth Sahib advises, and *amritdhari* Sikhs remember this through the steel wrist bands they keep on their right arms at all times. They might die, but they will die *as Sikhs*, standing up for truth as they know it, fearless. As Paulo Freire commented about the death of Tiradentes, "[they] could quarter his body, but they could not erase his witness" (1993:158). Khalsa Sikhs would understand this sentiment implicitly. And in a climate in which, as described in the first section of this chapter, the lives and deaths of Sikhs seem not to be taken seriously, the image of the Sikh militant, defiantly and seriously *present*, is an appealing one indeed. It is not surprising that it garnered so much ready, if covert, support. In his or her very undeniability and unignorability, the *amritdhari* Sikh gave expression to a population whose realities had come to be denied and ignored.

Martyrdom and love

There remains, however, the further and more enigmatic component of Sikh martyrological consciousness centered on the notion of love. There is something about the idea of living and dying for a principle that reminds us of puritanism; we can understand it, even admire it, since many of our own cultural heroes lived and died similarly. More problematic is the atmosphere of great joy that permeates the militant Sikh community, now largely in exile, an atmosphere seemingly at odds with the portraits of deceased friends that decorate the walls of many homes. Captured by photographers in poses of militancy, holding AK-47s, bandoliers across the shoulder, the martyred militants are regularly described as "gentle," "quite soft," "full of love," "humble," "quiet and calm," "very spiritual." They died of an excess of love, wrote Yeats about the heroes of the Irish uprising, but again, he could have been talking about Sikhs. Surrounded by death, much of the talk in militant Sikh households is of love.

When Guru Hargobind established the dual swords of *miri* and *piri*, worldly and spiritual power, as emblematic of the Sikhs, he was drawing on the Indian tradition which had long distinguished *shakti* and *bhakti* as two complementary forms of power. Joining them together produces the peculiarly Sikh conception of *chardhi kala*, "rising spirits," as the exercise of temporal power leads to greater spiritual power, and the exercise of greater spiritual power to greater temporal power, and so on in a grandly escalating cycle. The Sikh militant who went on combat missions with hymns on his headset and a gun in his hands was expressive of just this combination, which is more complex than the common gloss which words like "fanaticism" can indicate. The rising spirits of the *amritdhari* Sikh today, in which weapons and prayer are intertwined, are the logical outcome of a tradition which has long celebrated orthopraxy, the way one lives, more than orthodoxy, what one believes (the terms are T. N. Madan's, 1991:594–625). "Truth is the highest good," said Guru Nanak, "but higher still is truthful living."

The steel wrist bands worn by Sikhs carry multiple meanings for individuals involved in militancy. The steel that represents pure truth is part of the symbolism, but the notion that the bracelet "handcuffs" the wearer to the world is another aspect brought out by several of the militants I know. They are unable, that is, to interpret their adherence to truth as renunciation, as they perceive happened in other South Asian religious traditions. "It is a bond of love," one told me, "not only to my brothers and sisters of the *panth* but to all human beings." This person kept on his wall a portrait of Guru Teg Bahadur, the ninth Guru, who is believed to have sacrificed himself for the right of Hindus to worship freely. "He was so full of love [for humanity], he martyred," the militant commented. "Sikhs should be in Bosnia or Somalia or wherever people need help. That's the real role for the Sikhs." At the moment this person is busy fighting for Khalistan, but conceives this to be only a jumping-off point for the more universalist mission of the Sikhs. He has the motto *Deg Teg Fateh*, Kettle Sword Victory, on his wall as well; with the kettle to feed the hungry and the sword to defend the weak, we shall be victorious, he explains.

Within the Khalsa, the bond among initiates is more obvious. When "sisters" are sexually dishonored (a common experience in custody), "brothers" react with anger and shame. In the militant community, sheltering of such fictional brothers and sisters in Punjab and monetary and other support for them outside gives expression to the notion of familiarity among those who have taken *amrit*. Men frequently remember not their own experience of torture in prison but the cries of their comrades; women not their own rapes but the insults to their sisters, mothers, and daughters.

I suggest that the immediacy of the sense of siblinghood with others within and outside of the *panth* influences the behavior of Sikh militants in two ways. The first relates to the torture situation, in which, as Elaine Scarry (1985) points out insightfully, the major effect is the radical narrowing of the world of the victim to the space of the pain inflicted, with a corresponding widening of the world of the torturer, which becomes hegemonic. Resistance to torture, or more accurately, ability to survive torture, depends heavily on the victim's hold on a world wider than his or her pain, and it is in this context that the "handcuffed" quality of a Sikh to the world becomes critically important. One may, out of adherence to principle and individual courage, "refuse to talk" under torture. But surviving it with spirit intact depends on the ability to mentally and physically reject the narrowing of one's world that is the ultimate aim of the torture enterprise, and the elevated attention to the cries of a cellmate or the shame of a sister one hears in narratives of Sikh militants are best understood as part of this attempt to retain a shred of a space, a world, beyond and outside of one's own searing, demanding pain. A tradition which celebrates community bonds is one, in fact, with the latent capacity to mobilize these bonds as a form of resistance, and in the Khalistani insurgency we see this mobilization at the deepest and most personal levels.

When we come to the ultimate physical affront, death, the capacity of bonds of love to mold individual experience are at their strongest. A death conceived as martyrdom turns what looks like defeat into victory; the individual died, but in his or her bloody witness the truth lives on; the individual died, but the community to which he or she was linked continues. The embracing of death by Khalistani guerrillas is itself often conceptualized as an expression both of witness and of love. Sukha and Jinda, who were hanged for the murder of General Vaidya, said in their farewell address that they imagined the hangman's rope as the embrace of a lover, longing for death as for the marital bed, and hoping that their dripping blood, the outcome of this union, would fertilize the fields of Khalistan. Others compared the martyr's death to a shower of fireworks, which illuminates and guides the entire community; to provide light, the martyr selflessly grasped death. Death in struggle is defined here not only as a feature of courage, but as a feature above all of generosity, of selflessness, of love. Hence descriptions of martyred young men and women as kind, soft, and gentle, and immediate repudiation of leaders who, however bold, acquire the reputation of being greedy, inflated, or selfish. The Sikh who plays Nanak's game with head in hands is, I suspect, the "true revolutionary" of Che Guevara, who as quoted above feared being thought ridiculous as he commented about the spirit of love that infused the insurgents he knew.

Unlike Islam, a religious tradition with an equally prominent tradition of martyrdom, Sikhs who die in battle do not look forward to an eternal life in paradise. Though some elements of reincarnation have crept into Sikh popular religion, on the whole this is a tradition nearly wholly concerned with this life as the only life there is. Resistance to injustice is an existential stance, as something one does as a mode of worship with no other necessary aim than the fact of resistance itself. "I resist, therefore I am," wrote Camus (1961). One doesn't expect to get something out of it, either for oneself or even for one's movement. One engineering student who was part of the Bidar massacre in the late 1980s explained that he had been far removed from his Sikh origins until, as a Hindu mob bore down on the temple in which the students had taken refuge, someone handed him a *kirpan* (the sword or dagger carried by *amritdhari* Sikhs). "What was I supposed to do with a *kirpan?*" he recounted. "But I kind of held it out in front of me and you know, somehow I suddenly felt like a real Sikh. In that gesture I knew what being a Sikh meant. I didn't know if we would get out of there or if I would actually kill anybody, but just the feel of that dagger made me realize my faith." Although Sikh history contains ample elements of both resistance to power and complicity with power (Pettigrew 1991), it is in postures of resistance that *amritdhari* Sikhs today feel most fully at home, most fully Sikh. The essentially non-instrumental quality of Sikh resistance, its basic independence from rationally strategic political or military goals, is what enables the continuing florescence of militancy despite the low probability of its immediate success. Leaders who accept the rationalistic criticism that this strain in Sikhism may attract recruits and may foster extraordinary bravery, but is in the end non-productive in that it produces more martyrs than survivors, face an uphill battle in convincing the many enthusiastic fighters they "command" that the effects, not just the process, of militant actions are critical to the eventual success of the campaign.

In the Buddhist tradition, a distinction was traditionally made between *nibbana* (enlightenment) as a state of mind and the *nibutta*-person (adjectival form of *nibbana*), the person who is "cooled" of desires and attachments. Applying this analytical framework to Sikhism, it is clear that it is the active mode, the adjectival understanding of enlightenment, that would resonant with Sikh experience. The central concept here is the *gurumukh*, the Guru-oriented person, one liberated from all selfish attachments and entirely in tune with a larger reality. The fact that the *nibutta*-person in Buddhism was also classically tied to the ideal of loving compassion for all beings also compares usefully to the *gurumukh*, who in his very unselfishness is filled with love for all. Ready to face his own mortality without equivocation, because he is already unattached to the narrow self that fears it, his courage in the military sense is of one piece with his love for the world.

Despite the many occasions in which Sikh militants saved one another's lives, they typically talk about these episodes without the heightened sense of drama such stories would usually provoke in the Western military tradition. Rather, they are narrated in quite matter-of-fact tones: "X stayed behind, so that Y and I could go on with the second part of our mission." Since X, Y and Z were already walking around in a state of total dedication, of already-presumed martyrdom, the actual embrace of death by X is a matter of personal sorrow, of course, but not of radical heroism. All are perceived as heroic. What seems a cold-blooded recollection of the demise of a friend – the kind of hyper-rationality that many fear characterizes "terrorists" – is in fact a phenomenon of an entirely different order. We need to understand the philosophy behind it to comprehend in human terms what Sikh militancy is all about. The friends "were in love with" each other (a commonly used phrase to describe comradely bonds), but felt more strongly their common commitment to the cause than their selfish attachments to each other as individuals. Their efforts on behalf of their broader love (for Guru, for Sikhi) were what was being narrated above, not their narrower and more selfish love for each other as friends. Life as a game of love means life unafraid of death, for oneself or for others.

Militancy and martyrdom: Does the paradigm have a future?

One of the key features of the guerrilla insurgency in Punjab, in structural terms, was its diffuse and decentralized quality. Although there was an early attempt to organize the entire community under the leadership of a council of five (Panthic Committee), factionalization was rife from the beginning and several different Panthic Committees at various times have claimed to speak for the Khalistani Sikh *panth*. There have been at least five major guerrilla forces, which split up, joined back together, and split up again regularly. Even at snapshot moments in time when a logical command structure could be pointed out, small groups of individuals had considerable autonomy in deciding on and carrying out missions. This lack of disciplined organization is alternately praised as indicative of the essentially democratic nature of the *panth*, or condemned as militarily inefficient. What is clear is that the "passionate" quality of Sikh martyrdom, as described above, is often at odds with military strategy in the strict sense of the word. The incongruity between effective militancy and the philosophy and rhetoric of martyrdom is increasingly brought to the fore in Khalistani Sikh discussions, which at the moment, facing the undeniability of the ebbing of insurgent power in Punjab, are taking a particularly urgent tone.

The atomistic quality of Sikh militancy over the past ten to fifteen years was probably responsible for the attraction it provided to young men in particular, for whom the heady experience of holding a gun was coupled with almost unbounded freedom to decide what to do with it. It is also clear that, religious ideals aside, substantial atrocities were committed by these undisciplined groups of youths, some of whom took advantage of the militancy to carry out personal vendettas or to commit crimes, and others who probably simply didn't understand what the insurgency was actually all about. There were, for example, many "communal" killings, directed against the Hindu population of Punjab, although Khalistani leaders have always been firm on the point that they are not against Hindus per se but against the government of India and its representatives. Bombs went off in crowded Hindu neighborhoods; women and children were massacred on buses. The predominantly young men involved in these actions were rarely disciplined by higher-ups in the militant organizations, and if reprimanded, they could always turn to one of the other guerrilla units. The major human rights organizations have all criticized the abuses carried out by militant groups, at the same time as they criticised the violations carried out by the state. Though the Khalistani militancy never lacked for recruits, it did admit practically anyone who wanted to fight. In this lack of discrimination it risked what in fact happened: the crumbling of the movement from within as well as its repression from without. Many villagers eventually became disillusioned with the militants as well as tired of suffering at the hands of police.

Where do the heroic aspects of martyrdom, as described above, fit into this less-than-romantic picture of the Khalistani insurgency? It would be a mistake, I believe, to discount the former because of the depradations of the latter, as tends to happen in most accounts of Sikh militancy. The tendency to view the philosophy of martyrdom as a sort of secondary or after-the-fact justification for violence is particularly unhelpful, its skeptical attitude towards Sikh religious commitment being more a function of secular Western ethnocentrism than a facet of Khalistani reality. Though the infiltration of the Khalistani guerrilla forces by people totally uninterested in faith is undoubted, the backbone of the movement remained, and remains today, a core of spiritually dedicated individuals. Rather than using the gap between the ideal of martyrdom and the reality of less-than-perfect guerrilla fighters to point to the lack of applicability of ideals, I see the Sikh conceptualization of martyrdom as itself leaving the door open to the kind of military free-for-all that has characterized phases of the Khalistan movement. People who see themselves as primarily attuned to Guru, as described above, clearly do best in situations in which individual motivation is called for, and less well in situations in which that primary connection has to be constrained by organizational priorities. This gives the movement a certain resiliency, but also leaves it open to abuses. Furthermore, the passionate commitment of individual fighters to Khalistan, to Sikhism, and to each other is the foundation of, but can also seriously hamper, strategic military and political efforts.

The lack of centralization in the Khalistan movement has a strong historical foundation, however, and leaders are hesitant to tamper with it. When Guru Gobind Singh, the tenth and last Guru, asked for volunteers who would be willing to give their heads for the faith, five men stood up, forming the basis for the initial Khalsa siblinghood. After their initiation by *amrit*, Gobind Singh asked the five, henceforward called "Five Beloved Ones", to in turn initiate *him* into the Khalsa order. This gesture radically decentered the Sikh community, vesting the power even to initiate a Guru with five ordinary people. Any five Sikhs who come together can in fact still be called "Five Beloved Ones" and can make decisions as representatives of the *panth*. The spirit of the entire community is thus condensed primarily in face-to-face groups, which both encourages personal involvement and disperses authority dramatically.

When this localization of decision-making is combined with a martyrological tradition emphasizing dying for truth and love – concepts which are open to a fair amount of individual interpretation – the result can be chaotic. Who is or is not a "true Sikh" is in fact highly contested in the militant milieu. It is the tenor of these arguments, sometimes quite shrill, that leads to the accusation of "fundamentalism" from those excluded from the "true Sikh" category and from Western scholars who see resonances of Khomeini and Falwell in the narrowness of the debates. The linkage of the political movement for a sovereign Khalistan with the broader notion of serving and protecting "the faith" clearly leads to a certain volatility in the guerrilla movement. The owner of a chain of newspapers which published "anti-Sikh" tracts was assassinated; did this action effectively serve the cause, or was it simply an emotional response by an individual offended by perceived blasphemy? The same ambiguity surrounds many other acts of violence committed by militants over the past ten to fifteen years of insurgency. The sincerity of the responses and the courage exhibited in carrying them out were applauded, but it was often less clear what the practical results were.

While most militant Sikhs defend the varied actions of Khalistani militants as all part and parcel of the general struggle, as indicative of the flexibility and breadth of the movement, there is an increasingly vocal group calling for a more tightly disciplined approach. Particularly in the current climate in which at least surface quiet in Punjab makes talk of mass uprisings seem rhetorical at best, a strategy of investing a smaller group of militants with the symbolic power of a whole population seems a likely response and one which is shared with similar movements in other parts of the world. The smaller spearhead group would then focus on international pressure and on key persuasive events rather than encouraging the kind of deeply personal responses and encounters that have thus far flourished. If events do develop in this direction, it will be interesting to see how the traditional conception of the saint-soldier, always at the ready to fight and die for his faith, evolves. One Sikh leader, after a particularly motivational speech, had several young people rush up afterwards saying they "wanted to die." He had to use all his powers of persuasion to convince them that they could best be of service in some other capacity than as martyrs. In this context, the classic paradigm of an organized, strategic group affecting events through carefully planned actions (what could be called the professional model) is at odds with the Sikh tradition of militancy, a populist one based on the idea of the citizen-as-saint, citizen-as-soldier. When you celebrate a tradition in which the "true Sikh" is the Sikh who fights, how do you justify restricting fighting to a narrower group than the entire population?

Given the continuing unwillingness of the Indian government to "come clean" on what actually happened during Operation Blue Star, on its complicity in the anti-Sikh pogroms following the Gandhi assassination, and on the human rights abuses going on in Punjab still, the gold figure of the *amritdhari* Sikh who will go to his death but will not be silenced remains an important symbol for people whose concerns and humanity seem to have been dismissed by the state of which they form a part. That these militants have also committed acts of terror and violence seems to their supporters less atrocious, not only because of the cause on whose behalf the acts were carried out but also because of the forthrightness with which the militants accept the necessity for such violence as part of the "war" they are fighting. What for one side is "war" for the other side is "crime," and it is this discrepancy that provokes amplifying messages of revolutionary violence on one side, and draconian punishment on the other. Whatever concessions are made to professional strategy on the part of Khalistani militants, the figure of the passionate martyr as the ultimate symbol of legitimate Sikh struggle is sure to persist. It is, I suggest, enhanced by each government attempt to minimize Sikh suffering, to criminalize Sikh heroes, and to sweep the last decade or two under the rug as if nothing had happened.

Scholars in arenas of violent conflict obviously face many methodological and ethical challenges (Sluka 1990). The philosophical challenge of coming to grips with an existential stance radically different from one's own is less easily talked about. Anthropologists, I suggest, with their orientation to cultural difference and to suspending judgment while investigating other realities, are in a particularly good position to try to understand what motivates individuals to put their lives on the line for a cause, whatever that cause may be. Refraining from false exoticization of such people while recognizing the very different perspectives on life and death they hold is the task facing us as we attempt to build a bridge between the Other – the martyr – and ourselves. And crossing back and forth on that bridge as we engage in our job of translating across cultural divides without abandoning our own values, without condoning assassins and bombers, is a hefty challenge indeed.

Martyrdom is often a tactic of the weak, who have to expect many deaths in confrontation with the powerful and therefore find a way to make these meaningful. That Sikhs, as a small minority in a small corner of a large and overpopulated subcontinent, have developed a philosophically sophisticated tradition of martyrdom, is therefore not surprising. The celebration of martyrdom on the part of the weak is also, of course, greatly feared by the strong, who have always to worry that by winning battles they are creating more martyrs and hence feeding the flames they seek to extinguish. Certainly the ethnographic study of the Sikh militant community, with full attention to the central role played by martyrdom in Sikh theology, makes clear that the way that the government of India has handled "the Punjab crisis" was a Pyrrhic victory in this sense. It has crushed the Sikh militant movement by force, but there is little doubt that the seeds sown in this effort will sooner or later bear fruit, in one form or another. To expect otherwise is, I believe, to fail to learn from history, and to fail to take seriously the passions that animate Sikhs.

Bibliography

Amnesty International 1991 *Proposed Amendments to the Constitution Affecting Fundamental Rights*. London: Amnesty International.

— 1992 *Disappearances and Impunity in Punjab and Kashmir.* London: Amnesty International.

Arendt, H. 1965 *Eichmann in Jerusalem: A Report on the Banality of Evil.* New York: Viking.

Asia Watch 1991 *Punjab in Crisis: Human Rights in India.* New York: Human Rights Watch.

Brar, K. S. 1993 *Operation Blue Star: The True Story.* Delhi: UBS Publishers.

Camus, A. 1961 *Resistance, Rebellion and Death.* Trans. Justin O'Brien. New York: Alfred A. Knopf.

Connor, W. R. 1991 "Why Were We Surprised?" *American Scholar* (Spring).

Corbin, J. R. 1977 "The Anthropology of Violence." *International Journal of Environmental Studies* 10:107–11.

Elon, A. 1995 "One Foot on the Moon." *New York Review of Books,* April 6.

Freire, P. 1933 *Pedagogy of the Oppressed.* Trans. Myra Bergman Ramos. New York: Continuum.

Guevara, E. C. 1968 *Venceremos: The Speeches and Writings of Che Guevara.* John Gerassi, ed. London: Weidenfeld and Nicholson.

Human Rights Watch/Physicians for Human Rights 1994 *Dead Silence: The Legacy of Abuses in Punjab.* New York: Human Rights Watch.

Madan, T. N. 1991 "The Double-Edged Sword: Fundamentalism and the Sikh Religious Tradition." *In Fundamentalisms Observed* (M. E. Marty and R. Scott Appleby, eds.). Scott. Chicago: University of Chicago Press.

Pettigrew, J. 1991 "Betrayal and Nation-Building Among the Sikhs." *Journal of Comparative and Commonwealth Politics* 29(1):25–43.

— 1992 "Martyrdom and Guerilla Organization in Punjab." *Journal of Comparative and Commonwealth Politics* 30(3):387–406.

— 1995 *The Sikhs of the Punjab: Unheard Voices of State and Guerrila Violence.* London: Zed Books.

Scarry, E. 1985 *The Body in Pain: The Making and Unmaking of the World.* New York: Oxford University Press.

Sluka, J. A. 1990 "Participant Observation in Violent Social Contexts." *Human Organization* 49(2):114–205.

9

A Head for an Eye: Revenge in the Cambodian Genocide

Alexander Laban Hinton

In April 1975 the Khmer Rouge overthrew the U.S.-backed Lon Nol regime, thus ending a bloody civil war in which perhaps six hundred thousand Cambodians had died.[1] The Khmer Rouge quickly reorganized Democratic Kampuchea (DK) along strict communist lines that glorified peasant life. The cities were emptied and their inhabitants sent to live and work in the countryside as "new" people (*brâcheachon tmey*) who constituted the bottom social stratum below cadre, soldiers, and "old" people (*brâcheachon chas*) who had lived under Khmer Rouge rule during the war. Economic production and consumption were collectivized, Buddhism banned, and the family subordinated to the Party Organization, Ângkar. As a result of starvation, overwork, disease, and outright execution, over one and half million of Cambodia's eight million inhabitants – more than 20 percent of the population – perished by the time Vietnam invaded the country in January 1979 (Kiernan 1996).

How do such genocides come to take place?[2] While social scientists in other fields have addressed this question, anthropology has remained largely silent on the origins of large-scale genocide (DeWaal 1994; Kuper 1981; Lewin 1992; Shiloh 1975). Anthropologists have conducted some research on the atrocities committed during the Holocaust (e.g., Connor 1989; Dumont 1986; Gajek 1990; Jell-Bahlsen 1985; Lewin 1993; Stein 1993) and, more recently, in Bosnia (e.g. Bringa 1993, 1995; Denich 1994; Hayden 1996). Even less material has been written on the genocides that have occurred in non-European countries like Cambodia and Rwanda (but see Ebihara 1990, 1993; Hinton 1996, 1997; Malkki 1995, 1996; Marston 1985, 1994).

American Ethnologist 25(3):352–77. Copyright © 1998, American Anthropological Association.

Nevertheless, there are encouraging signs that anthropology stands poised to begin making a significant contribution to the comparative study of genocide. In recent years, the number of anthropological analyses of political violence has greatly proliferated as anthropologists have attempted to explain the origins of conflicts in Sri Lanka (e.g. Daniel 1996; Kapferer 1988; Tambiah 1986, 1992), Ireland (e.g., Aretxaga 1995, 1997; Feldman 1991; Sluka 1989), Argentina (e.g., Robben 1996; Suárez-Orozco 1990), and other locales (Besteman 1996; Coronil and Skurski 1991; Das 1990; Desjarlais and Kleinman 1994; Lan 1985; Nordstrom 1997; Nordstrom and Martin 1992; Nordstrom and Robben 1995; Riches 1986; Tambiah 1989, 1996; Taussig 1987; Warren 1993; see also Nagengast 1994). These scholars have demonstrated the crucial ways in which violence is linked to social and cultural factors.

In this chapter, which is based on fifteen months of fieldwork in Cambodia, I provide an example of how such anthropological insights can be applied to large-scale genocide. In particular, I will show how the Cambodian cultural model of disproportionate revenge (*karsâng-soek*) contributed to the genocidal violence that occurred during DK. In contrast to a biblical conception of revenge that is premised on the talion principle of "an eye for an eye," the Cambodian model of disproportionate revenge involves disproportionate retaliation against one's enemy, what I call "a head for an eye." In the first section of this article I summarized *Tum Teav,* a violent epic poem that enacts an extreme version of this cultural model; it concludes with King Rama's (*Reamea*) obliteration of Governor Archoun's (*Ârchoun*) family line seven generations removed. I then describe the Cambodian cultural model of disproportionate revenge in greater detail, noting that it may vary in severity and scale. In the third section I demonstrate how the most lethal forms of this model were directly manipulated in Khmer Rouge ideological discourse about a "class grudge," thus providing a template for much of the group vengeance that took place in DK.

I should note, however, that the cultural model of disproportionate revenge does not guide Cambodian behavior in a deterministic manner. Cultural models may be differentially internalized, vary in their distribution and saliency across contexts, and have disparate degrees of motivational force for people (D'Andrade and Strauss 1992; Shore 1996; Strauss and Quinn 1994).[3] Moreover, when a person acts, he or she often has a variety of available options. Cambodians who are publicly insulted will therefore not automatically seek disproportionate revenge (Hinton 1997). Drawing on an alternative set of Buddhist norms, they may choose "to block/control [their] hearts" (*tuap chett*) or to "disperse [their] anger" (*rumsay komhoeng*). Other Cambodian strategies for controlling anger include internalization, the use of culturally constituted defense mechanisms, and low-level or indirect expression. Even if individuals come to hold a grudge for the insult, they choose when, how, and whether to seek revenge.

Such choices, however, are not made in a vacuum. Human behavior is both enabled and constrained by sociocultural structures – including cultural models that are an important part of what scholars have variously termed "habitus" (Bourdieu 1977, 1990), "practical consciousness" (Giddens 1984), "discourse" (Foucault 1979, 1980), and "hegemony" (Williams 1977). Just as the Kabyle sense of honor consists of internalized generative schemes ("structured structures") that organize ("structuring structures") Kabyle practice (Bourdieu 1977), so too is the cultural model of disproportionate revenge a form of knowledge which most Cambodians have internalized and may be inclined to enact in given circumstances. Such cultural knowledge constitutes a crucial site upon which genocidal regimes can work. Within an appropriate historical and sociocultural context, those who articulate genocidal ideologies often use these highly salient cultural models to motivate individuals to commit violent atrocities (e.g., Goldhagen 1996; Hinton 1997; see also Kapferer 1988). As we shall see, this is exactly what happened during DK, as the exponents of Khmer Rouge ideology invoked the Cambodian cultural model of disproportionate revenge.

The story of *Tum Teav*

The Cambodian cultural model of disproportionate revenge is clearly embodied in *Tum Teav* (Sânthor Mok 1986), the most famous romantic epic in Cambodia. The story of *Tum Teav*, which bears some similarity to *Romeo and Juliet*, was first composed or put into writing by the nineteenth-century poet Sânthor Mok and is thought to have a partial basis in historical fact. (Because Sânthor Mok's manuscript was in poor shape, a poet named Saom reworked *Tum Teav* in 1915.) *Tum Teav* is taught in schools throughout the country, recounted orally by village elders and parents, and sometimes dramatically enacted on special occasions. Almost all Cambodians are thus familiar with this legend, which has never been translated into English.

Set in the sixteenth century, *Tum Teav* begins when Tum, a handsome young monk, sets out with a fellow monk and friend, Bic, to sell bamboo rice containers for their pagoda. When they arrive at a village in Tbaung Khmum province, the inhabitants coax Tum, who has a lovely voice, into singing religious chants. Teav, a beautiful young girl who is just entering womanhood, hears Tum sing, falls in love with him, and sends Tum a message telling him about her feelings. After Tum returns to his pagoda, he cannot eat or sleep because he misses Teav so much. Tum decides to disrobe against the will of the chief monk, who has foreseen that Tum will soon die if he does this. Tum and Bic return to Tbaung Khmum. Meanwhile, the powerful governor of the province, Archoun, has asked Teav's mother for permission to marry Teav to his son. Teav's mother is jubilant about the prospect of her daughter's marriage into a family of great wealth and honor. Teav, however, refuses to consent to the marriage because she longs for Tum. When Tum arrives in Tbaung Khmum, he goes to Teav's house and professes his love for her. She invites him to stay with her and they sleep together. The next day, Teav's mother returns from an overnight trip to find Tum there. Not knowing that Tum and Teav are lovers, she agrees to let Tum stay at the house.

The king of Cambodia, Rama, hears of Tum's wonderful singing and sends for him to come and sing at the palace. King Rama is so impressed by his singing that he asks Tum to remain at the palace as a court singer. Meanwhile, the king has sent emissaries throughout the land to find him a wife. In Tbaung Khmum, the emissaries see Teav and decide she would be a perfect match for the king. Hoping to curry favor with the king, Archoun agrees to break off his son's engagement to Teav. Teav's mother is even more pleased at this marriage prospect. Teav and Tum continue to long to be together. When Teav arrives at the palace, King Rama calls for Tum to come and sing for his prospective bride. Upon seeing that the bride is Teav, Tum decides to risk death by singing about his love affair with Teav. The king becomes extremely angry, but Teav tells the King that Tum has spoken the truth. King Rama's anger diminishes and he arranges for the two of them to be married.

Upon hearing that her daughter has married the impoverished Tum, Teav's mother becomes very upset. She decides to send a message to Teav saying that she is gravely ill and asking Teav to return home to nurse her back to health. Meanwhile, she goes to see the powerful provincial governor, Archoun, and arranges for Teav to be married to Archoun's son. When Teav discovers her mother's real intentions, she is heartbroken and sends Tum a letter explaining what has transpired. Tum becomes furious and immediately returns to Tbaung Khmum.

Tum and Bic arrive in Tbaung Khmum on the day of the wedding. After working his way through the crowd, Tum calls out of Teav who comes and reaffirms her love for him. Upon seeing Tum, Archoun is filled with rage and orders his guards to kill Tum. They capture Tum and beat him until he falls dead under a Bo tree. Teav runs to the spot, takes out a knife, cuts her throat, and then dies on top of Tum's body. After these events, Bic returns to the palace and tells the king what has happened. King Rama becomes irate that Archoun has killed Tum and disregarded his authority, and orders his army to prepare to go to Tbaung Khmum. When they arrive, Archoun, who is extremely frightened, brings gifts and food to the king in order to assuage his anger. King Rama ignores his supplications and commands that Archoun's family and relatives seven generations removed be buried up to their necks in the ground and then have their heads raked off by an iron plow and harrow. In addition, all the members of Archoun's political faction are to be boiled alive and the residents of the district forbidden to leave the area. After King Rama's subordinates carry out his orders to eliminate Archoun's family line and faction in this way, King Rama returns to his palace. In the next section, I will explain how King Rama's actions embody the Cambodian cultural model of disproportionate revenge.

A head for an eye: the Cambodian cultural model of disproportionate revenge

One of the most chronic and volatile sources of violence in Cambodia is a "grudge" (*kum, kumkuon, kumnum, kongkuon*) that leads to the desire for "disporportionate revenge" (*karsângsoek*). One women's rights worker succinctly described the origins of a grudge to me as follows: "A person will hold a grudge when he or she understands that another person has done something very bad to him or her; he or she will have this one thought kept inside his or her heart." While such a grudge most often arises when another person (or group) makes the individual in question (or that person's group) suffer (e.g., by murdering a family member), lose power (e.g., by deposing that person from office), and/or lose face (e.g., by dishonoring that person by a slight), it almost always involves anger, shame, and the desire to "defeat" (*chneah*) a foe.

Vengeance has a distinct moral basis in Cambodian culture. The root of the word *sângsoek, sâng,* refers to the moral obligation "to return (an object), to pay back (debt), to pay for damage" (Headley 1977:1039). One of the greatest virtues in Cambodia is repaying (*sâng*) the "kindness" (*kun*) of others. Thus, Cambodians are morally obliged to "repay the good deeds" (*sângkun*) that their parents, relatives, teachers, and patrons have done for them. An ingrate who ignores this debt *(romilkun)* is widely detested. Whereas in many Judeo-Christian societies such moral debts are often viewed as analogous to a commercial transaction (Johnson 1993), in Cambodia they frequently create a personalized relationship between the two parties involved. In general, those who receive a good deed will acknowledge their debt through greater respect, loyalty, and attachment to the benefactor, although the intensity and structure of the bond will vary according to the situation and the respective status of each person in the dyad. The increased respect given to the person who does the good deed signals the benefactor's elevation in hierarchical standing vis-à-vis the debtor.

By extension, we can see that revenge is the moral inverse of gratitude (see Benedict 1946). Just as people must return a good deed, so too are they morally obliged to repay a bad deed. The word *sângsoek* literally means "to pay back" (*sâng*) "the enemy" (*soek*). Moreover, the injured party's obligation to repay an enemy for whatever the latter has done creates a bond between them. A Cambodian bearing malice is often said to be "tied, linked" (*châng*) to an enemy by anger or a grudge (*châng komhoeng, châng kumnum*). During the post-Khmer Rouge communist period (SOC/PRK), for example, the government sponsored a national holiday on May 20 that was popularly known as the "Day to Remain Tied in Anger" (or, sometimes, the "Day of Hate"). In each district, people would gather at the local DK killing field to listen to government officials and victims speak about the atrocities that had occurred under the Khmer Rouge regime. Villagers often carried knives, axes, clubs, or placards saying things like "Defeat to Pol Pot, Khieu Samphan, Ieng Sary Clique" or "Remember Life under Pol Pot who tried to Destroy the Cambodian Lineage." The holiday no doubt served as an effective device to keep many people "tied in anger" against the Khmer Rouge, who were still engaged in guerrilla warfare against the government.

This type of grudge can result from either a single "happening" (*preuttekar*) or a series of smaller events that gradually add up. On the one hand, a person will often desire revenge when someone else does "something very bad" to that individual. Thus Tum has a grudge against Archoun who is attempting to remarry Teav to his son, and a large porportion of the Cambodian populace continues to bear malice toward the Khmer Rouge who were responsible for their great suffering and the deaths of family members. Similarly, in November of 1994, when the American evangelist Mike Evans arrived in Cambodia promising to cure the blind and heal the crippled, people from all over the country sold their possessions to come to Phnom Penh to attend his healing and proselytizing rallies. While he gave out free Bibles, Evans failed to provide any miracle cures. By the third night, the attendees realized that they had been duped by a foreigner and began to riot. One police officer predicted that if "he stays, he dies" *(Phnom Penh Post* 1994:21). Evans barely escaped Cambodia with his life; he continues to have enemies there who want to pay him back for his bad deed. (After Evans had returned to the United States, he reported to his American congregation that his trip to Cambodia had been a great success.)

Alternatively, a grudge may gradually develop as a person endures a series of small yet memorable "happenings." While usually able to manage their anger so that open disputes do not break out, Cambodians do not always simply forget about a matter. Lim, a research assistant who had formerly been a soldier, once told me, "Cambodians never forget – they remember things forever. After several little anger-provoking happenings, they will begin to hold a grudge." This pattern of silently harboring resentment may be initially modeled for children when they fight. Parents will separate quarreling children and tell them not to argue, but usually do not tell them to apologize to or to make peace with their adversaries. To do so would involve a slight loss of face for both the child and the parents. As one informant explained, "To say 'excuse me' makes them too lowly. It is like saying 'please let me lose.' Sometimes the parents of a kid who loses a fight will become extremely angry." The result is that children often "do not learn how to forget their anger" and will occasionally hold a small grudge and may stop speaking to those with whom they have been fighting for several days, months, or even forever afterward.

Cambodians have a variety of phrases that express the idea of storing away the memory of events that have angered them. They sometimes say that a person takes such anger (or a grudge) and "hides it inside the body" (*leak tuk knong kluen*), "puts (or keeps) it in the head" (*tuk knong khuor kbal*), or "buries (or hides) it in the heart" (*bângkap/leak knong chett*). For example, a young man named Tic, who was from a moderately poor family, was invited to attend a wedding at the home of one of the richest families in Kompong Cham city. When Tic arrived at the receiving line, however, the parents and the bridal couple did not smile or politely greet him. He stated, "I lost face and had a small heart. These rich people were not paying adequate respect to me because I am poor. I got drunk at the wedding and hid my anger so they wouldn't know." While Tic said that he did not have a grudge against the family, he was nevertheless "hiding his anger inside his heart." A series of such minor incidents can make a person resentful and angry, a condition that Cambodians sometimes call being "seized with painful anger" (*chheu chap*). As we shall see, such a build-up of class resentment proved quite lethal during DK when Khmer Rouge ideology encouraged the poor to take revenge upon the rich for past abuses.

What is common to the above examples of malice is a pattern in which an event or a series of smaller incidents causes a person to suffer or be shamed, which, in turn, leads to anger, resentment, and, ultimately, the desire for revenge. A Cambodian who has a big grudge is sometimes said to want to "eat the flesh and sip the blood" (*si sach hot cheam*) of the enemy. Despite this strong desire to take revenge, however, Cambodians recognize that it is often not propitious to repay a bad deed immediately. A grudge thus contains an element of latent potentially and is frequently long-lasting. One religious wise man (*achar*) explained, "A grudge is packaged anger that has not yet come out; it remains inside, always hot, but it doesn't leave. It keeps waiting until 'I' (*ânh*) have the opportunity to strike immediately." To maintain an element of surprise or to prevent a powerful adversary from taking the initiative, Cambodians bearing malice will often try to hide their animosity from their foes. Like anger, a grudge is usually kept hidden. During everyday interactions, Cambodians may therefore smile and act politely toward an enemy; when the appropriate occasion arises, however, they will act.

Those who are unable to seek revenge in person may decide to hire a killer or order a subordinate to perform the deed. Several Cambodian journalists have been murdered by assassins weeks or months after having written insulting articles about government officials and businessmen. Alternatively, people sometimes hire sorcerers to cast black magic upon their adversaries (see also Wikan 1990 on the Balinese). After Mike Evans had fled Cambodia, for example, it was reported that some Cambodians harassed and attacked his Christian followers with black magic (Mang 1995:17). Many Cambodians are extremely frightened of black magic, which, they believe, can make a person terminally ill, and will try to protect themselves by wearing such magical objects as a pig's fang, a fragment of an elephant's tusk, a piece of gold, a magical string, an inscribed cloth, a Buddha amulet, or some combination of these.

Why does a Cambodian grudge frequently lead to revenge that, is "much more damaging than the original injury?" Earlier I pointed out that benefactors gain respect, elevate their status, and create moral debts by performing good deeds. Conversely, the prepetrator of a bad deed shows disrespect toward, lowers the status of, and "defeats" (chneah) the recipient who, in turn, has a moral obligation to repay the bad action. Merely to repay this debt with an equivalent act, however, would leave the parties on an equal footing. Because Cambodians are strongly motivated to want to be "higher than" others, they will strive to defeat – and thus rise above – their adversaries by doing something even worse to them. As Ngor notes, "If I hit you with my fist and you wait five years and then shoot me in the back one dark night, that is *kum*" (1987:9). Such an action can at least partially "purify one's honor" (*star ketteyos*) and destroy the enemy's reputation. Thus, the head of a Buddhist society explained that Cambodians who hold a grudge "desire to take vengeance in a manner that exceeds the initial offense because they want to win and not to be ashamed before others. When they win, they have honor and others will look at them and not think that they are inferior."

One night, for example, a Kompong Cham policeman named Hong got drunk and began arguing with someone. After the conflict escalated, Hong began firing his AK-47 in the air and yelling loudly. Another policeman, Moly, went to intercede. Hong pointed his gun at Moly and threatened him, "If you come any closer, I'll blow you away." Moly was extremely angry and, when he returned to his station, said, "So, little Hong was trying to be hard with me (*ânh*). Well, I'm strong, too, and I'm going to defeat him." Moly called a relative who was Hong's superior and explained what had happened. Perhaps twenty minutes later, the chief and several policemen arrived on the scene, arrested Hong, and threw him in jail. To frame this example in the terms of my argument, Hong did "something bad" to Moly and made him lose face and appear "inferior" (*an*). Moly's resulting shame and anger quickly developed into a grudge. Moly took revenge that exceeded Hong's original bad deed by having him imprisoned. By doing so, Moly restored his own honor, "defeated" Hong, and demonstrated that he was the superior person.

Lim told me an even more violent story that occurred when he was an officer during the post-Khmer Rouge communist period (SOC) and Vietnamese troops were still on Cambodian soil. After a drunken Vietnamese soldier had threatened to rape a local Cambodian woman, Lim sent one of his soldiers over to the Vietnamese barracks to intercede. Perhaps after an argument had broken out, some of the Vietnamese soldiers shot and killed one of Lim's men. Lim stated, "At that point my heart stopped being afraid and I wanted to kill any Vietnamese that I saw." That night, Lim deployed his troops around the area. Several heavily armed Vietnamese soldiers broke into a house and raped a different woman. When they came out, Lim's troop killed them all. Afterward, they cut the hands and heads off the dead Vietnamese soldiers who had murdered his private and left the dismembered bodies by the side of the road for all to see. Lim explained that he had a grudge against the Vietnamese because he lost face when they killed his soldier and disregarded his authority. By daring to exact revenge against them, Lim restored his honor.

The desire to seek such disproportionate vengeance may be partially rooted in socialization practices related to honor and shame. From a young age, children are taught to seek praise and to avoid losing face. Children are frequently punished by shaming and given warnings that they should not behave in ways that would make them and their families "shamed before others." The resulting acute sensitivity to the opinion of others may be reinforced by parental comments about how they and their family must never lose standing or otherwise be inferior to others. Such lessons take on heightened meaning as children grow older, begin to be evaluated in earnest, and feel anger when slighted. While young adults may internalize various strategies for managing anger, such as those prohibitions taught by Buddhism, they also learn an alternative moral basis for harboring resentment and avenging insults that damage their honor. They may draw this conclusion from real-life observations, the lack of parental pressure to "make up" fights, a vindictive animistic cosmos, moral beliefs about returning (*sâng*) a good or bad deed, the extreme cultural valuation of being "higher than" others, and stories like *Tum Teav* and the *Reamker*, the Cambodian version of the *Ramayana*. One teacher explained that, as a result of such enculturation, Cambodians who feel that they have been greatly wronged or shamed may "hold a grudge and want to defeat their foes to the point of eating their flesh and sipping their blood. The Cambodian character is such that these people will strive on; they cannot lose and stop thinking about the matter."

The second crucial reason why a Cambodian grudge results in disproportionate revenge is the view that a person must "completely defeat the enemy" (*phchanh phchal*) in order to deter further retaliation. The phrase *phchanh phchal* literally means "to defeat, vanquish" in such a manner as "to cause [the opponent] to be afraid and not dare to repeat the same act" (Headley 1977:614; see also Bun 1973:179ff.). Cambodians who bear malice realize that after they have exacted revenge, their victims will in turn desire to repay the bad deed. To prevent the cycle from continuing, it is in the avenger's best interest to make a preemptive strike that will mute this desire by fear or by death. As one informant explained, "Phchanh phchal means that you want the enemy to see what you have done and to be scared and respect you ... to be so afraid that [that person] won't dare to fight back." Those who can successfully *phchanh phchal* thus end up on top and stay there, looking down on their completely defeated (or dead) foes.

When Moly defeated Hong, for instance, he demonstrated his superiority and power in such a way that Hong and others would be afraid to challenge him in the future. Likewise, Lim claimed that after he had dismembered the corpses of the Vietnamese soldiers and left them lying by the side of the road, "the other Vietnamese soldiers were so scared that they didn't dare go far from their barracks or try to take revenge against me." Another example of *phchanh phchal* comes from a contemporary Cambodian movie, *Revenge by Marriage*, in which a young man, Sakun, marries a woman in order to exact revenge upon her brother who had severely beaten Sakun in the past. After the marriage, Sakun takes a second wife and treats the first wife like a servant. Her family, in turn, can do nothing because if they kill him she will be a widow and if she leaves him she will be a divorcée – both situations that can bring great shame to women in Cambodia. Sakun's revenge thus "completely defeats" his enemy, the first wife's brother.

The extreme form of *phchanh phchal* consists of killing one's enemies and possibly their family lines as well. While people may exact revenge in such a manner that their adversary has been completely defeated for the moment, it is possible that the vanquished foe's fortune may later change for the better, allowing an opportunity for revenge. In fact, several Cambodian proverbs warn of the danger that a person who currently shows fear and respect may rise to a powerful position in the future (Fisher-Nguyen 1994). One way to prevent such potential retribution is to suppress its root cause: to kill the enemy in order to preempt the possibility of revenge. Thus the polite, soft-spoken, young Cambodian male cited at the beginning of this section stated that he always tried to control his heart and to avoid getting into a major dispute because he knew that he would have to beat his adversary to death in order to prevent that person from taking revenge on a later day. A further problem arises, however, since it is likely that someone in the deceased foe's family will seek disproportionate revenge for the death. The head of a Cambodian nongovernmental organization pointed out, "When a son sees people kill his father, he will be seized with painful anger (*chheu chap*). After he has grown up, he will try to kill all of the people connected to his father's death. He won't just kill one person, he will kill many."

While only possible in situations in which a person has great power, the most extreme Cambodian solution to this predicament is to kill the enemy and "cut off his or her family line" (*phtach pouch, sângsoek suor pouch, prâlay pouch sas*). The origins of this tradition go far back in Cambodian history to times when, after winning a war, a victorious Cambodian king would sometimes attempt to kill the opposing king and his entire family line (Bun 1973). As we shall see, much DK violence can be viewed as a modern example of "cutting off a familial line." Other parallels also exist. During the Sihanouk regime, for example, the families of Sihanouk's political enemies were sometimes harassed, imprisoned, or both (Bun 1973). Similarly, Lim told me that when he was in the army he was once stationed in an area that was renowned for its high prevalence of sorcery. At one point, several soldiers died after their stomachs had swollen up, a sign of black magic. Lim and his troops gathered together the families of all the suspected sorcerers, over fifty people in all, and executed every one of them. Lim explained, "We had a grudge against them after they cast black magic and killed our soldiers, so we took disproportionate revenge. If we had just killed the sorcerers, their children would have been angry and tried to kill us later on. So we cut off the entire family line, just like during the Pol Pot period."

During the recent political upheaval in Cambodia, several incidents of "cutting off the family line" were rumored to have occurred. First, in a desperate attempt to hold onto power in June 1997, Pol Pot was said to have had Son Sen (his former DK Minister of Defense), the latter's wife Yun Yat, and ten of their family members and relatives executed (Barber and Chaumeau 1997:3). Some reports held that, after killing them, Pol Pot's troops ran over their heads with a truck. Second, during the July 1997 coup rumors abounded that Hun Sen's troops had killed the families of some of Prince Ranariddh's loyalists. Ranariddh's top general, Nhek Bun Chhay, alleged, "Hun Sen's forces not only killed the men who are soldiers, but he killed the families of [Ranariddh's Funcinpec Party] soldiers. Whole families, women and children" (Barber 1997:7). His claims, however, have never been substantiated. Finally, between 1993 and 1997, the Khmer Rouge supposedly conducted internal purges in which entire families were annihilated (Levy 1998). Krom Khuon, a former Khmer Rouge soldier, recalled, "Sometimes I would see a car full of soldiers come ... They would take the whole family into the forest in a truck. Then the soldiers would come back without the family" (cited in Levy 1998). Thousands of these victims were said to be buried in a massive killing field called "Gravel Hill."

The tradition of "cutting off a family line" is also clearly enacted in *Tum Teav*. When Tum hears that Teav is to be remarried to Archoun's son, he becomes incensed at Archoun and Teav's mother, both of whom clearly look down on him because he is from a lower-class background. Tum sets out to Tbaung Khmum to restore his honor by avenging the slight and taking back Teav. But the sad truth is that a poor youth like Tum stands little chance of defeating Archoun who is powerful and has many guards. By daring to go to the wedding and to call for Teav, Tum is able to make Archoun lose face before his followers and guests. Archoun, however, quickly retaliates by having Tum killed. In the end, it is left to Tum's patron, King Rama, to take symbolic revenge for Tum. King Rama both literally and figuratively takes "a head for an eye" by ordering that Archoun and his relatives seven generations removed be buried up to the neck in the ground and that their heads be cut off by plow and harrow. By "cutting off the family line," King Rama guarantees that none of Archoun's relatives will seek revenge against him in the future. To ensure further that no members of Archoun's faction will attempt subsequent retaliation, King Rama has them boiled alive. This sequence of events clearly illustrates the Cambodian cultural model of disproportionate revenge – albeit in its most extreme form of "completely destroying" the enemy – and provides a culturally salient root metaphor of "little" people who gain a powerful patron to help them exact revenge on enemies who have done "something bad" to them.

In the next section, I will show how the Cambodian cultural model of disproportionate revenge embedded within the story of *Tum Teav* provided a legitimizing and highly motivating basis for much violence during DK. After describing traditional sources of peasant resentment toward the rich, I will point out how the Khmer Rouge often tried to use ideological discourse to turn these feelings into a class grudge. Like Rama, the Khmer Rouge often attempted to exact revenge in such a manner as to destroy the former supporters of Lon Nol completely.

Disproportionate revenge in Democratic Kampuchea

In early 1967 hundreds of peasants from the Samlaut subdistrict in Battambang province revolted. Fed up with the government's new policy of directly purchasing the rice crop from farmers at prices far below the black market rate, high levels of debt, heavy-handed treatment by local soldiers, corruption, and the reallocation of their land, peasant rebels murdered two soldiers and stole their weapons on the morning of April 2 (Chandler 1991; Kiernan and Boua 1982; Martin 1994). Carrying banners denouncing the government and U.S. imperialism, the peasants destroyed a youth agricultural camp, attacked two government outpost, and killed a local official later that day. During the next few weeks, the revolt quickly expanded. In order to put down this threat to civil order, Sihanouk's government sent additional troops into the area and used increasingly brutal tactics to suppress the "red" rebellion. Peasant villages were razed to the ground. Suspects were beaten, imprisoned, and summarily executed. There were even rumors that the government paid a bounty for the severed heads of rebels (Kiernan and Boua 1982:173). Estimates of the number of the dead ranged from hundreds to thousands.

While the Samlaut rebellion did not overthrow the Sihanouk government, it illustrated the existence of a substantial base of disaffected peasants who could potentially be incited to join the Khmer Rouge movement. In fact, between 1952 and 1970, the proportion of landless peasants rose from 4 to 20 percent of the population (Kiernan 1985; Kiernan and Boua 1982); still others remained heavily in debt or owned only a small amount of land. (Landlordism was highest in the Battambang region where the Samlaut rebellion broke out.) These numbers undoubtedly rose as the civil war progressed and the U.S. carpet bombing of Cambodia increased. The number of disaffected peasants "probably never formed a majority in the Cambodian countryside. But they were numerous enough for Pol Pot to build a viable recruitment strategy targeting poor peasants, and particularly their teenage children" (Kiernan 1996:7; see also Vickery 1984).[4] Many of these people harbored a great deal of anger toward the rich and urban dwellers and quickly embraced Khmer Rouge ideology about class struggle.

One major source of resentment was the disrespectful way in which many rich people treated the poor. Like the Japanese (Lebra 1976:128), Cambodians lose face and become extremely upset when others act arrogantly toward them. Such behavior implies that the arrogant person is making the evaluation (*aoy tamlei*) that one is "inferior" and can be "looked down upon" (*moel ngeay*). As demonstrated by Tum's rage toward Archoun and Tic's anger after he was slighted at the rich family's wedding, the memory of such shameful events is usually "buried in the heart" and may induce a strong desire for revenge.

A second grievance the poor had against the rich was a sense of the relatively greater suffering they had been made to endure, frequently as a direct result of exploitation by the rich and powerful. While many Cambodians were indebted to money lenders who frequently charged an interest rate of more than 10 percent (Delvert 1961; Kiernan and Boua 1982), the poorest of all were often forced to farm for landlords. Even those who owned land were resentful of how little they received for their hard work in comparison to the rich. Albeit in a much more moderate form, such animosity toward the rich persists, partially explaining why the Khmer Rouge continue to enjoy popular support in some rural areas. A peasant told me, "The farmers feel that they work hard but only get a little for their effort. They only have a little money to purchase things. Rich people, in contrast, have it easier and have lots of money. They also make a profit from the farmers to whom they sell and from whom they profit." One can only imagine how angry peasants would become if forced to sell their crops to the government at a price far below the potential value. The Samlaut rebellion illustrated the explosiveness of such feelings.

Finally, the civil war itself was a source of great anger for the poor. After being deposed and allying himself with the Khmer Rouge, Prince Sihanouk appealed to his rural "children" to take arms with him against the traitorous and illegitimate Lon Nol government.[5] Thus, a man named Khel stated that he and many other youths in his village joined the Khmer Rouge because "in general the people loved the king and he was the head of the Khmer Rouge military front." U.S. bombing also greatly increased rural discontent. During the course of the war, American bombers dropped 540,000 tons of explosives on Cambodian soil, resulting in economic destabilization, the deaths of up to 150,000 people, and the displacement of tens of thousands of others (Kiernan 1996; see also Shawcross 1987). Many Cambodians joined the Khmer Rouge out of anger at the destruction of their homes and the deaths of loved ones. Khel explained, "The American B-52s dropped too many bombs. It made the people become seized with painful anger (*chheu chap*) and want to fight against the Lon Nol regime." Another cadre explained that the bombing made it "easy for the Khmer Rouge to win the people over" (Kiernan 1996:23).

Khmer Rouge ideology took the resentment stemming from all these sources and gave it a common focus (class struggle) and target (the urban population). Political education sessions were geared to "create class ardor and fury." Recruits were taught basic communist doctrine, which held that the suffering of the poor (*vonnah âtun*) was due to the exploitation (*chih choan;* literally "to ride" and "step on," see Headley 1977:240, 259 and Chandler 1991:242) of the capitalist class *(vonnah neaytun).* Lohr, a former guard at the infamous Tuol Sleng prison and interrogation center in Phnom Penh, explained that the Khmer Rouge "told us that the poor were poor because of the rich and the rich were rich because of the poor. They wanted us to become seized with painful anger about this exploitation, to hate and to fight bravely against the capitalist, feudal, and landlord classes, the rich big people who harmed the poor."

Criticism and self-criticism meetings, propaganda sessions, disciplinary precepts, and revolutionary songs, slogans, and plays were all geared to developing this proper revolutionary "consciousness" *(sâte'aram)* that would be filled with "burning rage toward the enemy" (Carney 1977:51). The very notion of "class struggle" *(Tâsou vonnah)* drew on a Cambodian cultural model of warriors who "struggle" or "fight bravely" *(neak tâsou* see Headley 1977:311) against the enemy. Like Tum, the poor were supposed to be filled with anger and heroically fight back against their arrogant oppressors. Thus, while a person like Khel might have joined the Khmer Rouge because Sihanouk was overthrown, he was quickly indoctrinated into communist ideology: "Their political education consisted of telling us to be seized with painful anger against the oppressor class. They spoke about this all the time." The dispossessed and the young, who were likened, in a Maoist metaphor, to "a blank page on which we can write anything we want" (Picq 1989:60), proved most susceptible to this propaganda. On returning from political indoctrination sessions, many of these recruits were described as dedicated and well-disciplined "fanatics" (Quinn 1976:24).

Khmer Rouge ideologies attempted to focus the "burning rage" of these fanatics upon the urban centers, the bastions of capitalism. This goal was often not difficult to achieve given the initial resentment many of the poor felt toward rich city people who allegedly looked down upon them, enjoyed a much easier life, and supported Lon Nol, who was responsible for the overthrowing of Sihanouk and the carpet bombing of the countryside. Khmer Rouge propaganda employed slogans such as "trees in the country, fruit in the town" (Soth 1980:44) to inflame still further this rural animosity toward the cities. A current government official explained, "They brainwashed people to believe that the Lon Nol regime was a capitalist regime, and that the very poor, who had been oppressed and swindled by the rich, had to fight bravely to defeat Lon Nol." Moreover, the cities were portrayed as corrupt and immoral centers of undue foreign influence. On the one hand, rich city people were reported to spend their time living in luxurious houses, eating well, sipping cognac, and visiting prostitutes (the "cognac and concubine circuit") while the peasants toiled in the countryside producing their "fruit." On the other hand, Phnom Penh was said to be filled with "American lackeys" and to contain a disproportionately large number of ethnic Chinese and Vietnamese (Kiernan 1996:5). City people were not only capitalist exploiters, but also not "real Khmer." They were, rather, a hated enemy who should be "crushed" (*kamtech khmang*) by "class ardor and fury."

By drawing on preexisting resentment and focusing it on the city, Khmer Rouge ideology effectively fostered a rural class grudge (*kumnum vonnah*) against the urban population. The city people had done "something bad" to the poor by making them suffer and lose face. One or more of these "happenings" led the poor to be "seized with painful anger" (*chheu chap*), which they stored inside themselves. The Khmer Rouge inflamed this hidden resentment into a class grudge that motivated many of the poor to want to "eat the flesh and sip the blood" of their enemies. One "new" person explained that the Khmer Rouge "sometimes called this 'igniting class anger.' They made people in the countryside have a grudge against the urbanites by teaching them about class contradiction. When we left the cities, the rural population considered us their enemies." Like Tum, the poor needed a powerful patron to help them exact disproportionate revenge against this hated enemy. The Khmer Rouge Party Organization, or Ângkar, fulfilled this role.

This class grudge facilitated a great deal of violence during DK. By the end of the war, the "ignited class anger" was burning at full force. In Battambang province, for example, Khmer Rouge appeared "contemptuous and aloof" just after liberation and later reportedly admitted that they had been "fired by 'uncontrollable hatred' for members of the 'old society.' 'We were so angry when we came out of the forest,' one speaker allegedly said, 'that we didn't want to spare even a baby in its cradle'" (Chandler et al. 1976:2, 9). This hatred was quickly directed at the first targets of revenge, the Lon Nol government and military. Leading officials were rounded up and executed, and a concerted attempt was made to identify other potential enemies. Urbanites being evacuated out of the cities were asked to give background information about their former occupations. Many who told the truth were taken away to be killed. Others were sent to be "re-educated" in special camps or through rural peasant life. Up to 200,000 people may have been killed during this first wave of DK killing (Thion 1993:166). Like King Rama, the Khmer Rouge sought to "destroy the enemy completely" by annihilating the entire leadership of the Lon Nol regime, a point to which I shall return.

Instead of ending the vengeance after this initial period of violence, the Khmer Rouge attempted to keep the class grudge inflamed. Haing Ngor, who was a "new" person during DK, related how, during a public propaganda dance, costumed cadres would pound their chests with clenched fists and repeatedly shout at the top of their lungs: "'BLOOD AVENGES BLOOD!' ... Blood avenges blood. You kill us, we kill you. We 'new' people had been on the other side of the Khmer Rouge in the civil war ... Symbolically, the Khmer Rouge had just announced that they were going to take revenge" (Ngor 1987:140–1). In fact, the color of blood, red, was a prominent theme in Khmer Rouge propaganda and provided a metaphoric call for revenge. The national anthem contained numerous mentions of spilled "blood," which provided a reason for people to maintain their "unrelenting hatred." In a September 27, 1977 speech, Pol Pot explained that a "blood call has been incorporated into our national anthem. Each sentence, each word shows the nature of our people's struggle. This blood ha been turned into class and national indignation" (FBIS 1977:H25). Similarly, the Khmer Rouge flag was red and glorified by "The Red Flag" song, often sung in unison before meetings:

Glittering red blood blankets the earth – blood given up to
liberate the people: the blood of workers, peasants, and intellectuals;
blood of young men, Buddhist monks, and girls.
The blood swirls away, and flows upward, gently, into the
sky, turning into a red, revolutionary flag.
Red flag! red flag! flying now! flying now!
O beloved friends, pursue, strike and hit the enemy.
Red flag! red flag! flying now! flying now!
Don't leave a single reactionary imperialist (alive): drive
them from Kampuchea. Strive and strike, strive and strike,
and win the victory, win the victory!

[Chandler et al. 1976:14]

Like the national anthem, "The Red Flag" song, with its analogy between blood sacrifice and the color red and its encouragement to "strike and hit the enemy," urged cadres to maintain their class grudge until not "a single reactionary imperialist" was left alive.

Realizing to whom such ideology would have the greatest appeal, the Khmer Rouge placed the extreme poor and the young in local-level positions of power during DK. These individuals had the greatest reason to hate their "class enemies" and to be loyal to their powerful new patron, Ângkar. Khmer Rouge propaganda attempted to keep their memory fresh about how the city people had caused them to suffer and feel humiliated. One radio broadcast reminded the poor, "Our brothers and sisters lived a most miserable life, enduring all manner of hardships. … They never had enough food, never were happy and never had an opportunity to receive [an education]. Our brothers and sisters were looked down upon, regarded as animals" (FBIS 1976 H1). Such propaganda, combined with basic political education about class struggle, was often effective in encouraging low-level cadres to seek revenge against their class enemies. One "old" person recounted how his village leader, Boan, was changed by such Khmer Rouge ideology: "At first Boan was like us. After they had brainwashed him, however, his heart and thoughts changed. He became angry at the people, particularly the rich and soldiers. Boan was an ignorant person and couldn't write much … but he loved Ângkar and would report on people who were then killed." Ngor once made a pun to some other "new" people in his work group that such Khmer Rouge cadre were not "communist" (*kommuyonis*) but "revenge people" (*Kum-monuss*). "'That's what they are at the lower level,' I said, 'revenge people.' 'All they know is that city people like us used to lord it over them and this is their chance to get back. That's what they are, communist at the top and kum-monuss at the bottom'" (Ngor 1987:159).

Revenge against the "new" people was further legitimated by a variety of dehumanizing practices. If the poor had disproportionately suffered in comparison to, and been looked down upon by, the rich, the situation was now reversed. While the pattern and scope of conditions varied (Vickery 1984), "new" people tended to receive less food, be treated more harshly, have fewer rights, and be killed more readily than "old" people. Long work hours, starvation rations, a lack of freedom, miserable living conditions, and constant terror quickly robbed them of their humanity.[6] One "New" person described what happened to people in a particularly difficult region of Cambodia: "We were hungry, too tired to wash or clean our clothes, and we lost all sense of hygiene. We didn't care what we ate as long as we could put something in our stomachs. We didn't mind where we had a shit, or who saw us. Disease spread through the village – cholera, malaria, dysentery, diarrhoea and skin infections" (May 1986:165). Such "new" people were "depositees," the lowest level of a new tripartite DK social structure that included "candidates" and "full rights people." Suspect from the start as "class enemies" who were tainted by city life and no longer "pure" Khmer, they constituted the bottom stratum of society, one that was greatly devalued and became the explicit target of persecution.

In many cases, "new" people were regarded as analogous to animals. Like water buffalo, they were sometimes required to pull a plow or cart and might be whipped if they failed to work hard enough (see, for example, Stuart-Fox 1985:60; Szymusiak 1986:147). One "new" person recounted how at meetings cadres often urged people to be like oxen: "Comrad Ox never refuse to work. Comrad Ox was obedient. Comrad Ox did not complain. Comrad Ox did not object when his family was killed" (Yathay 1987:171). A soldier told another "new" person that it would be better for her sick mother to die "than [it would be for] a cow. The cows are good. They help us a lot and do not eat rice. They are much better than you pigs" (Moyer 1991:123). Since "new" people were like animals, cadres were justified in harming them. A "new" person who did something wrong could therefore be "discarded" (*veay chal*) without much of a qualm. Several people interviewed mentioned a chilling Khmer Rouge saying that was invoked in such situations or as a threat: "To keep you is no gain; to destroy you is no loss" [*tuk min chomnenh yok chenh min khat*]. One Cambodian-American refugee has even used this slogan as the title of her book about her experiences during DK (Criddle and Mam 1987).

Given such dehumanization and the Khmer Rouge ideology that fostered a sense of class grudge and glorified violence against the enemy, it is not surprising that revenge killings continued to take place long after the first wave of DK executions. Having annihilated most of the Lon Nol government's leadership, the Khmer Rouge began gradually to kill off other "class enemies" such as rich "capitalists," intellectuals, professionals, and lower-ranking soldiers, police, and government employees. Local cadres continued to research people's backgrounds. Upon arriving at a new village, a woman named Yum explained that a cadre "asked my husband what he had done. He lied and told them he had ridden a cyclo bike and guarded a house. The cadre said, 'if so, why are your hands, legs, and face so nice?' They asked him to prove that he was really from the countryside by plowing a rice field and doing other peasant tasks." Because he had grown up performing such labor in a rural village, Yum's husband was able to do successfully what the cadre asked. In the end, however, the Khmer Rouge still found out that her husband had been a soldier. Yum added, "There were people from our village living there who knew my husband's occupation. Whoever hated us told the Khmer Rouge that my husband had been a soldier." After learning about this family of Lon Nol soldiers, the district security office gave orders for them to be executed. Yum began to cry as she recounted how her husband's brother, who worked at the district office, arrived that evening with some guns and provisions and fled with his brothers into the rainy night, never to be seen again.

The family of a young woman named Gen experienced a similar tragedy, which I will recount in detail. When local officials began researching people's backgrounds, her family could not hide the fact that her father, Tak, had been a teacher during the Lon Nol period, since he had taught in the area. Tak eventually went to the local hospital because his stomach had become swollen because of the lack of food. A few days later, Tak was told to gather his things because he was being transferred to the regional hospital. Instead of going there, Tak was taken to an area behind the hospital and killed. Witnesses told Gen that when the killers returned, they were covered in blood.

One of them, Tralok, had been a student of Tak's. Gen explained, "My father was an extremely strict teacher and would frequently hit his students in order to make them want to learn. Tralok was a particularly lazy and disobedient student and was beaten often. These beatings really hurt, so Tralok became angry at and held a grudge against my father." Afterwards, Tralok was overheard bragging that, before killing Tak, he told him (using superior-to-inferior prefixes), "When you (*hâ'aeng*) were my (*ânh*) teacher, you beat me and made me hurt. Now, I will repay your 'good' deeds (*sângkun*) in turn. I will kill and discard you, so that you can no longer be such a mean teacher."

Perhaps two months later, Gen's mother went to the hospital to get an injection to make her feel better. Before administering the shot, the doctor, Khon, supposedly asked, "Are you Tak's wife?" When she responded affirmatively, Khon filled the syringe with a white liquid. Gen's mother died immediately after receiving the shot. Earlier in the day, cadres had been asking where Gen's mother was and then, upon hearing that she had gone to the hospital, went and spoke to Khon. Gen has no doubt they ordered Khon to kill her mother.

Three of Gen's sisters were the next to be killed. The oldest, Srey, had a silk scarf (*krâma*) that had been used in their parents' wedding ceremony. The subdistrict head, Rom, saw the scarf and "suggested" that Srey give it to her, but Srey refused because the scarf had such sentimental value. Gen explained, "When my elder sister didn't give the scarf to her, Rom became very angry with this new person who thought she was better than an old person. Rom held a grudge against my sister and waited for an opportunity to get back at her." A few days later, Srey was plowing a field and swore at one of her oxen. Rom was nearby and claimed that Srey had sworn at her. That evening, one of Rom's minions told Srey that Rom wanted to see her. Gen's other elder sister insisted upon coming along because she was afraid something bad would happen to Srey; they took along their youngest sibling who was just an infant.

Later, after DK, Heng, a person who worked with Rom at the subdistrict office, told Gen that Srey and her sister were tied up and led away to a local killing field by Rom and a group of five or six other people. Rom reportedly said to Srey (using superior-to-inferior prefixes), "So, you were trying to act tough with me and wouldn't give me your scarf. This is what you get." Upon hearing this, Srey, despite having her arms tied, began to kick wildly at her captors, managing to tear some of their clothes. Rom was incensed. Gen recounted what supposedly happened next: "They stripped off her clothes and made her stand there naked in front of the group, some of whom were men. One of them then grabbed my infant sister and smashed her head against a tree stump. Her head burst open with a pop and she died at once." Next, they made Srey watch as her other sister was executed. Rom and the other executioners then began to beat Srey all over the body. "Rom told my sister, 'It's going to be a long time before you are dead.' They punched and kicked her all over until she was finally finished off. She suffered so much. It's so sad." A few days later, Gen and her younger sister made a dramatic escape from the village. Unfortunately, Gen's four younger brothers were still in the area living with an uncle. Rom sent for them and had them work at the local pagoda, which was being used by the Khmer Rouge as a prison. Their job was to carry out the prisoners' excrement. Just before the end of DK, the boys were all executed after being forced to dig their own graves.

The destruction of Gen's entire family illustrates how the Khmer Rouge attempted to take disproportionate revenge in such a manner as to "destroy completely" (*phchanh phchal*) their class enemies. Because the Khmer Rouge were so powerful, they were able to engage in the most extreme form of *phchanh phchal* – killing off the enemy's line. Gen sadly explained. "The Khmer Rouge had a grudge against my family because my father had been a government worker during the previous regime. They were seized with painful anger and wanted to take revenge against 'new' people like us. They wanted to cut off our entire familial line so no one would be left to seek vengeance against them on a later day." Many other Cambodian family lines were similarly destroyed during DK. For example, eight out of nine of Yum's husband's siblings (seven of whom had been in the army) were executed. Every person in four of these siblings' families were killed. In some cases, the Khmer Rouge would simply load families of "new" people into trucks and take them to local execution centers to be exterminated. The Khmer Rouge actually had a saying which encouraged such slaughter: "To dig up grass, one must also dig up the roots" [*chik smav trauv chik teang reus*]. Echoing the explanation of many others, a former DK village chief of Gen's village told me that this phrase meant that cadres "were supposed to 'dig up' the entire family of an enemy – husband, wife, kids, sometimes from the grandparents down – so that none remained ... to kill off the entire line at once so that none of them would be left to seek revenge later, in turn."

Thus the severity of much DK killing can be seen as following the script of the Cambodian model of disproportionate revenge illustrated by the story of *Tum Teav*. Like Tum, many of the poor were angry at the rich and powerful who looked down upon them and made them suffer. The Khmer Rouge used this ideology to inflame this feeling of resentment even further, trying to make its followers completely "seized with painful anger" (*chheu chap*) to the point of wanting to avenge their class grudge. Khieu Samphan's brother explained, "The destruction of the Cambodian people can be [largely] understood in terms of the resentment (*chheu chap*) of the destitute (*neak ât*) who suffered and were looked down upon. ... Their resentment became a grudge that was repaid (*sâng*) when they had power ... they repaid [this debt] by killing."

Just as King Rama took revenge for Tum, so too Ângkar provided a means for the poor and the young to wreak vengeance upon these "class enemies," most of whom were, at least during the first phase of DK, "new" people. Moreover, like King Rama, the Khmer Rouge exacted revenge that was disproportionate to the initial offense and "completely destroyed" their enemy. King Rama cut off the heads of Archoun's relatives seven generations removed and boiled his associates to death. The Khmer Rouge first killed off virtually the entire military and governmental leadership of the Lon Nol regime and then set out to eradicate other suspected enemies and, in many cases, part or all of their family lines. By taking "a head for an eye," King Rama and the Khmer Rouge were attempting both to demonstrate their superiority over a foe who had previously done "something bad" to them and to prevent the cycle of vengeance from continuing thereafter.

As is illustrated by the revenge killings that took place at the end of DK, the Khmer Rouge were not totally successful in preventing such retaliation. One women described how Son, a harsh village head whom she had watched kill two ethnic Vietnamese, was himself killed by an irate mob: "They were angry at him for all he had done. I went and watched as a great number of people beat him and cut off his head." Similarly, one of Rom's associates named Phat fled into the jungle when the Vietnamese invaded Cambodia. After hiding for a few days, Phat tried to sneak into a village to steal some food one night and was shot and wounded. A crowd soon gathered and began to beat Phat. Another woman whose husband had been killed by Phat said, "More and more people kept coming, grandfathers and grandchildren. They really hated her because she had killed so many people. I hit her two times, too. I hated her because she had killed my husband. We wanted revenge." Most Cambodians can relate a similar violent story about the post-DK revenge killing of former Khmer Rouge cadres. As illustrated by Son's murder, many of these stories involve decapitation, perhaps a symbolic act that indexes the avenger's desire to take "a head for an eye" (see, for example, May 1986:241ff.; Ngor 1987:362; Stuart-Fox 1985:152; Szymusiak 1986:209).

Conclusion

Many Cambodians who suffered greatly during DK continue to hold a grudge against the Khmer Rouge. When I asked her how she feels when she sometimes see Tralok, for example, Gen responded, "I get really hot and angry inside my heart. My heart is still tied in wanting revenge. I want to ask him, 'What did my father do to you to make you kill him? You were beaten because you were lazy.' When I think about him, I get so angry." Such feelings were no doubt what the post-Khmer Rouge communist government (SOC/PRK) was trying to exploit when they held the "Day to Remain Tied in Anger." Because the cultural model of disproportionate revenge remains so entrenched in Cambodian society, it is difficult to prevent such cycles of revenge from occurring.

Nevertheless, potential solutions do exist. As I noted in my introductory remarks, Cambodians have alternatives to taking revenge. Individuals who have been slighted or harmed may choose to invoke Buddhist norms of emotion control and foregiveness. Others may take comfort in the Buddhist notion that the form of future rebirth is determined by actions in the present. Thus some Cambodians, like Gen, say that Pol Pot will be reincarnated as a *bret,* perhaps the most hideous, despicable, and evil spirit in the Cambodian religious cosmology (Ang

1987; Ebihara 1968). On an institutional level, legal and educational practices could be modified. If the rampant corruption within the Cambodian judicial system were reduced, for example, Cambodians bearing malice might feel less desire to exact revenge personally. Moreover, a Nuremberg-like trial of the surviving Khmer Rouge leaders, now made possible by the Cambodian Genocide Program, might satisfy many Cambodians, as a symbolic severing of the collective Khmer Rouge head. Alternatively, during class sessions on texts like *Tum Teav,* teachers could analyze, point out the detrimental results of, and explain the different options to the cultural model of disproportionate revenge. Whatever the means, Cambodians would benefit greatly if the destructiveness that often results from the cultural model of disproportionate revenge were to be prevented.

In conclusion, I have attempted to provide an example of how anthropology can contribute to our understanding of large-scale genocide. In particular, I have demonstrated how the Cambodian cultural model of disproportionate revenge served as a template for part of the genocidal violence that occurred in DK. It is crucial for anthropologists to point out how cultural models come to serve as templates for violence, since such implicit cultural knowledge often provides fodder for genocidal ideologies. As Naomi Quinn and Dorothy Holland have noted, "To be successful, ideologies must appeal to and activate pre-existing cultural understandings, which are themselves compelling ... though ideologues may mold and adapt cultural models to their own devices" (1987:13). Thus Khmer Rouge ideology about class struggle, which played upon the traditional suffering and humiliation of the poor, served to transform the anger and resentment of many of the regime's followers into a class grudge. These cadres and soldiers in turn used the traditional cultural model of disproportionate revenge as a template for committing genocidal atrocities. The result was the death of hundreds of thousands of "enemies" and, often, of their families. Pointing out how cultural knowledge is employed in this lethal manner constitutes one important way in which anthropologists can increase our knowledge about the genocidal events that have occurred in Turkey, Nazi Germany, and Cambodia, and have more recently taken place in Bosnia and Rwanda.

Notes

1. After leading his country to independence from the French in 1953, Prince Sihanouk dominated the political scene in the Kingdom of Cambodia. International affairs (the Vietnam War and the Cold War) contributed to his

downfall in 1970, when a coup took place. General Lon Nol then headed the newly formed Khmer Republic until 1975, when his government was overthrown by the Khmer Rouge, a group of Maoist-inspired communist rebels who gained legitimacy and a great deal of rural support when Sihanouk joined them after the coup. During the next four years, Democratic Kampuchea (DK) was reorganized along strict communist lines that glorified peasant life and the revolution. Khmer Rouge antagonism and military raids into Vietnam eventually led the Vietnamese to invade in January of 1979. The Vietnamese army routed the Khmer Rouge and set up the People's Republic of Kampuchea (PRK), which was opposed by guerrilla forces located on the Thai border. After the Vietnamese army withdrew in 1989, the PRK renamed itself the State of Cambodia (SOC) and initiated a series of reforms to improve the country's image both within and outside the country. This government held power until 1993 UN-sponsored elections, when the new Royal Government of Cambodia (RGC) was established. Sihanouk was crowned King and the government was jointly run by his son, First Prime Minister Prince Ranariddh, and the ex-leader of SOC, Second Prime Minister Hun Sen. The increasingly contentious relations between the Prime Ministers led Hun Sen to launch a coup on July 5, 1997. At the time of writing, an internationally brokered agreement has allowed Ranariddh and other opposition candidates to return from exile and participate in national elections scheduled for July 26, 1998.

2. Article II of the United Nations Genocide Convention defines genocide as "acts committed with intent to destroy, in whole or in part, a national, ethnical, racial or religious group, as such" (see Kuper 1981). Given the conceptual vagueness of this definition, there has been some debate about whether the violence that took place in Cambodia can be accurately classified as genocidal (Kiernan 1993). I believe that it is appropriate to use this term in this case because ethnic groups (Muslim Chams and ethnic Vietnamese, Chinese, and Thai) and religious groups (Buddhists and Christians) were subject to systematic elimination, both through outright execution and through the imposition of extremely harsh living conditions (see also Fein 1993; Hawk 1988, 1990; Kiernan 1986, 1988; Stanton 1993). Moreover, the original Genocide Convention definition excluded political groups and social classes because of pressure from countries like the Soviet Union that feared being indicted. To correct for this bias, many genocide scholars have redefined genocide in a more inclusive manner (e.g., Chalk and Jonassohn 1990; Chamy 1994; Fein 1990; Kuper 1981). Thus Fein defines genocide as "sustained purposeful action by a perpetrator to physically destroy a collectivity directly or indirectly, through interdiction of the biological and social reproduction of group members, sustained regardless of the surrender or lack of threat offered by the victim" (1990:24). Under this definition and given the purges, the attack on "new" people, and the execution of members of the Lon Nol military and government, the repression under DK can clearly be classified as genocide. See Andreopoulos 1994 for an examination of the historical and conceptual issues surrounding the use of the term *genocide*.

3. It is important to recognize that, by conceptualizing cultural models in this manner, scholars are able to discuss notions of "culture" and "ethos" without falling into the overly reductive stereotyping of "national character" studies.

As Strauss and Quinn have noted, cultural models may be both shared and differentially internalized, since they have "centripetal" and "centrifugal" tendencies (1994; see also Shore 1996). On the one hand, cultural models may be durable (learned patterns that are established through experience), historically enduring (while the potential for transformation exists, cultural models inform an individual's publicly enacted behavior and beliefs and therefore tend to be re-created in later generations), thematic (some cultural models are highly salient across a variety of contexts and constitute an important part of what is often called an "ethos" or "worldview"), and shared (because members of a culture are often exposed to and internalize similar schematic patterns). On the other hand, cultural models are never completely identical (because people have distinct life histories and unique experiences that give rise to idiosyncratic models or alter the emotional and motivational valences associated with given cultural models) and may be socially distributed (individuals and social groups often have differential access to knowledge and are exposed to disparate types of experiences that shape their cultural models in distinct ways). Thus, while the Cambodian cultural model of disproportionate revenge is widely shared by and highly salient for many Cambodians, it is not a generic part of their "national character."

4. While Cambodian scholars generally agree that the Khmer Rouge were successfully able to draw recruits from the ranks of the extreme poor and the young, some disagree over how widespread such peasant support was before 1975 (see Frieson 1991; Kiernan 1996; Kiernan and Boua 1982; and Vickery 1984). This debate dovetails with larger academic discussions about how peasant grievances, often of long duration, are mobilized by revolutionary movements within a particular set of sociocultural, economic, political, and historical circumstances (see Moore 1966; Popkin 1979; Scott 1976; Skocpol 1979; Thaxton 1983; Wolf 1969). Interestingly, although analyses of peasant revolutions often mention revenge as a motivating factor, none delineates the precise cultural form it takes in given societies. I would argue that doing so is of crucial importance since revolutionary leaders must adapt their ideological discourse to pre-existing cultural models that make sense to their followers. Disparate cultural models of revenge also have different entailments. Thus, within an appropriate set of historical and socioeconomic conditions, the culture-specific form of the Cambodian cultural model of disproportionate revenge facilitated genocide. In other revolutions, indigenous concepts of "revenge" might not do so. Accordingly, scholars must take such cultural factors into account in order to fully explain the origins of genocide.

5. Sihanouk's actions can also be partially explained as the result of a grudge. When he was overthrown, Sihanouk lost a great deal of power and face, particularly given all of the disparagement that the new government cast upon him and his family. In order to pay back Lon Nol and Sirik Matak for their "bad deed" and to restore his own honor, Sihanouk allied himself with the Khmer Rouge, who potentially could provide him with the revenge he desired. One informant explained:

> Sihanouk was the one who gave Lon Nol power, but Lon Nol deposed him. Sihanouk was really angry and had a grudge against Lon Nol ... The people loved King Sihanouk and fled into the forest to struggle with him.

The Khmer Rouge would never have defeated Lon Nol if they hadn't had Sihanouk on their side.

Sihanouk's actions resemble those of other Cambodians who hold such great malice that they are willing to lose everything for the sake of vengeance.
6. Clearly, "old" people also suffered greatly during DK. Echoing the sentiments of many other "old" people with whom I spoke, one Banyan villager told me that Khmer Rouge cadres "treated us like animals. Like a chicken, we didn't have the right to protest. We didn't dare say anything for fear they would kill us. They could discard us like an animal." Since I am examining class revenge in this article, my analysis is primarily geared to exploring the way in which the Khmer Rouge used ideological discourse and policy to encourage the impoverished and young cadres and soldiers, whom they put in positions of power, to take revenge against their former oppressors. While many other "old" people may also have enjoyed seeing their former "class enemies" executed, not all the poor hated city people. Some "old" people were friendly toward, and even tried to help, "new" people.

Bibliography

Andreopoulos, George J., ed. 1994. *Genocide: Conceptual and Historical Dimensions.* Philadelphia: University of Pennsylvania Press.

Ang Chouléan 1987 *Les êtres surnaturels dans la religion populaire Khmère.* Collection Bibliothèque Khmère, Série Travaux et Recherches. Paris: Centre de Documentation et de Recherche sur la Civilisation Khmere.

Aretxaga, Begoña 1995 "Dirty Protest: Symbolic Overdetermination and Gender in Northern Ireland Ethnic Violence." *Ethos* 23:123–48.

— 1997 *Shattering Silence: Women, Nationalism, and Political Subjectivity in Northern Ireland.* Princeton, NJ: Princeton University Press.

Barber, Jason 1997 "Leaner Bun Chhay Vows to Fight On." *Phnom Penh Post,* August 15:7.

Barber, Jason, and Christine Chaumeau 1997 "Power Struggle Shatters KR Leadership." *Phnom Penh Post,* June 27:3.

Benedict, Ruth 1946 *The Chrysanthemum and the Sword: Patterns of Japanese Culture.* Boston: Houghton Mifflin.

Besteman, Catherine 1996 "Violent Politics and the Politics of Violence: The Dissolution of the Somali Nation-State." *American Ethnologist* 23:579–96.

Bourdieu, Pierre 1977 *Outline of a Theory of Practice.* Richard Nice, trans. New York: Cambridge University Press.

— 1990 *The Logic of Practice.* Richard Nice, trans. Stanford, CA: Stanford University Press.

Bringa, Tone 1993 National Categories, National Identification and Identity Formation in "Multinational" Bosnia. *Anthropology of East Europe Review* 11(1–2):27–34.

— 1995 *Being Muslim the Bosnian Way: Identity and Community in a Central Bosnian Village.* Princeton, NJ: Princeton University Press.

Bun Chân Mol 1973 *Châret Khmaer* (Cambodian character). Phnom Penh: Kehâdtan 79, distributor.

Carney, Timothy, ed. 1977 *Communist Party Power in Kampuchea (Cambodia): Documents and Discussion.* Ithaca, NY: Cornell University Southeast Asia Program.

Chalk, Frank, and Kurt Jonassohn 1990 *The History and Sociology of Genocide: Analyses and Case Studies.* New Haven, CT: Yale University Press.

Chandler, David P. 1991 *The Tragedy of Cambodian History: Politics, War, and Revolution since 1945.* New Haven, CT: Yale University Press.

Chandler, David P., Ben Kiernan, and Muy Hong Lim 1976 *The Early Phases of Liberation in Northwestern Cambodia: Conversations with Peang Sophi.* Melbourne: Monash University Centre of Southeast Asian Studies Working Papers.

Charny, Israel W. 1994 "Toward a Generic Definition of Genocide." In *Genocide: Conceptual and Historical Dimensions.* George J. Andreopoulos, ed. pp. 64–94. Philadelphia: University of Pennsylvania Press.

Connor, John W. 1989 "From Ghost Dance to Death Camps: Nazi Germany as a Crisis Cult." *Ethos* 17:259–88.

Coronil, Fernando, and Julie Skurski 1991 "Dismembering and Remembering the Nation: The Semantics of Political Violence in Venezuela." *Comparative Studies in Society and History* 33(2):288–337.

Criddle, Joan D., and Teeda Butt Mam 1987 *To Destroy You Is No Loss: The Odyssey of a Cambodian Family.* New York: Anchor Books.

D'Andrade, Roy, and Claudia Strauss, eds. 1992 *Human Motives and Cultural Models.* New York: Cambridge University Press.

Daniel, E. Valentine 1996 *Charred Lullabies: Chapters in an Anthropography of Violence.* Princeton, NJ: Princeton University Press.

Das, Veena, ed. 1990 *Mirrors of Violence: Communities, Riots, and Survivors in South Asia.* Delhi: Oxford University Press.

Delvert, Jean 1961 *Le Paysan Cambodgien.* Paris: Mouton.

Denich, Bette 1994 "Dismembering Yugoslavia: National Ideologies and the Symbolic Revival of Genocide." *American Ethnologist* 21: 367–90.

Desjarlais, Robert, and Arthur Kleinman 1994 "Violence and Demoralization in the New World Order." *Anthropology Today* 10(5):9–12.

De Waal, Alex 1994 "Genocide in Rwanda." *Anthropology Today* 10(3):1–2.

Dumont, Louis 1986 *Essays on Individualism: Modern Ideology in Anthropological Perspective.* Chicago: University of Chicago Press.

Ebihara, May Mayko 1968 "Svay, A Khmer Village in Cambodia." Ph.D. dissertation, Columbia University. Ann Arbor, MI: University Microfilms.

— 1990 "Revolution and Reformulation in Kampuchean Village Culture." In *The Cambodian Agony.* David A. Ablin and Marlowe Hood, eds. pp. 16–61. Armonk, NY: M. E. Sharpe.

— 1993 "A Cambodian Village under the Khmer Rouge, 1975–1979." In *Genocide and Democracy in Cambodia: The Khmer Rouge, the United Nations, and the International Community.* Ben Kiernan, ed. pp. 51–63. New Haven, CT: Yale University Southeast Asia Studies.

FBIS (Foreign Broadcast Information Service) 1976 *Asia and Pacific Report.* Springfield, VA: U.S. Department of Commerce. January 1: H1.

— 1977 *Asia and Pacific Report.* Springfield, VA: U.S. Department of Commerce. October 4: H25.

Fein, Helen 1990 "Genocide: A Sociological Perspective." *Current Sociology* 38(1):1–126.

— 1993 "Revolutionary and Antirevolutionary Genocides: A Comparison of State Murders in Democratic Kampuchea, 1975 to 1979, and in Indonesia, 1965 to 1966." *Comparative Studies in Society and History* 35:796–823.

Feldman, Allen 1991 *Formations of Violence: The Narrative of the Body and Political Terror in Northern Ireland*. Chicago: University of Chicago Press.

Fisher-Nguyen, Karen 1994 "Khmer Proverbs: Images and Rules." In *Cambodian Culture since 1975: Homeland and Exile*. May M. Ebihara, Carol A. Mortland, and Judy Ledgerwood, eds. pp. 91–104. Ithaca, NY: Cornell University Press.

Foucault, Michel 1979 *Discipline and Punish: The Birth of the Prison*. Alan Sheridan, trans. New York: Vintage.

— 1980 *The History of Sexuality, Volume 1: An Introduction*. Robert Hurley, trans. New York: Vintage.

Frieson, Kate G. 1991 "The Impact of Revolution on Cambodian Peasants: 1970–1975." Ph.D. dissertation, Monash University, Australia. Ann Arbor, MI: University Microfilms.

Gajek, Esther 1990 "Christmas under the Third Reich." *Anthropology Today* 6(4):3–9.

Giddens, Anthony 1984 *The Constitution of Society: Outline of the Theory of Structuration*. Berkeley: University of California Press.

Goldhagen, Daniel Jonah 1996 *Hitler's Willing Executioners: Ordinary Germans and the Holocaust*. New York: Alfred A. Knopf.

Hawk, David 1988 "The Cambodian Genocide." In *Genocide: A Critical Bibliographic Review*. Israel Charny, ed. pp. 137–54. New York: Facts on File.

— 1990 "International Human Rights Law and Democratic Kampuchea." In *The Cambodian Agony*. David A. Ablin and Marlowe Hood, eds., pp. 118–45. Armonk, NY: M. E. Sharpe.

Hayden, Robert M. 1996 'Imagined Communities and Real Victims: Self-Determination and Ethnic Cleansing in Yugoslavia." *American Ethnologist* 23:783–801.

Headley, Robert K., Jr., *et al.* 1977 *Cambodian–English Dictionary,* vols. 1 and 2. Washington, DC: Catholic University of America Press.

Hinton, Alexander Laban 1996 "Agents of Death: Explaining the Cambodian Genocide in Terms of Psychosocial Dissonance." *American Anthropologist* 98:818–31.

— 1997 "Cambodia's Shadow: An Examination of the Cultural Origins of Genocide." Ph.D. dissertation, Emory University. Ann Arbor: University Microfilms.

Jackson, Karl D. 1989 "The Ideology of Revolution." In *Cambodia 1975–1978: Rendezvous with Death*. Karl D. Jackson, ed., pp. 37–78. Princeton, NJ: Princeton University Press.

Jell-Bahlsen, Sabine 1985 "Ethnology and Fascism in Germany." Dialectical Anthropology 9:313–35.

Kapferer, Bruce 1988 *Legends of People, Myths of State: Violence, Intolerance, and Political Culture in Sri Lanka and Australia*. Washington, DC: Smithsonian Institution Press.

Kiernan, Ben 1985 *How Pol Pot Came to Power: A History of Communism in Kampuchea, 1930–1975*. London: Verso.

— 1986 "Kampuchea's Ethnic Chinese under Pol Pot: A Case of Systematic Social Discrimination." *Journal of Contemporary Asia* 16(1):18.

— 1988 "Orphans of Genocide: The Cham Muslims of Kampuchea under Pol Pot." *Bulletin of Concerned Asian Scholars* 20(4):2–33.

— 1996 *The Pol Pot Regime: Race, Power, and Genocide in Cambodia under the Khmer Rouge, 1975–79*. New Haven, CT: Yale University Press.

Kiernan, Ben, ed. 1993 *Genocide and Democracy in Cambodia: The Khmer Rouge, the United Nations, and the International Community*. Monograph Series 41. New Haven, CT: Yale University Southeast Asian Studies.

Kiernan, Ben, and Chanthou Boua, eds. 1982 *Peasants and Politics in Kampuchea, 1942–1981*. Armonk, NY: M. E. Sharpe.

Kuper, Leo 1981 *Genocide: Its Political Use in the Twentieth Century*. New Haven, CT: Yale University Press.

Lan, David 1985 *Guns and Rain: Guerrillas and Spirit Mediums in Zimbabwe*. Berkeley: University of California Press.

Lebra, Takie Sugiyama 1976 *Japanese Patterns of Behavior*. Honolulu: University of Hawaii Press.

Levy, Marc 1988 "Tales of Cambodia's Latest 'Killing Field.'" *Camnews* 1(634.3):June 8.

Lewin, Carroll McC. 1992 "The Holocaust: Anthropological Possibilities and the Dilemma of Representation." *American Anthropologist* 94:161–6.

— 1993 "Negotiated Selves in the Holocaust." *Ethos* 21:295–318.

Malkki, Liisa H. 1995 *Purity and Exile: Violence, Memory, and National Cosmology among Hutu Refugees in Tanzania*. Chicago: University of Chicago Press.

— 1996 "Speechless Emissaries: Refugees, Humanitarianism, and Dehistoricization." *Cultural Anthropology* 11:377–404.

Mang Channo 1995 "The Stones Being Thrown at Christians." *Phnom Penh Post*, March 10:17.

Marston, John 1985 "Language Reform in Democratic Kampuchea." M.A. thesis, University of Minnesota.

— 1994 "Metaphors of the Khmer Rouge." In *Cambodian Culture since 1975: Homeland and Exile*. May M. Ebihara, Carol A. Mortland, and Judy Ledgerwood, eds., pp. 105–18. Ithaca, NY: Cornell University Press.

Martin, Marie Alexandrine 1994 *Cambodia: A Shattered Society*. Mark W. McLeod, trans. Berkeley: University of California Press.

May, Someth 1986 *Cambodian Witness: The Autobiography of Someth May*. New York: Random House.

Moore, Barrington, Jr. 1966 *Social Origins of Dictatorship and Democracy: Lord and Peasant in the Making of the Modern World*. Boston: Beacon.

Moyer, Nancy 1991 *Escape from the Killing Fields: One Girl Who Survived the Cambodian Holocust*. Grand Rapids, MI: Zondervan.

Nagengast, Carole 1994 "Violence, Terror, and the Crisis of the State." *Annual Review of Anthropology* 23:109–36.

Ngor, Haing 1987 *A Cambodian Odyssey*. New York: Macmillan.

Nordstrom, Carolyn 1997 *A Different Kind of War Story*. Philadelphia: University of Pennsylvania Press.

Nordstrom, Carolyn, and JoAnn Martin, eds. 1992 *The Paths to Domination, Resistance, and Terror*. Berkeley: University of California Press.

Nordstrom, Carolyn, and Antonius C. G. M. Robben, eds. 1995 *Fieldwork under Fire: Contemporary Studies of Violence and Survival*. Berkeley: University of California Press.

Phnom Penh Post 1994 "They Said It … The Movers and Shakers." December 30:21.

Picq. Laurence 1989 *Beyond the Horizon: Five Years with the Khmer Rouge*. New York: St. Martin's Press.

Popkin, Samuel 1979 *The Rational Peasant: The Political Economy of Rural Society in Vietnam*. Berkeley: University of California Press.

Quinn, Kenneth M. 1976 "Political Change in Wartime: The Khmer Krahom Revolution in Southern Cambodia, 1970–1974." *U.S. Naval War College Review* (Spring):3–31.

Quinn Naomi, and Dorothy Holland 1987 "Culture and Cognition." In *Cultural Models in Language and Thought*. Dorothy Holland and Naomi Quinn, eds. pp. 3–40. New York: Cambridge University Press.

Riches, David, ed. 1986 *The Anthropology of Violence*. New York: Basil Blackwell.

Robben, Antonius C. G. M. 1996 "Ethnographic Seduction, Transference, and Resistance in Dialogue about Terror and Violence in Argentina." *Ethos* 24:71–106.

Sâthor Mok 1986 *Tum Teav*. Paris: Centre de Documentation et de Recherche sur la Civilisation Khmere.

Scott, James C. 1976 *The Moral Economy of the Peasant: Rebellion and Subsistence in Southeast Asia*. New Haven, CT: Yale University Press.

Shawcross, William 1987 *Sideshow: Kissinger, Nixon and the Destruction of Cambodia*. New York: Simon and Schuster.

Shiloh, Ailon 1975 "Psychological Anthropology: A Case Study in Culture Blindness?" *Current Anthropology* 16:618–20.

Shore, Bradd 1996 *Culture in Mind: Cognition, Culture, and the Problem of Meaning*. New York: Oxford University Press.

Skocpol, Theda 1979 *States and Social Revolutions: A Comparative Analysis of France, Russia, and China*. New York: Cambridge University Press.

Sluka, Jeffrey A 1989 *Hearts and Minds, Water and Fish: Support for the IRA and INLA in a Northern Irish Ghetto*. Greenwich, CT: JAI Press.

Soth Polin 1980 "Pol Pot's Diabolical Sweetness." Index on Censorship 5:43–5.

Stanton, Gregory H. 1993 "The Khmer Rouge and International Law." In *Genocide and Democracy in Cambodia: The Khmer Rouge, the United Nations and the International Community*. Ben Kiernan, ed. pp. 141–61. Monograph Series 41. New Haven, CT: Yale University South East Asia Studies.

Stein, Howard F. 1993 "The Holocust, the Self, and the Question of Wholeness: A Response to Lewin." *Ethos* 21:485–512.

Strauss, Claudia, and Naomi Quinn 1994 "A Cognitive/Cultural Anthropology." In *Assessing Cultural Anthropology*. Robert Borofsky, ed., pp. 297–312. New York: McGraw-Hill.

Stuart-Fox, Martin 1985 *The Murderous Revolution: Life and Death in Pol Pot's Kampuchea Based on the Personal Experiences of Bunheang Ung*. Chippendale, Australia: Alternative Publishing Cooperative.

Suárez-Orozco, Marcelo M. 1990 "Speaking of the Unspeakable: Toward a Psychosocial Understanding of Responses to Terror." *Ethos* 18: 353–83.

Szymusiak, Molyda 1986 *The Stones Cry Out: A Cambodian Childhood, 1975–1980*. Linda Coverdale, trans. New York: Hill and Wang.

Tambiah, Stanley Jeyaraja 1986 *Sri Lanka: Ethnic Fratricide and the Dismantling of Democracy*. Chicago: University of Chicago Press.

— 1989 "Ethnic Conflict in the World Today." *American Ethnologist* 16:335–49.

— 1992 *Buddhism Betrayed?: Religion, Politics, and Violence in Sri Lanka*. Chicago: University of Chicago Press.

— 1996 *Leveling Crowds: Ethnonationalist Conflicts and Collective Violence in South Asia*. Berkeley: University of California Press.

Taussig, Michael 1987 *Shamanism, Colonialism, and the Wild Man: A Study in Terror and Healing.* Chicago: University of Chicago Press.

Thaxton, Ralph 1983 *China Turned Rightside Up: Revolutionary Legitimacy in the Peasant World.* New Haven, CT: Yale University Press.

Thion, Serge 1993 *Watching Cambodia: Ten Paths to Enter the Cambodian Tangle.* Bangkok: White Lotus.

Vickery, Michael 1984 *Cambodia 1975–1982.* Boston: South End Press.

Warren, Kay B., ed. 1993 *The Violence Within: Cultural and Political Opposition in Divided Nations.* Boulder, CO: Westview.

Wikan, Unni 1990 *Managing Turbulent Hearts: A Balinese Formula for Living.* Chicago: University of Chicago Press.

Williams, Raymond 1977 *Marxism and Literature.* Oxford: Oxford University Press.

Wolf, Eric R. 1969 *Peasant Wars of the Twentieth Century.* New York: Harper and Row.

Yathay, Pin 1987 *Stay Alive, My Son.* New York: Simon and Schuster.

10
Dirty Protest: Symbolic Overdetermination and Gender in Northern Ireland Ethnic Violence

Begoña Aretxaga

Introduction

In a personal interview a man arrested for Irish Republican Army (IRA) activity described a prison scene of the late 1970s that became known as the Dirty Protest. He recalled the first contact with his comrades – already immersed in the protest – shortly upon arrival to Long-Kesh prison:

> We went to Mass – it was Sunday. Afterwards I walk into the canteen and if you can imagine this yourself ... there were about 150 people in the canteen and all that they were wearing was trousers. Other than that they were naked, and had nothing on their feet. They had matted long beards and long hair, and they were stinking, really filthy ... can you imagine? I walked in there and I said to myself, "They are all mad!" Everybody had big staring eyes, and they were all talking fast, firing questions and very nervous ... you know, all this. And I was seeing fellows in the canteen I had known outside [prison] and they were all just ribs, very thin. I thought they were really crazy ... mad. I was really taken aback.

From 1978 to 1981 IRA and Irish National Liberation Army (INLA) male prisoners in Northern Ireland undertook an extraordinary form of protest against prison authorities and the British government. They refused to leave their cells either to wash or to use the toilets, living instead in the midst of their own dirt and body waste. In 1980 they were joined by their female comrades, thus adding menstrual blood to the horrendous excretal imagery of the protest. Unlike the hunger strike on which the prisoners would embark in 1981, the Dirty Protest

Ethos 23(2): 123–48. Copyright © 1995, American Anthropological Association.

had no precedent in the existing political culture. This action, which resonated with notions of savagery, irrationality, and madness, was shocking and largely incomprehensible to the public in Ireland and Britain. Not only did relatives and supporters of the prisoners admit this popular incomprehensibility, but the main newspapers treated the protest as "a bizarre and foul exercise," to use the not uncommon words of the English *Times*. The striking form of this political action, coupled on the one hand with the strong emotional reactions that it provoked and on the other with its genderized character, makes the Dirty Protest a particularly suitable case for the exploration of how subjectivity, gender, and power are articulated in situations of heightened political violence.

Bodily violence has been extensively theorized as a disciplinary mechanism (Asad 1983; Feldman 1991; Foucault 1979; Scarry 1985). In *Discipline and Punish* Foucault powerfully analyzed punishment as a political technology of the body aimed at the production of submissive subjects. In the modern prison discipline and punishment are directed at the subjective transformation of individuals from dangerous criminals to docile citizens. In Foucault's analysis the body ceases to be the repository of signs to become the material through which subjectivities are molded (1979:23). What Foucault has not addressed are the points at which the technology of normalization breaks down, the moments in which rational disciplines of the body fail to produce docile subjects, either because the subjects refuse to be normalized, even at the cost of death, or because the exercise of punishment indulges in an excess that betrays its rational aims; becoming a drama of its own rather than merely a political tactic, as recent work has well shown (Graziano 1992; Obeyesekere 1992; Suarez-Orozco 1992; Taussig 1987).

In his extensive study of the Dirty Protest, Allen Feldman (1991) has criticized the unidirectionality of Foucault's analysis. For Feldman, the prisoners themselves instrumentalized their bodies against the technologies of domination first applied to them. Feldman's critique of Foucault remains, however, inside the Foucaudian paradigm. In his analysis the body continues to be an artifact, an instrument subject to political technologies managed now by both the prisoners and the guards. Feldman, like Foucault, belies the question of subjectivity. Disciplines of the body are permeated by an emotional dynamic that includes powerful feelings of fear, desire, and hate that are crucial to the political operativity of the body. This emotional dynamic is entangled in cultural forms such as myth, religious images, stories, and the like. It is not only a product of the disciplines of the body used in the prison; it also plays an important part in the excess of violence characterizing those disciplines. Carceral violence has been used against political prisoners all over the world, including Ireland, yet there is no other case in which prisoners resisted with something like the Dirty Protest. The excreta and menstrual blood that characterized the protest exposes an excess of meaning that reveals the very character of violence as an intersubjective relation that must necessarily be interpreted. This interpretative approach does not negate, however, Foucault's important understanding of the body as political field. Instead, it invests such political field (the body) with the intersubjective dynamic through which power takes place. For Lacan (1977:50–2), subjectivity is always grounded in history – a history that includes the scars left by forgotten episodes and hidden discourses as much as conscious narratives.

The Dirty Protest is a good case for an approach that combines a Foucaudian critique of power with an interpretative anthropology sensitive to the "deep play" of subjectivity. To develop this analysis I conceptualized the feces and menstrual blood that characterized the Dirty Protest not as artifacts but as overdetermined primordial symbols. I do not mean by *primordial* an ontological essence. I use *primordial symbols* here for lack of a better word to refer to those symbols that resort to physiological material of great psychological significance and that are elaborated in one form or another in all cultures. Following Sapir, Victor Turner (1967) called them "condensation symbols," Mary Douglas (1966), "natural symbols." I mean overdetermination in the Freudian sense of the term, as the condensation of different strands of meaning, none of which are in themselves necessarily determinant. Obeyesekere has noted that the power of symbols is derived from their capacity to tap into diverse areas of experience (1990:280). The prisoners' excreta and menstrual blood tap into the interconnected domains of prison violence, colonial history, unconscious motivation, and gender discourses.

Resisting normalization

With the escalation of the political crisis that followed the riots of 1969 in Northern Ireland, large numbers of people in the working-class Catholic communities of Belfast were arrested. Most of them were accused of crimes against the state, a general label that included a wide variety of actions ranging from the wearing of combat jackets to participation in demonstrations to the use of firearms. After a hunger strike in 1972, the British government agreed to give the prisoners "special category" status, regarding them as de facto political prisoners. These included members of Irish paramilitary organizations, both Republican and Loyalist.[1]

In 1976 the British government, as part of a more general counter-insurgency operation, withdrew "special category" status from Republican and Loyalist prisoners, who were then to be considered and treated as ODCs (Ordinary Decent Criminals), in British legal parlance. This entailed the use of prison uniforms instead of personal clothes and the cancellation of rights of association, internal organization, and free disposal of time. Republican prisoners resisted government regulations by refusing to wear the prison uniforms. Since other clothes were lacking, the prisoners covered themselves with blankets. The prison administration penalized their insubordination with an array of disciplinary measures: 24-hour cell confinement, inadequate food, lack of exercise and intellectual stimulation, curtailment of visits, frequent beatings, and recurrent body and cell searches. The prisoners (three-quarters of whom were between the ages of seventeen and twenty-one) left their cells only for trips to the toilet, weekly showers, Sunday mass, and monthly visits. Physiological necessities such as food and excretory functions became a focus of humiliating practises. The already inadequate diet was frequently spoiled with defiling substances such as spit, urine, roaches, or maggots. Access to the toilet was controlled by the permission of guards who would delay or deny it at will. After a year of this situation the prison administration forbade wearing blankets outside the cells. Prisoners had to leave their cells naked on their way to toilets and showers. Harassment increased at these times, leaving prisoners especially vulnerable to beatings, guards' mockery and sexual insults, as well as the hated body searches. These were described to me by an IRA ex-prisoner:

> They made you squat on the floor on your haunches. You wouldn't do that so they beat you, they sat over you and probed your back passage, and then with the same finger some would search your mouth, your nose, your hair, your beard, every part of your body, there was nothing private about your body.

According to prisoners, it was the increased harassment and heightened violence accompanying the use of toilets that sparked the Dirty Protest in 1978. In a co-ordinated action, prisoners refused to leave their cells except to go to mass and visits. At first they emptied the chamber pots through windows and peepholes of the doors. When the guards boarded them up prisoners began to dispose of feces by leaving them in a corner of their cells. This, however, allowed the guards to mess the mattresses and blankets of prisoners with the feces during cell-searches. Finally, prisoners began to smear their excreta on the walls of their cells.

In 1980 the Republican women in Armagh prison joined their male comrades in the Dirty Protest. They had also been resisting the changes of status from political prisoners to criminals since 1976 by refusing to do mandatory prison work and were also enduring similar disciplinary measures. But in contrast to the male prisoners in Long-Kesh, Republican women were allowed to use their own clothes – as were all female prisoners in Britain. Although harassment and tension had been rising inside the jail, what prompted women into the Dirty Protest was not humiliation accompanying use of the toilets but an assault by male officers – the second of its kind – followed by two days' lock-up in their cells. What justified this assault was the search of "subversive garments." If in Long-Kesh male prisoners spurned the prison uniform to assert their political identity, in a similar metonymic move Armagh women used their clothes to improvise IRA uniforms. It was in search of those small pieces of apparel – berets, black skirts; trivial in themselves yet full of significance in the encoded world of the prison – that military men in full riot gear entered the cells of IRA prisoners on February 7, 1980, kicking and punching the women. The following quote from a report smuggled out of jail by one of the prisoners illustrates the sexual overtones of the assault:

At around 3:45pm on Thursday Feb. 7th, numerous male and female screws [guards] invaded my cell in order to get me down to the governor. They charged in full riot gear equipped with shields. I sat unprotected but aware of what was going to happen as I had heard my comrades screaming in pain. I was suddenly pinned to the bed by a shield and the weight of a male screw on top of me. Then my shoes were dragged off my feet. I was bodily assaulted, thumped, trailed and kicked. I was then trailed out of my cell, and during the course of my being dragged and hauled from the wing both my breasts were exposed to the jeering and mocking eyes of all the screws, there must have been about twenty of them. While being carried, I was also abused with punches to the back of my head and my stomach. I was eventually carried into the governor, my breasts were still exposed. While I was held by the screws the governor carried out the adjudication, and I was then trailed back and thrown into a cell.[2]

Sexual harassment by state forces has been a systematic complaint during the last twenty years that reappears in informal conversations with women as well as in their narratives of encounters with security forces.[3] For the prisoners, the assault was as much a political attempt to discipline through punishment as a humiliating assertion of male dominance. Moreover, at the time of the assault, there was a lot of pain, grief, and anger among women prisoners. In addition to health problems and increasing petty harassment, a high percentage of women lost close relatives in shootings by Loyalist paramilitaries or the British army during their time in jail. The devastating emotions of mourning were repressed to preserve collective morale and inner strength as well as to avoid special targeting from guards. The assault and enforced lock-up in the cells provoked a strong response. Shortly after the beginning of the protest, Mairead Farrell, leader of the women prisoners, described their situation in a letter smuggled out of jail:

> The stench of urine and excrement clings to the cells and our bodies. No longer can we empty the pots of urine and excrement out the window, as the male screws [guards] have boarded them up. Little light or air penetrates the thick boarding. The electric light has to be kept constantly on in the cells; the other option is to sit in the dark. Regardless of day or night, the cells are dark. Now we can't even see out the window; our only view is the wall of excreta. The spy holes are locked so they can only be opened by the screws to look in. Sanitary towels are thrown into us without wrapping. We are not permitted paper bags or such like so they lie in the dirt until used. For twenty-three hours a day we lie in these cells.[4]

The Dirty Protest was by any standard of political culture, and certainly by that of Ireland, an unusual political action. The British national press, upon visiting Long-Kesh for the first time, called it "the most bizarre protest by prisoners in revolt against their goalers" and "self-inflicted degradation" (*Guardian* and *Daily Telegraph*, March 16, 1979). It was as incomprehensible to the general public as it was to prison officers and government administration. In the Catholic communities, massive support for the prisoners was not reached, for instance, until the end of the Dirty Protest and the beginning of the hunger strike. The Dirty Protest provoked an inexpressible horror and a rising spiral of violence inside and outside the jails. If the men's Dirty Protest was incomprehensible, the women's was unthinkable, generating in many men, even among the ranks of supporting Republicans, reactions of denial. It was no doubt a form of warfare, a violent contest of power, as Feldman (1991) has noted. But why this form and not another?

Humiliation and violence: the deep play of subjectivity

Feces are a primordial symbol of revulsion as well as a primary mechanism of aggression and the assertion of will to power. As we know from Freud, they become especially significant in childhood, during the period of sphincter training; an early systematic discipline applied on the body and a crucial step in socialization. The disciplines and ritual punishments enacted in jail are deliberately aimed at socializing the prisoners into the new social order of the prison. To that end the identity of the prisoner as a political militant had to be destroyed. The random beatings, scarce diet, constant visibility, body searches, and denial of control over their excretory functions were directed at defeating the will of autonomous individuals and transforming them into dependent infantilized subjects through physical pain and humiliating practises. This divestment of individual identity is, in more or less drastic forms, characteristic of what Goffman (1959) called "total institutions." Once the power battle was displaced to the psychological arena of childhood and the prisoners were left in a state of absolute powerlessness with nothing but their bodies to resist institutional assault, they resorted to the primordial mechanism of feces, at once a weapon and a symbol of utter rejection. Thus, an ex-prison officer admitted to anthropologist Allen Feldman that "[h]umiliation was a big weapon. Prisoners were constantly propelled into an infantile role. You could see the Dirty Protest as virtually resistance to toilet training in a bizarre way" (Feldman 1991:192). That is to say, the Dirty Protest can be interpreted as simultaneously literal and symbolic resistance to prison socialization and the accompanying moral system that legitimized it. Feldman has suggested that the prisoners carried out this resistance by utilizing the excretory function as a detached weapon (1991:178). The use of excreta as a weapon of resistance was not, however, the only bodily weapon available to the prisoners. The hunger strike, to which the prisoners resorted later on, was a more likely and socially understandable form of political resistance. Neither was the Dirty Protest very effective in attracting international sympathy. Amnesty International, for example, concluded upon examination of the case that the prisoners' conditions were self-inflicted.[5] Any socialization process implies an emotional dynamic that Feldman does not analyze. After a year of close contact an IRA male ex-prisoner openly admitted the turmoil of emotions provoked by our lengthy conversation on the Dirty Protest:

> I feel funny now, my emotions are mixed. You suffer a lot in jail, some people more than others. Some people remember the good things about jail, the laughs. You don't want to remember the times you felt like crying ... It was just strange. You are on your own, you worry sick no matter how much you laugh or share, you have irrational fears. People cry in jail. A lot of strange things happen to you.

I would like to suggest that far from being a detached weapon, the Dirty Protest entailed a deep personal involvement, a process that was tremendously painful psychologically and physically.

Physical pain, insufficient diet, and constant humiliation evoked in the prisoners, in acute and extreme form, the vulnerability and powerlessness of childhood. The sense of permanent physical insecurity produced, as is frequently the case in these situations, anxieties about disfigurement (Goffman 1959:21; Scarry 1985:40–1). Fantasies of dismemberment, dislocation, and mutilation accompanied any venture outside the cells and were particularly present during body searches, forced baths, and wing shifts.[6] In a personal interview, an IRA ex-prisoner recalled the terror experienced at being suspended in the air held spread-eagled by four officers who were pulling his arms and legs during a body search while another inspected his anus: "It was very, very frightening because there were times when you thought you were going to tear apart." Forced baths entailed heavy scrubbing with rough brushes that left the body bruised and scarred. They also involved forced shaving of beard and hair with the frequent result of skin cuts. Not only physical pain but the images of mutilation triggered by the hostility of warders made the baths terrifying experiences:

> They used scrubbing brushes to wash you. The whole thing was very violent, a terrifying experience. After they finished they dragged me to the sink and one cut my head with a razor and they cut my head in a whole lot of places while all the time they were making fun of me. Then they threw me to the floor, spread eagle. I had massive dark bruises all over my ribs and they painted them with a white stuff, I don't know what it was and they painted my face too.

The terror was augmented by the association of cleaning and death in other contexts. For example, another ex-prisoner of the same affiliation commented, apropos of the situation: "It just reminded me of the Jews in the concentration camps because every man in the [visiting] room was bald and we were all very thin and frightened" (see also Feldman 1991).

The prison dynamic of punishment and humiliation fueled feelings of hate and anger that threatened to overcome the psychological integrity of the prisoners. The following quotes from two prisoners interviewed by Feldman illustrate best the force of these feelings:

I hated the screws [prison officers]. I used to live for the day that I got out. I would have taken three days before I killed a screw. I was wrapped up in the hatred thing and it wasn't political motivation at all. (1991:196–7)

The hate, I found out what hatred was. I used to talk about hate on the outside, but it was superstitious, it was depersonalized. There were wee people you didn't like. But it was in jail that I came face to face with the naked hatred. It frightened the life out of me when I saw it for what it was. When you thought of getting your own back on the screw, how much you would enjoy it, it really frightened you. You just blacked those thoughts out of your mind. At the end of the day I knew I was smarter than the screws. But I knew the road of black hatred. I just got a glimpse of it. It scared the balls clean out of me. (1991:197)

The Dirty Protest was simultaneously a sign of rejection and an instrument of power, but one that constituted also the symbolic articulation of dangerous feelings that could not be expressed in other forms without risking madness or serious physical injury. The feces constituted not so much the instrument of a mimetic violence, as Feldman has suggested, but the crystallization of a conflict between the desire of mimetic violence against prison officers and the need for restraint to preserve some physical and psychological integrity. In this sense, the feces appear as a compromise formation, a symptom in the Freudian sense of the term. However, unlike the hysterical symptom, the Dirty Protest had conscious meaning and political intentionally for the prisoners. Its significance was elaborated by them in the idiom of Republican resistance, which is part of Northern Ireland's nationalist culture. The prisoners' political beliefs arise out of a shared social experience of the working-class ghettos and are essential to the protest in that they provide its rationale and moral legitimation, as the ethnographies of Burton (1978) and Sluka (1989) have well shown. In other words, the prisoners knew why they were smearing their cells with excrement and under which conditions they would cease to do so. They were also aware that their political language made sense to an audience outside the jail, even when their action remained largely uncomprehended. Thus, if we consider the Dirty Protest as an emotionally loaded compromise formation meaningful to the actors yet not to the larger society, we can read it as a symptom of profound alienation midway between the elusive hysterical symptom and the graspable cultural symbol. Here is where Obeyesekere's concept of personal symbols (1981,1990) becomes useful. Obeyesekere has defined personal symbols as symbols that have meaning at the personal and cultural levels. Yet while Obeyesekere's personal symbols arise out of unconscious motivation, the feces as symptom-symbol arise out of a situation of violent political conflict capable of triggering powerful unconscious associations. Republican consciousness, then, is crucial in understanding the experience of the Dirty Protest, yet it does not exhaust it. To understand the Dirty Protest we need to look beyond what is experienced "subjectively" by the individuals (Lacan 1977:55; Scott 1991). This requires a deeper probing into the kind of relation in which prisoners and guards were engaged and the larger discourses in which such relation was embedded.

The prison experience since 1976 evoked for Republicans in extreme form the historical experience of neglect and the desire for social recognition that characterized the lives of working-class Catholics in Northern Ireland. The claim to political status was so important to them precisely because it implied a deep existential recognition, the acknowledgement that one's being-in-the-world mattered. Recognition can only come from an "other." At the closest level the significant "other" was represented by the Loyalist guards with whom prisoners interacted daily. Although in terms of profession the guards occupied the lower ranks of the social structure, as Protestants they occupied a position of social superiority vis-à-vis Catholics. Thus, the relation between prisoners and guards was mediated by a relation of social inequality larger and historically more significant than that existing in the prison universe. At a more removed level, however, the position of the "other" was occupied by the British government, which became the embodiment of the "Law of the Father." Britain became the absent presence whose law threatened to erase the prisoners by eliminating their political identity. The desire of recognition from Britain was implicit in the prisoners' and supporters' representation of the protest as a battle between Ireland and Britain. The prison disciplines, with their uniformity, the substitution of names for numbers, and extreme forms of humiliation, constituted an ultimate form of erasure.

If existential recognition was essential to the prisoners – literally a matter of life and death – the Dirty Protest must be understood as a violent attempt to force such recognition without succumbing to physical elimination, which could ultimately happen – as it did happen in 1981 – with a hunger strike. In this context, which links prison power relations with larger social-political arenas, the feces of the Dirty Protest tap into a whole new domain of meaning. They are not just a symbolic and material weapon against the prison regime, and a symptom of the alienation of the prisoners qua prisoners, but also a social symptom that must be understood in historical perspective.

The symptom appears initially as a trace, as a return of a repressed history. In the words of Slavoj Zizek, "[I]n working through the symptom we are precisely bringing about the past, producing the symbolic reality of the past" (1989:57). In the case of the Dirty Protest what we have is the re-elaboration of Anglo–Irish history. The excreta on the walls of the cells made visible the hidden history of prison violence; furthermore, it appeared to the world as a record of Irish history. The Catholic Primate of Ireland, Archbishop Tomas O'Fiaich, upon visiting the Long-Kesh jail, declared publicly that the situation of the prisoners was inhuman. He denounced the inflexibility of the British government that was violating the personal dignity of the prisoners and voiced concern about beatings and ill-treatment of the prisoners (*Times* and *Guardian,* August 2, 1978). Archbishop O'Fiaich's press declaration unleashed a polemic storm. The British government emphatically denied any liability for the protest as well as any mistreatment of the prisoners: "These criminals are totally responsible for the situation in which they find themselves .... There is no truth in those allegations [of mistreatment]" (*Times*, August 2, 1978).While unionist and conservative parties accused O'Fiaich of IRA sympathy (*Times*, August 3, 1978), Nationalist parties supported the Archbishop's concern. The Presbyterian church, on the other hand, attacked O'Fiaich for his "grave moral confusion" (*Guardian* and *Times*, August 5, 1978). The prison violence came to occupy an important place in public political discussions in Ireland and England, attracting also the attention of the international media. The connection between prison and colonial violence was drawn during the years of the Dirty Protest not only by the prisoners and their Republican supporters. The *Washington Post* compared the inflexibility of the British government with the "iron-fisted rule of Oliver Cromwell" (quoted in the *Times*, November 22, 1978).

Even the European Court of Human Rights, while ruling that the prisoners were not entitled to political status, expressed its concern "at the inflexible approach of the State authorities which has been concerned more to punish offenders against prison discipline than to explore ways of resolving such a serious deadlock" (European Law Centre 1981:201).

The rigidity of the British government, which held onto the banner of "The Law" with an intransigence highly evocative of paternal authority, as well as the refusal by prison officers to acknowledge any responsibility in the emergence of the Dirty Protest echoed the historical denial of British responsibility in the dynamics of violence in Ireland.

Historical amnesia, though common enough, is never trivial or accidental (De Certeau 1988). Such emphatic negation of any relation to the dirty prisoners, coupled with the inability to end the protest, reveals perhaps a stumbling block in the history of Britain and Ireland that remains to be explained. In this context the power of feces as a symptom of the political (dis)order of Northern Ireland may lie not so much in what it signified, but precisely in that which resisted symbolization: its capacity to tap into unconscious fears, desires, and fantasies that had come to form part of ethnic violence in Ireland through a colonial discourse of dirtiness. This discourse provided yet another arena, or another field of power, if you will, in which the Dirty Protest acquired a new set of cultural resonances appearing as a materialization of the buried "shit" of British colonization, a de-metaphorization of the "savage, dirty Irish."

Excrement and the fiction of civilization

Dirtiness has been a metaphor of barbarism in British anti-Irish discourse for centuries. From Elizabethan writings to Victorian accounts of Ireland there have been recurrent descriptions of the dirtiness, misery, and primitiveness of the country and its people. "Irish" and "primitive" soon implicated each other, and the image of the dirty, primitive Irish became familiar to the English imagination through jokes, cartoons, and other popular forms of representation. Such images have proliferated at times of political turmoil in Ireland, with the Irish frequently depicted with simian or pig-like features (Curtis 1971; Darby 1983). After the partition of Ireland, "dirty" continued to be a favorite epithet to debase Catholics in Northern Ireland. My Nationalist informants were acutely aware of the operativity of this discourse, and many, like this middle-aged woman, recalled growing up hearing that they were dirty: "You would hear people saying that Catholics were dirty, and live like rats, and had too many children … and you suddenly realized that was you and your family."

The investment of excrement and dirt with intense feelings of disgust, which are then associated with aggression and fear of racial contamination, is well known and need not be underscored here. Notions of dirt and purity are crucial, as Mary Douglas (1966) noted, in organizing ideas of savagery and civilization and highly significant in establishing social boundaries and cultural differentiations. For many people in England and Ireland the prisoners living amid their own excreta constituted the image par excellence of the uncivilized, the erasure of categorical distinctions that structure human society, the regression to a presocial state, with its concomitant power of pollution and contagion. In the women's prison of Armagh officers wore masks, insulating suits, and rubber boots that shielded them from the polluting conditions of the prisoners' wing. Prisoners noted that the guards did not like to touch anything belonging to the prisoners even though they used gloves. Prison officers felt defiled coming in contact with the prisoners. As the women looked increasingly dirty, the guards tried to counteract defilement by increasing their care in making themselves up and having their hair done. Similarly, in Long-Kesh physical contact with the prisoners was abhorrent for guards.

The images of the prisoners surrounded by excreta seemed to reinforce stereotypes of Irish barbarism, yet the inability of government and administrators to handle the situation reveals other effects. Thus, I would argue that the fantasies of savagery projected onto Catholics were appropriated, literalized, and enacted by the prisoners. This materialization inevitably confronted the officers in an inescapable physical form with their own aggressive fantasies, which produced shock, horror, and the futile attempt to erase them by increasing violence, forced baths, and periodic steam cleaning of cells – acts of cleansing that, like the dirtying of the prisoners, were both literal and symbolic (Feldman 1991:185). The "Dirty Irish" had became *really* shitty. In so doing they were transforming the closed universe of prison into an overflowing cloaca, exposing in the process a Boschian vision of the world, a scathing critique of Britain and, by association, of civilization. One cannot help but find a parallel of this critique in the writings of that polemic Irishman, Jonathan Swift.

Swift utilized the excretory function as a satiric weapon against the pretentiousness and self-righteousness of English civilization. His "excremental vision" (Brown 1959:179) is sharply displayed in part 4 of *Gulliver's Travels*. In "A Voyage to the Country of the Houyhnhnms," Gulliver encounters the Yahoo. Although Yahoos possess a human form, they are filthy and nasty, have a strong smell and bad eating habits, and use excrement as an instrument of self-expression and aggression (Swift 1967[1726]:270, 313). Immediately after their encounter the Yahoos shoot feces at Gulliver, who tries failingly to stay clear of them. If the Yahoo represents the archetype of human savagery, its juxtaposition with Gulliver's narrative of English life soon makes clear that the civilized human is nastier than the savage Yahoo. In other words, Swift made excremental aggression the hidden core of civilization, an insight hard to swallow.

In the context of the Anglo–Irish colonial relation in which it emerged, the Dirty Protest, like the Yahoo, acted as a mirror of colonial barbarism that reflected back to prison officers and British public an obscured image of themselves that challenged their identity as a civilized nation. This excremental image literally entered the center of gravity of British civilization when two supporters of the prisoners hurled horse dung to the startled members of Parliament (*Guardian*, July 7,1978).

Guards and government alike responded to this image with absolute denial, voiced in the argument that the "prisoners' condition was self-inflicted." Yet the guards' rising brutality reproduced on the incarcerated bodies the same barbarity attributed to the prisoners. Such mimesis seems inherent to the colonial production of reality, which frequently uses the fiction of the savage (or the terrorist) to create a culture of terror (Bhaba 1984; Taussig 1987). In Northern Ireland the fiction of criminality of Republican prisoners ultimately exposed and reproduced the savagery of state policies. Inside Long-Kesh positions had been reversed: from objects of a defiling power, the prisoners had come to be the subjects that controlled it (Feldman 1991). Yet the prisoners were inescapably locked in a political impasse characterized by a vicious cycle of projection–reflection that spilled the violence from the prison onto the wider society.[7] While the men's Dirty Protest was locked in its own violence, the women's provoked a movement of social transformation. The impulse of such transformation came from the articulation of menstrual blood as a symbol of sexual difference with ongoing feminist discourse.

Dirt and blood: the meaning of sexual difference

Inside the walls of Armagh prison filthiness was tainted with menstrual blood. An additional set of meanings resonated there. Journalist Tim Coogan, who visited the jail at that time, wrote:

I was taken to inspect "A" wing where the Dirty Protest is in full swing. This was sickening and appalling. Tissues, slops, consisting of tea and urine, some feces, and clots of blood – obviously the detritus of menstruation – lay in the corridor between the two rows of cells … I found the smell in the girls' cells far worse than at Long-Kesh, and several times found myself having to control feelings of nausea. (1980:215–16).

What can make thirty dirty women more revolting than four hundred dirty men if not the exposure of menstrual blood – an element that cannot contribute much to the fetid odors of urine and feces but can turn the stomach. What Coogan expresses with his body – it literally makes him sick – is the horror and repulsion triggered by the sight of "that" which constitutes a linguistic and optic taboo, a horror that he cannot articulate linguistically. Through his own body Coogan also inscribes a crucial difference between men and women prisoners. Ironically, it was this difference that Armagh women were trying to eradicate by joining the Dirty Protest.

Women did not belong to prison in popular consciousness, even though they had participated in armed operations and had been imprisoned in rising numbers since 1972. Most Nationalists perceived women's presence in jail as a product of an idealistic youth and the freedom from family commitments. Through the course of my fieldwork, some women ex-prisoners acknowledged that Republican men still assumed that after marriage women would abandon political activities that entail a risk of death or imprisonment. Although this frequently happens it is by no means always the case. On the other hand, the image of male prisoners did not have an age reference. Although the majority of male prisoners were young, it was not rare for them to be married and have children. In contrast to male prisoners, female prisoners were permanently thought of as girls. Their cultural space was in this sense limited. Neither men nor completely women, they were perceived at a general social level as gender neutral.

Women prisoners did not consider gender a significant element of differentiation either. Female members of the IRA had fought to be part of this organization rather than part of its feminine counterpart, Cumman na mBan. Thus, they had consciously rejected gender as a differential factor in political militancy. To prove that gender was irrelevant to military performance in a male organization de facto entailed downplaying women's difference and interiorizing men's standards. At the level of consciousness gender difference was at the beginning of the Dirty Protest completely accidental to its meaning. From the point of view of Armagh women their Dirty Protest was not different from that of the men: it was the same struggle undertaken by equal comrades for political recognition. The emphatic reassertion of the sameness of prisoners' identity regardless of gender must be understood as an attempt to counteract the overshadowing of women prisoners under the focus of attention given to male prisoners. Such an eclipse was partly a consequence of the fact that women were not required to use prison uniforms and thus were not subjected to the dramatic conditions that the men were. That fact asserted from the start a gender difference that worked against their political visibility. At this level the Dirty Protest was for Armagh women an attempt to erase that gender difference introduced by the penal institution and to thus reassert their political visibility. Yet, unintentionally, the menstrual blood brought to the surface the contradictions involved in this process, shifting the meaning of the protest. It objectified a difference that women had carefully obliterated in other dimensions of their political life. That is, while their political identity as members of the IRA entailed at one level a cultural desexualization, and the Dirty Protest a personal defeminization, at a deeper level the exposure of menstrual blood subverted this process by radically transforming the asexual bodies of "girls" into the sexualized bodies of women. In so doing, the menstrual blood became a symbol through which gender identity was reflected upon, bringing to the surface what had been otherwise erased.

Menstruation as an elemental sign of womanhood also marks women's social vulnerability. At the level of representation it is a metonym linking sex and motherhood, a sign of the dangerously uncontrolled nature of women's flesh in Catholic ideology from which only the mother of God escaped (Warner 1983); a tabooed and polluting substance that must be hidden from discourse as it is from sight. In the context of arrest it is a sabotage of the body. The meaning of this sabotage has been forcefully expressed by Northern Ireland writer and Republican ex-prisoner Brenda Murphy in a short story entitled "A Curse." An arrested young woman gets her period in between interrogation shifts and is forced to talk about it to a male officer:

> "I've taken my period" she said simply. "I need some sanitary napkins and a wash." He looked at her with disgust. "Have you no shame? I've been married twenty years and my wife wouldn't mention things like that." What is the color of shame? All she could see was red as it trickled down her legs. (1989:226–7)

When it comes to women, impotence and shame have color, not name. Mary Cardinal, in the superb fictional account of her own madness (1983), calls the permanent flow of her menstrual blood "the thing." Her cure entailed a process of inscribing meaning in language, of finding "The Words To Say It." In choosing the theme of menstruation to talk about the experience of arrest, Brenda Murphy – who participated in the Dirty Protest – broke a taboo of silence that made Nationalist women's personal and political experience invisible. One can read her story as a commentary on the Armagh Dirty Protest. Indeed, on her release Maureen Gibson, one of the protesting prisoners, said:

> I do get the impression that people outside [the prison] don't fully realize that there are actually women in Armagh. They don't understand what the women are going through both physically and psychologically. You go through a lot with your menstrual cycle. (*Republican News*, September 27,1980)

The shocking character of the imagery that the words of released prisoners evoked was recalled to me by Mary, a middle-aged Republican woman:

> I remember one rally in which a girl released from Armagh spoke about what it was for them during their periods. It was very hard for her to talk about menstruation, to say that even during that time they could not get a change of clothes, could not get washed. And some people, including Republican men, were saying "How can she talk about that?" They did not want to hear that women were being mistreated in Armagh jail during their menstruation. And so, the Republican movement did not talk about it. They only talked about the men, but they did not want to hear about girls. Some people just could not cope with that.

What the Nationalist community did not understand and could not cope with was *women's* pain. Not a mother's suffering, which ultimately roused the emotions of Nationalist people in support of the prisoners. Nor the suffering of incarcerated young men, whose image, naked and beaten, resembled that of Jesus Christ. Unintentionally, the women prisoners in Armagh brought to the fore a different kind of suffering, one systematically obscured in social life and in cultural constructions, devalued in Catholic religion and Nationalist ideologies: that women's pain of which menstruation is a sign and a symbol.

If the men's Dirty Protest represented the rejection of the civilizing mission of British colonialism, the Armagh women permeated that rejection with gender politics. At one level it encapsulated the negation of dominant models of femininity embedded in the idealized asexual Catholic mother and elaborated in Nationalist discourse around the image of Mother Ireland. This model provokes high ambivalence in many Nationalist women for whom motherhood is at once a source of comfort and support and a restrictive social role.[8] On the other hand, the women's Dirty Protest represented also a rejection of male violence fused, as noted below, with political dominance in colonial discourse and practice. In the prison context the visibility of menstrual blood can be read as a curse redirected from the bodies of women to the male "body politic" of colonialism.[9]

As symptom, symbol, and weapon, the Dirty Protest involved an enormous suffering. The young women in Armagh, like the men in Long-Kesh, conceptualized their physical and psychological pain within the parameters of a religious ethic of salvation acting in the political arena. At the level of conscious purpose it was for them a necessary requisite to save Ireland from colonization and re-establish a just and equal society in a reunited Irish land. This ethic of salvation acted as an interpretative language for pain that would otherwise be meaningless. Yet if a religious–political frame can provide meaning to the prisoners' pain, it cannot express it. Their suffering eludes language. Republican women could narrate the events of the Dirty Protest, but the emotional experience was encountered with painful silence and the explicit admission of lacking words to describe it.

For Elaine Scarry (1985), inexpressibility is what characterizes pain, which needs to be objectified in order to be comprehended. But pain does not operate in the same way for women and men. In Armagh, the prisoners' suffering became objectified in the menstrual blood, a complex symbol that inscribed their suffering inside the symbolic contours of what Gayatri Spivak has called "the space of what can only happen to a woman" (1988:184). As this space had been actively silenced in the cultural logic of nationalism, tensions were bound to arise on the different shades of the political horizon.

Mimesis or the power of transgression: the feminist debate

The feminist movement in Ireland grew bitterly divided as the Dirty Protest went on.[10] Mainstream feminists were sharply critical of the male-dominated Republican movement, whose use of violence, they argued, divided women. At the head of these feminists was the Northern Ireland Women's Rights Movement (NIWRM), a broadly defined organization founded in 1975 and very hostile to nationalism in general and Republicanism in particular. The NIWRM refused any support to Armagh prisoners on the grounds that they were aping their male comrades. Other women's groups such as the Socialist Women's Group and the Belfast Women's Collective quite literally agonized over the meaning and degree of support of the prisoners. The Republican movement, on the other hand, was not less hostile to feminism, which they easily dismissed as being pro-British. Preoccupied with the large number of male prisoners, Republicans had largely ignored the existence of women in jail, seeing them at best as an appendix to the men's protest. Was the Armagh women's protest a mimetic enactment? I think so, but one that had important political implications. Drucilla Cornell has argued that mimesis constitutes not a simple repetition but a reappropriation entailing a process of refiguration (1991:182). It is in this light that we must interpret the Armagh protest.

When the Armagh women demanded to be part of the IRA, rejecting its feminine branch, they were criticizing a genderized system that set them in the position of political subsidiaries. This critique already modified the terms of the system. Similarly, by mimetically reappropriating the Dirty Protest, the Armagh women at first negated gender difference, stating that their struggle was the same as that of the men. Yet this attempt to transcend a genderized context by negating the feminine was negated in turn by the objectification of sexual difference that the menstrual blood represented. Thus, the mimetic appropriation of the Dirty Protest entailed a process of rewriting a (hi)story of resistance, a rewriting that specified the feminine in its most transgressive form. But it also entailed a refiguration of the feminine inasmuch as it was affirmed not as a shared essence but as existentially inseparable from class and ethnic positions.

The rising tensions exploded publicly when Nell McCafferty, a journalist from Derry City, wrote in the pages of the *Irish Times,* "There is menstrual blood in the walls of Armagh prison in Northern Ireland."[11] McCafferty shouted aloud in the main Irish newspaper what most people had been refusing to hear, that there was a specific women's pain, and that in Northern Ireland it was inextricably linked, but not reduced, to colonial oppression. Such link was encapsulated in the menstrual blood as a symbol of an existence, of a being-in-the-world that could not be represented by dominant feminist and Nationalist discourses, even less by the discourse of the *law*. The menstrual blood stood as a symbol of that reality excluded from language. In so doing it acted as a catalyst of cultural change, a vehicle of reflection and discussion about the meanings of gender difference in Northern Ireland. The most public manifestation of such – often bitter – debate was McCafferty's article. As time went on, Armagh prisoners began to inscribe their difference in language, translating the dirt and menstrual blood into a critique of a ready-made feminist subject that failed to represent them. In a letter published in the *Irish Times* in 1980, Armagh prisoners answered the NIWRM, which had contended that the predicament of the prisoners did not concern feminists, with a demand for a redefinition of feminism:

> It is our belief that not only is our plight a feminist issue, but a very fundamental social and human issue. It is a feminist issue in so far as we are women, and the network of this jail is completely geared to male domination. The governor, the assistant governor, and the doctor are all males. We are subject to physical and mental abuse from male guards who patrol our wing daily, continually peeping into our cells ... If this is not a feminist issue then we feel that the word feminist needs to be redefined. (quoted in Loughran 1986:64)

The articulation of the symbol of menstrual blood with ongoing political and feminist discourses forced a discussion among Nationalists and feminists alike on the exclusionary politics of the very categories of feminism and nationalism, which had a social effect.

By the end of 1980, a policy document on women's rights was approved for the first time in the Republican movement. Two years later, in 1982, a Women's Center was opened also for the first time in the working-class Nationalist ghetto of Falls Road. It set to work amid the discomfort and protest of many Nationalist men. Women flowed in with a hitherto muted knowledge. A Republican woman recalled that "there were battered women, incest, rape, appalling poverty. We had been too busy with the war and didn't realize until the Women's Center that all those problems were there too." Another kind of shit had surfaced. As it gained social visibility, the stinking reality of male violence against women disputed both Catholic models of gender and Nationalist heroic epics. Since then the Nationalist community, and Republicanism in particular, have not been able to ignore easily gender politics. Neither have Irish feminists been able to ignore Nationalist politics. Yet the problem of defining a Nationalist-feminist subject is fraught with difficulties as Irish nationalism – like other postcolonial nationalisms – continues to use gender discourse to advance political claims. Nationalist-feminists have to contend in Northern Ireland with a permanent split between anti-imperialist positions and feminist positions that both exclude them. It is precisely this self-conscious, split political identity that may open the political field in Northern Ireland to new critical possibilities.

Conclusion

I have attempted to show that a Foucaudian notion of power as force relations is not incompatible with an interpretative anthropology sensitive to the "deep play" of subjectivity. Departing from the premise that the Dirty Protest was a violent contest of power, I have tried to elucidate the dynamics that organized it in that form and not others, as well as its social and political consequences in a shared universe of meaning. I have conceptualized the feces and blood characterizing the protest as primordial symbols. These symbols are invested with political power; contrary to Mary Douglas, though, they are not just an expression of the social order. Neither are they locked in unconscious motivation. They partake of both domains and are simultaneously instrumental in that, like speech acts, they have a performative character. The excreta and menstrual blood arose out of a situation of violent political conflict that became overdetermined by tapping into the interconnected domains of prison violence, colonial history, unconscious motivation (infantile fantasies, fears, and desires) and gender discourse, *all* of which constituted the political field at the particular historical moment of the Dirty Protest. It was precisely this overdetermination that gave the protest its shocking power, simultaneously allowing the prisoners to endure its suffering by crystallizing inexpressible and contradictory emotions. The meanings of the Dirty Protest were not fixed, but shifted with each domain of experience into which they tapped, acting simultaneously as weapon, symbol, and symptom. In so doing, they also revealed the gender organization of power.

I regard gender not just as a dimension of violence but as an intrinsic component of it, crucial to the understanding of its meanings, deployments, and ends. My analysis suggests that political violence performed on and from the body cannot escape the meaning of sexual difference. Despite the shared political consciousness and goals of men and women prisoners, their protests had different significance. While the men's protest was articulated through an intense dynamic of violence, the women's protest was crystallized around the meaning of sexual difference. Armagh women provoked, albeit unintentionally, a reformulation of feminine subjectivity. Inasmuch as sexual difference is, in Ireland as everywhere else, inseparable from class, ethnic, and even political positions, such reformation in turn sparked a transformation of dominant discourses of feminism and nationalism.

I have suggested in this chapter that ethnic and political violence predicated on the bodies of women cannot be considered as an addendum to violence performed on men's bodies. As I have shown, it might have disparate meanings and effects that are crucial to both the construction of sexual difference and the construction of ethnic identity.

Notes

1. Republicans favor Irish reunification and independence from Britain; they include the IRA and INLA. Loyalists are pro-British and radically opposed to Irish reunification.
2. *Republican News*, February 16, 1980; McCafferty 1981; Women against Imperialism 1980. The sexual overtones of the assault were confirmed by personal interview.
3. In relation to colonialism and sexuality, see Chatterjee 1989, Kelly 1991, Sangari and Vaid 1990, and Stoler 1991, among others.
4. *Republican News*, February 23, 1980; report by Women against Imperialism, April 9, 1980, p. 27.
5. Amnesty International Report on Long-Kesh 1977.
6. These images are characteristic of childhood aggressiveness and the formation of the image of one's body. They belong to the repertoire of the unconscious and thus appear frequently in dreams, myth, art, and so on. They are, however, easily triggered under special physical or psychological duress. See Lacan 1977:10–11.
7. As the violence inside the prison augmented, so did IRA and Loyalist assassinations and military repression. The brutalization of the warders had a direct effect in isolating them from their own communities and increasing conflicts in their domestic life. See Coogan 1980 and Feldman 1991.
8. This ambivalence emerged in recurrent comments made by Nationalist women during my fieldwork. Particularly important were the discussions following the screening in the Nationalist districts of Belfast and Derry of the documentary *Mother Ireland*, directed by Anne Crilly and produced by the Derry Film and Video Company, and of the play about the Armagh women, *Now and at the Hour of our Death,* produced by the theater group Trouble and Strife.
9. In this sense the Armagh women's Dirty Protest is reminiscent of the kind of symbolic warfare enacted by women in some parts of Africa. Ardener and Ifeka-Moller have documented women's exposure of genitals as a powerful sexual insult used against men violating their dignity and rights. This display publicly states disrespect, denial of dominance, and nonrecognition of authority. See Ardener 1975 and Ifeka-Moller 1975.

10. In relation to the history and composition of the feminist movement in Northern Ireland, see Evason 1991, Loughran 1986, and Ward 1987 and 1991.
11. Nell McCafferty, "It is my belief that Armagh is a feminist issue." *Irish Times,* June 17, 1980.

Bibliography

Amnesty International 1997. Report of an Amnesty International Mission to Northern Ireland, June.
Ardener, Shirley 1975 "Sexual Insult and Female Militancy." In *Perceiving Women.* Shirley Ardener, ed. pp. 29–54. London: Dent and Sons.
Asad, Talal 1983 "Notes on Body Pain and Truth in Medieval Christian Ritual." *Economy and Society* 12:1.
Bhabha, Homi 1984 "Of Mimicry and Man: The Ambivalence of Colonial Discourse." October 28:123–33.
Brown, Norman O. 1959 *Life against Death: The Psychoanalytical Meaning of History.* Middletown, CO: Wesleyan University Press.
Burton, Frank 1978 *The Politics of Legitimacy: Struggles in a Belfast Community.* London: Routledge & Kegan Paul.
Cardinal, Marie 1983 *The Words to Say It: An Autobiographical Novel.* Cambridge: Van Vactor & Goodheart.
Chatterjee, Partha 1989 "Colonialism, Nationalism and Colonized Women: The Contest in India." *American Ethnologist* 16(4):622–33.
Coogan, Tim Pat 1980 *On the Blanket: The H-Block Story.* Dublin: Ward River Press.
Cornell, Drucilla 1991 *Beyond Accommodation: Ethical Feminism, Deconstruction and the Law.* New York: Routledge.
Curtis, L. Perry 1971 *Apes and Angels.* Washington, DC: Smithsonian Institution Press.
Darby, John 1983 *Dressed To Kill: Cartoonists and the Northern Ireland Conflict.* Belfast: Appletree.
De Certeau, Michel 1988 *The Writing of History.* New York: Columbia University Press.
Douglas, Mary 1966 *Purity and Danger: An Analysis of the Concepts of Pollution and Taboo.* London: Routledge & Kegan Paul.
European Law Centre 1981 *European Human Rights Reports,* Part 10.
Evason, Eileen 1991 *Against the Grain: The Contemporary Women's Movement in Northern Ireland.* Dublin: Attic Press.
Feldman, Allen 1991 *Formations of Violence: The Narrative of the Body and Political Terror in Northern Ireland.* Chicago: University of Chicago Press.
Foucault, Michel 1979 *Discipline and Punish: The Birth of the Prison.* New York: Vintage Books.
Goffman, Erving 1959 *Asylums: Essays on the Social Situation of Mental Patients and Other Inmates.* New York: Anchor Books.
Graziano, Frank 1992 *Divine Violence: Spectacle, Psychosexuality and Radical Christianity in the Argentine Dirty War.* Boulder, CO: Westview Press.
Ifeka-Moller, Caroline 1975 "Female Militancy and Colonial Revolt: The Women's War of 1929, Eastern Nigeria." In *Perceiving Women.* Shirley Ardener, ed. pp. 127–59. London: Dent and Sons.

Kelly, John 1991 *A Politics of Virtue: Hinduism, Sexuality and Countercolonial Discourse in Fiji*. Chicago: University of Chicago Press.

Lacan, Jaques 1977 "Aggressivity in Psychoanalysis and Function and Field of Speech and Language." In *Ecrits* pp. 8–114. New York: Norton.

Loughran, Christine 1986 "Armagh and Feminist Strategy." *Feminist Review* 23:59–79.

McCafferty, Nell 1981 *Armagh Women*. Dublin: Co-op Books.

Murphy, Brenda 1989 "A Curse." In *Territories of the Voice. Contemporary Stories by Irish Women Writers*. L. DeSalvo, K.W. D'Arcy, and K. Hogan, eds. pp. 226–7. Boston: Beacon Press.

Obeyesekere, Gananath 1981 *Medusa's Hair: An Essay on Personal Symbols and Religious Experience*. Chicago: University of Chicago Press.

— 1990 *The Work of Culture: Symbolic Transformation in Psychoanalisis and Anthropology*. Chicago: University of Chicago Press.

— 1992 *The Apotheosis of Captain Cook: European Myth Making in the Pacific*. Princeton: Princeton University Press.

Sangari, K., and S.Vaid 1990 *Recasting Women: Essays in Indian Colonial History*. New Brunswick: Rutgers University Press.

Scarry, Elaine 1985 *The Body in Pain: The Making and Unmaking of the World*. New York: Oxford University Press.

Scott, Joan 1991 "The Evidence of Experience." *Critical Inquiry* 17:773–97.

Sluka, Jeffrey 1989 *Hearts and Minds, Water and Fish: Support for the INLA in a Northern Irish Ghetto*. Greenwich, CT.: Al Press.

Spivak, Gayatri 1988 "Forward to 'Draupadi' by Mahasweta Devi." In *In Other Worlds: Essays in Cultural Politics*. New York: Routledge.

Stoler, Ann L. 1991 "Carnal Knowledge and Imperial Power: Gender, Race and Morality in Colonial Asia." In *Gender at the Crossroads of Knowledge: Feminist Anthropology in the Postmodern Era*. Micaela di Leonardo, ed. pp. 51–101. Berkeley: California University Press.

Suarez-Orozco, Marcelo 1992 "Dirty War and Post Dirty War in Argentina." In *The Paths of Domination, Resistance and Terror*. C. Nordstrom and J. A. Martin, eds. pp. 219–60. Berkeley: California University Press.

Swift, Jonathan 1967 (1726) *Gulliver's Travels*. London: Penguin.

Taussig, Michael 1987 *Shamanism, Colonialism and the Wild Man*. Chicago: University of Chicago Press.

Turner, Victor 1967 *The Forest of Symbols. Aspects of Ndembu Ritual*. Ithaca, NY: Cornell University Press.

Ward, Margaret 1987 "A Difficult, Dangerous Honesty. Ten Years of Feminism in Northern Ireland. A Discussion." Belfast.

— 1991 "The Women's Movement in the North of Ireland: Twenty Years On." In *Ireland's Histories: Aspects of State, Society and Ideology*. S. Hutton and P. Steward, eds. pp.149–63. London: Routledge.

Warner, Marina 1983 *Alone of All Her Sex: The Myth and the Cult of the Virgin Mary*. New York: Vintage.

Women against Imperialism 1980 "Women Protest for Political Status in Armagh Gaol." April 9.

Zizek, Slavoj 1989 *The Sublime Object of Ideology*. New York: Verso.

11
Surfacing Gender: Reconceptualizing Crimes Against Women in Time of War

Rhonda Copelon

Introduction

Historically, the rape of women in war has drawn occasional and short-lived international attention. Most of the time rape has been invisible, or comes to light as part of the competing diplomacies of war, illustrating the viciousness of the conqueror or the innocence of the conquered. When war is done, it is comfortably cabined as a mere inevitable "by-product of war," a matter of indiscipline, of soldiers revved up by war, needy, and briefly "out of control."

Military histories rarely refer to rape, and military tribunals rarely either charge or sanction it. This is true even where rape and forced prostitution are mass or systematic, as with the rape of women in both theaters of the Second World War;[1] it is even true where the open, mass and systematic rape has been thought to shock the conscience of the world, such as in the "rape of Nanking"[2] or the rape of an estimated 200,000 Bengali women during the war of independence from Pakistan.[3] Though discussed in the judgment of the International Military Tribunal in Tokyo, rape was not separately charged against the Japanese commander as a crime. In Bangladesh, amnesty was quietly traded for independence.

The question today is whether the terrible rape of women in the war in the former Yugoslavia will likewise disappear into history or at best will survive as an exceptional case. The apparent uniqueness of the rape of women in Bosnia-Herzegovina, directed overwhelmingly against Bosnian-Muslim women, is a product of the invisibility of the rape of women through history as well as in the present. Geopolitical factors – that this is occurring in Europe, is perpetrated by white men against white, albeit largely Muslim women, and contains the seeds of

193

a new world war – cannot be ignored in explaining the visibility of these rapes. By contrast, the rape of 50 percent of the women of the indigenous Yuracruz people in Ecuador by mercenaries of an agribusiness company seeking to "cleanse" the land is invisible, just as the routine rape of women in the civil wars in Peru, Liberia, and Burma, for example, has gone largely unreported.[4]

Moreover, just as historically the condemnation of rape in war has rarely been about the abuse of women as a crime of gender, so the mass rape in Bosnia has captured world attention and remains there largely because of its association with "ethnic cleansing," or genocide. In one week, a midday women's talk show opened with the script, "In Bosnia, they are raping the enemy's women ...," and a leading Croatian-American scholar blithely distinguished "genocidal" rape from "normal" rape. Our ad hoc Women's Coalition against Crimes against Women in the Former Yugoslavia spoke of rape as a weapon of war whether used to dilute ethnic identity, destabilize the civilian population, or reward soldiers. But the public was nodding: Yes, when rape is a vehicle of genocide.

The elision of genocide and rape in the focus on "genocidal rape" as a means of emphasizing the heinousness of the rape of Muslim women in Bosnia is thus dangerous. Rape and genocide are separate atrocities. Genocide – the effort to destroy a people based on its identity as a people – evokes the deepest horror and warrants the severest condemnation. Rape is sexualized violence that seeks to humiliate, terrorize, and destroy a woman based on her identity as a woman. Both are based on total contempt for and dehumanization of the victim, and both give rise to unspeakable brutalities. Their intersection in the Serbian and, to a lesser extent, the Croatian aggressions in Bosnia defines an ineffable living hell for women. From the standpoint of these women, they are inseparable.

But to emphasize as unparalleled the horror of genocidal rape is factually dubious and risks rendering rape invisible once again. Even in war, rape is not fully recognized as an atrocity. When the ethnic war ceases or is forced back into the bottle, will the crimes against women, the voices of women, and their struggles to survive be vindicated? Or will condemnation be limited to this seemingly exceptional case? Will the women who are brutally raped for domination, terror, booty, or revenge – in Bosnia and elsewhere – be heard?

Whether the rape, forced prostitution, and forced impregnation of women will be effectively prosecuted before the recently created UN ad hoc International Tribunal,[5] whether the survivors will obtain redress, or whether impunity will again be the agreed-upon or de facto cost of "peace" is up for grabs. The pressure of survivors and their advocates, together with the global women's human rights movement, will make the difference. The situation presents a historic opportunity as well as an imperative to insist on justice for the women of Bosnia as well as to press for a feminist reconceptualization of the role and legal understanding of rape in war.

To do this, we must surface gender in the midst of genocide at the same time as we avoid dualistic thinking. We must critically examine the claim that rape as a tool of "ethnic cleansing" is unique, worse than or not comparable to other forms of rape in war or in peace, at the same time as we recognize that rape together with genocide inflicts multiple, intersectional harms.[6] This combination of the particular and the general is critical if the horrors experienced by women in Bosnia are to be appreciated and if that experience is to have meaning for women brutalized in less-known theaters of war or in the byways of daily life.

This chapter examines the evolving legal status of rape in war with attention to both the particular and the general as well as to the tension between them. The opening section focuses on the two central questions of conceptualization. The first is whether these gender crimes are fully recognized as war crimes under the Geneva Conventions, the cornerstone of what is called "humanitarian" law – that is, the prohibitions that have made war itself permissible. The second is whether international law does or should distinguish between "genocidal rape" and mass rape for other purposes. In this regard it examines the limitations and the potential in the concept of "crimes against humanity" as well as the relation between gender and nationality/ethnicity in the crimes committed against women in Bosnia. The second section looks at the viability of the ad hoc International Tribunal as well as the gender issues presented.

Reconceptualizing rape, forced prostitution, and forced pregnancy in war

Is rape a war crime?

Although news of the mass rapes of women in Bosnia had an electrifying effect and became a significant factor in the demand for the creation of an international war crimes tribunal, the leading question for a time was whether rape and other forms of sexual abuse are "war crimes" within the meaning of the Geneva Conventions and the internationally agreed-upon norms that bind all nations whether or not they have signed the Conventions. The answer is not unequivocal.

The question is not whether rape is technically a crime or prohibited in war. Rape has long been viewed as a criminal offense under national and international rules of war.[7] The 1949 Geneva Conventions as well as the 1977 Protocols regarding the protection of civilians in war explicitly prohibit rape, enforced prostitution, and any form of indecent assault and call for special protection of women, including separate quarters with supervision and searches by women only.[8] Yet it is significant that where rape and other forms of sexual assault are explicitly mentioned, they are categorized as an outrage upon personal dignity, or crimes against honor.[9] Crimes of violence, including murder, mutilation, cruel treatment, and torture, are treated separately.

The concept of rape as a crime against dignity and honor as opposed to a crime of violence is a core problem. Formal sanctions against rape range from minimal to extreme. Where rape has been treated as a grave crime, it is because it violates the honor of the man and his exclusive right to sexual possession of his woman as property. Thus, in the United States the death penalty against rape was prevalent in southern states as a result of a combination of racism and sexism.[10] Similarly, the media often refer to the mass rape in Bosnia as the rape of "the enemy's women" – the enemy in this formulation being the male combatant and the seemingly all-male nation, religious, or ethnic group.

Under the Geneva Conventions, the concept of honor is somewhat more enlightened: rape is a crime against the honor and dignity of women.[11] But this too is problematic . Where rape is treated as a crime against honor, the honor of women is called into question and virginity or chastity is often a precondition.[12] Honor implies the loss of station or respect; it reinforces the social view, internalized by women, that the raped woman is dishonorable. And while the concept of dignity potentially embraces more profound concerns, standing alone it obfuscates the fact that rape is fundamentally violence against women – violence against a woman's body, autonomy, integrity, selfhood, security, and self-esteem as well as her standing in the community. This failure to recognize rape as violence is critical to the traditionally lesser or ambiguous status of rape in humanitarian law.

The issue then is not whether rape is a war crime, but whether it is a crime of the gravest dimension. Under the Geneva Conventions, the term is "grave breach." The significance of a war crime's being a "grave breach" is threefold. On the level of discourse it calls attention to the egregiousness of the assault. On the practical level, it is not necessary that rape be mass or systematic: one act of rape is punishable. Finally, only crimes that are grave breaches give rise to universal jurisdiction under the Geneva Conventions. Universal jurisdiction means that every nation has an obligation to bring the perpetrators to justice through investigating, arresting, and prosecuting offenders in its own courts or extraditing them to more appropriate forums. The existence of universal jurisdiction also provides a legal rationale for trying such crimes before an international tribunal and for the obligation of states to cooperate. If rape were not a "grave breach" of the Geneva Conventions, some international jurists would argue that it can be redressed only by the state to which the wrongdoer belonged or in which the wrong occurred, and not by an International Tribunal.[13]

The relevant portions of the Geneva Conventions do not specifically mention rape in the list of crimes considered "grave breaches." Included are "willful killing, torture, or inhumane treatment" and "willfully causing great suffering or serious injury to body or health."[14] Clearly these categories are broad and generic enough to encompass rape and sexual abuse.[15] But in addition to qualifying as "willfully causing great suffering or serious injury to body or health" or as "inhumane treatment," it is important that rape be recognized as a form of torture.

When the Geneva Conventions were drafted, the view that torture was a method of extracting information was dominant. Today, however, this distinction has been largely abandoned, although it endures in popular thinking. The historian Edward Peters writes: "It is not primarily the victim's information, but the victim, that torture needs to win – or reduce to powerlessness."[16] Recent treaties define torture as the willful infliction of severe physical or mental pain or suffering not only to elicit information, but also to punish, intimidate, or discriminate, to obliterate the victim's personality or diminish her personal capacities.[17] Thus torture is now commensurate with willfully causing great suffering or injury. Moreover, it is not simply or necessarily the infliction of terrible physical pain; it is also the use of pain, sensory deprivation, isolation, and humiliation as a pathway to the mind. Indeed, in the contemporary understanding of torture, degradation is both vehicle and goal.[18]

Although largely ignored until recently by human rights advocates, the testimonies and studies of women tortured by dictatorial regimes and military occupations make it clear that rape is one of the most common, terrible, and effective forms of torture used against women.[19] Rape attacks the integrity of the woman as a person as well as her identity as a woman. It renders her, in the words of Lepa Mladjenovic, a psychotherapist and Serbian feminist antiwar activist, "homeless in her own body."[20] It strikes at a woman's power; it seeks to degrade and destroy her; its goal is domination and dehumanization.

Likewise, the testimonies in this book of raped women, whether they were attacked once or forced into prostitution, make it clear that rape is both a profound physical attack and a particularly egregious form of psychological torture. They document the intersection of contempt for and conquest of women based on their sex as well as on their national, religious, or cultural identity. They demonstrate the significance of the threat, fear, or reality of pregnancy as well as of the fact that in Bosnia the rapists are in many cases former colleagues, neighbors, or even friends.

Indeed, torturers know well the power of the intimate in the process of breaking down their victim.[21] Because rape is a transposition of the intimate into violence, rape by acquaintances, by those one has trusted, is particularly world shattering and thus a particularly effective tool of ethnic cleansing. It is no wonder that local Bosnian Serbs are being incited and, in some cases, recruited to rape. Their stories in this collection, notwithstanding their self-justificatory quality, reflect the common methods of training torturers – exposure to and engagement in increasingly unthinkable violence and humiliation.[22]

Despite the fact that rape in Bosnia has drawn substantial international condemnation, the United Nations' position on the status of rape as a grave breach of humanitarian law is not clear. The UN Human Rights Commission condemned "the abhorrent practice of rape and abuse of women and children in the former Yugoslavia which, *in their circumstances,* constitutes a war crime" and urged all nations to "exert every effort to bring to justice ... all those individuals directly or indirectly involved."[23] While this implies that rape is a "grave breach," the limitation to the particular "circumstances" could be read as a limitation to the context of ethnic cleansing. The Declaration of the 1993 World Conference of Human Rights in Vienna, though strongly worded, is limited to "systematic" rape and abuse.[24]

Most significantly, the Report subsequently adopted by the Security Council that constitutes the statute establishing the jurisdiction of the International Tribunal largely tracks the Geneva Conventions' definition of grave breach and does not explicitly list rape as a grave breach or describe it as implicit in the recognized categories.[25] But if, as a consequence of women's pressure, it is prosecuted as such and the various bodies of the UN begin to refer to rape as a grave breach, then this practice will effectively amend or expand the meaning of grave breach in the Conventions and Protocols. This emphasizes the importance, from a practical as well as a moral perspective, of insisting that all rape be subject to punishment, not only mass or genocidal rape. It should be noted that under the Geneva Conventions, responsibility is imputed to commanders where they knew, or should have known, of the likelihood of rape and failed to take all measures within their power to prevent or suppress it.[26]

It is also important to point out the importance of the Vienna Declaration's explicit inclusion of forced pregnancy in its condemnation of the mass atrocities in the former Yugoslavia. This is clearly a product of the intensive women's mobilization that preceded the World Conference. As the testimonies in this book indicate, forced pregnancy must be seen as a separate offense: the expressed intention to make women pregnant is an additional form of psychological torture; the goal of impregnation leads to imprisoning women and raping them until they are pregnant; the fact of pregnancy, whether aborted or not, continues the initial torture in a most intimate and invasive form; and bearing a child of rape, whether placed for adoption or not, has a potentially lifelong impact on the woman and her place in the community.[27]

Genocidal rape versus "normal" rape: when is mass rape a crime against humanity?

"Crimes against humanity" were first formally recognized in the Charter and Judgment of the Nuremberg Tribunal; they do not depend on adherence to a treaty, and they too give rise to universal jurisdiction. Since crimes against humanity can be committed in any war, it is irrelevant whether the war in the former Yugoslavia is international or internal.

Rape has been separately listed, and forced prostitution acknowledged, as a "crime against humanity" in the Report establishing the stature of the International Tribunal.[28] This is not without precedent. After the Second World War, Local Council Law No. 10, which provided the foundation for the trials of lesser Nazis by the Allied forces, also listed rape as a crime against humanity, although no one was prosecuted.[29] Nonetheless, the Security Council's reaffirmation that rape is a "crime against humanity," and therefore among the most egregious breaches of civilization, is profoundly important. But the meaning of this designation and its import for other contexts in which women are subjected to mass rape apart from ethnic cleansing are not clear. The danger, as always, is that extreme examples produce narrow principles.

The commentary on this aspect of the jurisdiction of the current Tribunal signals this danger. It explains crimes against humanity as "inhumane acts of a very serious nature, such as willful killing, *torture or rape,* committed *as part of* a widespread *or* systematic attack against any civilian population on national, political, ethnic, racial, or religious grounds."[30] Several aspects of this definition deserve comment.

First, on the positive side, the statute correctly encompasses violations that are widespread but not necessarily systematic. The law wisely does not require massive numbers but specifies patterns of abuse. Particularly with rape, numbers are unprovable: a small percentage of women will ultimately come forward, and the significance of rape threatens to become drowned in statistical claims. Moreover, the statute does not require that rape be ordered or centrally organized. Commanders can be held responsible where widespread violence is known and tolerated.[31] In Bosnia, rape is clearly a conscious tool of war and ethnic cleansing. It is politically and ethically important for the Tribunal to investigate and prove the chain of command, but it is likewise important that leaders can be held legally responsible without proof that rape was systematic or committed under orders.

Second, the commentary on the statute does rank rape with torture, at least where it is widespread or systematic. But it undercuts this by appearing to conflate what were originally understood as two separate and independent criteria of crimes against humanity: gross acts of violence *and* persecution-based offenses. Under the original concept, rape should qualify as a gross act of violence and accordingly, if widespread or systematic, would independently qualify as a crime against humanity. By merging the criterion of gross violence with persecution-based offenses, the commentary could limit prosecution to rape that is undertaken as a method of persecution on the specified grounds. Since the statute of the Tribunal lists rape and persecution separately, it is not clear, until put in practice, whether the broader understanding will prevail.

The narrow view is quite prevalent, however. The international and popular condemnation of the rapes in Bosnia tends to be either explicitly or implicitly based on the fact that rape is being used as a tactic of ethnic cleansing. Genocidal rape is widely seen not as a modality of rape but as unique. The distinction commonly drawn between genocidal rape and "normal" rape in war or in peace is proffered not as a typology, but rather as a hierarchy. But to exaggerate the distinctiveness of genocidal rape obscures the atrocity of common rape.

Genocidal rape often involves gang rapes, is outrageously brutal, and is done in public or in front of children or partners. It involves imprisoning women in rape "camps" or raping them repetitively. These are also characteristics of the most common rape in war – rape for booty or to boost the morale of soldiers; and they are common characteristics of the use of rape as a form of torture and terror by dictatorial regimes.[32]

The notion that genocidal rape is uniquely a weapon of war is also problematic. The rape of women is a weapon of war where it is used to spread political terror, as in the civil war in Peru. It is a weapon of war where, as in Bosnia and elsewhere, it is used against women to destabilize the society and force families to flee, because in time of war women are the mainstay of the civilian population, even more than in peacetime.[33]

The rape of women, where permitted or systematized as "booty" of war, is likewise an engine of war: it maintains the morale of soldiers, feeds their hatred and sense of superiority, and keeps them fighting. The Japanese military industrialized the sexual slavery of women in the Second World War: 200,000 to 400,000 mostly Korean, but also Philippine, Chinese, and Dutch women from Indonesia were deceived or disappeared into "comfort stations," raped repeatedly and moved from battlefield to battlefield to motivate as well as reward the Japanese soldiers. Genocide was not a goal, but it is believed that 70 to 90 percent of these women died in captivity, and among the known survivors, none were subsequently able to bear children.[34] For similar reasons, the United States military in Vietnam raped Vietnamese women and established brothels, relying on dire economic necessity rather than kidnapping to fill them.[35] Indeed, the foregoing testimonies of the Bosnian Serbian rapists reveal an admixture of all these goals.

At the same time, genocidal or ethnic cleansing rape, as practiced in Bosnia, does have some aspects that are particularly tailored to its goals of driving women from their homes or destroying their possibility of reproducing within and "for" their community. As the preceding testimonies suggest, that women are raped by men familiar to them exacerbates their trauma and the impulse to flee the community because trust and safety are no longer possible. This is particular to the Bosnian situation, where war and propaganda have made enemies out of neighbors.

The second and more generally distinctive feature of genocidal rape is the focus on women as reproductive vessels. The explicit and common threat to make Muslim women bear "Serbian babies" (as if the child were the product of sperm only) justifies repetitive rape and aggravates her terror and potential unacceptability to her community. Bengali women were raped to lighten their race and produce a class of outcaste mothers and children. Enslaved African women in the southern United States were raped as property to produce babies bartered, sold, and used as property.[36] While intentional impregnation is properly treated as a separate offense, it should also be noted that pregnancy is a common consequence of rape. In situations where women are raped repeatedly, most fertile women will become pregnant at some point. When the United States navy took over Saipan, for example, one observer reports that virtually all the women, who had been enslaved as comfort women for the Japanese army, were pregnant.[37]

These distinctive characteristics do not place genocidal rape in a class by itself; nor do they reflect the full range of atrocities, losses, and suffering that the combination of rape and ethnic cleansing inflicts. The women victims and survivors in Bosnia are being subjected to crimes against humanity based on ethnicity and religion, and based on gender. It is critical to recognize both and to acknowledge that the intersection of ethnic and gender violence has its own particular characteristics.

This brings me to the third concern: the complete failure of the United Nations and the international community in general to recognize that persecution based on gender must be recognized as its own category of crimes against humanity. The crystallization of the concept of crimes against humanity in the wake of the Holocaust has meant that "it" is popularly associated with religious and ethnic genocide. But the concept is a broader one, and the categories of persecution are explicitly open-ended, capable of expanding to embrace new understandings of persecution.

With respect to women, the need is to acknowledge that gender has historically not been viewed as a relevant category of victimization. The frequency of mass rape and the absence of sanction are sufficient evidence. In the Holocaust, the gender persecutions – the rape and forced prostitution of women as well as the extermination of gay people – were obscured.[38] The absence of gender as a basis for persecution is not peculiar to the concept of crimes against humanity. A parallel problem exists in the international standards for political asylum, which require a well-founded fear of persecution, but do not explicitly recognize gender as a source of persecution.[39] The expansion of the concept of crimes against humanity to include gender is thus part of the broader movement to end the historical invisibility of gender violence as a humanitarian and human rights violation.

Moreover, the particular goals and defining aspects of genocidal rape do not detract from, but rather elucidate the nature of rape as a crime of gender as well as ethnicity. Women are targets not simply because they "belong to" the enemy, but precisely because they keep the civilian population functioning and are essential to its continuity. They are targets because they too *are* the enemy – because of their power as well as vulnerability as women, including their sexual and reproductive power. They are targets because of *hatred* of their power as women; because of endemic objectification of women; because rape embodies male domination and female subordination.

The crime of forced impregnation – central as it is to genocidal rape – also elucidates the gender component. Since under patriarchy women are viewed as little more than vessels for childbearing, involuntary pregnancy is commonly viewed as natural – divinely ordained perhaps – or simply an unquestioned fact of life. As a result, the risk of pregnancy in all rape is treated not as an offense, but as a sequela. Forced pregnancy has drawn condemnation only when it reflects an intent to harm the victimized race. In Bosnia, the taunt that Muslim women will bear Serbian babies is not simply an ethnic harm, particularly in light of the prevalence of ethnically mixed families. When examined through a feminist lens, forced pregnancy appears as an assault on the reproductive self-determination of women; it expresses the desire to mark the rape and rapist upon the woman's body and upon the woman's life.

Finally, that the rape of women is also designed to humiliate the men or destroy "the enemy" itself reflects the fundamental objectification of women. Women are the target of abuse at the same time as their subjectivity is completely denied. The persistent failure to acknowledge the gender dimension of rape and sexual persecution is thus a most effective means of perpetuating it.

In sum, the international attention focused on Bosnia challenges the world to squarely recognize sexual violence against women in war as torture. Moreover, it is not enough for rape to be viewed as a crime against humanity when it is the vehicle of some other form of persecution; it must also be recognized as a crime against humanity because it is invariably a persecution based on gender. This is essential if the women of Bosnia are to be understood as full subjects as well as objects in this terrible victimization and if the international attention focused on Bosnia is to have meaning for women subjected to rape in other parts of the world.

Conclusion

Given the formidable pressure being brought to bear by women survivors and the women's movement globally, it may well be that some few men will be indicted and even tried before the International Tribunal or national courts, at least if impunity is not again the price of peace. This would be precedent-setting in international law and offer symbolic vindication to the untold number of women this war has rendered homeless in so many senses. Unless the gender dimension of rape in war is recognized, however, it will mean little for women where rape is not also a tool of genocide.

Emphasis on the gender dimension of rape in war is critical not only to surfacing women as full subjects of sexual violence in war, but also to recognizing the atrocity of rape in the time called peace. When women charge rape in war they are more likely to be believed, because their status as enemy, or at least "the enemy's" is recognized and because rape in war is seen as a product of exceptional circumstances. When women charge rape in everyday life, however, they are disbelieved largely because the ubiquitous war against women is denied.

From a feminist human rights perspective, gender violence has escaped sanction because it has not been viewed as violence and because the public/private dichotomy has shielded such violence in its most common and private forms.[40] The recognition of rape as a war crime is thus a critical step toward understanding rape as violence. The next is to recognize that rape that acquires the imprimatur of the state is not necessarily more brutal, relentless, or dehumanizing than the private rapes of everyday life.

This is not to say that rape is identical in the two contexts. There are differences here, just as there are differences between rape for the purpose of genocide and rape for the purpose of booty. War tends to intensify the brutality, repetitiveness, public spectacle, and likelihood of rape. War diminishes sensitivity to human suffering and intensifies men's sense of entitlement, superiority, avidity, and social license to rape. But the line is not so sharp. Gang rape in civilian life shares the repetitive, gleeful, and public character of rape in war. Marital rape, the most private of all, shares some of the particular characteristics of genocidal rape in Bosnia: it is repetitive, brutal, and exacerbated by betrayal; it assaults a woman's reproductive autonomy, may force her to flee her home and community, and is widely treated as legitimate in law and custom. Violation by a state official or enemy soldier is not necessarily more devastating than violation by an intimate.[41]

Every rape is a grave violation of physical and mental integrity. Every rape has the potential to profoundly debilitate, to render the woman homeless in her own body and destroy her sense of security in the world. Every rape is an expression of male domination and misogyny, a vehicle of terrorizing and subordinating women. Like torture, rape takes many forms, occurs in many contexts, and has different repercussions for different victims. Every rape is multidimensional, but not incomparable.

The rape of women in the former Yugoslavia challenges the world to refuse impunity to atrocity as well as to resist the powerful forces that would make the mass rape of Muslim women in Bosnia exceptional and thereby restrict its meaning for women raped in different contexts. It thus demands recognition of situational differences without losing sight of the commonalities. To fail to make distinctions flattens reality; and to rank the egregious demeans it.

Notes

1. See , e.g., Susan Brownmiller, *Against Our Will: Men, Women, and Rape* (New York, 1975), pp. 31–113.
2. The "rape of Nanking" refers to the brutal taking of Nanking by Japanese soldiers, which involved mass and open killing, looting, and rape that went on for several months. It is estimated that 20,000 women were raped in the first month. See Friedman, *The Law of War: A Commentary/History*, vol. 2 (New York, 1972), p. 46.
3. Brownmiller, *Against Our Will*, pp. 78–86. Among the motives for these rapes was a genocidal one – to destroy the racial distinctiveness of the Bengali people.
4. Presentation of Guadelupe Leon, Panel on Military Violence and Sexual Slavery, 1993 UN Conference on Human Rights, NGO Parallel Activities, June 1993; Americas Watch and Women's Rights Project, *Untold Terror: Violence against Women in Peru's Armed Conflict* (New York, 1992); Asia Watch and Women's Rights Project, *Burma: Rape, Forced Labor, and Religious Persecution in Northern Arakan* (Washington, D.C. 1992); Shana Swiss, *Liberia: Women and Children Gravely Mistreated* (Boston,1991). For other examples, see Shana Swiss and Joan E. Giller, "Rape as a Crime of War," *JAMA* 270 (August 4, 1993):612.
5. The full title is International Tribunal for the Prosecution of Persons Responsible for Serious Violations of International Humanitarian Law Committed in the Territory of the Former Yugoslavia since 1991. See *Report of the Secretary-General Pursuant to Paragraph 2 of the Security Council Resolution 808 (1993)*, S/25704 (May 3, 1993), para. 25, p. 8.
6. On the concept of the significance of the intersection of categories of oppression, see Kimberle Crenshaw, "Demarginalizing the Intersection of Race and Sex: A Black Feminist Critique of Anti-Discrimination Doctrine, Feminist Theory, and Antiracist Politics," *University of Chicago Legal Forum*, 1989, pp. 139–67.
7. See, e.g., Yougindra Khusalani, *Dignity and Honour of Women as Basic and Fundamental Human Rights* (Boston, 1982).
8. *Geneva Conventions Relative to the Protection of Civilian Persons in Time of War*, common art. 3, I(a) and (c); arts. 27 and 76, 97 (hereafter, *Geneva Convention IV): Protocol Additional to the Geneva Conventions of 12 August*

1949, and relating to the Protection of Victims of International Armed Conflicts (Protocol I), art. 76, and *Protocol Additional to the Geneva Conventions of 12 August 1949, and relating to the Protection of Victims of Non-International Armed Conflicts (Protocol II)*, art. 4, reprinted in Center for Human Rights, *Human Rights: A Compilation of International Instruments*, vol. I (second part) (New York, 1993), pp. 799–939.

9. See, e.g., Ibid., *Geneva Convention IV*, art. 27, para. 2; *Protocol II*, art. 4.
10. This was recognized by the U.S. Supreme Court in striking the death penalty in *Coker v. Georgia*, 433 U.S. 584 (1977).
11. Khusalini, *Dignity and Honour*, pp. 39–76.
12. See, e.g., Americas Watch and Women's Rights Project, *Untold Terror*.
13. It should be noted here that the concept of "grave breach" applies only to international conflict and not to civil war. Although there is debate about whether the conflict in the territory of the former Yugoslavia is international or internal, the UN has taken the position that the warring parties have agreed to abide by the rules governing international conflicts. *Report of the Secretary General*, para. 25, p. 8.
14. *Geneva Convention IV*, art. 147; *Protocol I*, arts. II and 85(3).
15. Khusalani, *Dignity and Honour*, pp. 39–76.
16. Edward Peters, *Torture* (New York, 1985), p.164.
17. *UN Convention against Torture*, art. I; *Inter-American Convention against Torture*, art. 2, reprinted in J. Herman Burgers and Hans Danelius, *The United Nations Convention against Torture – A Handbook on the Convention against Torture and Other Cruel, Inhuman and Degrading Treatment or Punishment* (Boston, 1988), appendix.
18. Amnesty International, *Report on Torture* (New York, 1974).
19. See, e.g., Ximena Bunster-Burotto, "Surviving beyond Fear: Women and Torture in Latin America," in *Women and Change in Latin America*, ed. June Nash and Helen Safa (Boston, 1986), pp. 297–325; F. Allodi and S. Stiasny, "Women as Torture Victims," *Canadian Journal of Psychiatry* 35 (March 1990):144–8; Inge Lunde and Jorge Ortmann, "Prevalence and Sequelae of Sexual Torture," *Lancet* 336 (August 1990):289–91. While not the subject here, the rape of men is also a devastating crime of gender, designed as it is to humiliate through feminization.
20. Testimony before the Global Tribunal on Violations of Women's Human Rights, part of the NGO Parallel Activities,1993, World Conference on Human Rights, Vienna, June 15, 1993.
21. See Amnesty International, *Report on Torture*; Elaine Scarry, *The Body in Pain: The Making and Unmaking of the World* (New York, 1985), p. 41; Judith Lewis Herman, *Trauma and Recovery* (New York, 1992).
22. See, e.g., Stanley Milgram, "Some Conditions of Obedience and Disobedience to Authority," *Human Relations* 18 (1965):57–74. On the training of torturers, see Amnesty International, *Torture in Greece: The First Torturers' Trial, 1975* (New York, 1977); Mika Haritos-Fatouros, "The Official Torturer: A Learning Model for Obedience to the Authority of Violence," *Journal of Applied Social Psychology* 18 (1988):1107–20.
23. UN Commission on Human Rights, *Rape and Abuse of Women in the Territory of the Former Yugoslavia*, report on the 49th sess., February 1–March 12,

1993, Economic and Social Council suppl. No. 3, E/CN4/1993/122 (emphasis supplied).

24. The Conference agreed: "Violations of the human rights of women in situations of armed conflict are violations of the fundamental principles of international human rights and humanitarian law. All violations of this kind, including in particular murder, systematic rape, sexual slavery, and forced pregnancy, require a particularly effective response." *Report of the Drafting Committee, Addendum, Final Outcome of the World Conference on Human Rights,* A/conf.157/PC/add. 1 (June 24, 1993) (hereafter "Vienna Declaration").

25. Article 2 identifies as grave breaches "(a) willful killing; (b) torture or inhuman treatment, including biological experiments; (c) willfully causing great suffering or serious bodily injury to body or health." *Report of the Secretary-General,* art. 2, paras, 37–40, pp. 10–11.

26. *Protocol I,* art. 86.

27. Anne Tierney Goldstein, *Recognizing Forced Impregnation as a War Crime under International Law* (New York: Center for Reproductive Law and Policy, 1993), examines forced impregnation under the Geneva Conventions and as a means of genocide and enslavement.

28. *Report of the Secretary-General,* art. 5, paras. 47–9, p. 13.

29. Khusalani, *Dignity and Honour,* pp. 13–38, esp. p. 23.

30. *Report of the Secretary-General,* art. 5, para. 48, p. 13.

31. Ibid., art. 7, *Draft Code of Offenses against Peace and Security of Mankind, UN GAOR, 6th sess. (1951), suppl. 9, doc. A/1858, art. 2(11).*

32. See, e.g., Brownmiller, *Against Our Will;* Bunster-Burrotto, "Surviving beyond Fear"; Amnesty International, *Woman on the Frontline* (New York, 1991).

33. Americas Watch and Women's Rights Project, *Untold Terror;* Swiss and Giller, "Rape as a Crime of War."

34. Testimony of Bok Dong Kim before the Global Tribunal on Violations of Women's Human Rights, NGO Parallel Activities,1993 World Conference on Human Rights, Vienna, June 15, 1993. See also *Hearings before the United Nations Secretary-General* (February 25, 1993) (testimony of Hyo-chai Lee, MA, Soon-Kum Park, and Chung-Ok Yum, MFA, Korean Council for the Women Drafted for Military Sexual Service in Japan); Lourdes Sajor, "Women in Armed Conflict Situations," MAV/1993/WP.1 (September 21, 1993), prepared for Expert Group Meeting on Measures to Eradicate Violence against Women, UN Division for the Advancement of Women.

35. Brownmiller, *Against Our Will,* pp. 86–113.

36. Angela Y. Davis, *Women, Race and Class* (New York, 1983), p. 172.

37. Conversation with D. B.

38. See Brownmiller, *Against Our Will,* pp. 48–78, for the unrecognized sexual violence against women on the part of Allied as well as Axis forces. See also Erwin J. Haeberle, "Swastika, Pink Triangle, and Yellow Star: The Destruction of Sexology and the Persecution of Homosexuals in Nazi Germany," in *Hidden from History: Reclaiming the Gay and Lesbian Past,* ed. Martin Duberman, Martha Vicinus, and George Channcez Jr. (New York,1990), pp. 365–79 (noting the gender aspect of the Nazi attacks on homosexuals reflected in the use of the pink triangle and charges of emasculation).

39. The Convention relating to the Status of Refugees recognizes persecution based on race, religion, nationality, membership in a particular social group, or political opinion. The "social group" category is currently being expanded to encompass gender claims, but this is not enough. See Pamela Goldberg and Nancy Kelly, "International Human Rights and Violence against Women," *Harvard Human Rights Journal* 6 (spring 1993).

40. See, e.g., Charlotte Bunch, "Women's Rights as Human Rights: Toward a Revision of Human Rights," *Human Rights Quarterly* 12 (1990):486; Rhonda Copelon, "Intimate Terror: Understanding Domestic Violence as Torture"; and Celina Romany, "State Responsibility Goes 'Private': A Feminist Critique of the Public/Private Distinction in International Human Rights Law," in *International Women's Human Rights,* ed. Rebecca Cook (Philadelphia, 1994).

41. Herman, *Trauma and Recovery.*

Part III
The Normalization of Violence

12

Culture of Terror – Space of Death. Roger Casement's Putumayo Report and the Explanation of Torture

Michael Taussig

This chapter is about torture and the culture of terror, which for most of us, including myself, are known only through the words of others. Thus my concern is with the mediation of the culture of terror through narration – and with the problems of writing effectively against terror.

Jacobo Timerman ends his book, *Prisoner without a Name, Cell without a Number,* with the imprint of the gaze of hope in the space of death.

> Have any of you looked into the eyes of another person, on the floor of a cell, who knows that he's about to die though no one has told him so? He knows that he's about to die but clings to his biological desire to live, as a single hope, since no one has told him he's to be executed.
>
> I have many such gazes imprinted upon me ....
>
> Those gazes which I encountered in the clandestine prisons of Argentina and which I've retained one by one, were the culminating point, the purest moment of my tragedy.
>
> They are here with me today. And although I might wish to do so, I could not and would not know how to share them with you.[1]

The space of death is crucial to the creation of meaning and consciousness, nowhere more so than in societies where torture is endemic and where the culture of terror flourishes. We may think of the space of death as a threshold, yet it is a wide space whose breadth offers positions of advance as well as of extinction. Sometimes a person goes through it and returns to us to tell the tale, like Timerman, who entered it, he says, because he believed the battle against military dictatorship had to be fought.[2]

Timerman fought with words, with his newspaper *La Opinion*, in and against the silence imposed by the arbiters of discourse who beat out a new reality in the prison cells where the torturers and the tortured came together. "We victims and victimizers, we're part of the same humanity, colleagues in the same endeavor to prove the existence of ideologies, feelings, heroic deeds, religions, obsessions. And the rest of humanity, what are they engaged in?"[3]

The construction of colonial reality that occurred in the New World has been and will remain a topic of immense curiosity and study – the New World where the Indian and the African became subject to an initially far smaller number of Christians. Whatever conclusions we draw as to how that hegemony was so speedily effected, we would be most unwise to overlook or underestimate the role of terror. And by this, I mean us to think through terror, which as well as being a physiological state is also a social fact and a cultural construction whose baroque dimensions allow it to serve as the mediator *par excellence* of colonial hegemony. The space of death is one of the crucial spaces where Indian, African, and white gave birth to the New World.

This space of death has a long and rich culture. It is where the social imagination has populated its metamorphosing images of evil and the underworld: in the Western tradition, Homer, Virgil, the Bible, Dante, Bosch, the Inquisition, Baudelaire, Rimbaud, *Heart of Darkness*; in Northwest Amazonian tradition, zones of visions, communication between terrestrial and supernatural beings, putrefaction, death, rebirth, and genesis, perhaps in the rivers and land of maternal milk bathed eternally in subtle green light of coca leaves.[4] With European conquest and colonization, these spaces of death blend as a common pool of key signifiers or caption points binding the culture of the conqueror with that of the conquered. The space of death is preeminently a space of transformation: through the experience of death, life, through fear, loss of self and conformity to a new reality; or through evil, good. Lost in the dark woods, then journeying through the underworld with his guide, Dante achieves paradise only after he has mounted Satan's back. Timerman can be a guide for us, analagous to the ways Putumayo shamans I know are guides to those lost in the space of death.

An old Ingano Indian from the Putumayo once told me of this space:

With the fever I was aware of everything. But after eight days I became unconscious. I knew not where I was. Like a madman I wandered, consumed by fever. They had to cover me up where I fell, mouth down. Thus after eight days I was aware of nothing. I was unconscious. Of what people were saying, I remembered nothing. Of the pain of the fever, I remembered nothing; only the space of death – walking in the space of death. Thus, after the noises that spoke, I remained unconscious. Now the world remained behind. Now the world was removed. Well, then I understood. Now the pains were speaking. I knew that I would live no longer. Now I was dead. My sight had gone. Of the world I knew nothing, nor the sound of my ears. Of speech, nothing. Silence. And one knows the space of death, there ... And this is death – the space that I saw. I was in its center, standing. Then I went to the heights. From the heights a star-point seemed my due. I was standing. Then I came down. There I was searching for the five continents of the world, to remain, to find me a place in the five continents of the world – in the space in which I was wandering. But I was not able.

We might ask, what place in the five continents of the world will the wanderer in the space of death find himself? And by extension, where will a whole society find itself? The old man fears the evil of sorcery, the struggle for his soul. Between himself, the sorcerer, and the curing shaman, the five continents are sought and fought for. Yet here there is laughter too, puncturing the fear of the mystery, reminding us of Walter Benjamin's comment on the way in which romanticism may perniciously misunderstand the nature of intoxication. "Any serious exploration of occult, surrealistic, phantasmagoric gifts and phenomena," he writes,

> presupposes a dialectical intertwinement to which a romantic turn of mind is impervious. For histrionic or fanatical stress on the mysterious side of the mysterious takes us no further; we penetrate the mystery only to the degree that we recognize it in the everyday world, by virtue of a dialectical optic that perceives the everyday as impenetrable, the impenetrable as everyday.[5]

From Timerman's chronicle and texts like Miguel Angel Asturias's *El señor presidente* it is abundantly clear that cultures of terror are based on and nourished by silence and myth in which the fanatical stress on the mysterious side of the mysterious flourishes by means of rumor and fantasy woven in a dense web of magical realism. It is also clear that the victimizer needs the victim for the purpose of making truth, objectifying the victimizer's fantasies in the discourse of the other. To be sure, the torturer's desire is also prosaic: to acquire information, to act in concert with large-scale economic strategies elaborated by the masters and exigencies of production. Yet equally if not more important is the need to control massive populations through the cultural elaboration of fear.

That is why silence is imposed, why Timerman, the publisher, was so important, why he knew when to be silent and close off reality in the torture chamber. "Such silence," he tells us,

> begins in the channels of communication. Certain political leaders, institutions, and priests attempt to denounce what is happening, but are unable to establish contact with the population. The silence begins with a strong odor. People sniff the suicides, but it eludes them. Then silence finds another ally: solitude. People fear suicides as they fear madmen. And the person who wants to fight senses his solitude and is frightened.[6]

Hence, there is the need for us to fight that solitude, fear, and silence, to examine these conditions of truth-making and culture-making, to follow Michel Foucault in "seeing historically how effects of truth are produced within discourses which are in themselves neither true nor false."[7] At the same time we not only have to see, we also have to see anew through the creation of counterdiscourses.

If effects of truth are power, then the question is raised not only concerning the power to speak and write, but as to what form shall that counterdiscourse take. This issue of form has lately been of much concern to those involved in writing histories and ethnographies. But faced with the endemicity of torture, terror, and the growth of armies, we in the New World are today assailed with a new urgency. There is the effort to understand terror, in order to make *others* understand. Yet the reality at stake here makes a mockery of understanding and derides rationality, as when the young boy Jacobo Timerman asks his mother, "Why do they hate us?" And she replies, "Because they do not understand." And after his ordeal, the old Timerman writes of the need for a hated object and the simultaneous fear of that object – the almost magical inevitability of hatred. "No," he concludes, "there can be no doubt my mother was the one who was mistaken. It is not the anti-Semites who must be made to understand. It is we Jews."[8]

Hated and feared, objects to be despised, yet also of awe, the reified essence of evil in the very being of their bodies, these figures of the Jew, the black, the Indian, and woman herself, are clearly objects of cultural construction, the leaden keel of evil and of mystery stabilizing the ship and course that is Western history. With the cold war we add the communist. With the time bomb ticking inside the nuclear family, we add the feminists and the gays. The military and the New Right, like the conquerors of old, discover the evil they have imputed to these aliens, and mimic the savagery they have imputed.

What sort of understanding – what sort of speech, writing, and construction of meaning by any mode – can deal with and subvert that?

On one thing Timerman is clear. To counterpose the eroticization and romanticization of violence by the same means or by forms equally mystical is a dead end. Yet to offer one or all of the standard rational explanations of the culture of terror is similarly pointless. For behind the search for profits, the need to control labor, the need to assuage frustration, and so on, lie intricately construed long-standing cultural logics of meaning – structures of feeling – whose basis lies in a symbolic world and not in one of rationalism. Ultimately there are two features; the crudest of empirical facts such as the electrodes and the mutilated human body, and the experience of going through torture. In his text Timerman does create a powerful counterdiscourse, precisely because, like torture itself, it moves us through that space of death where reality is up for grabs, to confront the hallucination of the military. His text of madness and evil establishes a revolutionary and, to my mind, sound poetics because it finds its counterweight and sanity in what I take to be the most difficult of political positions marked out by a contradictory space between socialism and anarchism. He is to Victor Serge as V. S. Naipaul is to Arthur Koestler and Joseph Conrad.

The Putumayo report

At this point it is instructive to analyze briefly Casement's Putumayo report, which was submitted to Sir Edward Grey, head of the British Foreign Service, and published by the House of Commons on July 13, 1913 when Casement was forty-nine years old.

The essence of his 136-page Putumayo report, based on seven weeks of travel in 1910 through the rubber-gathering areas of the jungles of the Caraparaná and Igaraparaná affluents of the middle reaches of the Putumayo river, and on some six months in the Amazon basin, lay in its detail of the terror and tortures together with Casement's explanation of causes and his estimate of the toll in human life. Putumayo rubber would be unprofitable were it not for the forced labor of local Indians, principally those called Huitotos. For the twelve years from 1900, the Putumayo output of some 4,000 tons of rubber cost thousands of Indians their lives. Deaths from torture, disease, and possibly flight had decreased the population of the area by around 30,000 during that time.[9]

The British government felt obliged to send Casement as its consular representative to the Putumayo because of the public outcry aroused in 1909 by a series of articles in the London magazine, *Truth*; the series depicted the brutality of the rubber company, which since 1907 had been a consortium of Peruvian and British interests in the region. Entitled "The Devil's Paradise: A British Owned Congo," these articles were the work of a young "engineer" and adventurer from the United States named Walter Hardenburg, who had with a companion entered the remote corner of the Amazon basin from the Colombian Andes in 1907 and had been taken prisoner by the Peruvian Rubber Company founded by Julio César Arana in1903. Hardenburg's chronicle is to an important extent an elaboration on a text basic to the Putumayo saga, an article pubished in the Iquitos newspaper *La Sanción* shortly before its publication was suspended by the Peruvian government and Arana.

Asserting that the rubber trees are in rapid decline and will be exhausted in four years' time because of the rapacity of the production system, the article continues by declaring that the peaceful Indians work night and day collecting rubber without the slightest remuneration. They are given nothing to eat or wear. Their crops, together with the women and children, are taken for the pleasure of the whites. They are inhumanly flogged until their bones are visible. Given no medical treatment, they are left to die after torture, eaten by the company's dogs. They are castrated, and their ears, fingers, arms, and legs are cut off. They are also tortured by means of fire, water, and crucifixion tied head-down. The whites cut them to pieces with machetes and dash out the brains of small children by hurling them against trees and walls. The elderly are killed when they can no longer work. To amuse themselves, company officials practice shooting, using Indians as targets, and on special occasions such as Easter Saturday – Saturday of Glory – shoot them down in groups or, in preference, douse them in kerosene and set them on fire to enjoy their agony.[10]

In a letter written to Hardenburg by an employee of the company we read how a "commission" was sent out by a rubber-station manager to exterminate a group of Indians for not bringing in sufficient rubber. The commission returned in four days with fingers, ears, and several heads of Indians to prove the orders had been carried out.[11] On another occasion, the manager called in hundreds of Indians to assemble at the station:

> He grasped his carbine and machete and began the slaughter of these defenseless Indians, leaving the ground covered with over 150 corpses, among them men, women and children. Bathed in blood and appealing for mercy, the survivors were heaped with the dead and burned to death, while the manager shouted, "I want to exterminate the Indians who do not obey my orders about the rubber that I require them to bring in."

"When they get drunk," adds the correspondent, "the upper-level employees of the company toast with champagne the man who can boast of the greatest number of murders."[12]

The drama perhaps most central to the Putumayo terror, quoted from an Iquitos newspaper article in 1908, and affirmed as fact by both Casement and Hardenburg, concerns the weighing-in of rubber brought by the Indians from the forest:

> The Indian is so humble that as soon as he sees that the needle of the scale does not mark the ten kilos, he himself stretches out his hands and throws himself on the ground to receive the punishment. Then the chief [of the rubber station] or a subordinate advances, bends down, takes the Indian by the hair, strikes him, raises his head, drops it face downwards on the ground, and after the face is beaten and kicked and covered with blood, the Indian is scourged. This is when they are treated best, for often they cut them to pieces with machetes.[13]

In the rubber station of Matanzas, continues the writer, "I have seen Indians tied to a tree, their feet about half a yard above the ground. Fuel is then placed below, and they are burnt alive. This is done to pass the time."

Casement's report to the House of Commons is staid and sober, somewhat like a lawyer arguing a case and in marked contrast to his diary covering the same experience. He piles fact on brutal fact, suggests an over-all analysis, and makes his recommendations. His material comes from three sources: what he personally witnessed; testimony of 30 Barbados blacks who, with 160 others, were contracted by the company during 1903–04 to serve as overseers, and whose statements occupy 85 published foolscap pages; and, interspersed with Casement's direct observations, numerous stories from local residents and company employees.

Early on in the report, in a vivid throwaway line, he evokes the banality of the cruelty. "The employees at all the stations passed the time when not hunting Indians, either lying in their hammocks or in gambling."[14] The unreal atmosphere of ordinariness, of the ordinariness of the extraordinary, can be startling. "At some of the stations the principal flogger was the station cook – two such men were directly named to me, and I ate the food they prepared, while many of their victims carried my baggage from station to station, and showed often terrible scars on their limbs inflicted at the hands of these men."[15]

From the evidence of scarring, Casement found that the "great majority" (perhaps up to 90 percent) of the more than 1,600 Indians he saw had been badly beaten.[16] Some of the worst affected were small boys, and deaths due to flogging were frequent, either under the lash, or more frequently, a few days later when the wounds became maggot-infested.[17] Floggings occurred when an Indian brought in insufficient rubber and were most sadistic for those who dared to flee. Flogging was mixed with other tortures such as near drowing, "designed," as Casement points out, "to just stop short of taking life while inspiring the acute mental fear and inflicting much of the physical agony of death."[18] Casement was informed by a man who had himself often flogged Indians that he had seen mothers flogged because their little sons had not brought in enough rubber. While the boy stood terrified and crying at the sight, his mother would be beaten "just a few strokes" to make him a better worker.[19]

Deliberate starvation was resorted to repeatedly, sometimes to frighten, more often to kill. Men and women were kept in the stocks until they died of hunger. One Barbadian related how he had seen Indians in this situation "scraping up the dirt with their fingers and eating it." Another declared he had seen them eating the maggots in their wounds.[20]

The stocks were sometimes placed on the upper verandah or residential part of the main dwelling house of the rubber stations, in direct view of the manager and his employees. Children, men, and women might be confined in them for months, and some of the Barbados men said they had seen women raped while in the stocks.[21]

Much of the surveillance and punishment was carried out by the corps of Indian guards known as the *muchachos*. Members of this armed corps had been trained by the company from an early age, and were used to control *salvajes* other than those to whom they were kin. Casement thought them to be generally every bit as evil as their white masters.[22] When Barbados men were present, they were frequently assigned the task of flogging, but, Casement emphasizes, "no monopoly of flogging was enjoyed by any employee as a right. The chief of the section frequently himself took the lash, which, in turn, might be wielded by every member of the civilized or 'rational staff.'"[23]

"Such men," reports Casement, "had lost all sight or sense of rubber-gathering – they are simply beasts of prey who lived upon the Indians and delighted in shedding their blood." Moreover, the station managers from the areas where Casement got his most precise information were in debt (despite their handsome rates of commission), running their operations at a loss to the company which in some sections ran to many thousands of pounds sterling.[24]

It is necessary at this point to note that although the Indians received the brunt of the terror, whites and blacks were also targets. Whether as competitors for Indian rubber-gatherers, like the independent Colombian rubber traders who first conquered the Putumayo and were then dislodged by Arana's company in 1908, or as employees of the company, extremely few escaped the ever-present threat of degradation and torture. Asked by Casement if he did not know it to be wrong to torture Indians, one of the Barbados men replied that he was unable to refuse orders, "that a man might be a man down in Iquitos, but 'you couldn't be a man up there.'"[25] In addition, most of the company's white and black employees were themselves trapped in a debt-peonage system, but one quite different from the one the company used in controlling its Indians.

From the testimony of the Barbados men it is clear that dissension, hatred, and mistrust ran riot among all members of the company – to the degree that one has to consider seriously the hypothesis that only in their group ritualization of torturing Indians could such anomie and mistrust be held in check, thus guaranteeing to the company the solidarity required to sustain it as an effective social unit.

To read Casement's secondhand and Hardenburg's eyewitness accounts of the company attacks against independent white Colombian traders is to become further aware of the ritualistic features which assured the violence of the Putumayo rubber boom of its success as a culture of terror.

Casement's analysis

Casement's main line of analysis lies with his argument that it was not rubber but labor that was scarce in the Putumayo, and that this scarcity was the basic cause of the use of terror. Putumayo rubber was of the lowest quality, the remoteness of its source made its transport expensive relative to rubber from other zones, and wages for free labor were very high. Hence, he reasons, the company resorted to the use of forced labor under a debt-peonage system, and used torture to maintain labor discipline.

The problem with this argument, which assumes the purported rationality of business and the capital-logic of commodities (such as labor), is that it encounters certain contradictions and, while not exactly wrong, strikes me as giving insufficient weight to two fundamental considerations. The first consideration concerns the forms of labor and economic organization that local history and Indian society made available, or potentially available, to world capitalism in the jungles of the Putumayo. The second, put crudely, is that terror and torture do not derive only from market pressure (which we can regard here as a trigger) but also from the process of cultural construction of evil as well. "Market pressure" assumes the paradigm of scarcity essential to capitalist economism and capitalist socioeconomic theory. Leaving aside the question of how accurate a depiction of capitalist society results from this paradigm, it is highly dubious that it reveals much of the reality of the Putumayo rubber boom where the problem facing capitalist enterprise was precisely that there were no capitalist social institutions and no market for abstract labor into which capital could be fed and multiplied. Indeed, one could go further to develop an argument which begins with the premise that it was just this lack of commoditized social relationships, in interaction with commodity forces emanating from the world rubber market, that accounts for the production of torture and terror. We can say that the culture of terror was functional to the needs of the labor system, but that tells us little about the most significant contradictions to emerge from Casement's report, namely, that the slaughter of this precious labor was on a scale vast beyond belief, and that, as Casement himself states, not only were the station managers costing the company large sums of money but that "such men had lost all sight or sense of rubber-gathering – they were simply beasts of prey who lived upon the Indians and delighted in shedding their blood." To claim the rationality of business for this is to claim and sustain an illusory rationality, obscuring our understanding of the way business can transform the use of terror from the means into an end in itself.

The consideration of local history and economic organization requires far fuller treatment than can be attempted here. But it should be noted in passing that "scarcity" of labor cannot refer to a scarcity of Indians, of whom there seems to have been an abundance, but rather to the fact that the Indians would not work in the regular and dependable manner necessary to a large-scale capitalist enterprise. Casement downplayed this phenomenon, now often referred to as "the backward sloping supply curve of labor," and did so even though in the Congo he had himself complained that the problem was that the natives would not work;[26] he felt sure that if paid with more goods, the Indians would work to the level required by the company without force. Many people with far longer experience in the Putumayo denied this naïve assertion and pointed out, with logic as impeccable as Casement's, that the scarcity of labor and the ease with which the Indians could live off the forest obliged employers elsewhere in the Putumayo to treat them with consideration.[27] In either case, however, with or without use of coercion, the labor productivity obtained fell far short of what employers desired.

The contradictions mount further on close examination of the debt-peonage system, which Casement regards as slavery. It was a pretext, he says, that the Indian in such a relation was in debt, for the Indian was bound by physical force to work for the company and could not escape.[28] One then must ask why the company persisted in this pretense, especially given the means of coercion at its disposal.

Accounts of advances paid in goods (such as machetes, cloth, shotguns) were supposedly kept for each rubber-gatherer; the advances were roughly equal to fivepence per pound weight of rubber, which was fetching three shillings tenpence on the London market in 1910. (In West Africa, natives were paid an equivalent of between two shillings and two shillings and sixpence per pound of "Ibi Red niggers'" rubber, equal in quality to the Putumayan).[29] A station manager told Casement that the Indians never asked the price or value of rubber. Sometimes a single coin was given, and Casement met numbers of Indian women wearing necklaces made of coins.[30] Joaquin Rocha writes that the Indians of the Tres Esquinas rubber station valued money not as a means of exchange but as a precious object; they would beat coins into smooth and shining triangular shapes to use as nose rings or ear pendants.[31] Yet, it would be naïve to suppose that the Indians lacked interest or understanding of the terms of trade and of what the whites got for rubber in the outside world. "You buy these with the rubber we produce," said an Indian chief as one entranced, looking through Casement's binoculars.[32] Casement was told that the station managers would fix the quantity of rubber due from each individual according to the goods that had been advanced, and in this connection Father Gridilla relates an episode of interest from when he travelled up the Caraparaná in 1912.

It was at a time when thousands of Indians came to the rubber station of La Occidente to deliver rubber. First there was a great dance lasting five days – the sort of event Joaquin Rocha a decade earlier likened to a harvest festival. Then the rubber was handed over and goods were advanced, Father Gridilla commenting "the savages don't know money, their needs are very limited, and they ask only for shotguns, ammunition, axes, machetes, mirrors, and occasionally hammocks." An Indian he described as a corpulent and ugly savage declined to accept anything and, on being pressed, replied, "I don't want anything. I've got everything." The whites insisted again and again that he must ask for something. Finally he retorted, "I want a black dog!" "And where am I going to find a black dog or even a white one if there aren't any in all of Putumayo?" responded the station manager. "You ask me for rubber." replied the savage, "and I bring rubber. If I ask for a black dog you have to give me one!"[33]

Relying on stories told him, Hardenburg wrote that the Indians received their advances with great pleasure, because if they did not, they were flogged to death.[34]

Pretext as it was, the debt which ensured peonage was nonetheless real, and as a pretense its magical realism was an essential to the labor organization of the Putumayo rubber boom as is the "commodity fiction" Karl Polanyi describes for a mature capitalist economy.[35] To analyze the construction of these fictional realities we need now to turn to some of their more obviously mythic features, enclosed as they are in the synergistic relation to savagery and business, cannibalism and capitalism. Interrogated by the British Parliamentary Select Committee on Putumayo in 1913, Julio César Arana, the driving force of the rubber company, was asked to clarify what he meant when he stated that the Indians had resisted the establishment of civilization in their districts, that they had been resisting for many years, and had practiced cannibalism. "What I mean by that," he replied, "is that they did not admit of exchange, or anybody to do business with them – Whites, for example."[36]

Jungle and savagery

There is a problem that I have only hinted at in all of the accounts of the atrocities of the Putumayo rubber boom. While the immensity of the cruelty is beyond question, most of the evidence comes through stories. The meticulous historian would seize upon this fact as a challenge to winnow out truth from exaggeration or understatement. But the more basic implication, it seems to me, is that *the narratives are in themselves evidence of the process whereby a culture of terror was created and sustained.*

Two interlacing motifs stand out: the horrors of the jungle, and the horrors of savagery. All the facts are bent through the prism formed by these motifs which, in keeping with Conrad's theory of art, mediate effective truth not so much through the dissemination of information as through the appeal of temperaments through sensory impressions. Here the European and colonist image of the primeval jungle with its vines and rubber trees and domination of man's domination stands forth as the colonially apt metaphor of the great space of terror and deep cruelties. (Europe – late nineteenth century, penetrating the ancient forests of the tropics.) Carlos Fuentes asserts that Latin American literature is woven between the poles formed by nature and the dictator, in which the destructiveness of the former serves to reflect even more destructive social relations. A Colombian author, José Eustacio Rivera writes in the 1920s as a debt-entrapped peon in the Putumayo:

> I have been a *cauchero* [rubber-gatherer] and I will always be a *cauchero*. I live in the slimy mire in the solitude of the forests with my gang of malarial men, piercing the bark of trees whose blood runs white, like that of gods ... I have been and always will be a *cauchero*. And what my hand inflicts on the trees, it can also inflict on men.[37]

In *Heart of Darkness*, the narrator, Marlow, sits back, like a Buddha introducing his yarn, prefiguring the late nineteenth-century colonial exploration of the Congo by evoking a soldier of imperial Rome, moving through the marshes of the Thames.

> Land in a swamp, march through the woods, and in some inland post feel the savagery, the utter savagery, had closed around him – all that mysterious life of the wilderness that stirs in the forest, in the jungles, in the hearts of wild men. There's no initiation either into such mysteries. He has to live in the midst of the incomprehensible, which is also detestable. And it has a fascination, too, that goes to work upon him. The fascination of the abomination – you know,

imagine the growing regrets, the longing to escape, the powerless disgust, the surrender, the hate.

The Capuchin father, Gaspar de Pinell, who made a legendary *excursión apostólica* to the Huitotos and other savage tribes in the Putumayo forests in the late 1920s, records how his white guide, a man of much experience, sickened and sought cure from a Huitoto shaman (whom the padre calls a witch) rather than from the pharmacy of the whites. He died shortly thereafter, providing Father Pinell with the moral dilemma of the colonist: "This shows," he wrote, "that it is more likely that the civilized man will become a savage on mixing with Indians, than the Indians are likely to become civilized through the actions of the civilized."[38] And with a torrent of phenomenological virtuosity, his colleague, Father Francisco de Vilanova, addresses the same vexing problem, only here it is the Putumayo jungle which constitutes the great figure of savagery. In a book describing Capuchin endeavors among the Huitotos from the 1920s on, we read:

It is almost something unbelievable to those who do not know the jungle. It is an irrational fact that enslaves those who go there. It is a whirlwind of savage passions that dominates the civilized person who has too much confidence in himself. It is a degeneration of the spirit in a drunkeness of improbable but real circumstances. The rational and civilized man loses respect for himself and his domestic place. He throws his heritage into the mire from where who knows when it will be retrieved. One's heart fills with morbidity and the sentiment of savagery. It becomes insensible to the most pure and great things of humanity. Even cultivated spirits, finely formed and well educated, have succumbed.[39]

But of course it is not the jungle but the sentiments men project into it that is decisive in filling their hearts with savagery. And what the jungle can accomplish, so much more can its native inhabitants, the wild Indians, like those tortured into gathering rubber. It must not be overlooked that the colonially constructed image of the wild Indian here at stake was a powerfully ambiguous image, a see-sawing, bifocalized, and hazy composite of the animal and the human. In their human or human-like form, the wild Indians could all the better reflect back to the colonists the vast and baroque projections of human wildness that the colonists needed to establish their reality as civilized (not to mention business-like) people. And it was only because the wild

Indians were human that they were able to serve as labor – and as subjects of torture. For it is not the victim as animal that gratifies the torturer, but the fact that the victim is human, thus enabling the torturer to become the savage.

How savage were the Huitotos?

The savagery of the wild Indians occupied a key role in the propaganda of the rubber company. Hardenburg writes that the Huitotos "are hospitable to a marked degree," and that while the Church improves their morals, in the company's domain, priests have been carefully excluded. "Indeed," he continues, "in order to frighten people and thus prevent them from entering the region, the company has circulated the most blood curdling reports of the ferocity and cannibalism of these helpless Indians, whom travellers such as myself have found to be timid, peaceful, mild, industrious and humble."[40] Father Pinell has published a document from Peru describing a film commissioned by Arana's company in 1917. Shown in the cinemas of Lima, it portrayed the civilizing effect of the company on "these savage regions that as recently as 25 years ago were peopled entirely by cannibals. Owing to the energy of this tireless struggler [Arana] they have been converted into useful elements of labor."[41]

Propaganda usually flowers only where the soil has been long and well prepared, and it seems to me that Arana's was no exception since the mythology of savagery dates from times long before his. Yet, the passions unleashed by the rubber boom invigorated this mythology with a seductive power. Before probing further into the ways the rubber company acquired the savagery it imputed to the Indians, it is necessary to pause and examine the colonists' mythology and folklore concerning the Upper Amazon forest people.

Time and again Casement tells us that the Huitotos and all Upper Amazon Indians were gentle and docile. He downplays their cannibalism, says that they were thoughtless rather than cruel, and regards their docility as a *natural* and remarkable characteristic. This helps him to explain the ease with which they were conquered and forced to gather rubber.

An Indian would promise anything for a gun, or for some of the other tempting things offered as inducements to him to work rubber. Many Indians submitted to the alluring offer only to find that once in the "conquistadores'" books they had lost all liberty and were reduced to unending demands for more rubber and varied tasks. A cacique or "capitán" might be bought over to dispose of the labor of his clan, and as the cacique's influence was very great and the natural docility of the Indian a remarkable characteristic of Upper Amazon tribes, the work of conquering a primitive people and reducing them to a continual strain of rubber-finding was less difficult than might at first be supposed.[42]

Yet, on the other hand, such docility makes the violence of the whites even harder to understand.

Many points can be contested in Casement's rendering here, such as his assertion of the degree of chiefly power and the deceptive simplicity he evokes with regard to the issue of toughness and tenderness in a society so foreign to his own. It should also not be forgotten that the story he wanted to sell was one of innocent and gentle child-like Indians brutalized by the rubber company, and this controlling image gives his report considerable rhetorical power. In addition there was his tendency to equate the sufferings of the Irish with those of the Indians and see in both of their preimperialist histories a culture more humane than that of their civilizing overlords. (Conrad never indulged in that kind of transference.) Still another factor blended with the foregoing, and that was the innate tenderness of Casement's character and his ability to draw that quality out of others, as testified by numerous people. It is this aspect of his homosexuality, and not sexual lust, which should be dwelt on here, as shown, for example, in this note in his Putumayo diary:

> ... floggings and putting in guns and floggings with machetes across the back ... I bathed in the river, delightful, and Andokes [Indians] came down and caught butterflies for Barnes and I. Then a captain [Indian chief] embraced us laying his head down against our breasts. I never saw so touching a thing, poor soul, he felt we were their friends.[43]

Alfred Simson, an Englishman who travelled the Putumayo and Napo rivers in the 1880s and spent far more time there than Casement, conveys a picture quite different from Casement's. An example is his description of the Zaparos, who, like the Huitotos, were considered by the whites to be wild Indians. Noting that they raided other groups and abducted their children for sale to white traders, Simson goes on to state:

> When unprovoked they are, like really wild Indians, very shy and retiring, but are perfectly fearless, and will suffer no one, either

whites or others, to employ force with them. They can only be managed by tact, good treatment, and sometimes simple reasoning: otherwise resenting ill-treatment or an attempt to resort to blows, [they react] with the worst of violence ... At all times they are changeable and unreliable, betraying under different circumstances, and often apparently under the same, in common with so many of their class, all the most opposite traits of character, excepting perhaps servility – a true characteristic of the old world – and stinginess, which I have never observed in them. The absence of servility is typical of all the independent Indians of Ecuador.[44]

And he observes that "they also gain great enjoyment from the destruction of life. They are always ready to kill animals or people, and they delight in it."[45]

Simson was employed on the first steam launch to ascend the Putumayo, that of Rafael Rayes, later a president of Colombia. Hence he witnessed the opening of the region to modern commerce, and was in a special position to observe the institutionalization of ideologies concerning race and class. Not only does he present a contrary and more complex estimate of Indian toughness than does Casement: he also provides the clue and ethnographic motif necessary to understand why such contrary images coexist and flourish, how Indian images of wildness come halfway, as it were, to meet and merge with white colonial images of savagery, and, finally, how such imagery functions in the creation of terror.

It is first necessary to observe that the inhabitants of the Putumayo were according to Joaquin Rocha at the turn of the century, divided into two great classes of social types: whites and savage Indians. The category, whites (also referred to as "rationals," Christians, and "civilized"), included not only people phenotypically white, but also mestizos, negros, mulattos, Zambos, and Indians "of those groups incorporated into civilization since the time of the Spanish conquest."[46] Simson takes us further into this classification, and although his remarks here pertain to the *montaña* region at the headwaters of the rivers, they seem to me generally applicable to the middle reaches of the Putumayo as well, and are certainly relevant to the understanding of colonist culture.

Simson notes that what he calls the "pure Indians of the forest" are divided, by whites and Spanish-speaking Indians, into two classes: Indians (*Indios*) and heathens (*infieles*). The *Indios* are Quichua-speaking, salt-eating, semi-Christians, while the heathens, also known as *aucas*, speak distinct languages, eat salt rarely, and know nothing of baptism or of the Catholic Church.[47] In passing it should be observed that today, if not in times long past, the term *auca* also connotes cannibals who roam the forest naked, are without marriage rules, and practice incest.

Simson also states that the term *auca* as commonly understood bears "the full meaning it did anciently in Peru under the Incas. It includes the sense of infidel, traitor, barbarian, and is often applied in a malignant sense." In Peru it was used, he says, "to designate those who rebelled against their king and incarnation of their deity, the Inca".[48] Whether or not this assertion is historically accurate (as it certainly seems to be) is somewhat beside the point, for its importance lies in its character as a myth informing everyday life at the time of the rubber boom.

Simson's second major point about *aucas* concerns their animal-like qualities, so pronounced, he says, that they partake of the occult and spiritual. With reference to the Zaparos, for example, he writes that their perceptions of eye and ear are perfectly marvellous, and surpass those of the non-*auca* Indians considerably. Their knowledge of the forest is so perfect that they often travel at night in unknown parts. They are great fighters, and can detect sounds and footmarks where white men perceive nothing. On the trail of an animal, they suddenly swerve, then change again as if following the scent of their prey. Their motions are cat-like and they move unscathed through the entangled underwood and thorns. To communicate with each other, they generally imitate the whistle of the toucan or partridge – and all this is in marked contrast to non-*aucas* or civilized Indians, "who stand in fear and respect of them, but despise or affect to despise them as infidels behind their backs."[49]

I should add that the highland Indian shaman with whom I work in the Colombian Andes which overlook the Putumayo jungles regards the jungle shamans below as *aucas*, as animal/spirit hybrids possessing great magic. He singles out the Huitotos as a spiritual force with whom he makes a mystical pact in incantations and songs, with or without hallucinogens, to assure the success of his own magical battles with evil.

It is crucial to grasp the dialectic of sentiments involved here by the appelation *auca*, a dialectic enshrouded in magic and composed of both fear and contempt – identical to the mysticism, hatred, and awe projected onto the Zionist socialist Timerman in the torture chambers of the military. In the case of the *aucas*, this projection is inseparable from the imputation of their resistance to sacred imperial authority and the further imputation of magical power possessed by lowland forest dwellers as a class and by their oracles, seers, and healers – their shamans – in particular. Moreover, this indigenous, and what may well be a pre-Colombian, construction blends with the medieval European mythology of the Wild Man brought to the Andes and the Amazon by the Spaniards and Portuguese. Today, in the upper reaches of the Putumayo with which I am acquainted, the mythology of *auca* and Wild Man underlies the resort to Indian shamans by white and black colonists who seek cure from sorcery and hard times, while these very same colonists despise Indians as savages.[50] In the rubber boom, with its desperate need for Indian labor, the same mythology nourished incalculable cruelty and paranoia on the part of the whites. It is to this mythic endowment inherited by world capitalism in the jungles of the Putumayo that we need to pay attention if we are to understand the irrational "excesses" of the terror and torture depicted by Casement.

Fear of Indian rebellion

Casement mentions the possibility that, in addition to their drive for profit, the whites' fear of Indian rebellion impelled them toward viciousness. But in keeping with his stress on Indian docility, he gives four reasons why Indian rebellion was unlikely. Indian communities were disunited long before the advent of the rubber boom, while the whites were armed and well organized. The Indians were poorly armed and their blowpipes, bows, and lances had been confiscated. Most important in his opinion was the fact that the elders had been systematically murdered by the company for the crime of giving "bad advice."[51]

Rocha, who was in the area some seven years before Casement, thought differently. He claims that the whites feared the consequences of the Indians' hatred and that this fear was central to their policies and thought. "Life for the Whites in the land of the Huitotos," he declares, "hangs by a thread." Small uprisings were common, and he provides an account of one of these.

In 1903 the Colombian Emilio Gutiérrez navigated up the Caquetá from Brazil searching for Indians to use to establish a rubber station. Reaching the area whose conquest he desired, he sent the bulk of his men back to carry in merchandise, and he and three others remained. While asleep, Gutiérrez and the companions were killed by wild Indians. Hearing the news, other whites prepared to retaliate when news reached them that thirty of Gutiérrez's civilized Indian work force had also been killed, all at the same time yet in different parts of the jungle. Indians working for whites were set in pursuit of the rebels; some were caught and killed outright, some were taken as prisoners for the whites, and the majority escaped. A few were captured and eaten by the Indian mercenaries – so the tale goes.[52]

In 1910 Casement heard the same episode from a Peruvian, who introduced his story by saying that the methods used by Colombian conquerors were very bad. In this version, the rebel Indians decapitated Gutiérrez together with an unstated number of other whites and exposed their skulls on the walls of their "drum house," keeping the limbless bodies in water for as long as possible to show them off to other Indians. Casement's informant said he had found the bodies of twelve others tied to stakes, assuring Casement that the reason they had not been eaten was that Indians "had a repugnance to eating white men, whom they hated too much." Terrible reprisals subsequently fell upon the Indians, notes Casement.[53]

Considered separately, and especially in relation to Rocha's version, this account of Casement's establishes the point that the white fear of Indian rebellion was not unjustified, but that, in addition, such rebellion was perceived in a mythic and colonially paranoid vision in which the image of dismemberment and cannibalism glowed vividly.

Fear of cannibalism

Cannibalism acquired great ideological potency for the colonists from the beginning of the European conquest of the New World. The figure of the cannibal was elaborated and used for many sorts of ends, responding as it did to some of the most powerful symbolic forces known to humankind. It could be used to justify enslavement and as such was apparently important in the early economy of Brazil,[54] thereby affecting even the headwaters of the Amazon such as the Putumayo where cannibalism was kept luridly alive in the imagination of the whites down to the era of the rubber boom.

Rocha provides many examples. He signals his arrival at Huitoto territory writing of "this singular land of the cannibals, the land of the Huitotos conquered by a dozen valiant Colombians repeating the heroism of their Spanish ancestors."[55] The rubber traders, he emphatically asserts, have tried to stamp out cannibalism with severe punishments. Yet cannibalism is an addiction. The Huitotos think they can deceive the whites about this, but "they succumb to the satisfaction of their beastly appetites."[56] The most notorious of the modern *conquistadores*, the Colombian Crisóstomo Hernandez (a Colombian highlands mulatto who had fled the police and sought refuge in the jungle), had, so Rocha was told, killed all the children, women, and men of an Indian long house because they practiced cannibalism – a surprising story given the need for labor, yet typical of white folk tales in the Putumayo.[57]

Don Crisóstomo was the hero of another legendary story as well, one which makes the point that although Indian customs would conflict with those of whites, as, for example, in their "misunderstandings" over the value of money and of work, there were nevertheless ritual features of Indian culture which whites could harness to the needs of the rubber company. The practice of sometimes delivering rubber in conjunction with a great dance as a prelude to a sort of gift-giving exchange, as reported by Gridilla and Rocha, has been mentioned. Even more interesting is the rite the whites called *chupe del tabaco*, or tobacco-sucking, by adult Indian men during most if not all ritual occasions, a rite which perhaps fascinated the whites even more than it did the Indians.

Seated in a circle, usually at night, with the women and children set back in their hammocks but within earshot, the men took turns to place a finger in a thick concoction of cooked tobacco juice and then sucked it. Hardenburg reports that this ceremony was indispensable to any fiesta or to solemnize any agreement or contract. These were times when the men in general and the chief in particular held forth with great oratory lasting perhaps the entire night. "This is the Huitoto's solemn oath," writes Hardenburg, "and is never said to be broken. Whenever the whites wish to enter into any important agreement with the Indians, they always insist upon this ceremony being performed."[58] Casement says the same, yet goes on to quote from a French explorer, Eugenio Robuchon, under whose name it was written that this rite was one "in which the Indians recall their lost liberty and their actual sufferings, and formulate terrible vows of vengeance against the whites."[59]

Rocha was told that Crisóstomo Hernandez was a marvellously skilled orator, taking his place as a *capitán* or *capitán general* among the circle of Indian men. Gathering with a large assembly of chiefs around the tobacco pot, don Crisóstomo would orate in Huitoto language and style from eight in the evening till four in the morning, with such power of seduction that the chiefs unanimously adopted his proposals. This, says Rocha, was before he reigned through terror and military might; his dominion came to rest on force of arms, yet it was through oratory that he initiated his conquest, "because for the Huitotos, he was their king and god."[60]

The story which most impressed Rocha was the one about the Huitoto rite of judicial murder, or capital punishment. One can easily imagine the chords of exotic terror it provoked among the colonists and employees of the rubber company listening to it in the chit-chat of a jungle night.

All the individuals of the nation that has captured the prisoner retire to an area of the bush to which women are absolutely prohibited, except for one who acts a special role. Children are rigorously excluded also. In the center, a pot of cooked tobacco juice is placed for the pleasure of the men, and in a corner seated on a little bench and firmly bound is the captive.

Clasping each other's arms, the savages form a long line, and to the sound of drum beats advance dancing very close to the victim. They retreat and advance many times, with individuals separating to drink from the pot of tobacco. Then the drum stops for the dancing cannibals, and so that the unfortunate victim can see how much he is going to lose by dying, the most beautiful girl of the tribe enters, regally attired with the most varied and brilliant feathers of the birds of these woods. The drum starts again, and the beautiful girl dances alone in front of and almost touching him. She twists and advances, showering him with passionate looks and gestures of love, turning around and repeating this three or four times. She then leaves, terminating the second act of this solemn occasion. The third follows with the same men's dance as before, except that each time the line of dancers approaches the prisoner, one of the men detaches himself and declaims something like this: "Remember when your people killed Jatijiko, man of our nation whom you couldn't take prisoner because he knew how to die before allowing himself to be dragged in front of your people? We are going to take vengeance of his death in you, you coward, that doesn't know how to die in battle like he did." Or else: "Remember when you and your people surprised my sister Jifisina bathing, captured her and while alive made a party of her flesh and tormented her until her last breath? Do you remember? Now you god-cursed man we are going to devour you alive and you won't die until all traces of your bloody flesh have disappeared from around our mouths."

Following this is the fourth and last act of the terrifying tragedy. One by one the dancers come forward and with his knife each one cuts a slice of meat off the prisoner, which they eat half roasted to the sound of his death rattle. When he eventually dies, they finish cutting him up and continue roasting and cooking his flesh, eating him to the last little bit.[61]

Narrative mediation: epistemic murk

It seems to me that stories like these were the groundwork indispensable to the formation and flowering of the colonial imagination during the Putumayo rubber boom. "Their imagination was diseased," wrote the Peruvian judge Rómulo Paredes in 1911, referring to the rubber-station managers, "and they saw everywhere attacks by Indians, conspiracies, uprisings, treachery etc. and in order to save themselves from these fancied perils ... they killed, and killed without compassion."[62] Far from being trivial daydreams indulged in after work was over, these stories and the imagination they sustained were a potent political force without which the work of conquest and of supervising rubber gathering could not have been accomplished. What is essential to understand is the way in which these stories functioned to create, through magical realism, a culture of terror dominating both whites and Indians.

The importance of this fabulous work extends beyond the epic and grotesque quality of its content. The truly crucial feature lies in creating an uncertain reality out of fiction, a nightmarish reality in which the unstable interplay of truth and illusion becomes a social force of horrendous and phantasmic dimensions. To an important extent all societies live by fiction taken as reality. What distinguishes cultures of terror is that the epistemological, ontological, and otherwise purely philosophical problem of reality-and-illusion, certainty-and-doubt, becomes infinitely more than a "merely" philosophical problem. It becomes a high-powered tool for domination and a principal medium of political practice. And in the Putumayo rubber boom this medium of epistemic and ontological murk was most keenly figured and objectified as the space of death.

In his report, Paredes tells us that the rubber-station managers lived obsessed with death. They saw danger everywhere and thought solely of the fact that they were surrounded by vipers, tigers, and cannibals. It is these ideas of death, he writes, which constantly struck their imaginations, making them terrified and capable of any act. Like children who read the *Arabian Nights*, he goes on to say, they had nightmares of witches, evil spirits, death, treason, and blood. The only way they could live in such a terrifying world, he observes, was by themselves inspiring terror.[63]

Sociological and mythic mediation: the *muchachos*

If it was the telling of tales which mediated inspiration of the terror, then it behooves us to inquire a little into the sociological agency which mediated this mediation, namely, the corps of Indian guards trained by the company and known as the *muchachos*. For in Rómulo Paredes's words, they were "constantly devising executions and continually revealing meetings of Indians 'licking tobacco' – which meant an oath to kill white men – imaginary uprisings which never existed, and other similar crimes."[64]

Mediating as civilized or rational Indians between the savages of the forest and the whites of the rubber camps, the *muchachos* personified all the critical distinctions in the class and caste system of rubber production. Cut off from their own kind, whom they persecuted and betrayed and in whom they inspired envy and hatred, and now classified as civilized yet dependent on whites for food, arms, and goods, the *muchachos* wrought to perfection all that was horrifying in the colonial mythology of savagery – because they occupied the perfect sociological and mythic space to do so. Not only did they create fictions stoking the fires of white paranoia, they embodied the brutality which the whites feared, created, and tried to harness to their own ends. In a very literal sense, the *muchachos* traded their identity as savages for their new social status as civilized Indians and guards. As Paredes notes, they placed at the disposal of the whites "their special instincts, such as sense of direction, scent, their sobriety, and their knowledge of the forest."[65] Just as they bought rubber from the wild Indians of the forest, so the whites also bought the *auca*-like savage instincts of the Indian *muchachos*.

Yet, unlike rubber, these savages instincts were manufactured largely in the imaginations of the whites. All the *muchachos* had to do in order to receive their rewards was to objectify and through words reflect back to the whites the phantoms that populated colonist culture. Given the centuries of colonial mythology concerning the *auca* and the Wild Man, and given the implosion of this mythology in the contradictory social being of the *muchachos,* the task was an easy one. The *muchachos'* stories were, in fact, stories within a much older story encompassing the *muchachos* as objects of a colonialist discourse rather than as its authors.

The trading system of debt-peonage established by the Putumayo rubber boom was thus more than a trade in white goods for rubber gathered by the Indians. It was also a trade in terrifying mythologies and fictional realities, pivoted on the mediation of the *muchachos,* whose storytelling bartered betrayal of Indian realities for the confirmation of colonial fantasies.

The colonial mirror

I began this chapter by stating that my concern was with the mediation of the culture of terror through narration, and with the problems of writing against terror. In part my concern stemmed from my problems in evaluating and interpreting the "facts" constituted in the various accounts of the Putumayo atrocities. This problem of interpretation grew ever larger, eventually bursting into the realization that that problem is precisely what is central to the culture of terror – not only making effective talking and writing against terror extremely difficult, but, even more to the point, making the terrible reality of the death squads, disappearances, and torture all the more effectively crippling of people's capacity to resist.

While much attention is given to "ideology" in the social sciences, virtually none as far as I know is given to the fact that people delineate their world, including its large as well as its micro-scale politics, in stories and story-like creations and very rarely, if ever, in ideologies (as customarily defined). Surely it is in the coils of rumor, gossip, story, and chit-chat where ideology and ideas become emotionally powerful and enter into active social circulation and meaningful existence. So it was with the Putumayo terror, from the accounts of which it seems clear that the colonists and rubber company employees not only feared but also themselves created through narration fearful and confusing images of savagery – images which bound colonial society together through the epistemic murk of the space of death. The systems of torture they devised to secure rubber mirrored the horror of the savagery they so feared, condemned – and fictionalized. Moreover, when we consider the task of creating counterrepresentations and counterdiscourses, we must take stock of the way that most if not all the narratives reproduced by Hardenburg and Casement, referring to and critical of the atrocities, were similarly fictionalized, drawing upon the same historically molded source that men succumbed to when torturing Indians.

Torture and terror in the Putumayo were motivated by the need for cheap labor. By labor per se – labor as a commodity – did not exist in the jungles of the Caraparaná and Igaraparaná affluents of the Putumayo. What existed was not a market for labor but a society and culture of human beings whom the colonists called Indians, irrationals, and savages, with their very specific historical trajectory, form of life, and modes of exchange. In the blundering colonial attempt to dovetail forcibly the capitalist commodity-structure to one or the other of the possibilities for rubber-gathering offered by these modes of exchange, torture, as Casement alludes, took on a life of its own: "Just as the appetite comes in the eating so each crime led on to fresh crimes."[66] To this we should add that, step by step, terror and torture became *the* form of life for some fifteen years, an organized culture with its systematized rules, imagery, procedures, and meanings involved in spectacles and rituals that sustained the precarious solidarity of the rubber company employees as well as beating out through the body of the tortured some sort of canonical truth about Civilization and Business.

It was not commodity fetishism but debt fetishism drenched in the fictive reality of the debt-peonage institution, with its enforced "advances" and theater-like farce of business exchanges, that exercised the decisive force in the creation of terror, transforming torture from the status of a means to that of the mode if not, finally, the very aim of production.

From the reports of both Timerman and Casement it is obvious that torture and institutionalized terror is like a ritual art form, and that far from being spontaneous, *sui generis*, and an abandonment of what are often called "the values of civilization," such rites have a deep history deriving power and meaning from those values. What demands further analysis here is the mimesis between the savagery attributed to the Indians by the colonists and the savagery perpetrated by the colonists in the name of what Julio César Arana called civilization.[67]

This reciprocating yet distorted mimesis has been and continues to be of great importance in the construction of colonial culture – *the colonial mirror* which reflects back onto the colonists the barbarity of their own social relations, but as imputed to the savage or evil figures they wish to colonize. It is highlighted in the Putumayo in the colonist lore as related, for instance, through Joaquin Rocha's lurid tale of Huitoto cannibalism. And what is put into discourse through the artful story telling of the colonists is the same as what they practiced on the bodies of Indians.[68]

Tenaciously embedded in this artful practice is a vast and mystifying Western history and iconography of evil in the imagery of the inferno and the savage – wedded to and inseparable from paradise, utopia, and the good. It is to the subversion of that apocalyptic dialectic that all of us would be advised to bend our counterdiscursive efforts, in a quite different poetics of good-and-evil whose cathartic force lies not with cataclysmic resolution of contradictions but with their disruption.

Post-Enlightenment European culture makes it difficult if not impossible to penetrate the hallucinatory veil of the heart of darkness without either succumbing to its hallucinatory quality or losing that quality. Fascist poetics succeed where liberal rationalism self-destructs. But what might point a way out of this impasse is precisely what is so painfully absent from all the Putumayo accounts, namely, the narrative and narrative mode of the Indians which does de-sensationalize terror so that the histrionic stress on the mysterious side of the mysterious (to adopt Benjamin's formula) is indeed denied by an optic which perceives the everyday as impenetrable, the impenetrable as everyday. At least this is the poetics of the sorcery and shamanism I know about in the upper reaches of the Putumayo, but that is another history for another time, not only of terror but of healing as well.

Notes

1. Jacobo Timerman, *Prisoner without a Name, Cell without a Number* (New York: Vintage Books, 1982), p. 164.
2. Timerman, *Prisoner,* p. 28.
3. Timerman, *Prisoner,* p. 111.
4. Gerardo Reichel-Dolmatoff, *Amazonian Cosmos: The Sexual and Religious Symbolism of the Tukano Indians* (Chicago: University of Chicago Press, 1971).
5. Walter Benjamin, "Surrealism: The Last Snapshot of the European Intelligentsia," in the collection of his essays entitled *Reflections,* Edmund Jephcott, trans., Peter Demetz, ed. and intro. (New York and London: Harcourt Brace Jovanovich, 1978), pp. 189–90.
6. Timerman, *Prisoner,* p. 52.
7. Michel Foucault, "Truth and Power" in *Power/Knowledge,* Colin Gordon, ed. (New York: Pantheon, 1980), p. 118.
8. Timerman, *Prisoner,* pp. 62, 66.
9. Some authorities glean Casement's report and state the figure of 30,000 deaths from 1900 to 1912 as a fact, while others, who had some knowledge of the area and its history, either present different figures (a wide range) or state that it is impossible to give any figure because census taking was impossibly difficult. Furthermore, how much of the population decrease was due to disease (especially smallpox), and how much to torture or flight, is a very vexed question. Similarly, the number of Huitotos living in the Igaraparaná and Caraparaná region in the late nineteenth century is variously stated as around 50,000 all the way up to a quarter of a million, the latter estimate being that of Joaquin Rocha, *Memorandum de un viaje* (Bogotá: Editorial El Mercurio, 1905), p. 138. In any event, the number of Indians in the area seems to have been extremely large by Upper Amazon standards and an important cause for the establishment of rubber trading there. It is worth noting that Casement in his report was extremely cautious in presenting figures on population and population decrease. He gives details of the problem in his evidence presented to the British Parliamentary Select Committee on Putumayo (*House of Commons Sessional Papers, 1913, vol. 14, 30, #707*). Father Gaspar de Pinell, *Un viaje por el Putumayo el Amazonas* (Bogotá: Imprenta Nacional, 1924), pp. 38–9, presents an excellent discussion, as does his *Excursión apostólica por los ríos Putumayo, San Miguel de Sucumbios, Cuyabueno, Caquetá, y Caguán* (Bogotá:Imprenta Nacional, 1929 (also dated 1928)), pp. 227–35.
10. Walter Hardenburg, *The Putumayo: The Devil's Paradise. Travels in the Peruvian Amazon Region and an Account of the Atrocities Committed upon the*

Indians Therein (London: T. Fisher Unwin, 1912), p. 214. The first publication of Hardenburg's revelations, in the magazine *Truth* in 1909, began with this article from the Iquitos newspaper, *La Sanción*. These articles, and probably the later book, were possibly ghostwritten by Sidney Paternoster, assistant editor of *Truth*.

11. Hardenburg, *Putumayo*, p. 258.
12. Ibid., pp. 260, 259.
13. Ibid., p. 236. Also cited by Casement in his Putumayo report to Sir Edward Grey. Casement declares that this description was repeated to him "again and again ... by men who had been employed in this work." Roger Casement, "Correspondence respecting the Treatment of British Colonial Subjects and Native Indians employed in the Collection of Rubber in the Putumayo District." *House of Commons Sessional Papers,* 14 February 1912 to 7 March 1913. vol. 68 (hereafter cited as Casement, *Putumayo Report*), p. 35.
14. Casement, *Putumayo Report,* p. 17.
15. Ibid., p. 34.
16. Ibid., p. 33, 34.
17. Ibid., p. 37.
18. Ibid., p. 39.
19. Ibid., p. 37.
20. Ibid., p. 39.
21. Ibid., p. 42.
22. Ibid., p. 31. From various estimates it appears that the ratio of armed supervisors to wild Indians gathering rubber was somewhere between 1:16 and 1:50. Of these armed supervisors, the *muchachos* outnumbered the whites by around 2:1. See Howard Wolf and Ralph Wolf, *Rubber: A Story of Glory and Greed* (New York: Covici, Friede, 1936), p. 88; U.S. Consul Charles C. Eberhardt, *Slavery in Peru,* 7 February 1913, report prepared for U.S. House of Representatives, 62d Cong., 3d Sess., 1912, H. Doc. 1366, p. 112; Roger Casement, British Parliamentary Select Committee on Putumayo, *House of Commons Sessional Papers*, 1913, vol. 14, p. xi; Casement, *Putumayo Report*, p. 33.
23. Casement, *Putumayo Report,* p. 33.
24. Ibid., pp. 44–5.
25. Ibid., p. 55.
26. Inglis, *Roger Casement,* p. 29.
27. Rocha, *Memorandum de un viaje,* pp. 123–4, asserts that because the Indians are "naturally loafers" they postpone paying off their advances from the rubber traders, thus compelling the traders to use physical violence. Eberhardt, *Slavery in* Peru, p. 110, writes that "the Indian enters the employ of some rubber gatherer, often willingly, though not infrequently by force, and immediately becomes indebted to him for food etc. ... However, the scarcity of labor and the ease with which the Indians can usually escape and live on the natural products of the forest oblige the owners to treat them with some consideration. The Indians realize this and their work is not at all satisfactory, judging from our standards. This was particularly noticeable during a recent visit I made to a mill where "cachassa" or aguadiente is extracted from cane. The men seemed to work when and how they chose, requiring a liberal amount of the liquor each

day (of which they are all particularly fond), and if this is not forthcoming or they are treated harshly in any way they run to the forests. The employer has the law on his side, and if he can find the runaway he is at liberty to bring him back; but the time is lost and the almost useless task of trying to track the Indian though the dense forests and small streams makes it far more practical that the servant be treated with consideration in the first place."

28. Casement, British Parliamentary Select Committee on Putumayo, *House of Commons Sessional Papers,* 1913, vol. 14, p. 113, #2809.
29. E. D. Morel, British Parliamentary Select Committee on Putumayo, *House of Commons Sessional Papers,* 1913, vol. 14, pp. 553, 556. Also see the evidence of the British accounts H. Parr, of the Peruvian Amazon Company, in 1909–10, at the La Chorrera station (pp. 336–481).
30. Casement, *Putumayo Report,* p. 50.
31. Rocha, *Memorandum de un viaje.* p. 75.
32. Peter Singleton-Gates and Maurice Girodias, *The Black Diaries* (New York: Grove Press, 1959), p. 261.
33. P. Alberto Gridilla, *Un año en el Putumayo* (Lima: Colección Descalzos, 1943), p. 29. Rocha's description is of a Colombian rubber trading post, and not one of Arana's: Rocha, *Memorandum de un viaje,* pp. 119–20.
34. Hardenburg, *Putumayo,* p. 218.
35. Karl Polanyi, *The Great Transformation* (Boston: Beacon Press, 1957), p. 72, Cf. Michael Taussig, *The Devil and Commodity Fetishism in South America* (Chapel Hill: University of North Carolina Press, 1980).
36. Julio César Arana, Evidence to the British Parliamentary Select Committee on Putumayo *House of Commons Sessional Papers,* 1913, vol. 14, p. 488, #12,222.
37. See Carlos Fuentes, *La Nueva novela hispanoamericana* (Mexico, D.F.: Editorial Joaquin Mortiz,1969), pp. 10–11. José Eustasio Rivera, *La vorágine* (Bogotá: Editorial Pax, 1974), pp. 277–9.
38. Pinell, *Excursión apostólica.* p. 156.
39. P. Francisco de Vilanova, introduction to P. Francisco de Igualada. *Indios Amazonicas: Colección Misiones Capuchinas,* vol. VI (Barcelona: Imprenta Myria, 1948).
40. Hardenburg, *Putumayo,* p. 163.
41. Pinell, *Excursión apostólica,* p. 196.
42. Casement, *Putumayo Report,* pp. 27–8.
43. Singleton-Gates and Girodias, *Black Diaries,* p. 251.
44. Alfred Simson, *Travels in the Wilds of Ecuador and the Exploration of the Putumayo River* (London: Samson Low, 1886), p. 170.
45. Simson, *Travels.* pp. 170–1.
46. Rocha, *Memorandum de un viaje.* p. 64.
47. Simson,*Travel,* p. 58. It is worth noting that during the seventeenth or eighteenth century missionaries worked among at least some of the Indian groups Simson designates as *auca,* and thus it is not true that they (to quote Simson), "know nothing of the Catholic Church." See P. José Chantre y Herrera, *Historia de las misiones de la Companía de Jesus en el Marañon español, 1637–1767* (Madrid: Imprenta de A. Avrial, 1901) pp. 283, 321–8, 365–9.

48. Simson, *Travels*, p. 58. This meaning of rebel against the Inca is sustained, referring to the Auracanians of Chile, in John M.Cooper, "The Auracanians," in Vol. II of *The Handbook of South American Indians*, Julian H. Steward, ed. (New York: Cooper Square, 1963), p. 690. For the eastern montaña of the northern Andes, the term *auca* means pagan as against Christian Indians, according to Steward and Alfred Metraux, "Tribes of the Equadorian and Peruvian Montaña," in Vol. III of the *Handbook*, pp. 535–656, esp. p. 629 (Zaparos), p. 637 (Canelos/Napos), p. 653 (Quijos). Unlike Simson, the mere traveller, these anthropologists of the *Handbook* fail dismally to indicate the magical and mythic connotations of the term *auca*.

49. Simson, *Travels*, pp. 166, 168.

50. Michael Taussig, "Folk Healing and the Structure of Conquest," *Journal of Latin American Lore*, 6:2 (1980), 217–78.

51. Casement, *Putumayo Report*, p. 45.

52. Rocha, *Memorandum de un viaje*, pp. 125–6.

53. Casement, *Putumayo Report*, p. 30. Father Pinell was told of a large uprising by rubber-working and other Indians along the Igaraparaná in1917; the use of Peruvian troops was required to put it down. Pinell, *Un viaje*, pp. 39–40.

54. An excellent discussion of this is to be found in David Sweet, "A Rich Realm of Nature Destroyed: The Middle Amazon Valley, 1640–1750" (Ph.D. diss., University of Wisconsin, 1975), I, pp. 113–14, 116, 120, 126, 130–1, 141, 347.

55. Rocha, *Memorandum de un viaje*, pp. 92–3.

56. Rocha, Ibid., p. 118.

57. Rocha, Ibid., pp. 106–7.

58. Hardenburg, *Putumayo*, p. 155. For use of coca in the *chupe del tabaco*, see Joseph F. Woodroffe, *The Upper Reaches of the Amazon* (London: Methuen, 1914), pp. 151–5. With regard to the reliability and sources of Hardenburg's statements, it is perhaps of use to cite some of the evidence he gave to the British Parliamentary Select Committee on Putumayo, *House of Commons Sessional Papers*, 1913, vol. 14. Asked what he saw himself of actual cruelties to the Indians, Hardenburg replied, "Of actual crimes being committed I did not see anything, practically; all I saw was that the Indians in [the rubber station of] El Encanto were nearly naked and very thin and cadaverous-looking; I saw several scores of them, and I saw what they were being fed on" (p. 510, #12848). His information came through accounts from other people: "In fact, I think I might say that most of the people came through others. They would say, 'I know another man who could state this and that,' and they would bring them" (p. 511, #12881). Asked if he questioned these people in detail about their statements, Hardenburg replied, "I cannot say I did much of that" (p. 511, #12882). It was, said Hardenburg, general knowledge that the atrocities were occurring. This "general knowledge" is precisely what I have been at pains to track down not because I believe that the atrocities were less than described by the several authors upon whom I draw, but because it is this general knowledge in the shape of mythic narratives which acts as a screen and as a network of signifiers

without which "the facts" would not exist. Most specifically, the function of this screen of signifiers is to heighten dread and hence the controlling function of the culture of terror. Casement's evidence is altogether of another category, being more carefully gathered, cross-checked, etcetera, and as a result of it we can affirm reports, such as Hardenburg's, which are less well substantiated. Nevertheless, Casement's evidence serve not to puncture the mythic character so much as indicate its terrific reality.

59. Casement, *Putumayo Report*, p. 48. Robuchon's text appeared as a book "Official Edition"), printed in Lima in 1907 and entitled *En el Putumayo y sus afluentes*. It was edited by Carlos Rey de Castro, a lackey of Julio César Arana's and one-time Peruvian consul in Brazil, from Robuchon's papers after his mysterious death in the Putumayo rain forest. Judging from Rey de Castro's book on the Putumayo, *Los pobladores del Putumayo* (Barcelona: Imp. Vda de Luis Tasso, 1917), and his relation to Arana, one can surmise that it would be unwise to read the Robuchon text as though it were really Robuchon's unadulterated work. The chances are that it was edited with a view to presenting a case favorable to Arana. The importance of prehistory, "ethnohistory," and Indian history in the ideological war for world opinion is well brought out by Rey de Castro's bold stroke in his *Los pobladores del Putumayo,* in which he sets out to prove that the Huitotos and adjacent Indian groups are in reality descendant from the *orejones* of Cuzco in the interior of Peru – thus supposedly strengthening the Peruvian claims over the Putumayo rubber zone and its indigenous inhabitants.

60. Rocha, *Memorandum de un viaje*. p. 111.

61. Ibid., pp. 116–17.

62. Rómulo Paredes, "Confidential Report to the Ministry of Foreign Relations, Peru," September 1911, translated in Eberhardt, *Slavery in Peru*, p. 146. Paredes's work is explained and put into context in a mass of testimony in the book of Carlos A. Valcarcel, *El proceso del Putumayo* (Lima: Imp. Comercial de Horacio La Rosa, 1915).

63. Paredes, "Confidential Report," in Eberhardt, *Slavery in Peru,* p. 158.

64. Ibid., p. 147. I am grateful to Fred Chin and Judy Farquahar of the Department of Anthropology at the University of Chicago for impressing upon me the importance of the *muchachos* as a mediating force. Then of course one should not omit the role of the blacks recruited in Barbados, mediating between the whites and the Indians. In much the same way as the British army from the mid-nineteenth century on deployed different colonial and ethnic groups so as to maximize reputations for ferocity and checking one against the other, the British and Peruvian rubber company used its "ethnic soldiers" in the Putumayo.

65. Paredes, "Confidential Report," in Eberhardt, *Slavery in Peru*, p. 147.

66. Casement, *Putumayo Report*, p. 44.

67. See p. 222 above.

68. Illustrations of the way in which this following of the letter of the tale was enacted in the torture of Indians can be found in the rare instances of dialogue that Casement allows his witnesses in the section of his report given over to testimony by men recruited in Barbados, as, for example:

"And you say you saw the Indians burn?" Consul-General Casement asked Augustus Walcott, born in the Caribbean island of Antigua but twenty three years before.

"Yes."

"Burnt alive?"

"Alive."

"How do you mean? Describe this."

"Only one I see burnt alive."

"Well, tell me about that one?"

"He had not work 'caucho,' he ran away and he kill a 'muchacho,' a boy, and they cut off his two arms and legs by the knee and they burn his body..."

"Are you sure he was still alive – not dead when they threw him on the fire?"

"Yes, he did alive. I'm sure of it – I see him move – open his eyes, he screamed out ..."

"Was Aurelio Rodriguez [the rubber-station manager] looking on – all the time?"

"Yes, all the time."

"Giving directions?"

"Yes, Sir."

"He told them to cut off the legs and arms?"

"Yes."

There was something else the Consul-General could not understand and he called Walcott back to explain what he meant by saying, "because he told the Indians that we was Indians too, and eat those – "What he meant, Casement summarized, was that the station manager, Señor Norman, in order "to frighten the Indians told them that the negroes were cannibals, and a fierce tribe of cannibals who eat people, and that if they did not bring in rubber these black men would be sent to kill and eat them." (Casement, *Putumayo Report*, pp. 115, 118).

Another, more complicated, example follows:

"Have you ever seen Aguero kill Indians?" the Consul-General asked Evelyn Bateson, aged twenty five, born in Barbados, and working in the rubber depôt of La Chorrera.

"No, Sir; I haven't seen him kill Indians – but I have seen him send 'muchachos' to kill Indians. He has taken an Indian man and given him to the 'muchachos' to eat, and they have a dance of it ..."

"You saw the man killed?"

"Yes, Sir. They tied him to a stake and they shot him, and they cut off his head after he was shot and his feet and hands, and they carried them about the section – in the yard and they carries them up and down and singing, and they carries them to their house and dances ..."

"How do you know they ate them?"

"I heard they eat them. I have not witnessed it, Sir, but I heard the manager Señor Aguero tell that they eat this man."

"The manager said all this?"

"Yes, Sir, he did." (Casement, *Putumayo Report*, p. 103.)

This sort of stimulation if not creation of cannibalism by colonial pressure is also recorded in missionaries' letters concerning King Leopold's Congo Free State and the gathering of rubber there. See, for example, the account of Mr. John Harris in the work by Edmund Morel, *King Leopold's Rule in Africa* (New York: Funk and Wagnalls, 1905), pp. 437–41.

13

Male Gender and Rituals of Resistance in the Palestinian *Intifada*: A Cultural Politics of Violence

Julie Peteet

This chapter examines the attainment and enactment of manhood and masculinity among Palestinian male youths in relation to ritualized beatings and detention in the occupied West Bank. The beatings (and detention) are framed as rites of passages now central in the construction of an adult, gendered (male) self with critical consequences for political consciousness and agency. While central to discussions of bodily violence, a Foucaultian analysis does little to focus attention on the way in which the subaltern interpret the practices of violence and power. In shifting the discussion to the recipients of violent practices, the focus is on the symbolic and agential enmeshed in a dialogic of power and transformation. As a methodological strategy to approach the terrain of cultural resistance to domination, I examine ritual performances that, in effect, inscribe power on the body and their subsequent construal as a rite of passage by one set of performers – those who are beaten or imprisoned – as an instance of the social construction of a male gender and resistant subjectivity. The beating is cast as performance in the sense that interaction between participants and audience (Schieffelin 1985:710) is critical to the meaning and efficiency of the ritual in a social rather than simply cognitive sense. Brenneis calls our attention to audiences as "not solely targets for rhetorical strategies; they are, rather, active interpreters, critics and respondents" (1987:237).

This chapter illustrates the points elaborated above by examining the Israeli policy and practice of beating and imprisoning young Palestinian males in the Occupied Territories during the *intifada* (uprising) (1987–) as ones constitutive of gender and power. I will argue that a Palestinian

American Ethnologist 21(1):31–49. Copyright © 1994, American Anthropological Association.

construal of the practice of violence as a rite of passage into manhood that galvanizes political consciousness and agency is a creative and dynamic act of resistance, a trick, if you will. After a brief discussion of inscriptions of power on the body, I turn to an ethnographic account of applications of violence. The chapter concludes with a discussion of ritualized physical violence as a transformative experience that galvanizes one set of participants to unsettle power arrangements. At the same time, it both reaffirms and transforms internal Palestinian forms of power. As such, this text involves the intersection of several themes: ritual performance and political agency, bodily inscriptions of power and the construction of manhood in the Middle East, and the transformation and reproduction of relations of domination.

Ritual, opposed meanings, and reversal

The anthropological literature increasingly displays less hesitancy to view symbols and rituals from the perspective of empowerment and the establishment of authority (Aronoff 1982; Kertzer 1988). The anthropology of ritual often assumed a generalized continuity of cultural categories and meaning for the participants in ritual performances, given that the ethnography on rituals was, by and large, conducted on single-cultural groups, without however, assuming an essentializing homogeneity. As I shall argue and as Schieffelin suggests, participants in ritual

> may not all experience the same significance or efficacy. Indeed, unless there is some kind of exegetical supervision of both performance and interpretation by guardians of orthodoxy, the performance is bound to mean different things to different people. In the absence of any exegetical canon one might even argue that there was no single "correct" or "right" meaning for a ritual at all. (1985:722)

Kertzer calls attention to the multivocal quality of symbols in ritual to refer to their capacity to embody a variety of meanings (1988:11). Given the absence of a canon and the contingent, multivocal nature of rituals and symbols, I will show that, where power relations are vastly asymmetrical between ethnically and nationally distinct groups, ritual may have opposed rather than simply different meanings and may lead to a practice designed to overthrow the ritual itself and its political context. According to Schieffelin, the efficacy of a ritual, what it does and how it does it, is to be located less in the context and its cultural categories of meaning and more in the "emerging relation between the performer and the other participants (and the participants among themselves) while the performance is in progress" (1985:722).

I would like to take Schieffelin's argument about ritual performances meaning different things to different people in a novel direction, to a situation where people stand in rather starkly opposed positions of power and powerlessness as a consequence of belonging to different and opposed national and cultural groups. I would suggest, however, that if ritual performances take place in a highly charged atmosphere of domination and crisis and are then cast as relations of power, they may inform a political agency designed to overthrow the domination of one set of performers. Thus ritual, while certainly a system of meaning and its communication, can simultaneously foreground a human agency with consequences for the power of its performers. In short, the consequences of ritual can be manifested in attempts to reverse the social order of hierarchies and relations of domination.

If we acknowledge that the cultural meaning of symbols can be construed in diametrically opposed ways for the participants in a ritual who themselves stand in hierarchical opposition to one another, what does this mean then for the question of agency? The potential for agential empowerment arising from ritual has been noted by anthropologists who study ritual in the context of politics. Kertzer argues that rituals do more than simply maintain and reaffirm the status quo; they can be galvanized to accomplish things. They overturn political orders, and opposition politics can be expressed in "rites of delegitimation" (1988:2).[1]

Bodies

As the most personal and intimate realm of the self, bodies are the most striking sites for the inscription of power (Outram 1989) and the encoding of culture (Combs-Schilling 1991). Foucault eloquently captures the body/politics equation when he writes, "the body is also directly involved in a political field; power relations have an immediate hold upon it; they invest it, mark it, train it, torture it, force it to carry out tasks, to perform ceremonies, to emit signs" (1979:25). Combs-Schilling persuasively argues that "durable systems of domination are often ones in which the structures of power are so embedded within the body of self that the self cannot be easily abstracted from them" (1991:658). The daily inscription of power on the unwilling bodies of Palestinians, almost a routine occurrence, is an attempt to embed power in them as a means of fashioning a domesticated subject whose terrorized silence would confirm the mythical Zionist landscape of an empty Palestine. Through bodily violence, the occupier desires not just to fashion a laborer but equally to assure a quiescent population, one sufficiently terrorized so as not to engage in acts of rebellion.[2] But, unlike the Moroccan situation of which Combs-Schilling writes, it gives rise instead to an oppositional political agency.

Foucault's view of the body as text, as a site of inscription and exhibition by dominant forces, shows little concern with people's responses to having their bodies appropriated and designated as sites of inscription. In short, he does not concern himself much with the individuals' consciousness of himself or herself in the historical process. English historian E. P. Thompson's (1978:79) call for restoring the subject to the history-making process dovetails neatly with anthropology's contemporary concern with integrating history, culture, and the individual. One can do this by approaching the body from the standpoint of its owners, who are always more than inscriptive sites, as they creatively respond by challenging the prevalent political order (Outram 1989). Outram argues in her discussion of the French revolution that "bodies are active creators of new power relations and sustain individuals in their confrontation with and against systems of power" (1989:23). E. Martin astutely shows how an alternative discourse and conception of the body exists that challenges the legitimacy of the hegemonic medico-scientific discourse that constitutes knowledge of, and thus a crucial basis for control over, women's physiological processes from menstruation and childbirth to menopause. She also asserts that "Because their bodily processes go with them everywhere, forcing them to juxtapose biology and culture, women glimpse every day a conception of another sort of social order" (1987:200).

The occupation is, similarly, a daily accompanying presence governing one's physical state of being. Mobility, safety, and daily routine are out of the control of Palestinians under occupation. Occupation is a daily shared experience that is subject to continuous questioning and widespread rejection. A prominent mode of embedding the power of the dominant group is to beat, daily and publicly, Palestinian male bodies. Like monarchal spectacles of public torture, the public beating, widespread during the intifada, is a representation of the power of the occupier, encoding and conveying a message about the consequences of oppositional expressions and practices.

The body, however, does not merely represent. Bodies also signify contradictions in everyday experiences (Comaroff 1985:8). The

Palestinian interpretation and organization of this experience is strikingly at odds with the meaning underlying Israeli actions. With these measures, Israel intended to control, humiliate, and punish; the ultimate, publicly recognized, and reiterated aim was to quell resistance. In other words, public spectacles of violence serve as a means of encoding and reproducing the Palestinians as Israel's acquiescent, though not consenting, "other." The intent was not to normalize social life under occupation but to rule through what Taussig called in the Latin American context the "strategic art of abnormalizing" (1990:219). Public violence was not meant to fashion homeostasis but to give rise to a continuous situation of crisis and instability as a way of putting obstacles in the way of Palestinian political organizing.

But the Palestinians made of the signs something radically different. These were experiences of transformation and empowerment, not humiliation and pacification. These experiences have been construed as rites of passage into manhood, with its attendant status and responsibilities, and concomitantly as vehicles of entry and, to a large extent, initiation into underground political leadership. For the community under occupation, the signs inscribed on the individual bodies were read as a collective assault and a commentary on suffering (see Keesing 1985 and Peteet 1991). I set these opposed interpretations into a dialogic frame whereby meaning is created in the process of engagement between, in this case, two asymmetrical forces. The meaning of the beating and its construal as a rite of passage into manhood, with its attendant agential imperatives, has resonance throughout the occupied territories, upsetting established hierarchies of generation, nationality, and class yet reproducing and reaffirming other hierarchies such as gender.

Manhood and rites of passage in the Middle East

Masculinity is neither natural nor given. Like femininity, it is a social construct. Herzfeld argues that, in a Cretan village, there is more stress on how rather than on what men do – what counts is "performative excellence" (1985:16). Gilmore notes that a "critical threshold" is passed by various forms of tests and ordeals (1990:11). While cautious of the perils of essentializing the category of gender, male or female, it is fairly safe to say, on a reading of the anthropological literature on masculinity in the Arab world[3] and its conflation with the deed, that this conflation conforms to Gilmore's criterion of being "something almost generic ... a ubiquity rather than a universality" (1990:2–3).

Arab masculinity (*rujulah*) is acquired, verified, and played out in the brave deed, in risk-taking, and in expressions of fearlessness and assertiveness. It is attained by constant vigilance and willingness to defend honor (*sharaf*), face (*wajh*), kin, and community from external aggression and to uphold and protect cultural definitions of gender-specific propriety.[4]

The occupation has seriously diminished those realms of practice that allow one to engage in, display, and affirm masculinity in autonomous actions.[5] Frequent witnesses to their fathers' beatings by soldiers or settlers, children are acutely aware of their fathers' inability to protect themselves and their children.[6]

Manliness is also closely intertwined with virility and paternity, and with paternity's attendant sacrifices. Denying one's own needs while providing for others is such a signifier. The consequences of resistance to occupation is a category of sacrifice with long-term implications for the autonomy and security of the community and larger national collectivity.[7]

Several anthropologists have referred to the concept of honor as a defining frame for masculinity. Among North Yemeni tribesmen, Caton (1985) argues that honorable deeds can be expressed in oral form. While not explicitly concerned with masculinity, his study of poetic performance and the acquisition of honor is gendered in that he is dealing with a performative genre exclusive to men, at least in public occasions. To best one's opponent in games of oral poetry is to perform an honorable deed.[8]

Abu-Lughod explicitly uses honor as a point of departure. Among the Egyptian Bedouin, the notion of control is crucial in signifying "real men". Control is the lack of "fear of anyone or anything," for to exhibit such fear "implies that it has control over one" (1968:88). "Real men" are able to exact respect and command obedience from others while they themselves resist submitting to others' control (Abu-Lughod 1986:88–90). Among the Berbers of Algeria, Bourdieu locates the man of honor in the context of challenge and riposte. A challenge confers honor upon a man, because it is a cultural assumption that the "challenge, as such, requires a riposte and therefore is addressed to a man deemed capable of playing the game of honour" (Bourdieu 1977:11). The challenge provides an opportunity for males to prove their belonging to the world of men. A point to which I shall return later concerns Bourdieu's contention that challenges directed to men who are unable to take them up dishonors the challenger.

Elaborate, well-defined rites of passage to mark transitions from boyhood to adolescence to manhood are difficult to discern in Arab culture.[9] Manhood is always more than the culmination of a series of biological transformations. The transformations, and their markings by a loose set of rites, must be accompanied by performative deeds to convince and win public approval. Like honor, with which it is inextricably bound, manhood is easily lost if one is not vigilant about its display and protection.

Assumption of the tasks, authority, and status associated with masculinity is a gradual process of becoming a member of the world of adult men and acquiring *'aql* (reason) or social common sense.[10] *'Aql* has been described as the "faculty of understanding, rationality, judiciousness, prudence, and wisdom" (Altorki 1986:51). Males begin to acquire *'aql* around the age of twenty. While acquisition of this quality has no definable starting date, it does not grow with marriage, and most men attain it fully "no earlier than 40, or mature adulthood, when men are perceived to have achieved sufficient capacity to deal with the complex problems of social existence" (Altorki 1986:52). Milestones along this path to adulthood are circumcision, educational achievements, marriage, income earning, the birth of children, and the acquisition of wisdom that comes from knowledge of one's society and its customs.[11] Each of these points in time further reaffirms masculinity and belonging to the world of men. None of these milestones is violent, except perhaps circumcision. Having briefly discussed the Middle East literature on masculinity, manhood, and rites of passage, we will return to the question of constructing masculinity and rites of passage after an ethnographic discussion of inscriptions of violence on the Palestinian male body.

Background to beatings and imprisonment

Around 40 percent (approximately 2,100,000) of Palestinians live under Israeli rule, either in Israel proper (around 645,000), in the West Bank and East Jerusalem (around 938,000), or in the Gaza Strip (around 525,000).[12] From the beginning of the intifada in December 1987 through December 1990, an estimated 106,600 Palestinians were injured.[13] Beatings are not isolated in these statistics, so it is impossible to calculate with any certainty the numbers beaten.[14]

One would be hard pressed to find a young male Palestinian under occupation who has not been beaten or who does not personally know someone who has been. Under the political and military authority of a foreign power, Palestinians possess few, if any, political rights, nor do they possess or have access to technologies of domination. Their powerlessness is all the more pronounced given their occupation by a major military power. The juxtaposition of technologies is striking. Offensively and defensively, Palestinians wield stones, one of the earliest forms of weaponry known to humankind. As part of the natural environment and landscape, the stone bears minimal, if any, application of human technological skills.

The occupying authority continuously displays the potential for and the actuality of violence to stem opposition and to imprint upon the subject population its lack of autonomy. In spite of more than two decades of occupation and a generation of youths who have known no other way of life, Israel has not been able to "normalize" its power relations with those under occupation. Since the beginning of the occupation (1967), resistance has been common.[15] The inability to establish a "naturalness" to occupation has meant a continued recourse to physical violence along with the standard forms of structural violence.

One quickly discerns that beatings are a common occurrence. The anticipation of an encounter with occupation authorities that might lead to a beating influences the daily mobility of young men. They decline evening social invitations that necessitate driving after dark. Military personnel at roadblocks stop cars and randomly pull out men for beating. Parents hesitate to allow adolescent boys to go downtown unaccompanied, or even on short errands, fearing they might be pulled over for an identity check and in the process roughed up. In the alleys of the camps, children now are more careful to stay close to home because on their daily patrols, soldiers occasionally chase and rough up children and detain them for several hours until their parents pay a stiff fine.

Beatings have been a part of the apparatus of domination since the beginning of the occupation, both in public and as an integral part of the interrogation process that leads to the question of how do pre-intifada and intifada beatings differ? While framing beatings in the context of time periods, one must not draw too distinct a boundary. In the first weeks of fieldwork in a refugee camp in the West Bank, I would pose many of my questions in terms of a distinct set of time frames – "pre-intifada" and "intifada." Finally, one woman kindly, but with some exasperation, told me: "Look, we've been having an intifada here for forty years, since 1948! The difference now is the rest of the population of the occupied territories is involved, and the continuity of resistance is being sustained! Though this word *intifada* is new to us, we've been resisting for forty years."

Before the intifada, beatings were less public, usually taking place while in custody.[16] They were an integral part of an interrogation procedure, designed to break the will of prisoners and to extract confessions as to their alleged deeds and those of their acquaintances and to possible externally based political backing and material support for resistance against the occupation.[17]

Soon after the launching of the intifada in December 1987, beatings became an explicit policy of the occupation authorities. On January 19, 1988, Defense Minister Yitzhak Rabin announced a new policy of "might, power, and beatings" to quell the uprising. The international witnessing of the public beatings and bone-breaking evoked widespread alarm among Israel's supporters, particularly in the United States. Subsequently, Likud ministers barred the media from the territories. Until the ban (spring 1988), the beatings were featured prominently on the nightly news in the country. In diminishing the external witnessing of the infliction of pain, the occupying authorities were attempting to create a fictitious reality of nonviolent techniques of riot control for external consumption.

For the Israelis, the beatings were an encoded medium intended to convey a message regarding the consequences of opposition. The young male is a metonym for Palestinian opposition and struggle against domination, the idea and symbols of which must be rooted out and silenced: the Palestinian population must be made acquiescent to the colonizing project. Israeli violence proceeds on the assumption of collective guilt and responsibility among Palestinians. In the occupied territories, violence is directed at individual bodies as representations of a collective transgressive other.[18] This collective other, however, is denied a national identity. The pregiven defining power of the collective Palestinian body, which requires a violently negating intervention, lies precisely in its assertive national identity, which in its very existence denies the mythical Zionist landscape of Palestine. Taussig draws our attention to torture and terror as "ritualized art forms" that "far from being spontaneous, sui generis, and an abandonment of what are often called the values of civilization ... have a deep history deriving power and meaning from those very values" (1987:133). Unbowed males signified an assertive resistance to the colonial project and a Zionist self-identity.

The walking embodiment of power, the Israeli soldier, totes the modern technology of violence – automatic rifle, pistol, grenade, handcuffs, tear-gas canisters, and batons. Anthropologist and Israeli army captain Ben-Ari remarked that some soldiers, given their training for warfare, were very uneasy with their tasks of policing heavily civilian areas (1989:376).[19] This unease, he suggests, should be understood against the images soldiers had of the uprising. The mass media presentation was one of "mass demonstration, concentrated rock throwing and tire burning, and the constant use of Molotov cocktails." Ben-Ari frames the behavior of soldiers in the territories in terms of the metaphor of masks and disguises. He suggests "that for the limited period of *milium* (reserve duty) and the reservists cease to be the normally identified, circumscribed, constrained members of Israeli society who must be concerned with how they are regarded by themselves and by others" (1989:378).

Donning masks and disguises facilitates construction of "highly delimited – spatially as well as temporally – episodes during which they become an-other person" (Ben-Ari 1989:378–9). Rather than "donning masks" and becoming "an-other," I would cast their behavior as more analogous to what Taussig referred to as "colonial mirroring," where "the terror and tortures they devised mirrored the horror of the savagery they both feared and fictionalized" (1987:133).

Tolerance of physical abuse of Palestinians was underwritten by a regime of knowledge that cast them as lawless and socially primitive and violent – terrorists, threats to law and order, bands, gangs – and thus as amenable to violent extrajudicial measures. Beyond the pale, Palestinians were cast as possessing a fundamentally different set of morals and knowledge – commonly stated as "they only understand force." Their human status does not correspond to that of others. Israeli military announcements do not use the Hebrew word for "child" when reporting injuries or deaths of Palestinian children in confrontations with the military. The Israeli Palestinian writer Anton Shammas commented that "for twenty years now officially there has been no childhood in the West Bank and Gaza Strip ... [A] ten year-old boy shot by military forces is reported to be a 'young man of ten'" (1988:10). Military discourse bypasses childhood, collapsing male Palestinian life-cycle categories. This regime of knowledge, together with a widespread ideology of the rights of the occupiers to Palestinian land and resources, constitutive of a claim to an Israeli national identity, and a judicial system that tolerated systematic human rights violations, if not indeed encouraged them as Amnesty International (1991) argues, fostered an atmosphere where inflictions of bodily violence flourished.

Whether pre-intifada or intifada, the intent behind the beating was to re-constitute the Palestinian male as a nonresistant, though certainly not consenting, subject of colonization. Stone throwing, tire burning, demonstrating, or displaying symbols of Palestine, such as the flag or its colors, could bring a swift and violent response. But rather than being mute repositories or sites on which the occupier exhibited and constructed power and affirmed its civilization and identity, the meaning of the beating has been appropriated by the subject in a dialectical and agential manner.

Ethnography and beatings

The bodies of those under occupation are continuously called forth to present themselves to outsiders. Visits to families are punctuated by the display of bodies with the marks of bullets and beatings and are social settings for the telling of beatings, shootings, verbal exchanges with settlers and soldiers, and prison stories. After several visits to Um Fadi, I noticed that her children were always in the house or in the walled garden around the house with the gate locked. Once when I had to knock very loudly several times for the children to open, she rushed to open and explained that she no longer leaves the gate open or allows her children to play in the alleys of the camp. After we were seated in the house and drinking tea, she quietly motioned her eleven-year-old son and thirteen-year-old daughter to come stand in front of us. With the reluctance of children their age, they silently did so. In a subdued and controlled tone, she related how they once were caught by soldiers while playing in the alley. Soldiers regularly patrol the streets and alleys of the camp, and occasionally groups of children throw stones at them. Four soldiers claimed they had been stoned by children in the vicinity and accused Um Fadi's son and daughter. Both were beaten with batons and rifle butts directed to the kidneys, arms, and face. When he got up to run, the boy was shot in the side. She asked him to raise his t-shirt to show me the scar. During this telling, several neighbor women were present as well as friends of her children. There was hushed silence as she told the story. The older women would periodically interject, almost inaudibly: "In the name of God – how can they do this to children!", "What can we do?", "What kind of people are these!" The act of telling lends dramatic narrative form to a dialogic process. For the listener, a sense of community is evoked through empathy. Many families have experienced such pain, and, for those who have not, the possibility looms large.

The physical marks of beatings, rubber bullets, and live ammunition constitute crucial elements in dialogue with others, particularly Americans whose near official silence on the matter of Palestinian human rights violations by the occupying authorities is seen as a form of complicity. Given the levels and continuity of U.S. financial support for the occupying power, they consider it all the more appropriate to display the physical signs of their suffering to Westerners. The battered body is a representation fashioned by the Israelis but presented by Palestinians to the West. To the Palestinians, the battered body, with its bruises and broken limbs, is the symbolic embodiment of a twentieth-century history of subordination and powerlessness – of "what we have to endure" – but also of their determination to resist and to struggle for national independence.

A representation created with the intent of humiliating has been reversed into one of honor, manhood, and moral superiority. But bodies do more than represent. Torture and beatings are ordeals one undergoes as sacrifices for the struggle (*qadiyyah*). It should be firmly stated that this argument in no way is meant to imply that Palestinians make light of physical violence. It is rather to try to understand how culturally they make sense of it. Displaying physical marks of violence, that one is usually powerless to avoid, stands as a "commentary on suffering" (Keesing 1985; Peteet 1991) but also, I would suggest, as a commentary on sacrifice. As such they are poignant communicative devices. These displays are powerful statements belying claims of a benign occupation and resonate with the honor that comes from unmasking and resisting.

Becoming men

> One sign of things to come – amidst the jokes and nervous laughter there were signs of genuine excitement by some soldiers at the prospect of "teaching them not to raise their heads." (Israeli soldier in the occupied territories, quoted in Peretz 1990:122)

I first had an inkling of the meaning of the beating and imprisonment as rites of passage when Hussein, twenty-four years old and resident in Jalazon refugee camp, remarked casually and with a hint of resignation that, on his first evening home from a nine-month stint in prison, a neighbor had come to ask his help in mediating a dispute he was involved in with another neighbor. Hussein pleaded fatigue and the crush of visitors to avoid assuming this mantle of community responsibility, a responsibility that carries with it substantial moral authority.

To be a mediator is a position and task usually the preserve of well-respected, older men known for their sagacity and even temperament. Such men have achieved *'aql.* Hussein did handle the matter the next day, talking to both parties, eventually hammering out a compromise solution. Like many young men of his generation and experience, he suddenly found himself with the responsibility for community affairs, mainly such tasks as mediation in disputes and participating in popular tribunals to try suspected collaborators.[20]

During visits to Hussein's family, I began to notice the deference paid him by his father, an unusual state of affairs in Arab family relations where sons are usually deferential to their fathers. Much about hierarchy and submission can be read in seemingly mundane, everyday gestures. Seating patterns in Arab culture are spatial statements of hierarchy. Those who stand or sit closest to the door are usually subordinate, younger males, while those farthest from the door, and centrally positioned, are older, respected men who are able to command obedience. The spatial arrangement of visitors and family members when congregating at Hussein's home did not conform to the traditional pattern. Indeed Hussein often was centrally positioned with his father clearly on the periphery. During conversations where his father was present, along with other family members and friends, his father deferred to Hussein in speech, allowing his son to interrupt him. Hussein's father listened attentively as his son talked for lengthy periods of time before interjecting himself. In short, he gave Hussein the floor. When Hussein would describe his prolonged torture at the hands of the interrogators, his father was quiet, only to occasionally interject "Prison is a school, a university" and "Prison is for men."

In observing resistance activities in camps, villages, and urban neighborhoods, it was clear the older men played little, if any role. It was the preserve of the young (under twenty-five years of age), and as such they embodied the prestige and respect that come from, and yet give one access to, leadership positions. It did not take long to realize that Hussein was a member of the local underground leadership. He had spent nineteen months in jail on charges of organizing local forms of escalation, such as stone throwing and barricade building. Chased and publicly beaten in the camp's alleyways before being thrown into a jeep, he was then taken to prison and subjected to eighteen days of interrogation. Naked, deprived of food, water, and sanitation facilities for the first three days, he was subjected to beatings with fists, pipes, and rifle butts, which alternated with questioning over an eighteen-day period.

Once interrogation procedures are completed, prisoners join their fellow inmates in daily prison routine. Palestinian political prisoners are highly organized. Classes are conducted daily in a variety of subjects ranging from foreign language to math, science, and history. Classes in political theory and practice are the high points in this educational project. For this reason, it is commonplace in contemporary Palestinian discourse to hear the comment "Prison is a university." A leadership hierarchy emerges, and as young men are released they take up the leadership mantle of those who are newly detained. In this way, young men circulate between prison and leadership positions. This circulation of young men ensures a leadership in spite of the campaign of massive arrests and detention of young males.

Upon his release, Hussein returned home to several days of visitors – kin, friends, and neighbors – and new responsibilities in the camp leadership. Within the prisons, recruitment to political organizations flourishes, and leaders of each political faction emerge to lead their followers. From the prison they can have some voice in the daily actions and policies of the intifada as they confer instructions and ideas on prisoners about to be released. Upon returning to their communities, young men like Hussein have acquired the stature to lead. They have withstood interrogation and not given away information or become collaborators. More importantly however, they return "educated men." Hussein, and other released detainees, spoke of prison as a place where they learned not only academic subjects, but also about power and how to resist.

Another young man I became acquainted with in the West Bank was Ali. Ali's experience of bodily inflictions of violence began substantially before the intifada. Within a five-year period, he had been detained seventeen times. Politically inactive before he was taken away from home in the middle of the night during his last year of high school, the soldiers assured his frightened parents that they would just ask him a few questions and let him go. Handcuffed and blindfolded, he was placed on the floor of a jeep where he was repeatedly kicked and hit with rifle butts. He recalls that the jeep stopped and picked up someone else. Once they started beating the other fellow, and he screamed, Ali realized it was his friend Sami. Sami told him: "Don't cry or shout. Don't let them know it hurts." He told me:

At first, of course, I was scared to death and then once you're in that room and they slap your face and start hitting you – that's it, it goes away and you start being a different person. All of a sudden you have a power inside you – a power to resist – you want to resist. You can't help it; you feel very strong, you even want to challenge them though basically I had nothing to tell them since I had done nothing.

After his release several days later, Ali returned home. Two weeks later, soldiers appeared again and detained him, this time for about two weeks. Upon his release, he decided to join the underground resistance movement and after several months was active in the local-level leadership. He now had stature in the community as a result of the beatings, arrests, and interrogations. He was effective in mobilizing others to join in demonstrations, national celebrations, and the resistance movement on the university campus he later attended.

Physical violence can be construed by its recipients as "bridge-burning" activity (Gerlach and Hines 1970). One often hears comments such as "I've nothing left to lose" and "I've already paid the price, I might as well be active." Palestinian males need not necessarily do violence to become political agents as Fanon (1969) argued for the Algerian revolution. As its recipients, they acquire masculine and revolutionary credentials. Marks on the body, though certainly unwanted, signal a resistant, masculine subjectivity and agency. The pervasiveness of beatings/detention, their organizational format, and their construal by recipients as entry into the world of masculinity make possible their casting as a rite of passage.

In his classic study of rites of passage, Van Gennep (1961) identified three characteristic stages: separation, marginality, and aggregation. A logic of sequences is apparent in the transformative process of physical violence. In the initial phase, the individual is physically detached from the group. He is either taken from his home and family to the jeep and then the interrogation room, or he is detached from the crowd in public and held by soldiers or settlers who try to keep at a distance those who would intervene. The second, or liminal, stage is a state of marginality and ambiguity and is one fraught with dangers. The young novice exists outside of social time, space, and the categories of the life cycle. Social rules and norms are suspended. Interrogation, with its applications of physical violence, is such a liminal stage during which social hierarchies of age and class are diluted. Oppositions between normal social life and liminality (Turner 1977) can be applied to the one being beaten, especially those in custody who are frequently naked, in a state of humility and without rank or status, and who silently undergo pain and suffering.

Imprisonment is also a liminal period because communitas is achieved and expressed in the emergence of new hierarchies that rest on an ability to withstand physical violation and pain, political affiliation and rank, and ability to lead in the prison community.

The final sequence, aggregation or the postliminal re-entry into normal social life, is verified and enacted by the family and the community at large. The return home is marked by a fairly well-defined celebratory etiquette. Relatives, friends, and neighbors visit for several weeks to show respect to the released detainee and his family. Special foods, usually more expensive meat dishes, are prepared by the women of the household both to strengthen the detainees' often poor health as well as to show appreciation and respect for his endurance. New clothes are bought to mark re-entry into the community. The respect shown by deferential gestures to the former prisoner or beaten youth all mark his re-entry into society with a new status of respect and manhood.

In emerging from the beating unbowed and remaining committed to resistance activities, young men exhibit generosity to the point of sacrifice that asserts and validates a masculine self. The infliction of pain reveals, in the most intimate and brutal way, the nature of occupation and strengthens them, they contend, to confront it.

Endowed with qualities of adulthood, honor, and manhood, emergence from the ordeal dovetails with access to power and authority. In a reversal of meaning, the beating empowers the self and informs an agency of resistance. Palestinians, as participants in and as audience to the public spectacle of beatings have consciously and creatively taken a coherent set of signs and practices of domination and construed them to buttress an agency designed to overthrow political hierarchies.

The intifada: tremors in the construction of masculinity

The term *intifada* comes from the Arabic root n-f-d, which indicates a shaking, as in shaking the dust from (Harlow 1989:32). It implies a shaking off of foreign occupation and ties of economic and administrative linkage. While its eruption was fairly spontaneous, the intifada was the culmination of years of accumulated frustrations and outrage. A decade of grass-roots political and social organizing undergirded its direction and ability to sustain itself (Hiltermann 1991). The intifada brought to the forefront of international diplomacy an internally based Palestinian leadership. Equally, it signalled a generational shake-up. The young, armed only with stones and facing death and pain, were to sweep away the older generation in terms of political relevance and actual leadership. Shaking off also implicates forms of internal domination embodied in age, class, and gender hierarchies. The continuity created by life-cycle transitions such as marriage, employment, and reaching the state of '*aql* were destabilized by the actions of young boys.

The assertion that the male under occupation is reconstituted via violence implies that the creation of meaning is a matter of Palestinian control. The transformative power of the ritual lies in the individual who consciously commits himself to political action and in the community's ability to confer adult status. Ritual mediates between relations of violence and domination and political agency by subordinates in such a way as to defy any notion of directional unilineality between oppression and resistance. As Feldman argued in his discussion of political violence in Northern Ireland, "Political agency is not given but achieved on the basis of practices that alter the subject" (1991:1). Yet it is political practices by boys, many undertaken willingly and often spontaneously rather than given, that lead to further political agency via ritual.

As rites of passage, beatings and imprisonment are procedures that are not controlled or overseen by the family or kin group. It is an individual experience within a collectivity of young men. Thus a critical rite of passage into adulthood, with its corresponding privileges of power/authority/respect, is now accomplished earlier and is initially out of the bounds of the kin group. Indeed, it underscores the powerlessness of the kin group to protect its youth.

To return to Bourdieu's mapping of the relationship between masculinity and honor, we can now pose the question, what happens to the cultural categories and concepts around which honor is organized and expressed when challenge and riposte take place not between members of the same social group, but between a colonial entity, and its apparatus of force, and a subjugated, indigenous population? A man dishonors himself when he challenges a man considered incapable of "taking up the challenge" (Bourdieu 1977:11). When Israelis pursue and engage Palestinian youths, the cultural interpretation available to Palestinians is to consider the Israelis as lacking in the emotional moral qualities of manhood. Only men of little honor and thus dubious masculinity would beat unarmed youths while they themselves are armed with and trained in the use of modern implements of warfare. Because little or no effective riposte is possible at the instant, there is no challenge – and the encounter degenerates into mere aggression (Bourdieu 1977:12). Such aggression deprives its practitioners of claims to honor and morality.

Palestinians construe these aggressions as cowardly and immoral, rather than a challenge. But what has all this to do with manhood? Palestinians have changed the cultural categories of the encounter so that manhood comes from a "riposte" not to a challenge but to what Bourdieu distinguished as "mere aggression." And thus is constituted the national backdrop against which Palestinians are re-constructing defining elements of their culture and society. This will take on more meaning when read against the following scene.

Moral superiority: affirming cultural and national selves

On my way to an office in east Jerusalem, I was rushing to avoid the 1:00 p.m. closure of all commercial activity in the Palestinian sector of the city in observance of the general strike. Children were returning home from school, and shop shutters were hastily rolling down. As I rounded the corner, I saw two jeeps and about six or seven heavily armed soldiers. They had a ten-year-old mentally handicapped boy pressed against the stone wall, slapping him in the face, shaking him, and yelling in broken Arabic for him to admit throwing a stone at them. Being mentally handicapped, the boy could only whimper and cry – he was incapable of talking. I ran into our office to tell the others that they were beating the boy who lived across the alley. By this time several neighborhood women, by and large middle-class Jerusalemites, had also appeared. One of these women, fluent in English, calmly walked up to the group, which had now expanded to four jeeps and about fifteen soldiers. She politely asked why they were bothering this boy who is retarded and can barely speak. She kept repeating to the soldiers that the boy cannot understand and speak like a normal child. By now, she had a slight mocking smile on her face and appealed to the soldiers with a kind of sarcasm: "Can't you see he's retarded? It takes all of you soldiers and four jeeps to question a retarded boy!?" The other women were smirking and exchanging comments on what possesses these people to beat retarded children. Several of the soldiers were clearly embarrassed and physically distanced themselves, turning their backs on the boy and the two soldiers roughing him up. They smiled sheepishly to the women gathered there and shrugged their shoulders as if to say "What can we do?"

An audience of women defused a potential escalation of violence through mockery and joking. The imbalance of forces is so patently absurd that Palestinians find an almost comic relief in watching soldiers engaged in such morally revealing behavior. In imposing interpretation and meaning on the violence of the occupiers, Palestinians are (re)-constituting themselves in a moral sense. Violent encounters where Palestinians are both participants and audiences are public scenes where their moral qualities are dramatically juxtaposed with the occupiers'.

The re-constitution of a moral self via violence involved both men and women. To some extent, however, a gendered distinction appears in the practice of violence. While women have been active in all arenas, a task assigned to them early in the intifada, and one in tune with cultural notions of female propriety and "natural" concerns and mobility constraints, was to intervene in violent encounters. In other words, women were to witness and defuse rites of violence. A leaflet (*bayan*) distributed on March 8, 1988, and signed "Palestinian Women in the Occupied Territories" said, "Mothers, in camps, villages, and cities, continue confronting soldiers and settlers. Let each woman consider the wounded and imprisoned her own children."[21]

Despite a gendered division of roles, the moral reconstruction consequent to violent acts does indeed permeate gender boundaries. The re-constituting moral self, whether male or female, is a cultural category, in this case one with a national content, constructed as it currently is vis-à-vis a foreign other. As the witnessing audience, women provide a running commentary intended to shame soldiers to cease a beating or stop an arrest. "Don't you people have children?!" "Has God abandoned you?" is screamed at soldiers while entreating them to desist. While women's moral self is enacted and affirmed publicly in this act of witnessing, the male being beaten or arrested is also positioned performatively to place himself against an other. But how are nonparticipants positioned such that they also ultimately are enabled to construct a moral self? I would argue that the "telling," punctuated by moral and evaluative judgments that circulate throughout Palestinian society as people visit one another in the course of daily life, is one such event in which a moral constitution of the self unfolds.

Israeli behavior is considered rude and boorish. Palestinian discussions are punctuated by surprise at their bad manners. "These are supposedly educated peoples – why do they behave so obnoxiously?" They are regarded as lacking in ethics and morality. Most significantly, they are seen as deficient in empathy with the suffering of others.[22] In contemporary constitutions of self vis-à-vis their occupiers, Palestinians have recourse to a "poetics of contrast" (Comaroff and Comaroff 1987:205). Clear and defining distinctions are drawn between their behavior and the occupiers'. Palestinians consider themselves polite to others and reserved in public, personal qualities that are central to a

Palestinian etiquette. Images of contrast are rhetorical devices that lend meaning to the occupiers' behavior. The moral nature of these images provides Palestinians with the stuff of which they construct a collective self-image in a situation of subordination and an absence of autonomy.

Transforming hierarchies: class and generation

In the historical encounter, sociocultural systems are simultaneously transformed and reproduced (Sahlins 1981). Inscriptions of bodily violence and their construal as rites of passage both transform and reproduce certain structural, relational, and cultural features of Palestinian society. The intifada has had profound implications for class and generational structures and relations in the occupied territories. While the intifada is a popular uprising, those in the forefront of resistance to occupation are subaltern male youths from the refugee camps, villages, and urban popular quarters who are usually under twenty years of age and can be as young as ten.

The power and status of the older generation were eclipsed. Young males took over the tasks previously the preserve of more mature, often notable men. For example, disputes were mediated in new judicial tribunals organized and staffed by the underground leadership. A common lament was that the young were out of control, displaying little or no respect for their parents. It reached such a pitch that several leaflets in 1990 called for parents to reassert control and for youth to heed the voices of their parents and teachers.

The older generation, those over the age of thirty-five, played little, if any, visible role in the daily activities of the intifada. A telling incident occurred one day in a *service* (shared taxi) ride from Jerusalem to Ramallah. There were six passengers, myself included. As we approached a roadblock manned by soldiers, we could see several other cars stopped with young male passengers being searched and questioned. No one in our car seemed particularly worried or concerned. Our car came to a halt and the soldiers peered in, gave each of us a searching glance, and then motioned the driver to proceed. My husband commented to the rest of the passengers, "Why didn't they ask to see our identity cards or search us?" The other men in the car, none of whom appeared to be younger than thirty or thirty-five, turned around in their seats and looked at him with incredulity. One of them said "You think you're a boy! They aren't interested in men our age!"

Bodily inscriptions of violence are more prevalent in camps and villages and thus are somewhat class-bound. The politically active urban elite, often from notable families, who have traditionally striven for leadership, are not usually exposed to bodily inscriptions of violence though they may well undergo periods of administrative detention. Indeed, they can be subject to derision for assuming a mantle of leadership when they have not been credentialized by violence. Um Kamel is a forty-year-old mother and activist in a refugee camp. Her husband is in jail serving a ten-year sentence on the grounds of organizing anti-occupation activities. One son has spent considerable periods of time in prison, and a sixteen-year-old son had been shot twice in the stomach. Twice she has had homes demolished, with only a few hours notice, because of allegations of her sons' political activism. She commented sarcastically on the urban-based leaders: What do they know of suffering? Who are they to lead? They and their sons aren't beaten and they rarely go to jail. Their sons study here and abroad while our sons are beaten, shot and imprisoned!"

Reproducing hierarchies: gender

Contemporary rites of initiation into manhood articulate with and set in dramatic relief the social reproduction of asymmetrical gender arrangements, while a hierarchical male identity and notions of self-hood and political positions are reaffirmed in these rites of passage.

Given the casting of the beating as a zone of prestige for young men, what does it mean for women? The number of women beaten, arrested, and detained is small, and their status afterwards is more ambiguous than heroic. The number does not index women's level of involvement in the uprising, which has been extensive. It does indicate, however, their less visible role, and the tendency of the Israeli Defense Forces to go for males first. Ambiguity devolves for the women from the shame of having bodily contact with strange men, a stark transgression of the code of modesty and shame. Foremost on everyone's mind is the question of sexual violation. Women who violate the modesty code by engaging in illicit sexual activities (i.e., pre-marital sexual relations or adultery after marriage) risk incurring reprisals by kinsmen. But when the violator is a common enemy in whose face one's kinsmen hold no power and few means of recourse, ambiguity sets in. Ambiguity arises from the notion of will and intent. Arab women are seen as possessed of an active sexuality. When transgressions of the sexual code occur, the women can be held responsible. Yet, if a woman's nationalist activity set in motion a series of events that culminated in a beating and detention, and an interrogation procedure that included sexual torture, it is difficult to cast her as having violated the modesty code. The nationalist, patriotic cast of her intent and actions precludes the usual cultural interpretation. By the time of the intifada, ambiguity was giving way to a cautious respect for the woman detainee.

While femininity is no more natural than masculinity, physical violence is not as central to its construction. It does not reproduce or affirm aspects of female identity, nor does it constitute a rite of passage into adult female status. Women frame their physical violation as evidence of their equality with men and wield it to press their claims – "We suffer like men, we should have the same rights," quipped one former prisoner who had undergone a lengthy detention and was tortured during interrogation. While the violence visited upon males credentializes masculinity, that visited upon women indicates a potential equality of citizenship (Peteet 1991).

Women experience the phenomenon of beating from a multiplicity of subject positions. The "mother" saving boys from soldiers' blows is one of the most widespread and enduring images to emerge in the intifada. Mothers of the subaltern are extolled as the "mother of all Palestinians." Known in the camps as "a mother of all youths," Um Kamel explained her actions in intervening in public beatings: "I feel each and every one of those boys is my son. If it was my son, I would want other mothers to try to protect him." The mothers intervene during beatings, at once screaming for the soldiers to stop and pleading with them to show mercy. They hurl insults that highlight the soldiers' denial of the humanity of others: "Have you no compassion and pity?" "Aren't we human beings, too?" "Don't you have mothers and sons – how would your mother feel if you were treated this way; would you like to see your sons beaten like this?" "What kind of a people takes the land of another and then beats them when they protest?" This protective action of middle-aged mothers accomplishes several things: It can create a diversion that allows boys to escape. The noise and confusion it generates can quickly mobilize large groups of passersby and nearby residents to surround soldiers and try to intervene. But above all, it casts shame on soldiers by scrutinizing their moral qualities in a dramatic, public narrative. Women as mothers of all are a collective moral representation of a community testifying to the abusive nature of occupation.

Thus women are not silent witnesses to everyday violence. Witnessing is itself a form of political activism. When the occasional foreign journalist enters a camp, a delegation comes from abroad, or the anthropologist such as myself comes, the "mothers," those who risked their own safety to protect others, are called forth. Much like the vaunted position of the "mothers of the martyrs" in areas where Palestinian resistance takes the form of armed struggle (Peteet 1991), they are called upon to tell their stories, to assume the position of communal witnesses and tellers of suffering. The experience of a beating may not affirm a feminine identity and selfhood, yet it does evoke some female traits – stoicism and silence to protect the community.

While beatings reproduce a masculine identity, they also reproduce men's authority and physical domination in the family. Asymmetrical gender relations may be reaffirmed as a result of a young man's assumption of adult tasks and authority that in this case are assumed through violent rites of passage. Young wives and sisters complained that their husbands and brothers returned from interrogation and detention with a new authoritarianism expressed in attempts to assert control over their mobility. Style of dress was another arena of conflict, as women were pressured to wear head scarves. Domestic violence, wives and social workers claimed, was on the rise. Some men who were subjected to beatings and torture return home and inflict violence upon women.

Conclusion

The meaning of the beating is central to new conceptions of manhood and ultimately access to leadership positions. Violence has almost diametrically opposed meanings. For one, it is an index of a fictionalized fear and image of inferiority of a subject population and is intended to control and dishonor; for the others, it is constitutive of a resistant subjectivity that signals heroism, manhood, and access to leadership and authority. Practices that intimately situate Israelis and Palestinians are construed by Palestinians as transformative and agential. How did the experience of physical violence become construed as a rite of passage into manhood with its associated practices? In other words, can we identify a dynamic interplay between meaning and agency? The categories of experience, meaning, and agency should not be arranged in a unilinear manner so as to identify a direction of transformation. A more fruitful line of inquiry would cast these categories as existing in a relationship of mutual constitutiveness.

While beatings, bodies, and rite of passage are texts and structures of meaning, they are also historically grounded social constructions derived from particular signs and practices that galvanize a community to action. The call to action derives less from the actual structure of the ritual and more from its performative essence, in which the audience plays a crucial role in reversing the meaning intended by the dominant performers. The intifada abruptly and violently signalled an end to what Scott has referred to as the "public transcript"... the open interaction between subordinates and those who dominate" (1990:2). Israel's public performances to exact submission are no longer efficacious.

The act of incorporating beatings and imprisonment into a cultural criterion of manhood and assigning them status as a rite of passage is a "trick," if you will, that reverses the social order of meaning and leads to political agency. To let bodily violence stand as constitutive of an inferior and submitting social position and subjectivity without interpretation and challenge would be to submit to the dominant performers' meaning. For the anthropologist, to interpret it otherwise would leave it as a textual rather than an agential problematic.

The occupying authorities, with constant attention directed to detecting ripples of change in Palestinian cultural categories and social relations, have by now caught on to the way applications of bodily violence and imprisonment have empowered a generation committed to resistance. A new element of knowledge seems to be emerging in their regime of pseudoknowledge of the subject population. Interrogation procedures now contain a sexual practice designed to thwart the meaning and agency of physical violence as rites of passage to masculinity and manhood. Rape during interrogation is now being more widely discussed among some released prisoners, as is fondling by interrogators with photographs taken of these incidents. Sexual forms of interrogation deprive young men of claims to manhood and masculinity. One cannot return from prison and describe forms of torture that violate the most intimate realm of gendered selfhood. If knowledge of such sexual tortures circulates widely, violence and detention will be diluted of their power to contribute to a gendered sense of self informing political agency.

Notes

1. The Rites of Ashura, a ritual commemoration of the death of the Prophet's grandson Hussein, engaged in by the Shi'ites of the Middle East (Iraq, Southern Lebanon, and Iran), is such an example. The playing of specific roles in the play reflects the power structure of a society at a particular moment, and the ritual itself has opposed meanings for its participants. In Hegland's analysis of Ashura rituals during the Iranian Revolution of the late 1980s, she confirms that participation in a ritual "does not necessarily indicate that all participants share the same mindset or ideology or even that they all consider themselves to be or wish to be members of the same

social or political group" (1983:90). In representing a reversal of the social order, Ashura rituals in revolutionary Iran were crucial symbolic and real agents of the "complete overthrow of the political, economic, and social order" (1983:96). Gilsenan indicates that the drama of Hussein, while seemingly a fixed, immutable religious ritual central to Shi'ite belief and practice, is socially produced in specific social historical contexts. In both turn-of-the-century Iran and Lebanon, it gave dramatic expression and enactment to relations of powerlessness/powerfulness while also presenting, in the case of Iran, an image of the world that reverses the social order. In Southern Lebanon, the drama confirmed the existing social order when the "learned families," the sheikhs, were losing power and prestige to an emergent peasant-trade group (1982:55–74).

2. In the drive to create a state in 1948, Israel did not seek to win Palestinian consent to the Zionist project or ideology, only to ensure either flight or nonrebellion (by those who stayed).

3. Literature devoted explicitly to masculinity in the Arab world is rare, but the topic surfaces in a variety of works, not exclusively but largely based on ethnography in North Africa (Abu-Lughod 1986; Caton 1985, 1987; Davis and Davis 1989).

4. Unlike masculinity in the Mediterranean, especially Spain, public displays of lust and sexual bravado are not explicit components of Arab manhood. Indeed self-mastery of lust and romantic emotions are crucial to the construction and maintenance of Arab manhood (see Abu–Lughod 1986; Gilmore 1990:40). In Muslim thought, unregulated sexuality can lead to *fitna* (social chaos).

5. Autonomy is more than simply the ability to provide physical protection. It is also the ability to support one's family through labor. To adequately explain how the Palestinian economy has been harnessed to that of the occupying country, and in the process how labor categories, relations, and patterns have been transformed, is beyond the scope of this chapter.

6. In a study of the dreams of Palestinian children, Bilu (1991) noted that in nightmares of violent encounters between their families and Israeli soldiers or settlers, parents are unable to protect children from violence, whereas in Israeli children's nightmares of violence emanating from Arabs, salvation arrives in the form of fathers, families, and the army. In one case the nightmare is resolved, in the other it is simply a nightmare from which the children can find no escape. A study discussed by Peretz had a similar conclusion. In a study of children's dreams, a prominent theme was the presence of soldiers in their homes, smashing furnitures and beating parents. Peretz commented that "a major conclusion was that these children regard themselves as victims of violence initiated by armed men and that the family no longer provides security. The father almost never figures in these dreams; according to the analysis, he has lost his authority" (1990:116). His source is Amos Lavav "Jewish–Arab Psychoanalysis" *Sotf-Shavooa*, weekly supplement to *Maariv International Edition* 12–23–88.

7. See Peteet (1991:105–7) where I argue that, among the Palestinians in Lebanon, rituals of martyrdom for guerrillas were testimonials to their honor and immortality in the collective consciousness. Moreover, their cel-

ebratory spirit signalled defiance of death and the subordination it was supposed to overcome.

8. In another instance, Caton (1987) foregrounds power in language. The ability to persuade using verbal skills is central in establishing and displaying power and masculinity, I would contend, rather than fighting skills and achievements as is usually assumed.

9. Hamid Ammar, in his ethnography of an Egyptian village, offers one of the most detailed accounts of the Arab male maturation process (1954).

10. For an extensive discussion of the concept *'aql* see Rosen (1984).

11. See Granqvist (1931, 1935, 1947) for a description of circumcisions and weddings in Mandate Palestine.

12. See Hajjar and Beinin (1988). This is a primer designed to provide a very basic overview of twentieth-century Palestinian history and society.

13. This encompasses injuries sustained from live ammunition, which includes plastic bullets, rubber bullets, metal marbles, and tear gas.

14. The Palestine Human Rights and Information Committee (PHRIC) cautions that the figure of 106,600 should probably be doubled, especially the beatings. They receive their information from hospitals and clinics, and many people do not seek medical care. Moreover, they do not receive figures on beating cases treated in emergency rooms, in local or private clinics, or by the medical communities. The figures from the Gaza Strip for the month of December 1990 indicate 273 reported beatings (66 were of women, 45 of children) (Palestine Human Rights and Information Campaign 1990).

15. See Aronson (1987) for a detailed discussion of the forms of this resistance and its dating to the earliest days of the occupation.

16. Their actual numbers are somewhat harder to estimate because, with the intifada, human rights organizations began making a concerted attempt to keep monthly and annual figures on human rights violations, breaking them down into distinct categories.

17. Amnesty International (1991) states that in the occupied territories, Palestinian detainees are "typically subjected to forms of torture or ill-treatment, with the aim of obtaining information as well as a confession ... Torture or ill-treatment seem to be virtually institutionalized during the arrest and interrogation procedures ... The practices relating in particular to interrogation procedures have been officially endorsed or are generally condoned, and therefore effectively encouraged, by the authorities" (p. 45). Amnesty's report also questions the "fairness of military court trials" because of the prominent roles of confessions and "the apparent reluctance by judges to investigate claims of coerced statements" (p. 49). The report states that "the substantial evidence available indicates the existence of a clear pattern of systematic psychological and physical ill-treatment, constituting torture or other forms of cruel, inhuman, or degrading treatment, which is being inflicted on detainees during the course of interrogation" (p. 58).

18. Zionist fictionalizing, and I would add, fear of collective Arab sentiment and action, goes far in explaining why the shooting of an Israeli diplomat in London could be presented as justification for the 1982 invasion of Lebanon and yet why Israel has usually insisted on bilateral negotiations with Arab states.

19. See Peretz (1990) for a discussion of the complexity of views among soldiers serving in the occupied territories.
20. For discussion of Palestinian popular tribunals and popular justice committees during the intifada see McDowell (1989) and Peretz (1990). A similar process of legal development occurred in Lebanon under the PLO (Peteet 1987).
21. Leaflets are printed several times a month by the underground leadership of the intifada. They contain a listing of the strike days and days of confrontation, and additionally exhort people to boycott Israeli goods, to actively participate in popular committees; in general, to support the uprising.
22. Jewish theologian Mark Ellis suggests that "Holocaust theology" – emergent since the creation of Israel in 1948 – is a self-absorbed phenomenon based on a joining of religious heritage with loyalty to Israel. Such self-absorption diminishes Jewish capacity for empathy with Palestinian suffering (Neimark 1992:21; see also Lewis 1990).

Bibliography

Abu-Lughod, Lila 1986 *Veiled Sentiments: Honor and Poetry in a Bedouin Society.* Berkeley: University of California Press.

Ammar, Hamid 1954 *Growing Up in an Egyptian Village.* London: Routledge & Kegan Paul.

Amnesty International. Israel and the Occupied Territories. 1991 *The Military Justice System in the Occupied Territories: Detention, Interrogation and Trial Procedures.* New York: Amnesty International.

Altorki, Soraya 1986 *Women in Saudia Arabia: Ideology and Behavior among the Elite.* New York: Columbia University Press.

Aronoff, Myron 1982 *Culture and Political Change.* Political Anthropology Series, 2. New Brunswick, NJ: Transaction Books.

Aronson, Geoffrey 1987 *Creating Facts: Israel, Palestinians, and the West Bank.* Washington, DC: Institute for Palestine Studies.

Ben-Ari, Eyal 1989 "Masks and Soldering: The Israeli Army and the Palestinian Uprising." *Cultural Anthropology* 4:372–89.

Bilu, Yoram 1991 "The Other as Nightmare: The Articulation of Aggression in Children's Dreams in Israel and the West Bank." Paper presented at the 90th Annual Meeting of the American Anthropological Association, Chicago.

Bourdieu, Pierre 1977 *Outline of a Theory of Practice.* Cambridge: Cambridge University Press.

Brenneis, Donald 1987 "Performing Passions: Aesthetics and Politics in an Occasionally Egalitarian Community." *American Ethnologist* 14:236–50.

Caton, Steven 1985 "The Poetic Construction of Self." *Anthropological Quarterly* 58:141–51.

— 1987 "Power, Persuasion, and Language: A Critique of the Segmentary Model in the Middle East." *International Journal of Middle East Studies* 19:77–102.

Comaroff, Jean 1985 *Body of Power, Spirit of Resistance: The Culture and History of a South African People.* Chicago and London: University of Chicago Press.

Comaroff, John L. and Jean Comaroff 1987 "The Madman and the Migrant: Work and Labor in the Historical Consciousness of a South African People." *American Ethnologist* 14:191–209.

Combs-Schilling, Elaine 1991 "Etching Patriarchal Rule: Ritual Dye, Erotic Potency, and the Moroccan Monarch." *Journal of the History of Sexuality* 1:658–81.

Davis, Susan, and Douglas Davis 1989 *Adolescence in a Moroccan Town*. New Brunswick and London: Rutgers University Press.

Fanon, Frantz 1969 *The Wretched of the Earth*. Harmondsworth: Penguin Book Ltd.

Feldman, Allen 1991 *Formations of Violence: The Narrative of the Body and Political Terror in Northern Ireland*. Chicago: University of Chicago Press.

Foucault, Michel 1979 *Discipline and Punish: The Birth of the Prison*. New York: Vintage Books.

Gerlach, Luther, and Virginia Hines 1970 *People, Power and Change: Movements of Social Transformation*. Indianapolis: Bobbs-Merrill Educational Publications.

Gilmore, David 1990 *Manhood in the Making: Cultural Concepts of Masculinity*. New Haven and London: Yale University Press.

Gilsenan, Michael 1982 *Recognizing Islam: Religion and Society in the Modern Arab World*. New York: Pantheon Books.

Granqvist, Hilma 1931 & 1935 *Marriage Conditions in a Palestinian Village*. 2 vols. Helsingfors, Finland: Societas Scientiarum Fennica.

— 1947 *Birth and Childhood Among the Arabs: Studies in a Muhammadan Village in Palestine*. Helsingfors, Finland: Soderstrom & Co.

Hajjar, Lisa, and Joel Beinin 1988 "Palestine for Beginners." *Middle East Report* 154:17–20.

Harlow, Barbara 1989 "Narrative in Prison: Stories from the Palestinian Intifada." *Modern Fiction Studies* 35: 29–46.

Hegland, Mary 1983 "Ritual and Revolution in Iran." In *Culture and Political Change*, Political Anthropology Series, 2. Myron J. Aronoff, ed., pp. 75–100. New Brunswick, NJ: Transaction Books.

Herzfeld, Michael 1985 *The Poetics of Manhood: Contest and Identity in a Cretan Mountain Village*. Princeton, NJ: Princeton University Press.

Hiltermann, Joost 1991 *Behind the Uprising*. Princeton, NJ: Princeton University Press.

Keesing, Roger 1985 "Kwaio Women Speak: The Micropolitics of Autobiography in a Solomon Island Society." *American Anthropologist* 87:27–39.

Kertzer, David 1988 *Ritual, Politics, and Power*. New Haven, CT: Yale University Press.

Lewis, Mark 1990 *Beyond Innocence and Redemption: Confronting the Holocaust and Israeli Power*. San Francisco: Harper & Row Publishers.

Martin, Emily 1987 *The Woman in the Body: A Cultural Analysis of Reproduction*. Boston: Beacon Press.

McDowell, David 1989 *Palestine and Israel: The Uprising and Beyond*. Berkeley: University of California Press.

Neimark, Marilyn 1992 "American Jews and Palestine: The Impact of the Gulf War." *Middle East Report* 175:19–23.

Outram, Dorinda 1989 *The Body and the French Revolution: Sex, Class and Political Culture*. New Haven, CT: Yale University Press.

Palestine Human Rights and Information Campaign 1990 *Palestine Human Rights and Information Campaign* 3:13. Human Rights Update.

Peteet, Julie 1987 "Socio-Political Integration and Conflict Resolution in a Palestinian Refugee Camp." *Journal of Palestine Studies* 16(2):29–44.

— 1991 *Gender in Crisis: Women and the Palestinian Resistance Movement*. New York: Columbia University Press.

Peretz, Don 1990 *Intifada: The Palestinian Uprising*. Boulder, CO: Westview Press.

Rosen, Lawrence 1984 *Bargaining for Reality: The Construction of Social Relations in a Muslim Community*. Chicago: University of Chicago Press.

Sahlins, Marshall 1981 *Historical Metaphors and Mythical Realities: Structure in the Early History of the Sandwich Islands Kingdom*. Ann Arbor: University of Michigan press.

Schiefellin, Edward 1985 "Performance and the Cultural Construction of Reality." *American Ethnologist* 12:707–24.

Scott, James 1990 *Domination and the Arts of Resistance: Hidden Transcripts*. New Haven, CT: Yale University Press.

Shammas, Anton 1988 "A Stone's Throw." *New York Review of Books*, March 31:10.

Taussig, Michael 1987 *Shamanism, Colonialism, and the Wild Man: A Study in Terror and Healing*. Chicago: University of Chicago Press.

— 1990 "Violence and Resistance in the Americas: The Legacy of Conquest." *Journal of Historical Sociology* 3:209–24.

Thompson, Edward P. 1978 *The Poverty of Theory and Other Essays*. New York: Monthly Review Press.

Turner, Victor 1977 *The Ritual Process: Structure and Anti-Structure*. Ithaca, NY: Cornell University Press.

Van Gennep, Arnold 1961 *The Rites of Passage*. Chicago: University of Chicago Press.

14

Terror Warfare and the Medicine of Peace

Carolyn Nordstrom

Introduction to the war

What is the staging ground of political violence? Traditional political and military science situate studies of warfare primarily in political institutions and the actions of elites. This may be where political violence is conceived, but it is not where it is carried out. Political institutions and elites operate in war and in peace; their existence does not mark the inception of violence. If institutions and their ideologues are not the staging ground of war, where, then, is it? Logic supplies a single answer: war comes into existence when violence is employed. Political aggressions may become enflamed, threats may be flung back and forth, military exercises may take place, but it is only when weapons are employed and people are harmed and killed that war is said to exist. But war is far more than the maiming and killing of humans. War is a cultural system that becomes reproduced in the minutiae of daily living and the constructs of what it means to be human. And it is here that terror warfare is waged, resisted, and ultimately defeated. One of the best descriptions of war that I have heard comes from a young woman I spoke with at the height of the war in Mozambique:

> I don't know if anyone really knows war until it lives inside of them. A person can come here and see the war, fear the war, be scared of the violence – but their life, their very being, is not determined by the war. This is my country, the country of my parents, my family, my friends, my future. And the war has gotten into all of these. I

Medical Anthropology Quarterly 12(1):103–21. Copyright © 1998 American Anthropological Association.

know everyone has suffered a loss in this war: a family member killed, a loved one captured and never heard of again. But it goes much deeper than this, to the very heart of the country, to my very heart. When I walk on the road, I carry nervousness with me as a habit, as a way of being. When I hear a sharp noise, I do not stop and ask "what is that?" like a normal person. I start and fear my life is in jeopardy. And I do this for my family as well. Whenever I am parted from them I have this gnawing worry: will I ever see them again, is something terrible happening to them at this moment? I cringe for my very land, soaked in blood so it can't produce health-ily. This lives in me – it is a part of my being, a constant companion, a thing no one can understand if they only enter here and worry about their own safety from one day to the next. I want to leave Mozambique, to go away and work or study … I want to get away from all this, to run from it for a little while. But the even stronger feeling is that I can't stand to leave my country, for I can never leave the war. I will carry the war with me, and that inflames within me a passion to be here, to be a part of my country and help even in its worst moments. For if I leave, when I come home my most cher-ished things may be ashes, what is a part of me may have died, and I wouldn't have been here to know, to have tried to do something. The passion that makes me want to flee my country's problems binds me to my country so that I can't bear to leave.

In addition to portraying the ontological *fact* of war for those living on the frontlines, this woman's words are an introduction to the war that devastated Mozambique from the time of independence in 1975 to the peace accords in 1992. Though I have studied several severe war zones during the fifteen years I have researched political violence,[1] I focus on Mozambique in this chapter for two reasons: (1) the violence to which Mozambicans were subjected during the postindependence war was among the worst of contemporary times, and (2) the creativity employed by the average civilians to survive and defeat the war was as sophisticated a system of conflict resolution as I have seen.

The extent of the violence in Mozambique can be summed up in a few statistics. In the sixteen years of war, one million people, the vast majority noncombatant civilians, died of war-related causes. Half a million of those casualties were children. Fully one-half of the entire population of sixteen million people were directly affected by the war. They were subjected to attack, rape, torture, forced relocation, kidnap-ping, and forced servitude at an army base; many were forced to witness atrocities against loved ones or participate in violence. One-quarter of Mozambique's population fled their homes. Infrastructure was also heavily targeted: over one-third of schools and clinics were destroyed or closed by the war, roads were made virtually impassable due to troop attacks and landmines, and the market economy collapsed countrywide (Casimiro *et al.* 1990; Geffray 1990; Ministerio da Saude/UNICEF 1988; Minter 1994; Vines 1991).

As these numbers of casualties demonstrate, terror warfare was a mainstay of this war. This was due to the politics of apartheid and the Cold War ideologies that divided the world into violent binary oppositions. When Mozambique achieved independence from the Portuguese in 1975, the successful forces, Frelimo, established a Marxist-Leninist, black-majority government. The governments in neighboring Rhodesia and South Africa, which were pro-apartheid, viewed the new Mozambique government as a considerable threat. Rhodesia instigated the rebel force, Renamo, in Mozambique to destabilize the Frelimo government and undercut its support of independence fighters in Rhodesia. When Rhodesia became independent Zimbabwe, the apartheid-era South African Defense Forces stepped in to direct Renamo. Because the goal of these external forces was destabilization (in order to protect their own apartheid governments) and not political power, war strategies were largely destructive. Many claim that Renamo did not have internal support and lacked a political agenda altogether. While there is truth in this, Renamo did in fact enjoy pockets of support. But because much of the funding and training of soldiers came from pro-apartheid military personnel and from ex-colonists who had fought against independence, terror tactics more than nation-building were infused into military strategy and tactics.[2]

What these statistics do not show is the full extent of the war casualties. The first time a Mozambican said to me that the war had taken from them everything they had, including *who* they were, I realized that identity, self, and personhood, as well as physical bodies, are strategic targets of war. Identity, self, and personhood are those dynamic aspects of being by which we recognize and know ourselves, our selves in the world, ourselves as "being" human. They are also the locus of political will. If political will is a dynamic attribute of one's self and identity, killing a "body" will not necessarily kill the dynamic font of political will. Therefore, creative self-definition instead becomes the enemy to conquer. Terror warfare thus focuses less on killing the physical body than on terrifying the population as a whole into, the military strategists hope, cowed acquiescence. Strategic murder, torture, community destruction, sexual abuse, and starvation become the prime weapons in the arsenal of terror warfare.

But, as this chapter (as well as much of history) shows, terror ultimately fails to control populations.[3] People resist, and they do so in very creative ways. They literally create selves and worlds capable of withstanding and defeating rule by violence. The creativity that I saw during the war years in Mozambique constituted a core survival strategy and a profound form of resistance to political violence. It is one of the most sophisticated mechanisms for asserting personal agency and political will in the face of intolerable repression that I have seen in the years I have studied political violence. Contrary to the popular belief that morality and society break down in the brutal chaos of war, I have found that *most* people actively dedicate themselves to rebuilding their lives and societies, to working with others to find solutions to the deprivations of war, and to instituting conflict-resolution measures at the local level.

Shared realities in difference: methodology and cultures of violence and peace

Terror warfare does not constitute a single sweeping strategy, and casualties of war do not constitute a generic group. Precisely because violence is embodied, it is profoundly personal. Each person experiences war according to a unique intersection of history, culture, immediate contexts, and personality. War is not primarily about adult male soldiers doing battle. Combatants and noncombatants cannot be stereotyped into "mass" categories, nor can the lines between them be clearly demarcated. Children and adults, men and women, fight and die. The battlefields are home to rogues and honorable citizens: to old and young, rich and poor, political and apolitical. In all of these categories, each person has an individual experience of war, a unique "war story."

Yet in the case of Mozambique, it is not enough to say that women, men, children, farmers, politicians, refugees, soldiers, the wounded, and the dying all "live" war differently, or that each of the country's more than one dozen major language and cultural groupings survived violence in a distinct way. Clearly a woman who is shot by soldiers, a general at a military command post in an urban center, and a man who is physically unharmed but sees his village burned experience war differently. Sixteen million people lived in Mozambique at the time I was there, and fully half of them were directly affected by the war. The people I met and spoke with, or read about in my time there represent an exceedingly small fraction of the total population. Each met violence in a profoundly personal way. How responsible, how representation, can any generalization about death, suffering, and survival be?

Yet it is equally accurate to say that certain generalizations about the experience of war are possible. Both in Mozambique and across its borders soldiers entered new battlefields, refugees fled, healers tended broken bodies, and teachers tried to continue teaching children. Mothers and fathers worked hard to protect their families from the latest terror tactics and rogue troops, soldiers shared rations and strategies, and politicians bent ideologies to fit battlefield realities. Looters followed troops, traders followed looters, and arms merchants ensured that cycles of attack and defeat could be set into motion yet again. Through all of this, each person talks with the next, and together they forge a way of thinking about and acting within a war zone. These conversations take place across gender, age, language, social, cultural, and politico-military associations. While some people agree and some disagree, a vast interrelated compendium of information is gathered, shared, and learned. This shared information on war and surviving war links people war-wide and constitutes shared culture(s). Every piece of information is encoded with values, orientations, ethics, strategies for survival, and basic concepts of in/humanity. These accounts of war and peace are conveyed in spoken words and prose, poetry and song, dance and fighting, and fleeing and protecting; they are represented in parable, myth, and ideology. They resonate through the realities of life and death. War is fought, resisted, survived, and defeated by these cultures.

Violence, then, is a fluid culture. For this reason I released ethnography from its traditional moorings in *place* and located it instead in the study of *process*. Rather than looking at how war affects a certain group of people in a specific locale, I followed the ramifications of violence across people's lives linked by a war in all the ways that war makes meaningful, or inescapable. In answering the methodological "how" of this decision, I decided to investigate all that I could of the threads of war and resistance spun across the country. I spent several years in Mozambique during the height of the war in 1988, 1989, and 1990–91 (and in the postwar period in 1994, 1996, and 1997). I decided to make my base in the north central province of Zambezia, which was one of the most war-affected provinces in Mozambique. From there, I followed the war, and people's resistance to it, through a number of Mozambique's different language and cultural groups by traveling to the two northernmost provinces of Niassa and Cabo Delgado, the central Provinces of Sofala and Manica, and to Gaza and Maputo

Provinces in the southern part of the country. By weaving together hundreds of my discussions and shared experiences with a wide diversity of people countrywide over time and space, I hope to illuminate at least something of what it means to live on the frontlines of a war.

This ethnography reflects the reality of many Mozambicans' lives. Conflict, starvation, deprivation, and the demands of work, family, and health have produced an extremely fluid population. In responding to the threat of aggression, Mozambicans carried with them reworked notions of home, family, community, and survival as they fought, fled from fighting, and sought security. This study follows this flux of war. All of the material presented in this article was gathered during the war, not after. Thus my research reflects the war in areas I could travel to. Heavy landmining of roadways throughout Mozambique severely limited road travel of any kind. But because the Mozambican Ministry of Health graciously gave me countrywide travel permits, and pilots flying emergency supplies to embattled civilians gave me *boleia* (hitchhiking rides), I was able to visit a fairly representative sample of locations (though I did not spend time in Renamo secured bases). What emerged as paramount for me during these travels was not only the devastating impact of war on a country, but the remarkable creativity that average people employed in their efforts to defeat not one side or the other, but the whole notion of war itself. These topics comprise the remainder of this chapter.

Terror warfare

Terror warfare is predicated on a bastardized understanding of cultural transmission that posits that maiming and murder of a few will terrify the many into political acquiescence (Nordstrom 1997b). Terror warfare can be constructed along several different principles. In its most basic form, its power lies in the threat it poses to life, limb, and the basic normalcy of the world. Aerial bombing, the devastation of communities, destruction of food and water sources, and torture and murder of soldiers and civilians constitute mainstays of this form of assault. For the victims, life as they knew it is the casualty. One Mozambican summed up a common sentiment:

> Our life has been taken from us: a life where people go to their fields to work, produce the foods that nourish our families, build the houses where we will raise our children – a good life, a healthy life. People just want to eat, to play with their children, to be able to buy a chair for their house if they can, to visit with their family and

friends. These are things we can't do now, we suffer too much – our lives are suffering. The life here, the life in the world, is no good now, it has been broken by war. We eat suffering for dinner. We can't walk freely, we can't work freely, we can't eat freely, we can't live freely. The life of war is a damaged [*estragado*] life. (conversation with a Mozambican man in Zambezia, 1990)

In its more grotesque form, terror warfare is about destroying, not people, but what military strategists conceive of as humanity. This form of terror is not directed at the destruction of life and limb, but against all sense of a reasonable and humane world. The strategy here is not to control people through fear of force, but through the horror of it. Because of the prevalence of this form of warfare in Mozambique, the country was sometimes called "the killing fields of Africa" in international presses (Frelick 1989).

Thousands of children have seen their parents die before their eyes, hundreds of children have been boiled in the presence of their parents. Heads of old people are used as stools by the bandits, unwilling farmers are nailed to trees. Every refugee, child or adult knows such a story. (Dis 1991:44, translated from Dutch by A. Robben)

Somewhere between the basic strategies and the extremes of terror warfare are the everyday stories of people who survived a very brutal war as best they could.

They have made us inhuman. We sleep in the jungle like animals every night to avoid attack. We run from every sound like the animals we hunt, we scavenge for food in the countryside like animals because we cannot maintain our crops like humans. Our family is scattered on the wind – we don't know where our children and parents are, or even if they are alive. We can't even help and protect them – we are even worse than animals in this sense. Do you know what this does to a person, living like this?

One of the goals of terror warfare is to reproduce the hegemony of violence in the minutiae of everyday life. The normal, the innocuous, and the inescapable are infused with associations of lethal harm and control. Perpetrators do this by using common everyday items to produce terror. Kitchen items, household goods, water sources, and tools become weapons of torture and murder. Public spaces are cast as strategic battlegrounds: the maimed and murdered are often left in communal areas. Main thoroughfares, community centers, public parks, schoolyards, and markets become places in which the war is "brought home" to people. Places traditionally associated with safety and items traditionally used in the production of the ordinary are recast as inhumane and lethal. When a kitchen knife is used to mutilate a family member, or a post office becomes the site of a massacre, kitchen knives and post offices become attached to the production of violence in ways that last far beyond the conclusion of the war. It is unlikely that anyone who witnesses these atrocities will ever again use a similar knife or enter a post office without reexperiencing the impact of war (Herman 1992; Scarry 1985). Peace accords may be finalized, but for many the war never fully ends. Terror warfare is predicated on this principle: its goal is in part to undermine the fundamental ontological security of an entire society. This goal is not something confined to the "victims" of war – everyone is a victim of war. A culture of violence, far more complex, multifaceted, and enduring than the formal boundaries of war demarcated in military culture, takes root in the quotidian life of a country at war (Nordstrom 1992a, 1992b).

War accounts are all too often limited to interviews with adults, leaving the impression that while terror warfare may affect children, it primarily targets adults.[4] In truth, children often comprise a prime target in dirty wars (Nordstrom 1997c; Suarez-Orozco 1987), and nowhere is the fundamental security of daily life undermined more than in attacks on children. The following quote is similar to many I heard during the war in Mozambique. The quote comes from an acquaintance of mine who stopped by one day in 1991 to visit. "There is someone I would like you to meet," she said. Her little cousin had arrived from a Renamo military stronghold. She explained that the girl and her brother had been kidnapped by Renamo soldiers some time ago, and that while the little girl had managed to escape, her brother had not. Children were routinely kidnapped by military forces and taken to their bases to provide labor and sexual services, and to serve as forced conscripts.

> I don't know what to do. She is thin, sickly, and terribly depressed. But I cannot get her to eat, or to sleep. When I bring her food, she will eat nothing. All I can get her to eat are things like the most basic roots. And the little girl replies "How can I eat when I know my brother is starving?" She will not sleep in a bed or on a mat, but curls up on the ground. And she looks at me with big sad eyes and

says "How can I sleep in comfort when I know my brother is sleeping on the cold hard ground?" And when I try to give her a bath, take her to the clinic, or tend to her in any way, she just pulls away and says "How can I think of myself when I know how my brother is suffering?" When I try to talk to her about this, to tell her she must get better to help her brother when he comes home, she shakes her head sadly and says "I know what he is going through, it is so bad you can not imagine." But she will say nothing else.

As these examples show, terror warfare attacks not just the body, not even just the body politic – it attacks core definitions of humanity. The target is the font of political will and of creative world building – the loci of resistance. Terror warfare thus constitutes an attack on identity. One Mozambican summarized, "This war took away everything we had, including *who* we were." The events that befell the sister-in-law of a friend of mine have always stood as a poignant summary of the connection between violence and identity. Not long after we met, Duirno told me the plight of his brother's wife, Jacanta. Their hometown had been attacked two years previously in a particularly vicious raid. The family had scattered in different directions. Duirno made it to safety, walking several days through the bush to a re-location center. The rest of his family was not as lucky: one was killed and two – his sister-in-law and her mother – were missing. As weeks turned into months and no word came from them, he decided they must have been kidnapped by Renamo soldiers and taken back to their base, for their bodies were never found.

One day Duirno came to visit brimming with good tidings: Jacanta and her mother had just come home. They had arrived sickly, bedraggled, and scarred, but alive. They had in fact been kidnapped by Renamo during the raid. Both had been forced to walk, carrying on their backs for hundreds of kilometers to a Renamo base camp in the next Province the very goods that were looted from their town. What exactly had happened to Jacanta was difficult to ascertain: she had completely lost the ability to speak Chuabo, her native language. The Renamo base was located in a different language zone, and the majority of the people there spoke a completely different dialect from Jacanta. She learned to speak a bit of this dialect, but no one in her family could understand it. Duirno sat down with a frown and said to me,

You know, we have heard of this happening to others. Jacanta's mother told us some of the terrible things that happened to them during these last two years. They were raped, they were beaten, they saw others killed. They were forced to do difficult labor, and were given little to eat, and no medicines when they were sick. Jacanta's mother can still speak Chuabo, but she doesn't want to speak of the experiences much – we really do not know all that happened to them. But this thing with Jacanta, I think the experiences were just too horrible, she did not want them to be a part of her real life, so she forgot Chuabo so that these things could not touch her life. There was that life, and then there is her real life. She can speak of that awful life in the other dialect, and none of us understand, but she cannot speak of them in Chuabo. We are hoping as her life comes back to her, so will her language.

Questions concerning the nature of self, identity, and their relation to resistance for Duirno and his family are not idle speculations or abstract epistemological endeavors – they are a pressing reality. Self and identity constitute the hidden casualties of war. For an antagonistic military wishing to destroy, control, or subjugate a people, what more powerful "target" is there than self-identity and personal perceptions of reality? Human *will* is an intolerable threat to those who seek to dominate.

The irony in terror warfare is that the premises upon which it is based are inaccurate. People suffer the ravages of war and are changed by the experience of being forced to respond to violent events, but they are not controlled by these experiences. People resist the oppression of violence; they re-create viable worlds; they reforge political identities of their own making. The remainder of this chapter is devoted to an exploration of these processes of resisting violence and rebuilding war-torn worlds.

Creativity and the un-making of violence

Self, culture, and reality are (re)generative. People ultimately control the production of reality and their place in it. This is an interactive process. They produce themselves, and equally, they are produced within, and by, these cultural processes. As much as terror warfare tries to dismantle the viable person, people fight back.

Creativity as I use it here refers to this profound aspect of world building – the creating of self and world. The creativity employed to survive a devastating war is of a different order than that used to survive in a functional society.

When people look out over a land that should resonate with meaning and life but that instead stares back blankly with barren fields, scattered communities, broken bodies, and shattered realities, they are left with the choice of accepting a deadened world, or creating a livable one. Imagination and the will to carry it out become core features of survival. "Pain unmakes the world, and imagining makes it" (Scarry 1985:163).[5]

Talking about creativity and imagination is not easy within the confines of Western epistemology. Creativity is often presented as a cognitive aspect of specific individuals. A brilliant person, a flash of insight, and the arts are the provinces of creativity in popular Western conceptions. The actual processes of the creation of self and world are poorly understood.[6] There has also been a generalized tendency in the West to see imagination as flimsy recollections that are less vibrant, less meaningful than the "real" experience that is deemed to be the source of imagination. In this view, it is the world that provides the substance for imagination, not the other way around. Sartre (1948) provides a classic example of this when he points out how shallow and impoverished his "imagined" friend Pierre is in his head when compared to the complex vibrancy of his real friend Pierre in the flesh.[7]

Yet if we accept the view that humans author their own existence, creativity must be self-generating. Imagining must be capable of engendering more than flimsy pictures of the real world.[8] This is a fact of life of which people on the frontlines are well aware:

> So after the attacks we come home ... to what? To less than nothing. Our town is burned, our houses and all our possessions gone, our fields destroyed, our animals killed. Worst, people in the community, in our families, well, some didn't survive. What do we do, rebuild our communities? With what? All we have is ruins. How? Like it was before: open to yet more attacks? With what faith – that somehow our good will win out, like it did in the last attack? But if we leave it like this, if we give up, the war wins. So we have to make our lives again. We have to imagine a future, a future safe from war, and then try to make it.

Corbin (1969, 1972) provides better explanations of how the creative construction of self and world is embodied. He uses the term *mundus imaginalis* to refer to the creative imaginary. The creative imaginary constitutes a very precise order of reality, which corresponds to a very precise order of perception. For Corbin, the imagination is a noetic, cognitive power or "an organ of true knowledge" (Corbin 1972:13). Fundamentally and perceptually real, yet outside of *where*, the realm of the imagination, according to Corbin, mediates between sense and intellect, matter and mind, inside (self) and outside (self-in-world), the given and the possible (Corbin 1972:9).[9] Not only are people in the world, the world is *in* them. Rather than being situated, the cognitive process of the *mundus imaginalis* situates; more so, it is situating. Beyond being perfectly real, its reality is more irrefutable and coherent than that of the empirical world where individuals perceive reality through their senses. In this way, the creative imaginary is fundamentally embodied: inseparable from the processes of life, and essential to defining them.

Unlike Sartre, many Mozambicans are able to imagine their friends, their homes, and their society and culture as vibrantly as the "real thing." This is a sophisticated survival mechanism. When Sartre cannot imagine his friend Pierre as vibrantly as he experiences Pierre in the flesh, it is not a tragedy because he will see Pierre, he will enjoy his vibrancy of life in a few hours, tomorrow, next year. But when the Mozambican equivalent of Pierre – Mozambicans' loved ones – are dead, maimed, or have disappeared, and when the world that held them lays in ruins, people suffer a profound loss that will not be ameliorated in a few hours, tomorrow, next year, or when the war "goes away" and "people return home." The vibrancy of these lives lost to the war will not be renewed at a future encounter. In these conditions, when the Pierres of the world, and the world itself, are no longer there, people must create, and to do so, they must first imagine what it is they are going to create.

How does this translate into the realities of Mozambicans' lives? Selves and worlds are not created in flashes of insight or in the abstracted words of theory, they are forged and sustained in ongoing practice. In the following pages I give three examples of creativity common in wartime: (1) the creation of viable worlds, (2) the creation of viable selves, and (3) the creation of new orders of significance capable of challenging the hegemony of terror warfare. Because health and survival are linked phenomena, many frameworks of creativity and resistance in Mozambique and other parts of the world are coded in medicinal and healing systems. The three examples I give are therefore concerned with healing traditions. They should be read together as a larger example of the interlocking worldviews that are replicated in Mozambican traditions and daily actions. Taken as a whole they provide Mozambican citizens with the resources to withstand a very brutal war and ultimately transform it into peace. The nurse in the first example healed with conventional medicines, but she also drew on the values of nonviolence and the traditions that heal aggression that are described in the third example to sustain her fight against inhumanity. It is important to note that in addition to these examples, other people in many walks of life were engaged in similar activities, drawing upon the same values described here: teachers instituted trauma classes in primary schools for war-afflicted children, traders carried goods to stricken communities for little or no economic gain, and communities set up services for finding people who had been kidnapped by troops and for reuniting children with their families. Each of the following examples was chosen not because it is unusual, but precisely because it represented a norm of survival visible in virtually all the communities I visited during the war.

Three examples of creativity

The nurse

When military forces besieged a town, in addition to sacking buildings and destroying infrastructure they often persecuted and killed health care workers, teachers, administrators, and other service people. South African Defense Force communiqués to Renamo uncovered in 1987 stressed the destruction of the infrastructure and personnel. When health care facilities were ransacked, supplies and medicines were taken back to the soldiers' bases. Thus, when troops approached a town many service personnel fled before the soldiers arrived. Those that stayed behind did so at considerable risk. One such person sticks in my mind. She was a health care practitioner in an area under siege. The towns in the area had been heavily targeted, and most of the resources and infrastructure had been destroyed. During the first severe attack on her town, she ran to the clinic and grabbed as many supplies and medicines as she could run with, and then, with the other survivors, fled to the bush to hide until the soldiers left. The soldiers had her name and looked for her. Although she was warned by townspeople to flee the area, she decided to stay. As the area remained in the path of the frontlines, and troops passed by continually, she lived something of a nomadic existence, and did not stay in her family home fearing that the soldiers could easily find her there. She buried the medicines and supplies outside of town, and held "clinic hours" there. As in any dangerous situation, well-established communication networks transmitted survival information such as where health care and medicines could be obtained. The townspeople kept her secret from the troops and brought her patients ranging from children with physical illnesses to victims of gunshot wounds. She changed the location where she buried medicines and held clinics every so often to make it more difficult for troops to locate her. There was nothing forcing this woman to stay and treat patients. The town was cut off from outside help, and the Ministry of Health could neither pay her nor provide support. In fact, in those embattled times, they would not have known whether she was in the town or had fled to a refugee camp.

Through her actions, she provided much more than medicines and health care. It is difficult to conceptualize a society bereft of all institutions that ground social life. Without houses and crops, and without schools, clinics, and markets, life simply does not progress in a known way. Terror warfare is predicated on the assumption that if all the supports that make people's lives meaningful are taken from them, they will be incapacitated by the ensuing disorder such that whether as hapless victims or Hobbesian brutes, they will be shorn of political agency.

But terror warfare was defeated by the thousands of people like this health care practitioner. By the sheer act of staying rather than fleeing, Mozambicans like this woman defied danger, and their defiance amounted to an act of control. By the very practice of setting up "clinics" order was re-established in a disordered world. Compassion and creative peace building were supported over fear and warfare. Political will and personal identity were asserted in creative resistance, and they were reaffirmed in the telling of each story of these people's courage and services. Hiding medicines successfully was a taunt in the face of the firepower and intelligence networks of the military. Success was a political victory. Society was reforged with a humane component.

Healing the war

African medicine provided one of the most important resources during the war, elevating healing to a creative process. It was here that the re-creation of a healthy self and a viable social universe were most clearly interwoven. My field-notes show that the majority of conversations I had with Mozambicans during the war in one way or another reflected their preoccupation with both healing the wounds of war – physical, emotional, and social – and defusing the cultures of violence that the war had wrought. Every community I visited, from refugee camp to besieged village, had one or more Curandeiros or Curandeiras, African doctors, who specialized in "treating the war." They stood as reminders that under the most extreme circumstances, the majority of people work to re-create a viable society, not to demolish it. The following quote from a woman illustrates a typical response:

> When people come back to our community after having been kidnapped and spending time with the Bandidos [Renamo], or arrive here after their community has been destroyed by the war, there are a lot of things they need. They require food and clothing, they need a place to live, they need medical attention. But one of the most important things they need is calm – to have the violence taken out of them. We ask that everyone who arrives here be taken to a Curandeiro for treatment. The importance of the Curandeiros lies not only in their ability to treat the diseases and physical ravages of war, but in their ability to take the violence out of a person and to reintegrate them back into a healthy lifestyle. You see, people who have been exposed to the war, well, some of this violence can affect them, stick with them, like a rash on the soul. They carry this violence with them back to their communities and their homes and their lives, and they begin to act in ways they have never acted before – they become more confused, more violent, more dangerous, and so too does the whole community. We need to protect against this. The Curandeiros take the war out of them, they uneducate their war education. They remind them how to be a part of their family, to work their machamba, to get along, to be a part of the community. They cure the violence that others have taught.

Of course, creativity does not focus solely on the ultimate good of a society. People create dangerous systems of oppression and exploitation as well. Thus battle zones evince a constant tension between those who profit from violence and its dislocations, and those who work to refashion a stable peaceful existence. Each trader, teacher, healer, or civilian concerned with establishing some semblance of social order dealt with the harsh truth that they coexisted among people who exploited networks of violence for self-gain. Arms merchants, merchants, mercenaries, blackmarketeers, modern-day slavers, thieves, and murderers also set up, or placed their mark on, self-generated social institutions.

What is of particular interest is that *most* people did *not* create abusive systems of self-gain and power. Returning to the example of African medicine, every healer I spoke with, and this numbered in the hundreds, developed methods to help people survive the war in a humane fashion, and to institute peace-building processes in doing so. In all my conversations with Mozambicans during my stay in the country, I found only one person who did not consult with a Curandeiro when her problems became pressing. Curandeiros helped people reconstitute their worlds in the most profound ways. Their success was due in part to the fact that African medicine combines individual and collective resources: it is flexible, fluid, and enduring.

I participated in one ceremony that illustrates this process. It was conducted for a woman who had returned after having been kidnapped by soldiers and held at their base for months. She was physically sick and emotionally traumatized. The ceremony actually began days before the public gathering. Community members stopped by her place of residence to bring food, medicines, words of encouragement, and friendship. They helped the woman piece together a bit of decent clothing to wear, and collected bathwater for her. They sat patiently and told her stories of other atrocities: a constant reminder to her that she was not alone or somehow responsible for her plight. On the day of the ceremony, food was prepared, musicians were called in, and a dirt compound shaded by pleasant trees and plants was swept and decorated with lanterns and cloth. The ceremony itself lasted throughout the night, a mosaic of support and healing practices. A high point was the ritual bath the woman received at dusk. Numerous women picked up the patient, and carefully gave her a complete bath, which was said to cleanse her soul as well as her body. The bathing was accompanied with songs and stories about healing, dealing with trauma, reclaiming a new life, and being welcomed back into the community. The patient was then dressed in her new clothing and fed a nutritious meal. Shortly thereafter, the musicians began a new rhythm of music, and all the women gathered about the patient to carry her inside the hut. There they placed her on the floor and gathered around, supporting her emotionally as well as physically. The women tended to her wounds; they stroked her much like one would stroke a frightened child, and they quietly murmured encouragements and reassurances. After a while, the women began to rock the patient, and lifted her up among them. They held her up with their arms talking of rebirth in a healthy place among people who cared for her, far from the traumas of war and the past. They carried her outside where the community welcomed her as part of it. Everyone began to play music, the audience accompanying the musicians. After a while each member of the audience got up in front of the musicians and danced for the patient in a reaffirmation of life. Slowly the formal structure of the ceremony gave way to the more natural patterns of community interaction, and the patient was drawn into these interactions. Throughout the ceremony, the woman was continually reassured by supportive stories that highlighted two core themes: her need to blame the war, not her own actions for her plight; and her responsibility not to inflict on others the violence to which she had been subjected. Through this ritual, in story, song, and interaction, respected traditions and nonviolent values were made vital. With this, community was rebuilt for, and with, the patient.

I found it interesting that these healing resources were not restricted to the civilian victims of war. Demobilized soldiers were also carefully reintegrated into communities with similar ceremonies and assistance. As people explained, "We have to take the war out of these soldiers." While community members often had suffered at the hands of soldiers, maybe even from the very soldiers in their midst, they explained that to harbor revenge and anger would simply fan the flames of war and violence. If they were truly to defeat their opponents, they had to defeat the war, and that meant turning soldiers from warring to peaceful pursuits. If they were to banish former soldiers from their communities – from the possibility of home, family, and a civil livelihood – the soldiers would continue to use violence to sustain themselves. One of the most fascinating acts of civil resistance I saw in Mozambique involved civilians who kidnapped soldiers and took them back to their villages to put them through ceremonies to remove them from the war (and to remove the war from them) and to reintegrate them into civilian life. People told me they were often successful. Many "kidnapped" soldiers gave up the war and remained with the community, or returned to their own homes and families.

Unmaking violence

Healing as conceptualized in Mozambican-African medicine views social and political violence as a pathology that needs to be cured like any other illness or misfortune. Mozambicans are concerned not only with treating the wounds of violence, but with *treating violence itself* by defusing the cultures of violence that the war created. Mozambicans' commitment to "unmaking" violence stands in direct contrast to popular occidental views of violence. In the West, violence is subtly but powerfully presented as "thing-like." This is evident in the linguistic habits surrounding violence: violence is avoided; violence is controlled; violence is surmounted; violence is turned inward or outward in anger; violence is released in cathartic mock-aggression; violence is held in check. As a fixed phenomenon, violence becomes a manifest *thing*: set, enduring, concrete. In this worldview, violence *exists*; it has a specific *given* nature.[10]

Most of the Mozambicans with whom I spoke, and especially those in civil society, hold a much different conceptualization of violence. In their view, violence is a fluid cultural construct. It is crafted into action by those who seek to control others. It is *made*. Those exposed to violence learn violence, and are thus capable of perpetuating it. People who have been brutalized by the military often return home more abusive themselves, more likely to employ violence to solve their own domestic and interpersonal dilemmas.

But the people in Mozambique stressed that if violence is *made*, it can be *unmade* as well. The great majority of Curandeiros and Curandeiras with whom I spoke throughout Mozambique had developed sophisticated techniques to heal traumatized war victims in a way that reduced violence *in general*. The following quote from a Curandeiro reflects a widely held set of medicinal beliefs:

We healers, we have had to set up new ways of treating people with this war. This war, it teaches people violence. A lot of soldiers come to me. Many of these boys never wanted to fight, they did not know what it meant to fight. Many were hauled into the military, taken far from their homes, and made to fight. It messes them up. You see, if you kill someone, their soul stays with you. The souls of the murdered follow these soldiers back to their homes and their families, back to their communities to cause problems. The soldier's life, his family, his community, begin to disintegrate from the strain of this. But it goes further than this. These soldiers have learned the way of war. It was not something they knew before. They have learned to use violence. Their own souls have been corrupted by what they have seen and done. They return home, but they carry the violence with them, they act it out in their daily lives, and this harms their families and communities. We have to take this violence out of these people, we have to teach them how to live nonviolent lives like they did before. The problem would be serious enough if it were only the soldiers, but it is not. When a woman is kidnapped, raped, and forced to work for soldiers, when a child is exposed to violence in an attack, when people are subjected to assaults and terrible injuries, this violence sticks to them. It is like the soldier carrying the souls of those he has killed back into his normal life, but here, the soul carries the violence. You can see this even with the young children here who have seen or been subjected to violence: they begin to act more violently. They lose respect, they begin to hit, they lose their bearings – this violence tears at the order of the community. We can treat this, we have to. We literally take the violence out of the people, we teach them how to relearn healthy ways of thinking and acting. It is like with people who have been sent to prison. They go in maybe having stolen something, but they learn violence there, they learn it because they are subjected to violence. We treat this too, in war or in peace. Violence is a dangerous illness. And the thing is, people want to learn. This violence, it tears them up inside, it destroys the world they care about. They want to return to a normal life like they had before. Most work hard with us to put this violence behind them. The leaders of the wars, those people who profit from the wars, they teach this violence to get what they want, without regard to the effect on people and communities. It is our job to thwart this violence, to take it out of the people and the communities. We are getting good at this, we have had a lot of practice.

In fact, "unmaking" violence is not only a citizen's option, but his or her social obligation. One of the first responses Mozambicans instituted (average civilians as well as trained healers) in the midst of abusive injustice was to teach those affected by the war how to navigate life's responsibilities without perpetuating destructive patterns of interaction. This was not instituted by formal or governmental agencies, but by average civilians at the frontlines. The examples were legion. In addition to the health care specialists described above, primary school teachers began classes in relieving traumatization, knowing that children exposed to violence are prone to reproduce it. Community-generated committees evolved in virtually all areas where internally displaced persons, refugees, and returning kidnapees circulated in order to assist them in readapting to a peaceful existence.

Afetados (the war affected) were reintroduced into the rhythms of life and stable society. In the same way that Duirno's sister-in-law lost the ability to speak her native language following the trauma of her kidnapping and forced labor at the military base, other *afetados* lost equally important personal or social skills; they became aggressive, withdrawn, or antisocial; or they forgot core aspects of life such as how to farm, work, or take care of their families. Throughout Mozambique, "healing the wounds of war" included reintegrating *afetados* back into normal – as normal as the ongoing war permitted – community life. The traumatized and war-affected were reintroduced incrementally into peaceful and productive lifestyles. The first step focused on reteaching a person how to create a farm. (This was a core survival strategy as well. With the collapse of most trade routes, family farms often provided the only food available.) Those assisting the traumatized would often walk with them to the new plots, help them fashion tools, and remind them how to find and plant seeds. Through all this, community members gave the war-affected solace. They told traditional stories, redirected anger and vengeance into community building and positive political action, and reminded scarred and battered limbs how to work. Further steps focused on introducing people to the larger cycles of life that animated self and world. For example, in agricultural work people were not only linked with the cycles of planting and harvesting, they were relinked with their ancestors and the traditions that keep society sound. These creative acts took place not only at the individual level of crafting a person, but also at the larger level of people crafting society. Meaning is given form. It is embodied in the minutiae of daily living.

It is important to recognize that, at the most basic ontological level, creativity in no way depends on violence. Employing the metaphor of the phoenix rising from the ashes to account for creativity in warfare serves to justify destructive violence, something that those who use terror warfare depend on. Although creativity attends to violence, it is not promoted by violence in any cause–effect relationship. For many Mozambicans, creativity provided a means of resisting violence. If we return to the people introduced in the section on terror warfare, we can see that while terror warfare takes a profound toll on a society, it does not crush a people's political will and resistance. In remaining to help her country, the woman quoted at the beginning of the chapter defeated the paralysis that terror hopes to instill. By juxtaposing the broken life of war with remembrances of life "as it should be lived" – by refusing to accept the crippling control of political violence – the man lamenting the cost of war in human life kept alive the ideas and ideals that guided the reforging of a viable society. By building little huts and living on farming plots in war-afflicted areas, Mozambican civilians, no matter how battle-scarred, revivified war-barren landscapes. And, by rebuilding and replanting in the face of repeated attacks, they defied the war. They defied the assault on the present to construct their own future. When Duirno's sister-in-law forgot her native language during the traumas of captivity, she was forging a self that could withstand the war and the violence done to her. When people in the community sat and talked with her, helping her to reconstruct her language day by day, when they accompanied her to the fields and helped her rediscover the rhythms of planting and producing, and when they reminded her how to fight against violence rather than reproduce it through destructive politics or ideals of revenge, these people in the community were reforging new worlds and vital identities. When the little girl refused comfort because her brother was still suffering at the hands of enemy soldiers, she refused to let the horrific realities of war and those she loved be ignored. By illuminating them, she demanded they not only be solved, but respected. It was in such acts, and in the thousands like them that took place throughout Mozambique, that oppressive political violence was resisted and paths towards peace were created.

Postscript

A Peace Accord was signed in 1992, bringing Mozambique's war to an end. The first multiparty elections were held in 1994. Frelimo won, with Renamo holding a close second. I was an election observer, and many of the people I spoke with said that this was a vote for peace more than for a political party. Five years after the end of the war, the peace is still holding. Mozambique is the only country in which I have worked during the last fifteen years of studying political violence that has maintained its peace accord for such a substantial length of time. I give serious credit for this achievement to the cultures of creative peace building instituted during the war.

Notes

1. See Nordstrom 1991, 1992a, 1992b, 1995a, 1995b, 1996a, 1996b, 1997a, and 1997b for comparative work on political violence.
2. For more information on the war in Mozambique see Casimiro *et al.* 1990; Finnegan 1992; Geffray 1990; Gersony 1988; Hanlon 1984, 1991; Isaacman and Isaacman 1983; Jeichande 1990; Magaia 1988, 1989; Ministerio Da Saude/UNICEF 1988; Minter 1989, 1994; Nordstrom 1997; UNICEF 1989, 1990; UNICEF/Ministry of Cooperation 1990; Vines 1991; World Health Organization 1990.
3. To give a few from hundreds of examples: The Madres' role in toppling the dirty war regime in Argentina; the ongoing Tibetan resistance movement; the public outcry that launched the War Crimes Tribunals after the Holocaust of WWII and after the wars in ex-Yugoslavia (the latter including rape as a war crime for the first time, again, due to public outrage); the peaceful rebellion against Marcos in the Philippines; and the decades-long resistance in Central American countries suffering politico-military oppression and human rights violations. From the Khmer Rouge in Cambodia to the apartheid government in South Africa, repressive governments relying on the politics of force and terror have ultimately buckled under the weight of popular public resistance. Many responsible for successfully defeating

oppressive regimes in their home country then travel to other embattled locations to lend support and assistance, thus keeping alive the lesson that oppression can be defeated.

4. The plight of children in war is strongly politically silenced. For example, more children are killed in wars today than soldiers, but very little is known about the specifics of this (Nordstrom 1997c).

5. Scarry continues, "[Together] pain and imagining are the 'framing events' within whose boundaries all other perceptual, somatic, and emotional events occur; thus, between the two extremes can be mapped the whole terrain of the human psyche" (1985:163).

6. Much has been written on the cultural construction of reality: that being human entails more than anything else creating the cultural worlds we live in and endowing them with significance. Yet this research has been conducted for the most part in societies with functioning institutions. In this context, people do not create worlds anew, but fine tune the ones they are born into. Very little empirical data exists to show how people's worlds are newly crafted. How does cultural creativity take that first step into constructing the wholly new? At the epicenters of war, this question is particularly pressing: if people rebuild their lives and worlds as they were, they will simply be open to re-attack. Survival, then, involves crafting a new universe of meaning and action.

7. See Nordstrom 1995a for a discussion of Elaine Scarry's and Sartre's analysis of imagination.

8. Castoriadis (1975, 1994) has developed this aspect of the creative potential of the imagination in positing it as a core force in the forging of social institutions and culture. He casts imagination as a radical act, literally, as "socially instituting."

9. This mediating function is crucial – it makes it possible for all the universes of experience and meaning to "symbolize with each other" (Corbin 1972:9).

10. There is a dangerous aspect to this view of violence: if violence is a given, then there is nothing people can do other than to endure it, or to protect against it.

Bibliography

Casimiro, Isabel, Ana Loforte, and Ana Pessoa 1990 *A Mulher em Moçambique*. Maputo, Mozambique: Centre Estudos Africanes/NORAD.

Castoriadis, Cornelius 1975 *The Imaginary Institution of Society*. Cambridge: Cambridge University Press.

— 1994 "Radical Imagination and the Social Instituting Imaginary." In *Rethinking Imagination*. G. Robinson and J. Rundell, eds., pp. 136–54. New York: Routledge.

Corbin, Henry 1969 *Creative Imagination in the Sufism of Ibn Arabi*. Princeton, NJ: Princeton University Press.

— 1972 "Mundus Imaginalis, or the Imaginary and the Imaginal." *Spring: An Annual of Archetypal Psychology and Jungian Thought*, pp. 1–19.

Dis, Adriaan van 1991 *In Afrika*. Amsterdam: Meulenhoff.

Finnegan, William 1992 *A Complicated War: The Harrowing of Mozambique*. Berkeley: University of California Press.

Frelick, Bill 1989 "Renamo: The Khmer Rouge of Africa; Mozambique, Its Killing Fields." Testimony before the House Subcommittee on Foreign Operations. Washington DC, February 8.

Geffray, Christian 1990 *La Cause des Armes au Mozambique: Antropologie d'une Guerre Civile*. Paris: Editions Karthala.

Gersony, Robert 1988 "Summary of Mozambican Refugee Accounts of Principally Conflict-Related Experience in Mozambique." Report submitted to Ambassador Jonathon Moore, director, Bureau for Refugees Program, and Dr. Chester Crocker, assistant secretary of African Affairs. Washington, DC.

Hanlon, Joseph 1984 *Mozambique: The Revolution under Fire*. London: Zed Books.

— 1991 *Mozambique: Who Calls the Shots?* Bloomington: Indiana University Press.

Herman, Judith 1992 *Trauma and Recovery*. New York: Basic Books.

Issacman, Allen, and Barbara Issacman 1983 *Mozambique: From Colonialism to Revolution 1900–1982*. Hampshire, England: Gower.

Jeichande, Ivette Illas 1990 *Mulheres Deslocadas em Maputo, Zambezia e Inhambane (Mulher em Situacao Dificil)*. Maputo, Mozambique: OMM–UNICEF.

Magaia, Lina 1988 *Dumba Nengue: Run for Your Life. Peasant Tales of Tragedy in Mozambique*. Trenton, NJ: Africa World Press.

— 1989 *Duplo Massacre em Mocambique. Historias Tragicas do Banditismo – II*. Maputo, Mozambique: Colecçao Depoimentos – 5.

Ministerio Da Saude/UNICEF 1988 *Analise da Situacao da Saude*. Maputo, Mozambique, September.

Minter, William 1989 "The Mozambique National Resistance (Renamo) as Described by Ex-Participants." Research report submitted to Ford Foundation and Swedish International Development Agency. African-European Institute, Amsterdam, March.

— 1994 *Apartheid's Contras*. London: Zed Books.

Nordstrom, Carolyn 1991 "Women and War: Observations from the Field." *Minerva: Quarterly Report on Women and the Military* 9(1):1–15.

— 1992a "The Backyard Front." In *The Paths to Terror: Domination, Resistance and Collective Violence*. C. Nordstrom and J. Martin, eds., pp. 260–74. Berkeley: University of California Press.

— 1992b "The Dirty War: Culture of Violence in Mozambique and Sri Lanka." In *Internal Conflicts and Governance*. K. Rupesinghe, ed., pp. 27–43, New York: St. Martin's Press.

— 1995a "Creativity and Chaos: War on the Frontlines." In *Fieldwork under Fire: Contemporary Studies in Violence and Survival*. C. Nordstrom and A. Robben, eds., pp. 124–53. Berkeley: University of California Press.

— 1995b "Contested Identities/Essentially Contested Powers." In *Conflict Transformation*. K. Rupesinghe, ed., pp. 93–115. London: Macmillan, now Palgrave.

— 1996a "Rape: Politics and Theory in War and Peace." *Australian Feminist Studies* 11(23): 147–62.

— 1996b "Girls behind the (Front) Lines." *Peace Review* 8(3):403–9.

— 1997a "The Eye of the Storm: From War to Peace." In *Cultural Variations in Conflict Resolution: Alternatives to Violence*. D. Fry and K. Bjorkqvist, eds., pp. 91–103. Mahwah, NJ: Lawrence Erlbaum.

— 1997b *A Different Kind of War Story*. Philadelphia: University of Pennsylvania Press.

— 1997c *Girls and Warzones: Troubling Questions*. Uppsala, Sweden: Life and Peace Institute.

Sartre, Jean-Paul 1948 *The Psychology of Imagination*. New York: Philosophical Library.

Scarry, Elaine 1985 *The Body in Pain: The Making and Unmaking of the World*. Oxford: Oxford University Press.

Suárez-Orozco, Marcelo 1987 "The Treatment of Children in the 'Dirty War': Ideology, State Terrorism, and the Abuse of Children in Argentina." In *Child Survival*. Nancy Scheper-Hughes, ed., pp. 227–46. Boston: D. Reidel Publishing.

UNICEF 1989 *Children on the Frontline*. 1989 Update, Geneva: UNICEF.

— 1990 *Annual Report, Mozambique*.

UNICEF/Ministry of Cooperation 1990 *The Situation of Women and Children in Mozambique*. Maputo.

Vines, Alex 1991 *Renamo: Terrorism in Mozambique*. Bloomington: Indiana University Press.

World Health Organization 1990 *WHO/Mozambique Cooperation*. Organizaçao Mundial Da Saude Representaçao em Mocambique. Maputo, March.

Part IV
Conclusion

15
Conclusion: Political Violence and the Contemporary World

The topic of political violence covers an enormous array of overt, covert, subtle, intensive, low-intensity, unitary, and ongoing violent actions. Assassinations, terrorist attacks, mass rape, genocide, and war are examples of political violence; but for many so are unjust incarceration, human rights abuses, violent government rhetoric, and structural inequalities supported by state policies. Stretched far enough, the phrase "political violence" can incorporate such diverse things as criminal activity (by those who argue that discriminatory government policies make crime a promising alternative for the politically disenfranchised), domestic assault (by those who argue that politics are patriarchal and government policies against sexism are not strong enough), and poverty (by those who argue that the political structure supports social stratification and government policies support the elite). Although this book took a narrower view of political violence, analysts are increasingly interested in linking these forms of violence to political structures and the forces of globalization. This chapter reviews current research on political violence to highlight some of these connections.

Broadly, research on political violence groups around three primary themes. The first, represented in the volume's first section, is the involvement of the state itself in perpetrating violence through terrorism, genocide, torture, and human rights abuses as well as more subtle forms of state violence. A second prominent theme examines the relationship between political economy and violence. One concern in this literature is the impact of the Cold War and its conclusion on the stability of states and a global order based on states. A particularly important focus is the link between capitalism and localized political violence, especially because capitalism has become "the only relevant economic system" (Friedman 1999) since the fall of the Berlin wall. A third area of study takes the concept of culture as central, examining the role that cultural ideologies and practices play in fostering or sustaining political violence. Identifying these broad approaches serves a heuristic purpose; most studies of political violence intertwine these themes to investigate, for example, the links between state violence and capitalist expansion, or cultural ideologies and state-backed genocide. The following sections address each theme in turn, while showing how lines of inquiry move back and forth.

States and violence

The first section of the book introduced the question of how states define and claim legitimacy in the domestic and international arenas. Although claims about legitimate violence have always been murky at best, contemporary transformations in the global order pose profound challenges to the state monopoly on legitimate violence. States' moral claims to legitimacy and state control over flows of people, money, technology, and information have been eroded by revisionist postcolonial analyses of imperialism and colonialism, twentieth-century state-run genocides and human rights abuses in the name of state order, the threats posed by nuclear weapons and so-called "rogue" states, the criminalization of many post-Cold War states, the decline of conventional war and the rise of complex low-intensity conflicts, the influence of diasporic populations on politics in their natal states, and advances in information technology that give local voices an international audience. While citizens around the world are perhaps more willing to reject state claims to moral and legal legitimacy than are state governments, a global erosion of state power is feared or lauded in all sectors. Certainly, groups everywhere in the world have greatly expanded domestic and international fora for challenging violent state actions that state leaders claim are legitimate.

Nevertheless, Hobbes' argument that government is the only alternative to anarchic violence (the famous "warre of every man against every man" (Hobbes 1958:90)) continues to dominate the international position that states are institutions that operate to minimize rather than foster violence. Not surprisingly, Hobbesian understandings of the need for government to control the violent impulses of human nature have great currency among politically influential groups such as military analysts, political scientists, and politicians, whose careers and ideologies are centered on powerful states and state legitimacy. In the public sector, contemporary "doomsday" journalists who predict a global increase in anarchy, violence, and crime as a result of weakened state authority also reinforce Hobbesian visions of global (dis)order (see Kaplan 1994). To be sure, those who are inclined toward a Hobbesian view that violence results from a lack of government recognize that states make war as well as stability and peace. But the assumption remains that the global structure of states – predicated on international governmental agreements about violence, rules for war, and understandings of justice and morality – ensures stability and hinders violence.

Recently, the view that strong states reduce violence has acquired a further clarification in the American media and policy circles: that strong capitalist states reduce violence, and/or that a global capitalist system will reduce state violence. In this view, a global capitalist economic order is becoming the stabilizing force in the global political order of states. The laws of supply and demand, consumer power, free trade, and capitalist profit will govern international interaction, and countries and peoples dependent on trade will be loath to war against their trading partners (see Friedman 1999). For these writers peaceful economic competition will replace violent political competition. The globalization of capital will enhance the prospects for liberal democracy (reflected in the idea of constructive engagement through trade), which many believe will ensure less political violence than alternative political structures.

Proponents of the benefits of state making and an international order of (capitalist) states have a range of detractors. For reasons noted in the opening paragraph of this section, many social scientists promote a less sanguine view of the intimate link between states and violence (as well as capitalism and violence). These studies highlight the violence of state formation and note that the consolidation of state power often depends on violence. Tilly's chapter in this volume is representative of the literature that emphasizes the uses of violence during the eras of European state formation, imperialism and colonialism (see also Giddens 1985, Reyna 1999). Following upon the studies connecting the emergence of capitalism with violent struggles for control of people, territory, and goods during the period of state formation in Europe is another body of work that explains local violence through reference to the global capitalist economy. These studies, often inspired by Marxist theory, demonstrate how states use violence to foster capitalist expansion, how capitalism introduces hierarchies that produce conflict, how labor control and extractive technologies that sustain capitalism rely on violence, and how the global capitalist economy benefits from domestic and international militarization. The eras of European nation-state formation, imperialism, colonialism, and Western-based industrial Fordism produced a world united by a global capitalist system, and an international order of states in control of technologies of industrial warfare. By the Second World War, the European model of the nation-state was intimately linked to industrial militarism, capitalism, and the right of coercion over citizens. Anthropologists have come to realize that "tribal" warfare in many parts of the world during these eras was a response to state-supported capitalist penetration rather than a traditional pattern (Ferguson and Whitehead 1992, Wolf 1982).

Critical to the consolidation of European nation-states over the past several centuries were the riches drawn from imperial and colonial endeavors. While the imperial and colonial experiences were complex and nonuniform, much anti-colonial and post-colonial literature describes the violence inherent to European state-making efforts in the colonies. In addition to the violences of conquest and colonial rule, the extractive economies managed by colonial governments produced structural violences that imposed great hardships on the colonized. The violences of "pacification," missionization, commodity extraction, labor control, and racial domination are well documented, shocking in their descriptions of colonial excess and brutality. Taussig's chapter in this volume describing the "culture of terror" which permeated life in Colombia's rubber-making zone is one example. The historic connection between states, capitalism, and violence makes these studies relevant to contemporary concerns about the possible links between the new globalization of capital, new forms of political authority, and political violence.

Of course, the violence of state making did not end with European state consolidation after the First World War, or with decolonization in the rest of the world. State consolidation in many contexts has depended on violence to establish a preferred, ideal state order of 'acceptable' citizens. In the mid-twentieth century, state-run violence against domestic citizens probably took two to four times more lives than warfare (Fein 1993). Pursing questions about what kinds of states violently kill or torture large numbers of citizens and what justifications state governments offer for such actions have occupied researchers writing about the twentieth-century genocides in Nazi Germany, Armenia, Cambodia, Indonesia, Stalinist Russia, China, Rwanda, and Bosnia, and about state terror in states like Argentina, Chile, Guatemala, and South Africa. In contrast to much of the literature on European and colonial state formation, capitalism does not figure prominently in these analyses, which emphasize instead how violence emerges from authoritarian political structures, state uses of practices and discourses of modernity, and nationalist ideologies that use symbolically charged political rhetoric.

The comparative research on genocides cited in Fein (1993) shows that communist governments have been responsible for most late twentieth-century genocides, although anticommunist states have also utilized mass murder and/or torture (see also Courtois *et al.* 1999). Mass state violence occurs as a response to political crises and/or in relation to revolution (as part of the revolution or as a response to the threat of revolution). Genocidal regimes using massive violence in an attempt to establish legitimacy and authority often employ a sanitizing discourse of domestic hygiene to explain their actions. A new or refor-mulated language of nationalism and patriotism extols the virtues of building a strong state and protecting the "true" nation by purging cancerous, polluting, dangerous or foreign elements (see also Hinton, this volume). These cleansing efforts have been facilitated by scientific advances in technology and the organization of knowledge, as demon-strated in Bauman's analysis in this volume of how modernity made the Holocaust possible. Where capitalism has played a role in state-run mass violence, it has been primarily in the form of overt or complicit capitalist superpower support for murderous anticommunist govern-ments (Fein 1993, see also Uvin 1998). These studies of some of the most extreme episodes of state violence in recent history analyze states as killing machines in an effort to understand why some states develop genocidal ideologies and how these ideologies become normalized and accepted by nontargeted citizens. In addition to the opportunities for state-run terrorist campaigns against undesirable citizens in authoritar-ian political structures, these studies demonstrate the importance of nationalist rhetoric, administrative bureaucracy, and the efficiencies of modernity for mass murder.

Most states, of course, are not genocidal, and many studies of state making/consolidation do not define the state as primarily an institution that dominates its citizens by force or the threat of force. In exploring modes of state control, many researchers draw on Michel Foucault's work to focus on state activities that do not involve direct physical coercion, such as administrative/bureaucratic control, disciplinary control, and ideological control. Although their focus is not overt viol-ence, some of these analysts argue that such state practices may be inherently – if not physically – violent. Foucault's work on insanity, prisons, medicine, and sexuality suggests that the establishment of truth regimes supported by the state create certain categories of people as illegitimate and thus subject to state-sanctioned violence (through imprisonment or physical discipline). Scholars inspired by this line of thinking remark on the bodily violence of disciplinary technologies, including the state's role in disciplining the population for capitalist production. Scholars writing on globalization draw direct links between new system of flexible capitalism and the disciplining of populations marginalized by the system through new categories of criminality and imprisonment (James 1996, 1998, Kelley 1996).

Another type of indirect violence is attributed to states by scholars influenced by Pierre Bourdieu's notion of symbolic violence (1977:192). States (and the international capitalist order of states) produce "structural violences" of poverty, malnutrition, poor health, local violence, and crime resulting from implicit or overt state support of hierarchies based on gender, race, sexuality, language, and class. The violence of categorization and discipline, and the structural violence of poverty and inequality are important areas clearly linked to the study of political violence. These forms of violence are coming under increasing scrutiny in the post-Cold War era of flexible capitalism, which some see as responsible for producing poverty, marginalization, and the structural conditions for violence by the disenfranchised.

A final mode of state violence to be noted here is of growing importance in the post-Cold War "new global disorder" – the involvement of the state in criminal violence. Recent studies of the mafia in Italy and government corruption in Russia and African states draw attention to the relations between politicians, state functionaries, and violent criminal organizations who deal in drugs, arms, stolen goods, extortion, kidnappings, beatings, and assassinations (Bayart *et al.* 1999, Humphries 1999, Reno 1998, Schneider and Schneider 1994). These studies explore how state functionaries become complicit in or supportive of criminal violence and what ordinary citizens are doing to avoid becoming victims or to challenge the involvement of the state in violent criminal activity.

With the globalization of capital and information in the post-Cold War era, scholars are charting the changing contours of state power. While states will remain the central organizing structure of political authority for some time to come, what is less clear is the means by which states will claim legitimacy to control – by laws and by force – their citizens. Another question is the extent to which the globalization of information will offer international challenges to state-backed human rights abuses, and the extent to which globalization will nurture political freedoms for citizens within their states.

The Cold War and the new global (dis?)order

The backdrop of the Cold War provided a frame of reference for many analyses of political violence during that period (1945–89). While scholars note that twentieth-century communist governments have been more murderous than capitalist governments, comparing the violences of communism against the violences of capitalism is no longer of much interest. But the effects of the Cold War remain significant for its legacy of global militarization and nuclearism. Many studies of recent "tribal" or "ethnic" warfare, for example, argue that political violence in places like Mozambique, Angola, and Nicaragua was the local expression of Cold War-nurtured hostilities, fought with weaponry made plentiful by Cold War-inspired militarization. As states collapsed and civil wars spread in the post-Cold War period (in places like Somalia, Sierra Leone, Zaire/Congo, Yugoslavia, and Guatemala), social scientists explained how local governments propped up with superpower support in the absence of popular support became unsustainable. During the Cold War the global buildup of weaponry was intimately tied to local and global political economies, driving the economy in some areas (the industrial centers) and draining it in others (the nonindustrialized client states). In the context of other destabilizing factors, the present proliferation of civil wars and low-intensity conflicts can be linked to these arms buildups (because weapons are so easily accessible, sold alongside tomatoes and potatoes in local markets around the world), but also to superpower nuclearization.

Nuclearism, a product of state-directed technological development wedded to modern industrial capitalism, was another effect of the Cold War political order (Lutz and Nonini 1999). The implications of Cold War patronage, the arms race, nuclearization, and ideologies of militarization on how states manage their populations and how groups challenge state control demonstrate the profound legacy of the Cold War throughout the globe. The military historian Martin van Creveld (1991) argues that fears of nuclear weapons have reduced the likelihood of conventional war, replacing it with bloody, complex, guerrilla-style low-intensity conflicts. Cold War militarization and nuclearization in the post-Cold War world of declining state power and state legitimacy are producing a new kind of war, according to van Creveld and others – anarchic and unpredictable. Arendt's observation that the end of violence is not power, but the destruction of power seems particularly apt where toppled governments have been replaced by warlords, terror, and the rule by Nobody.

Many scholars agree that the economic restructuring of the past several decades (towards globalization and flexible capital) has produced global and local instabilities that characterize a new world order – or disorder. The new globalization of flexible capital has degraded state political and economic control within and across political borders. For some, this new global order is dangerous and violent, fostering such processes as the criminalization of the state, state fragmentation, low-intensity conflict, and the violences of economic dislocations caused by the rapid movement of capital around the globe. In their excellent review article linking forms of political economy and forms of violence, Lutz and Nonini (1999) suggest that the economic restructuring of the global capitalist system has produced a well protected "global urban archipelago of wealth" and a global periphery characterized by "brigandage, mafia-domination, and marauding private ethnic armies" (p. 96). New forms of flexible warfare (designed for low-intensity conflicts, guerrilla activity, and terrorism) match new forms of flexible capitalism. This view contrasts markedly with those who predict that a post-Cold War global turn to capitalism (and perhaps liberal democracy) will reduce political violence.

Two orientations are evident in recent work on the post-Cold War "disorder." One is predictive, warning that future political violence (for territory, power, wealth, autonomy) will be along cultural fault lines, motivated by cultural differences (as opposed to the ideological differences that characterized Cold War hostilities) (Huntington 1996, Kaplan 1994). The most extreme writings predict a terrifyingly violent future world in which waning state power is replaced by control by warlords and criminals. The other orientation is historical, consisting of carefully researched microstudies that trace the unique trajectories of state disintegration in particular areas, placing local history in the global context (Ferguson 2001, Reno 1998, Uvin 1999, Zartman 1995). These studies analyze the confluence of local and global factors that created instability and fragmentation in specific states.

One question of interest to both the predictive and historical writers is the extent to which democracy will become the leading political structure in the world. While the global spread of democratization has been noted (and applauded) in many corners, the processes of democratization are coming under increasing scrutiny (a critical research agenda no doubt facilitated by the fall of the Soviet Union). Social scientists recognize that democracy and political violence in fact may be linked in some contexts, and that the European history of democratiza-tion tied to citizenship, civil rights, and the rule of law may not be the global norm. (Others note that the emergence of democracy and liberal rights in Europe was cotemporaneous with the era of European states as "killing machines" (Reyna 1999:17)). The explosion of political viol-ence associated with democratization in places like Colombia and Brazil demonstrate that political definitions of democracy (which emphasize the electoral process) are unable to account for the violence of democratization (see Caldeira and Holston 1999). Culturally sensi-tive, historically informed ethnographic research is essential to illuminate how political violence may be associated with (rather than constrained by) democratization.

Research on the links between capitalism, the Cold War and its con-clusion, the new world order, and political violence thus raise a number of questions for future studies. Is the new era of flexible capital trans-forming social relations and state structures so as to promote violence? As the political order of the post-Cold War world shifts from a global dichotomy of liberalism and communism, how will new forms of state authority co-ordinate with new forms of capitalism to produce or minimize violence? If state power and the state monopoly on violence continue to decline, what kinds of interests will motivate future warfare, and in what ways will the system of flexible accumulation contribute to violence? To what extent will the vision of universal economic prosper-ity often heralded as a promise of the global capitalist system provide alternatives to violence? Or will war continue to offer more financial rewards for some than peaceful trade? Furthermore, although evidence demonstrates the links between the spread of capitalism and liberal democracy, democratization often occurs violently in non-Western set-tings. Continuing to study the linkages between new forms of capital-ism, new forms of political authority, and new forms of political violence will remain an important research agenda for the future.

Another important sub-theme in the scholarship on Cold War-inspired militarization is gender. Led by political scientist Cynthia Enloe's prolific work on how militarism shapes masculinity and gender roles, numerous social scientists have been exploring the relationship between militarization (militaristic ideologies, military training, milit-ary geographies, and the proliferation of weapons) and gender. Comparative research suggests militarization in a wide variety of social contexts is linked with increasingly circumscribed understandings of masculinity as violent, dominant, and heterosexual, coalescing around a "Rambo" image of the military man (Peteet, this volume, Linke 1997,

Moran 1997). These connections are seen with brutal clarity in the recent work on mass military rape in the context of warfare (Copelon, this volume, Stiglmayer 1994). John Borneman's work has extended this analysis to more fully incorporate an understanding of how territorial sovereignty linked to compulsive male heterosexuality could produce mass rape as a form of ethnic cleansing (1998). These studies suggest future directions in the study of the gendered dimensions of political violence.

The role of culture

While many researchers continue to analyze the origins of violence in political structures, economic systems, or the rhetoric of leaders, others focus more acutely on the textures of violence at the local level. This book has given particular attention to ethnographic approaches that seek to explain local understandings of political violence. Despite the tendency in the media to explain violence as the result of cultural differences (tribalism, ancestral ethnic hatreds, and so on) anthropologists are clear that cultural differences do not create conflict or by themselves produce violence. But people participate in and apprehend violence through cultural lenses. Future studies must identify the point at which the initial reasons for undertaking political violence recede, to be overwhelmed by a cultural poetics of violence. For understanding the trajectories of political violence, the most useful studies will analyze the factors that contribute to a shift from violence as a means to a political end, to a situation where violence becomes the culturally affirmed end in itself.

One obvious goal of studies of political violence is to offer solutions for mediating violence. In terms of resolving conflict, in what ways can a globalized world offer opportunities for a multicultural mediation of local or regional conflicts? Furthermore, what does a globalized world mean for universal standards of human rights and a universal agreement about what constitutes legitimate state-backed violence? Now that the recently dominant paradigm of liberalism versus communism has been retired, will more attention be devoted to understanding and undermining the structural violences of capitalism – violences that often find politically violent expression? How can new political/economic models emerge that offer alternatives to these forms of political violence? These questions are being asked by scholars across disciplines, political orientations, and countries, and form the core set of research agendas on political violence in the contemporary era.

Bibliography

Bayart, Jean-François, Stephen Ellis and Béatrice Hibou. *The Criminalization of the State in Africa* (Oxford: James Currey and Bloomington, Indiana: Indiana University Press, 1999.)

Borneman, John. *Subversions of International Order: Studies in the Political Anthropology of Culture.* (Albany: SUNY Press, 1998.)

Bourdieu, Pierre. *Outline of a Theory of Practice.* (Cambridge: Cambridge University Press, 1977.)

Caldeira, Teresa and James Holston. "Democracy and Violence in Brazil." *Comparative Studies in Society and History* 41(4) (1999):691–729.

Courtois, Stéphane, Nicolas Werth, Jean-Louis Panné, Andrzej Paczkowski, Karel Bartosek, Jean-Louis Margolin. *The Black Book of Communism: Crimes, Terror, Repression.* (Cambridge: Harvard University Press, 1999.)

Fein, Helen. "Revolutionary and Antirevolutionary Genocides: A Comparison of State Murders in Democratic Kampuchea, 1975–1979, and in Indonesia, 1965–1966." *Comparative Studies in Society and History* 35(4) (1993):796–823.

Ferguson, Brian, ed. *The State Under Siege: Political Disintegration in the Post Cold War Era.* (Amsterdam: Gordon and Breach, in press.)

Ferguson, Brian, and Neil Whitehead, eds. *War in the Tribal Zone: Expanding States and Indigenous Warfare.* (Santa Fe, New Mexico: School of American Research Press, 1992.)

Friedman, Thomas. *The Lexus and the Olive Tree.* (New York: Farrar, Straus, Giroux, 1999.)

Giddens, Anthony. *The Nation-State and Violence: Volume Two of a Contemporary Critique of Historical Materialism.* (Berkeley: University of California Press, 1985.)

Hobbes, Thomas. *Leviathon.* (New York: Liberal Arts Press, 1958.)

Humphries, Caroline. "Russian Protection Rackets and the Appropriation of Law and Order." In *States and Illegal Practices,* edited by Josiah McC. Heyman. (Oxford: Berg. 1999:199–232.)

Huntington, Samuel. *The Clash of Civilizations and the Remaking of World Order.* (New York: Simon and Schuster, 1996.)

James, Joy, ed. *The Angela Y. Davis Reader.* (Malden, MA: Blackwell, 1998.)

James, Joy. *Resisting State Violence: Radicalism, Gender, and Race in U.S. Culture.* (Minneapolis: University of Minnesota Press, 1996.)

Kaplan, Robert. "The Coming Anarchy." *The Atlantic Monthly* 273 (1994):44–75.

Kelley, Robin D. G. *Yo Mama's DysFUNKtional!: Fighting the Culture Wars in Urban America.* (Boston: Beacon Press, 1997.)

Linke, Uli. "Gendered Differences, Violent Imagination: Blood, Race, Nation." *American Anthropologist* 99(3) (1997):559–73.

Lutz, Catherine and Donald Nonini. "The Economies of Violence and the Violence of Economies." In *Anthropological Theory Today,* edited by Henrietta Moore. (Cambridge: Polity Press and Blackwell, 1999:73–113.)

Moran, Mary. "Warriors or Soldiers? Masculinity and Ritual Transvestism in the Liberian Civil War." In *Situated Lives: Gender and Culture in Everyday Life,* edited by L. Lamphere, H. Ragoné, and P. Zavella. (New York: Routledge, 1997:440–50.)

Reno, William. *Warlord Politics and African States.* (Boulder: Lynne Reinner, 1998.)

Reyna, S. P. "Introduction: Deadly Developments and Phantasmagoric Representations." In *Deadly Developments: Capitalism, States, and War*, edited by S. P. Reyna and R. E. Downs. (Amsterdam: Gordon and Breach, 1999:1–21.)

Schneider, Jane and Peter Schneider. "Mafia, Antimafia, and the Question of Sicilian Culture." *Politics and Society* 22(2) (1994):237–58.

Stiglmayer, Alexandra. *Mass Rape: The War Against Women in Bosnia-Herzegovina.* (Lincoln: University of Nebraska Press, 1994.)

Uvin, Peter. *Aiding Violence.* (London: Kumerian Press, 1998.)

van Creveld, Martin. *The Transformation of War.* (New York: The Free Press, 1991.)

Wolf, Eric. *Europe and the People Without History.* (Berkeley: University of California Press, 1982.)

Zartman, I. William. *Collapsed States: The Disintegration and Restoration of Legitimate Authority* (Boulder: Lynne Reinner, 1995.)

Index

Abda, Ahmed Shah, 121
Abu-Lughod, L., 249
Adi Granth, 124
administration, 15–16
    control of material means of, 16–18
afetados (war affected), 291–3
Africa, corruption, 304
African medicine, 285–9
    ceremonies, 288–9
    and returning soldiers, 289
    treating violence, 289–91
aggressiveness, innate, 26
Akal Takht, 120, 121, 122
Alberti, L.B., 73
Algeria, 103, 258
Ames, E., 42
Amnesty International, 175, 253
amrit, 124, 125, 127, 132
anarchism, 101, 105, 106, 107, 111
anger, controlling, 137–8
Ângkar (Khmer Rouge Party
    Organization), 136, 152, 154, 158
Angola, 305
antisemitism, 76
apartheid, 275
aql, 250, 256, 260
Arab-Israeli War, (1967) 110
Arana, Julio César, 216, 219, 222, 225,
    236
Ardant, G., 50
Arendt, H., 119
Argentina, 103, 137, 211
aristocracy, 17, 26
Arjun, Guru, 123–4
Armagh prison, 173, 181, 182–4,
    185–6, 187
armies, cost and organization, 50
artillery, improvement of, 45
Asturias, Miguel Angel, 213
auca, 227–9, 234

Bahadur, Guru Teg, 127
Bangaladesh, 193

Barbados, men from, 217–18, 219
Barkun, M., 111
Basque separatists, 103, 106
Battambang, 148–9, 152
Bean, R., 45
beatings of Palestinians
    background, to 250–4
    intifada and pre-intifada, 251–2, 254
    opposed interpretations of, 247–8,
        255, 260, 261–2
    physical marks, of 254–5
    as rites of passage, 244–5, 255–9,
        260, 266, 267
    role of women, 261, 262, 264–6
Bedouin, 249
Begin, Menachem, 107, 112
Belfast Women's Collective, 187
Ben-Ari, Eyal, 253
Bengal, rape, 193, 201
Benjamin, W., 213
Berbers, Algeria, 249
Bergson, H., 22
Bhindranwale, Sant Jarnail Singh,
    120, 122–3, 125
Bidar massacre, 129
biological weapons, 20–1
biomedical scientists, and Nazi policy
    90
black magic, 143, 147
body
    disciplines of, 170–1
    and inscription of power, 245,
        246–8
    intersubjective dynamic, 170–1
body searches, 172, 176
Bolshevik Revolution, 103
Bonanate, L., 105
Borneman, J., 308
Bosnia, 136, 160
    and rape, 193, 194–5, 198, 200–2,
        203, 205
    see also Yugoslavia
Bourdieu, Pierre, 249, 260, 261, 304

Bowyer Bell, J., 111
Brar, Lt Gen K.S., 120
Braudel, F., 40, 46
Brazil, 103, 307
Brenneis, D., 244
Breton separatists, 104, 106
Britain
  national debt, 48
  and recognition of political
      prisoners, 172, 178–9
  and responsibility for Dirty Protest,
      179–80
  taxation, 48–9
Buddhism, 129, 136, 145, 159
bureaucracy, 26, 50, 79–83
  and dehumanisation of objects,
      83–5
  and genocide, 84–5, 87, 94
  and Holocaust, 83, 85–7
  and moral conscience, 84
Burma, 194
Burton, F., 177

Cabo Delgado, 277
Cambodia, 136–63
  alternatives to revenge, 159–60
  and disproportionate revenge
      (*karsâng-soek*), 140–8
  judicial system, 160
  national anthem, 153
  peasant revolt, 148–9
  political education, 150–1
  US carpet bombings, 149, 150,
      151
  Vietnamese invasion, 159
  Vietnamese soldiers in, 144–5, 146
  see also Democratic Kampuchea
      (DK)
Cambodian Genocide Program, 160
Camus, A., 112, 129
cannibalism, 222, 225, 230–2, 236
capital accumulation
  and military expansion, 46–7
  and war making, 38–9, 44
capitalism, 36, 44, 301–3, 304, 307,
      308
Caquetá, 229
Caraparaná, 215, 222, 235
Cardinal, M., 185

Carnot, Marie François Sadi, 111
Casement, Roger, 215–16, 217–22,
      225, 230, 231, 235–6
Catholics, Northern Ireland, 180–1
Caton, S., 249
Chandler, D.P., 153
chardhi kala (rising spirits), 126
charismatic domination, 14, 15
Charles I, Britain, 52
Charles V, Spain, 47
children
  deaths of, 253
  and terror warfare, 280–1, 291
China, 41, 103
Churches, and Holocaust, 90–1
circumcision, 250
civil wars, proliferation of, 305
civilized society
  definition of, 77–8, 87
  and safeguards against violence, 88,
      91
  and savagery, 236
civilizing process, 75, 77, 78–9
civitas, 27
class struggle, 22, 150–1, 154, 160
Clausewitz, C. von, 20, 26, 118
Colbert, Jean-Baptiste, 47
Cold War, legacy of, 305–8
Collins, Michael, 103, 105, 108
Colombia, 307
  see also Putumayo, Colombia
Colombian rubber traders, 219, 230
colonialism
  and global capitalist system, 302
  and Ireland, 182
  and mythology of savagery, 223,
      224, 230, 234–7
  role of terror, 212
Combat Organization of the Socialist-
      Revolutionary party, 101, 102,
      106
Combs-Schilling, E., 246, 247
comfort stations, 201
communism, 136
  and genocide, 303
  indoctrination, 150–1, 152
  and violence, 305
concentration camps, 23
Connor, W.R., 118

Coogan, T.P., 182–3
Corbin, J.R., 119, 283–4
Cornell, D., 187
Corsican separatists, 106
creative imaginary (*mundus imaginalis*), 283–4
creativity, 282–5
  examples of, 285–93
Cromwell, Thomas, 48
Cuba, 103
Cumman na mBan, 183
Curandeiros, 286–8, 290
Czechoslovakia, 32, 33

Dacre family, 41
Davenant, Charles, 48
death, space of, 211–13, 215, 235
debt, war induced, 47–8, 49
debt-peonage system, 220, 221–2, 223, 234, 236
dehumanization, 83–5, 155, 279
democracy, 26, 28, 93
  as safeguard, 91
  and violence, 306–7
Democratic Kampuchea (DK), 136, 137, 138, 143, 147
  and disproportionate revenge (*karsâng-soek*), 148–59
  'new' people, 152, 154–5, 157
  see also Cambodia
Denmark, 50
detention of Palestinians
  background to. 250–4
  and education. 256, 257
  and recruitment to political organization. 257
  as rite of passage. 244–5, 255–9, 260, 267
  sexual torture, 267
  women, 264–6
diasporas, 300
dictatorship, 65
dirtiness, and anti-Irish discourse, 180–1
Dirty Protest, 169–71
  causes of, 171–4
  as contest of power, 189
  and emotions, 176–7
  and feminist debate, 186–9

meanings of, 177–8, 179, 189
  as mirror of colonial barbarism, 182
  reactions to, 174, 175
  and sexual difference, 182–6, 187–8, 189–90
  and stereotypes of Irish barbarism, 181
  symbolic resistance, 175, 177
  understanding, 178–80
  see also feces; menstrual blood
disproportionate revenge (*karsâng-soek*)
  Cambodian cultural model, 137–8, 140–8
  in Democratic Kampuchea (DK), 148–59
  and killing, 146–7
  killing families, 147–8, 155–8
  sociocultural context, 138, 145, 148, 160
  and superiority, 144, 158
domination, 25–6
  based on terror, 33–4
  cultural resistance to, 244, 246
  foreign invasion and occupation, 32
  justifications for, 14–15
  organized, 15–16
  and Palestinian beatings, 251, 252
  see also obedience; power
Douglas, M., 171, 181, 189

Easter Rising, (1916) 105
Ecuador, 194, 227
electronic battlefield, 95
Elias, N., 87, 88
Ellul, J., 95
Elton, G.R., 48
empowerment, 245, 246, 248, 267
Endlösung, 86
Engels, F., 20
England
  and decolonization of India, 32, 33
  national debt, 48
English Revolution, (1640) 52
Enloe, C., 307
etatization, 93
European Court of Human Rights, 180
European states
  and coercive exploitation, 36

and colonialism, 302
creation of 36, 38–42, 45–6, 52
maritime states, 45, 46
military organization, 45–6, 54–5
monopolizing violence, 40–2
and national debt, 47–8, 49
taxation, 48–9
Evans, Mike, 142, 143
evil, concept of, 34, 119
excreta *see* feces
existentialism, 22
extortion, 42–3
extraction
  and fiscal strategy, 50
  forms of, 49
  and state making, 51
  and war making, 38–9

fanaticism, 126, 151
Fanon, F., 22, 23, 24, 103, 258
Farrell, Mairead, 174
feces, 169, 177
  as primordial symbol, 171, 175,
    189
  as social symptom 179, 180, 181
  as weapon, 175
  see also Dirty Protest
Fein, H., 303
Feldman, A., 170, 175, 177, 260
femininity, 186, 265, 266
feminism, 186–9
  and Nationalist politics, 188–9,
    190
Figner, Vera, 113
'five K's', 124, 125
Foucault, M., 170, 171, 214, 246, 247,
  303–4
France
  anarchist terrorism, 101, 105, 107,
    111
  demilitarization of lords, 41
  national debt, 47–8
  taxation, 48
Francis I, Spain, 47
Freire, P., 126
Frelimo, 275, 293
French Revolution, (1789) 101, 103,
  247
Freud, S., 175, 177

Front de Libération Nationale (FLN),
  Algeria, 101, 102, 106, 108, 110, 112
Fuentes, C., 223

Gandhi, Indira, 121, 122, 133
Gandhi, Mahatma, 32, 109
Gaulle, Charles de, 30
Gaza, 277–8
gender
  and Irish Republican Army (IRA),
    183–4, 187
  and Palestinians, 244, 245, 248–50,
    255–61, 264–6
  and persecution, 202–3, 204
general strikes, 22, 24
Geneva Conventions, and rape, 195–9
Genghis Khan, 72
genocide, 23, 70–9, 136–63, 300,
  302–3
  and bureaucracy, 84–5, 87, 94
  and communism, 303
  and concept of evil, 119
  and disproportionate revenge,
    137–8
  and ideology, 73, 75
  justifications for, 303
  and modern civilization, 69, 75–9
  and political power, 94
  and rape, 194, 195, 198–203, 204
  and social engineering, 73–5, 87
  studies, 136–7
  systematic, 72, 76
  see also Holocaust
Germany
  final solution, 88, 94
  Nazism, 93, 160
Gibson, Maureen, 185
Giddens, A., 78
Gilmore, D., 248
globalization, 302, 304–5, 306, 307,
  308
Goffman, E., 175
Golden Temple complex, Amritsar,
  120, 121, 122
Gordon, S., 76
governments
  corruption, 304
  indirect rule via local magnates,
    41–2

monopolizing violence, 37–8, 39, 40–2, 44, 49
need for, 300–1
and protection, 37, 38, 42–5
as racketeers, 37–8, 42–3
Grabosky, P.N., 102
Gravel Hill, 148
Great Purge ,62, 65
Grey, Sir Edward, 215
Gridilla, Father, 222, 231
grudge, 140–5
class grudge, 137, 143, 149–55, 160
and disproportionate revenge (*karsâng-soek*), 143–5
guerrilla warfare, 31
rural, 108
urban, 102
Guevara, Che, 118, 128
Gurr, T.R., 101, 102
Guru Granth Sahib, 124–5
Guru Panth, 125, 127
gurumukh, 129
Gutiérrez, Emilio, 229–30

Habsburg Empire, 45
Hamilton, E.J., 48
Hardenburg, Walter, 216–17, 219, 222, 225, 231, 235
Hargobind, Guru, 125, 126
Harimandir Sahib, 120
Haussman, G.E., Baron, 102
Hegel, G.W.F., 22, 34
Henry VIII, 48
Hernandez, Crisóstomo, 230–1
Herzfeld, M., 248
hijacking, 102
Hilberg, R., 67, 86
Hindus, 131
Hitler, Adolf, 72, 74, 85–6, 90
Hobbes, T., 300–1
Hobsbawm, E.J., 102, 104
Holland, D., 160
Holocaust, 67–96, 136
and bureaucracy, 83, 85–7
and concentration of violence, 79
factors producing, 76–7
functionalist approach, 85–6
gender persecution, 202
intentionalist approach, 85

lack of explanation for, 67–8, 69
and modern civilization, 71–2, 75, 77, 303
normality of, 76–7
and role of science, 89, 90
unimaginable, 68–9
uniqueness of, 70–2, 76
see also genocide
Huitotos, 216, 224, 225–9, 230, 236
rite of judicial murder, 231–2
humanity, crimes against, 199–200, 202
Hun Sen, 147
Hungarian Revolution (1956), 29

Igaraparaná, 215, 235
imagination, 283–4
see also creativity
impotence, and violence, 33
India, 32, 33, 120
Indians
South American, 216–19
classification of, 227–8
and colonial imagination, 232–3, 236
docility of, 225–6
fear of rebellion by, 229–30, 233
forms of labor organization 220–1, 235
and savagery, 224–5, 226–9, 236
value of money and work, 221–2, 231
see also Huitotos; Putumayo Report
information technology, 94, 95, 300
intifada, 244, 247, 251, 259–61, 267
and class and generational structure, 263
Ireland, 102–3
and dirtiness, 180–1
feminist movement, 186–9
Irgun Zwai Leumi, 101, 106, 107, 110, 112
Irish National Liberation Army, (INLA) 169
Irish Republican Army (IRA), 101, 103, 105, 106, 110, 169
and gender, 183–4, 187
see also Dirty Protest
Irish Times, 187, 188

Islam, and martyrdom, 128
isonomy, 27
Israel, 108
  and beating and detention of
    Palestinians, 244–5, 247, 250–4
  soldiers, 252–3
Italy, 105, 304

Jalazon refugee camp, 255
Japan
  and sexual slavery, 201, 202
  terrorism, 105
Jehangir, 123
Jews, 85, 87
Jinda, 128
Jouvenel, Bertrand de, 25, 26, 28
June 2 Movement, West Germany,
  101
jungle, and savagery, 223–5

Kabyle, 138
Kaliayev, 112
Kertzer, D., 245, 246
Khalistan, Punjab, 118–19, 127, 132
Khalsa, 124–6, 132
Khmer Rouge
  class grudge, 137, 143, 149–55, 160
  and dehumanization, 155
  disproportionate revenge (*karsâng-
    soek*), 137, 138, 147–8, 155–7
  grudge against, 141, 159
  indoctrination, 150–1, 152, 154
  purging families, 147–8, 155–8
  and 'Red Flag', 153
  retaliation against, 158–9
  support for, 150
  see also Cambodia; Democratic
    Kampuchea (DK)
Kiernan, V.G., 47
King, Martin Luther, 109
Kristallnacht, 71
kulaks, 62

La Occidente rubber station, 222
labor, 22, 23
  forced, 216–17, 220
  organization, 220–1, 235
  shortage of, 220–1, 235
Labor Government, Britain, 63

Lacan, J., 171
Lacqueur, W., 99
Lane, F. 42–5, 46, 48, 49
Law of the Father, 178
leadership, and charisma, 14, 15
League of Nations, 54
legal domination, 14, 15
Lenin, V.I., 66
Liberia, 194
Lifton, R.J, 113
Lon Nol regime, 136, 150, 151, 152–3,
  155–6, 158
Long-Kesh prison, 169, 173, 174, 179,
  181, 182
  see also Dirty Protest
Louis XIII, 41, 47
Louis XIV, 47, 48
Lutz, C., 306

McCafferty, N., 187–8
Madan, T.N., 127
Madison, J., 27
mafia, 304
manhood, 244, 245, 248–50, 255,
  259, 266
  see also masculinity; rites of passage
Manica, 277
Mao Tse-tung, 21, 26
Maputo, 277–8
marginalization, 304
Marighela, C., 103, 108
Martin, E., 247
martyrdom, 118
  and conception of death, 128
  and love, 126–30, 132
  and selflessness, 123, 128, 129–30
  as tactic of weak, 134
  and truth, 122–6, 128, 132
Marx, Karl, 21–2, 24–5, 34
masculinity, 244, 248–50, 258
  and challenge, 249, 260, 261
  and control, 249
  and honor, 249, 260–1
  and militarism, 307–8
  see also manhood
massacre art, 122, 123
Matanzas, 217
Mazarin, Jules, 47
menstrual blood, 169, 182–6, 187

catalyst of cultural change, 188
as primordial symbol, 171, 187–8,
189
and women's pain, 185, 186, 187
see also Dirty Protest
menstruation, 184–5, 247
Meridor, Dan, 112
militarization, and gender roles, 307–8
Mill, J.S., 26, 27
millenarians, 106, 107, 109
miri, and *piri*, 125, 126
Mladjenovic, L. 197
Modelski, G., 53–4
modernity, 70–1, 75–9, 93
monarchy, 26, 28
Montesquieu, Baron de, 28
Morocco, 110
Mozambique, 273–94, 305
African medicine, 285–91
destruction of infrastructure, 285
elections, 293
extent of violence, 274–5
health care workers, 285–6
kidnap, 280, 281, 287
killing of service people, 285
Peace Accord (1992), 293
reintegration of war-affected, 291
and resistance, 284–5
shared experiences of war, 276–8
and survival mechanisms, 276
teachers, 291
terror warfare, 275–6, 278–82
unmaking violence, 289–93
Mubarak, Hosni, 121
muchachos, 218, 233–4
Murphy, Brenda, 184, 185

Nanak, Guru, 123, 124, 127
Nanking, rape, 193
Napoleonic Wars, (1792-1815) 48
Narodnaya Volya, 101, 102, 103, 105,
107, 111, 113
National Liberation Movements, 25
nationalism, 100, 103–4, 106, 303
naval warfare, 46
Nazism, 71, 76, 86, 90, 93
Needham, J., 90
'new global disorder', 304, 305–8
New World, role of terror, 212

Ngor, Haing, 144, 153, 154
Niassa, 277
nibbana, 129
nibutta-person, 129
Nicaragua, 305
Nobel, Alfred, 102
Nonini, D., 306
nonviolence movements, 23–4
North, D., 44
North Yemeni tribesmen, 249
Northern Ireland, 137, 169–90, 260
demonstrators fired on, 112
ill-treatment of prisoners, 172–4,
175, 176, 179
Protestant violence, 105
special category prisoners, 171–2,
173, 178–9, 180
see also Dirty Protest
Northern Ireland Women's Rights
Movement (NIWRM), 187, 188
nuclear weapons, 23, 300, 305
Nuremberg Tribunal, 199

obedience, 14, 15–16, 26–7
and material reward, 16, 42
and revolution, 29–30
and social honour, 16
to laws, 27
Obeyesekere, G., 171, 178
O'Fiaich, Tomas, 179
Ohnesorg, Beno, 105–6
oligarchy, 26
Operation Blue Star, 120, 121, 133
La Opinion, 212
Ordinary Decent Criminals (ODCs),
172
Outram, D., 247

Palestinians, 108, 110, 244–67
beatings, 247–8, 250–5, 260, 261–2,
264–6, 267
bodily inscription of power,
246–7
class and generational structures,
263–4
deaths of children, 253
detention, 244–5, 250–4, 255–9,
260, 264–6, 267
domestic violence, 266

gender, 244, 245, 248–50, 255–61,
        264–6
    and masculinity, 244, 248–50, 258
    moral superiority, 261–3
    and occupation, 247, 249
    rites of passage, 244–5, 248–50,
        255–9, 260, 266, 267
    weapons, 250–1
    women and violence, 261, 262,
        264–6

Panth, 125, 127, 132
Panthic Committees, 130
Paredes, Rómulo, 233–4
Paris, 102
passions, 118–19
    and military efficiency, 130
    see also martyrdom
peace, 31
Peacock, T.A., 48
Percy family, 41
Peru, 194, 201, 216, 228
Peruvian Rubber Company, 216–19
    culture of terror, 225, 233
    payment of Indians, 221–2
    punishment, 216–19
    slaughter of Indians, 216–17, 218,
        220
Peter the Hermit, 72
Peters, E., 197
Pettigrew, J., 119, 124
phchanh phchal, 145–6, 157
Phnom Penh, 142, 151, 152
Pinell, Gaspar de, 224, 225
Pol Pot, 141, 147, 149, 153, 159
Poland, 45, 71
Polanyi, K., 222
police state, 33–4
policing, 40, 42, 52
political asylum, 202
politics
    and power, 13–14, 27, 31–2
    and violence, 20–2, 25, 299, 306
Popular Front for the Liberation of
    Palestine, 101, 102
Portugal, 51
post-Khmer Rouge communist period
    (SOC), 141, 144, 159
poverty, 304

power
    bodily inscriptions of, 245, 246–8
    breakdown of, 29–30
    as check on power, 63, 64
    and deep play of subjectivity, 171,
        175, 189
    definitions of, 25–7
    and gender, 244–5
    legitimacy of, 31–2, 38
    and opinion of people, 27–8
    and politics, 14, 27, 31–2
    and ritual performances, 245
    of state over society, 92–3
    and support, 30–1
    terminology, 28
    and violence, 20–1, 25–6, 28–9,
        30–1, 32–3, 305–6
    and wealth, 21
pregnancy, forced, 194, 199, 201–2,
        203
prisoners in Northern Ireland
    discipline, 175
    female, 169, 173–4, 182–6
    hunger strikes, 171, 174, 175,
        179
    ill-treatment of, 172–4, 175, 176,
        179
    and individual identity, 175
    ODCs, 172
    political status, 171–2, 173, 178–9,
        180
    and punishment, 170–1, 174, 177
    sexual harassment of, 173–4
    socialization process, 175
    see also Dirty Protest
Proctor, R., 90
prostitution, forced, 193, 194, 196,
        199, 201, 202
protection, 36–7, 42–5, 49, 49–50, 51,
        55
protection rents, 42–4
Provisional IRA, 103, 105, 169
    see also Irish Republican Army
Prussian army, 50
punishment
    by Peruvian Rubber Company,
        216–19
    and humiliation, 177
    and normalization, 170–1

of prisoners in Northern Ireland,
170–1, 174, 177
Putumayo, Colombia
classification of social types, 227–8
and culture of terror, 223, 234–5
forced labor, 216–17, 220
ill-treatment of Indians, 216–19, 220
savagery, 222–9
and space of death, 212–13
see also Indians, South American;
Peruvian Rubber Company;
rubber production
Putumayo report, 215–19, 236
Casement's analysis, 219–22, 226

Québecois separatists, 104
Quinn, N., 160

Rabin, Yitzhak, 252
Ranariddh, Prince, 147
rape, 193–205
commanders' responsibility, 199,
200
as crime against honor, 196
as crime against humanity, 199,
200, 203
and ethnic cleansing, 194, 195,
198, 199, 200, 308
genocidal, 194, 195, 198–203, 204
and military tribunals, 193
and pregnancy, 194, 199, 201–2,
203
and soldiers' morale, 200, 201
as torture, 197–8, 199, 200, 203
and UN International Tribunal,
194–5, 197, 198, 199, 200, 203
and universal jurisdiction, 196–7,
199
unrecognised, 193–5, 202
as war crime, 195–9
as weapon of war, 194, 200, 201
Rapp, R., 42
rationality, 88, 90, 95
Ravachol, 111
Rayes, Rafael, 227
Reamker, 145
Red Army, Japan, 106
Red Army faction, West Germany, 106
Red Brigades, Italy, 106

'Red Flag', 'The', 153
Reichsicherheithauptamt, 83
reincarnation, 128, 159
Renamo, 275, 280, 281, 285, 287, 293
rentes sur l'Hôtel de ville, 47
resistance, 128–9
and creativity, 282–93
and healing systems, 284–5, 286–9
nonviolent, 109
responsibility, moral and technical,
79, 81–3
revenge
alternatives to, 159–60
see also disproportionate revenge
Revenge by Marriage, 146
revolution, 21–2, 24, 29–34, 52, 92, 93
and genocide, 303
and ideology, 103
and rapid change, 65
revolutionary socialism, 100
Rhodesia, 275
Richelieu, Duc de, 41, 47
rites of passage, 248–50
beatings and detentions, 244–5,
255–9, 260, 266, 267
stages of, 258–9
see also manhood
ritual
and empowerment, 245, 246
healing, 288–9
opposed meanings of, 245–6
and symbols, 245, 246
Rivera, J.E., 223
Robuchon, Eugenio, 231
Rocha, J., 221–2, 227, 229, 230–1, 236
'rogue states', 300
Rote Armee Fraktion (RAF), West
Germany, 101, 106, 108
rubber production, 216–17, 219–20,
302
culture of terror, 225, 233
ill-treatment of Indians, 216–19, 220
jungle and savagery, 222–5, 234
managers' fears, 233–4
payment of, Indians 221–2
shortage of labor, 220–1, 235
Rumania, 71
Russia, 45
corruption, 304

crowd violence, 71
and Czechoslovakia, 32, 33
revolutionary terrorism, 103, 104,
    105
see also Soviet Union
Rwanda, 136, 160

Saipan, 202
Samlaut rebellion, 148–9, 150
La Sanción, 216
Sânthor Mok, 138
Sartre, Jean-Paul, 22, 24, 25, 283, 284
savagery, 223–5, 226–9, 234, 236
    and colonial mirroring, 234–7, 253
Scarry, E., 127, 186
Schieffelin, E., 245–6
science
    as instrument of power, 88–90
    and Nazism, 90
    and rationality, 88, 90
Scott, J., 267
Second World War, rape, 193, 199,
    201
Secret Army Organization, Algeria,
    106–7
separatist movements, 103, 106, 109
sexual difference, 182–6, 187–8, 247
    see also gender; menstrual blood
shakti, and *bhakti,* 126
Shammas, A., 253
Sihanouk, Prince Norodom, 147, 149,
    150, 151
Sikh Reference Library, 120, 121
Sikhs
    amritdhari, 124–7, 132, 133
    atrocities by, 131
    and fearlessness, 125, 126
    future of militancy, 130–4
    Khalsa order, 124–6, 132
    and lack of disciplined
        organization, 130–3
    and martyrdom, 122–34
    massacre of, 121–2, 133
    militant movement, 118, 119–20
    and resistance, 128–9
    and selflessness, 129–30
    steel wrist bands, 127
    and symbols, 124, 125, 127
    threatened by Hinduism, 120

Simson, Alfred, 226–8
Singh, Baba Deep, 123
Singh, Bhai Mani, 123
Singh, Guru Gobind, 124–5, 132
Sluka, J., 177
Smith, Adam, 48
social engineering, 73–5
socialism
    and fanatical conviction, 64
    and individual freedom, 63
    and terror, 61, 62–3, 64
    see also Marx, Karl
Socialist Women's Group, 187
society, garden analogy, 73–4, 93
Sofala, 277
Soloviev, V.S., 111
Solzhenitsyn, A.I., 33
Son Sen, 147
Sorel, G., 22, 24, 25
South African Defense Forces, 275,
    285
Soviet Union, 53, 118
    and organized terror, 61–2, 64,
        65–6
    see also Russia
Spain, 52
Spivak, G., 186
Sri Lanka, 137
Stalin, Joseph, 33–4, 52, 66, 72, 74
starvation, deliberate, 218
state making, 49–50, 301–2
    and extraction, 51
    internal and external processes,
        53–4
    as organized crime, 35–55
    popular resistance to, 52
    state consolidation, 302
    and war making, 36, 38–9, 44,
        51–2, 53
state(s)
    activities of, 49–52
    coalitions, 53
    and criminal violence, 304, 306
    definitions of, 13, 25
    formation of, 2–3
    and genocide, 302–3
    legitimacy, 38, 39–40, 300
    new, 55
    and organized means of violence, 36

and physical force, 13–14, 18, 299,
   300–5, 307
Stepniak, S. (Kravchinski), 111
Stinchcombe, A., 38
Stone, L., 40
Strausz-Hupé, R., 26
subjectivity, 170–1, 175, 189
Sukha, 128
survivor-guilt, 113
Sweden, 50
Swift, Jonathan, 181–2
symbolic violence, 304
symbols
   personal, 178
   primordial, 171, 175, 189
   and ritual, 245, 246
   Sikhs, 124, 125, 127

Taussig, M., 248, 252, 253
taxation, 47–50
   displacement effect, 48
terror, 33–4
   and colonial hegemony, 212
   culture of, 211–44, 302
   functions of, 65–6
   impact of, 61–2
   narration, 211, 212, 214, 215,
      232–5
   nourished by silence, 121, 213–14
   and purges, 65–6
   and restriction of information, 62
   as ritualized art form, 236, 252
   understanding, 214–15
terror warfare, 275–6, 278–82
   and creativity, 282–93
   and dehumanization, 279
   effect on children, 280–1
   and resistance, 276
   and use of everyday items, 279–80
terrorism, 119
   anarchist, 101, 105, 106, 107, 111
   attacks on regimes, 107–8
   causes of, 99–114
      cross-national factors, 101
      and denied access to power, 104
      and discrimination, 103–4
      grievances of minorities, 103–4,
         108–9
      precipitating events, 101, 105–6

and revolutionary ideologies,
   100, 103, 106
   vengeance, 111–12
condoned, 103
contagion effect, 110
effects on public opinion, 108, 109
and elite disaffection, 104–5, 113
factional, 108
individual motivation, 111–13, 114
objectives of, 106–11
provocative, 108
and rationality, 106
and security measures, 103
settings for, 101–6
and social facilitation, 102
and student unrest, 105
and urbanization, 102
weapon of the weak, 109, 110
see also Irish Republican Army; Sikh
   militants; terrorists
terrorism organizations
   formation of, 100
   and impatience, 109–10
   and individual commitment, 111,
      114
   internal pressures, 110
   and shared guilt, 111, 112
terrorists
   and choice, 109, 114
   and risk of death, 112–13
   and survivor-guilt, 113
Third World, 35–6
   unity of, 25
Thomas, R.P., 44
Thompson, E.P., 247
Thornton, 107
Timerman, Jacobo, 211–12, 213–15,
   228, 236
Tiradentes, 126
tobacco-sucking, 231–2, 233–4
torture, 23, 211–12, 216–19, 220, 235
   resisting, 127–8
   as rite of passage, 256
   as ritualized art form, 236, 252
trace italienne, 45
traditional domination, 14, 15
transportation, by water, 46
Tres Esquinas rubber station, 221
tribute, 42–3

Trotsky, Leon, 13
Truth, 216
truth
    and martyrdom, 122–6, 128, 132
    and power, 214
Tudors, demilitarization of lords, 40–1
Tum Teav, 137, 138–40, 145, 148,
    158, 160
Tunisia, 110
Tuol Sleng prison, 151
Tupamaros, Uruguay, 101, 106
Turkey, 160
Turner, V., 171
tyranny, 28

Ulster Defence Association, 107
United Nations, 54
    and crimes against women, 194–5,
        198, 202
    Human Rights Commission, 198
    Security Council, 198, 199
United States, 53, 101, 105, 201
urbanization, 102
Uruguay, 101, 103, 105
utopianism, 64

Vaidya, General, 128
van Creveld, M., 305
Van Gennep, A., 258
Veblen, T., 83
vengeance, 111–12, 140–1
    see also disproportionate revenge
Venice, 52
Vienna Declaration, (1993) 198,
    199
Vietnam war, 23, 31, 201
Vilanova, Francisco de, 224
violence
    and arbitrariness, 20, 61–2
    bodily inscriptions of, 263–4
    and bureaucracy, 79–83, 85–7, 94
    centralization of, 78–9
    changing attitudes to, 223–4
    as conceptual, 119
    constant threat of, 87–8
    and cultural ideologies, 300
    and dehumanization of
        bureaucratic objects, 83–5
    and discipline, 170, 175

dissociation from moral evaluation,
    79–81, 83
and divisions of labor, 79–83
and economic development, 20, 44,
    45, 299–300, 301–2
elimination of, 77–8, 87–8, 308
and empowerment, 267
glorification of, 22, 24
and identity, 175, 281–2, 292–3
and implements of violence, 19, 32
justification for, 32
legitimacy, 38, 39–40, 300
Mozambican conception of, 290
and politics, 20–2, 25, 299, 306
and power, 20–1, 25–6, 28–9, 30–1,
    32–4, 305–6
predictions for future, 306, 307
responsibility, 79, 81–2
and revolution, 21–2, 24, 29–34
role of culture, 308
safeguards against, 88, 91, 94, 96
substitute for power, 33
unmaking, 289–93
    see also disproportionate revenge;
        terror; terror warfare; war
Voltaire, 26
Vries, J. de, 46–7

wanggar, 124
war
    and banditry, 39–40
    crimes against women, 193–205
    definitions of, 20, 26
    end of, 31
    exploitation of, 287
    increasing destructiveness of, 35
    instability after, 92
    as international relations, 53–5
    in Mozambique, 273–94
    and technological revolution,
        19–21, 23, 95
    terror warfare, 275–6, 278–82
war making, 49–51
    and capital accumulation, 38–9, 44
    and extraction, 38–9, 51, 53
    loans and supplies, 52–3
    as organized crime, 35–55
    and state making, 36, 38–9, 44,
        51–2, 53

Wars of Religion, France, 47
Washington Post, 179
weapons, 19, 20, 23
Weber, M., 25, 26
Weimar Republic, 93
Weizenbaum, J., 94
West Germany, 105, 105–6, 112
Western Civilization
  legitimizing myth of, 78
  potential for violence, 67–70, 95,
    96
Wild Man myth, 229, 234
Wiseman, J., 48
women, 247
  Catholic, 186
  Palestinian, 261, 262, 264–6
  rights, 188
  war crimes against, 193–205

  see also gender; menstrual blood;
    sexual difference
Women's Center, Belfast, 188
Women's Coalition against Crimes
  against Women in the Former
  Yugoslavia, 194
Wright Mills, C., 25

Yeats, W.B., 126
Yugoslavia, 193, 198, 199, 205
  see also Bosnia
Yun Yat, 147
Yuracruz, 194

Zambesia, 277
Zaparos, 226–7, 228
Zimbabwe, 275
Zizek, Slavoj, 179